RECOLLECTIONS OF MY LIFE AS A WOMAN

OTHER BOOKS BY DIANE DI PRIMA

This Kind of Bird Flies Backward
Dinners and Nightmares
The New Handbook of Heaven
Poet's Vaudeville
Seven Love Poems from the Middle Latin
Haiku
New Mexico Poem
Earthsong
Hotel Albert
Memoirs of a Beatnik
L.A. Odyssey
The Book of Hours
Kerhonkson Journal
Revolutionary Letters
The Calculus of Variation
Loba, Part I
Freddie Poems
Brass Furnace Going Out
Selected Poems
Loba, Part II
The Loba As Eve
Loba: Parts I–VIII
Wyoming Series
The Mysteries of Vision
Pieces of a Song
Seminary Poems
The Mask Is the Path of the Star

RECOLLECTIONS OF

My Life as a Woman

THE
NEW YORK
YEARS

A MEMOIR BY *Diane di Prima*

VIKING

VIKING
Published by the Penguin Group
Penguin Putnam Inc., 375 Hudson Street,
New York, New York 10014, U.S.A.
Penguin Books Ltd, 27 Wrights Lane,
London W8 5TZ, England
Penguin Books Australia Ltd, Ringwood,
Victoria, Australia
Penguin Books Canada Ltd, 10 Alcorn Avenue,
Toronto, Ontario, Canada M4V 3B2
Penguin Books (N.Z.) Ltd, 182–190 Wairau Road,
Auckland 10, New Zealand

Penguin Books Ltd, Registered Offices:
Harmondsworth, Middlesex, England

First published in 2001 by Viking Penguin,
a member of Penguin Putnam Inc.

10   9   8   7   6   5   4   3   2   1

Names and descriptive details of some of the individuals
appearing in this book have been changed.

Portions of this book, some in different form, first appeared in *Mama Bears
News and Notes, Mother Jones Magazine, VIA (Voices in Italian Americana),*
and *Growing Up Ethnic in America* edited by Maria Mazziotti Gillan and
Jennifer Gillan, Penguin Books.

Grateful acknowledgment is made for permission to reprint excerpts from the following copy-
righted works:
    The Cantos of Ezra Pound. Copyright © 1934, 1948 by Ezra Pound. Reprinted by permission
of New Directions Publishing Corp.
    Confucius, translation by Ezra Pound. Copyright © 1947, 1950 by Ezra Pound. Reprinted by
permission of New Directions Publishing Corp.

LIBRARY OF CONGRESS CATALOGING IN PUBLICATION DATA
Di Prima, Diane.
    Recollections of my life as a woman : the New York years / Diane di Prima.
      p.   cm.
    ISBN 0-670-85166-3
      1. Di Prima, Diane—Homes and haunts—New York (State)—New York.   2. Italian
American families—New York (State)—New York.   3. Poets, American—20th
century—Family relationships.   4. Women—New York (State)—New York—Biography.
5. Poets, American—20th century—Biography.   6. Di Prima, Diane—Childhood and youth.
7. New York (N.Y.)—Biography.   8. Di Prima, Diane—Family.   I. Title.
PS3507.I68 Z475 2001
811'.54—dc21
    [B]   00-043893

This book is printed on acid-free paper. ∞

Printed in the United States of America
Set in New Caledonia
Designed by Suvi Asch

for Jeanne, Dominique, Alexander, Tara, and Rudi
for Christopher and Chani and the grandchildren yet to come

and for artists everywhere
now and in the future

ACKNOWLEDGMENTS

I received so much love and support while working on this book, that I cannot begin to tell it all.

First of all, I want to thank Sheppard Powell, my partner and soulmate, who blessed the book every step of the way, and often was its fierce advocate against my own negativity and despair. Truly, this project would never have emerged into the light of day without his support, and all his editorial help: he read innumerable versions of certain passages and helped me make difficult decisions.

Thanks to my two brothers, Frank and Richard, for their belief in me and my work.

Thanks too to my editors at Viking: Dawn Seferian, David Stanford and Paul Slovak; to my agent Sandra Dijkstra and all the folks at her office, who go far beyond the usual job description and create an extended family—a safe place in the business world; to two brilliant therapists and good friends who helped to midwife the work—Ian Grand, and Diane Lee.

Thanks to the various friends who offered their ears and workspaces while I was on the road: Allen Ginsberg, Gerrit Lansing, Allice Molloy, Maria Mazziotti Gillan, Jean Claude van Itallie, Peter Warshall, Abigail Albrecht, Rachel Guido deVries, Laura Stortoni, Judith Serin, David Short. There are many, many others, and I thank you with all my heart for your kindness.

Certain institutions also provided invaluable time and workspace. They include Naropa Institute, Harbin Hot Springs, Shantigar Foundation, and the Atlantic Center for the Arts. The American Italian Historical Association gave this work-in-progress informed and interested hearings at several panels and readings over the years.

Most of all, I want to give my deepest humble gratitude to Lama Tharchin Rinpoche, my dharma teacher, who taught me that writing is a wonderful way to bring light and vastness into others' lives. It is my hope that in some small way this book will be helpful to others.

AUTHOR'S NOTE

Close as I can, this is how I remember it. I could be wrong about some things. Most everybody is.

chapter ONE

My earliest sense of what it means to be a woman was learned from my grandmother, Antoinette Mallozzi, and at her knee. It was a house of dark and mellow light, almost as if there were fire and kerosene lamps, but to my recollection there was electric light, the same as everywhere else. It is just that the rooms were so very dark, light filtering as it did through paper shades and lace curtains, and falling then on dark heavy furniture (mahogany and walnut) and onto floors and surfaces yellowed with many layers of wax, layers of lemon oil. The light fell as if on old oil paintings, those glazes, that veneer. Sepia portraits: Dante, Emma Goldman. There was a subtle air of mystery. The light fell on my grandmother's hands as she sat rocking, saying her rosary. She smelled of lemons and olive oil, garlic and waxes and mysterious herbs. I loved to touch her skin.

There was this mystery: she sat, saying her beads, but the beads and her hand never completely left her apron pocket. My grandfather was an atheist, and if she heard his step on the stair she would slip the beads out of sight and take up some work. They had lived thus for forty years, and the mystery was how much they loved each other. To my child's senses, already sharpened to conflict, there was no conflict in that house. He was an atheist, she a devout Catholic, and for all intents and purposes they were one. It would never do to argue with him about God, and so when he came into the room she slipped the beads away.

As for him, he never seemed to inquire. Though those clear blue eyes saw everywhere. The *I Ching* has the phrase: "He let many things pass without being duped".

My grandmother's Catholicism was of the distinctive Mediterranean variety: tolerant and full of humor. When I was a little older, I would frequently hear her remark, at some tale of transgression, sins of the flesh reported by a neighbor in hushed Neapolitan—"Eh"! (an exclamation whose inflection communicated humor and seriousness, and a peculiar, almost French, irony)—"Eh"! my grandmother would say, "The Virgin Mary is a woman, she'll explain it to God".

This response to the vagaries of human existence, the weakness of the flesh, especially female flesh, gave me pause for thought. It indicated on the one hand, that the Virgin Mary knew much better than God the ins and outs so to speak of human nature, what we were up to, and that she had a tolerance and intelligence and humor that was perhaps missing from the male godhead.

• • • • •

It was at my grandmother's side, in that scrubbed and waxed apartment, that I received my first communications about the specialness and the relative uselessness of men, in this case my grandfather. There was no doubt that he was the excitement of our days, the fire and light of our lives, and that one of his most endearing qualities was that we had no idea what he was going to do next. But it was the women, and there were many of them, who attended on all the practical aspects of life. In the view that Antoinette Mallozzi transmitted, there was nothing wrong or strange about this. We women had the babies, after all, and it was enormously more interesting to us than to any man to know that there would be food on the table.

Not that I wish in any way to denigrate my grandfather: he worked enormously hard for his family—*but he would at any time throw everything over for an ideal.* There were many stories of his quitting an otherwise okay job to protest some injustice to a fellow worker. At which point he would arrive home with the fellow worker and his entire family, at the very least for dinner. Often they stayed for weeks. My grandmother would set the table for that many more, and if a solution was not rapidly forthcoming she and the six girls would take in crochet beadwork to keep cash coming in until my grandfather found another, less unjust employer.

Now, this sort of thing was not still going on when I was little—by then my grandfather was no longer working for others as a custom tailor—but the stories and the memory of it were in the air. My grandfather was regarded somewhat as the family treasure: a powerful and erratic kind of lightning generator, a kind of Tesla experiment, we for some reason kept in the house.

It was clear to me that he was as good as it got. My father, a sullen man with a smoldering temper, was easily as demanding as Grandpa, but did not bring these endearing qualities of excitement and idealism, this demand for something more than we already had or knew, into our lives. It was like tending a furnace in which the fire had gone out.

Antoinette was always busy, but there was a way in which she communicated the basic all-rightness of things. I loved to watch her hands. As I think about it now, I realize that as a little person I was not separated from the old: the sight and feel of soft, dry wrinkled skin was associated with the sight and feel of love. Of those who had the time to listen, to tell a story. I learned to love the smells and feel of old flesh—I loved to put my round child's cheek up against her wrinkled one.

Her hands always smelled of garlic and onions, beeswax and lemons and a thousand herbs. There was that sense of cleanness and the good smells of the world. A sense of the things that went on. In the turbulent 1930s into which I was born, my grandmother taught me that the things of woman go on: that they are the very basis and ground of human life. Babies are born and raised, the food is cooked. The world is cleaned and mended and kept in order. Kept sane. That one could live with dignity and joy even in poverty. That even tragedy and shock and loss require this basis of loving attendance.

And that men were peripheral to all this. They were dear, they brought excitement, they sought to bring change. Printed newspapers, made speeches, tried to bring that taste of sanity and order into the larger world. But they were fragile somehow. In their excitement they would forget to watch the clock and turn the oven off. I grew up thinking them a luxury.

• • • • •

Antoinette Rossi and Domenico Mallozzi met in their hometown in Italy, a town whose name translates as Saints Cosimo and Demiano. Antoinette's family was the aristocracy of the town (hence, perhaps, her French first name—French was still to some extent the language of the upper classes) though how aristocratic or wealthy the aristocracy of this small town was, I can only guess. I do know that later in my life, when Antoinette undertook to improve my education, she taught me the fine arts of embroidery and hemstitching in linen—a delicate process in which you pull out the threads of the linen weft and rework the warp into intricate geometric patterns. Though I remember her hands endlessly darning old clothes and making practical pieces of clothing—skirts, aprons—when it came time to teach sewing to her granddaughter she went back to the work she'd been taught, and no doubt the only work it had been expected she would ever do: fine embroidery, working in linen, and crocheting lace.

I am not sure how, or under what circumstances, Antoinette met Domenico: he was of a much poorer family. I imagine, though, that in a town the size of Saints Cosimo and Demiano, everyone more or less knew everyone else. One of the things we grandchildren were frequently told about Domenico was that he had had to quit school in the third grade to help support his family. He had learned the trade of custom tailoring and become a fine tailor, and it was with this profession that he supported his numerous family later in America. Domenico was of a fierce and fiery disposition, and seems to have had a certain difficulty in getting along with folks in his native part of the world. He was for one thing, then as later, an atheist, and—fairly common in the Italy of that period, and not at all as far-out as it sounds to us now—an anarchist. The combination, together with a burning curiosity and intellectual zeal, and a love of argument for its own sake and as a tool to uncover Truth, whatever that might be, didn't make him a popular guy. Or that's the impression I get.

At some point, he and Antoinette encountered each other and fell in love. For all her wealth, she was in a state of serious servitude. Seems my grandmother had six brothers and a father, and her mother had died, and nobody in the family had any intention of letting her marry at all—she was living, it was quite apparent to the men of the household, solely to keep house for them and provide the womanly comforts, however they might have been conceived back then. (We are talking the last decades of the nineteenth century here.) Keeping house in her situation didn't have the onerous overtones it has for us—she mostly had to oversee the servants and make sure things were done right. Probably plan the menus and things like that. Though she was a very skilled cook and may well have done a bunch of the work herself, I don't have the sense that she had to. Or that any really grubby or depressing tasks fell her way.

Still, servitude isn't in the quality or quantity of the work, but simply in performing tasks that your heart isn't in. Where the True Will, to use a magickal term, isn't engaged.

I am not sure how many servants the Rossi household employed, but there were enough so that Antoinette had her own personal maid. This is crucial to the tale. When her brothers (and presumably her father—though my mother and aunts never mentioned him) found out that she was being courted—and by such a low-class type as Domenico!—they locked her up in her room. She was their property, clearly, and they weren't about to let the only woman in the house go anywhere. If there were going to be a marriage at all—which was unlikely—it would have been "arranged" for the family convenience. In any case, Antoinette's maid, who remains nameless in these stories, smuggled letters from Domenico to Antoinette and back again for some time, while Antoinette remained behind a locked door, refusing to yield. The maid eventually helped her escape. She eloped with Domenico, and for a time the couple lived at Domenico's house—probably quite a change for her. It must have been crowded there, and clearly uncomfortable to remain in the town after such a outré move. Eventually they emigrated to America.

I'm sure this was no fun either, though Grandma never complained, and to my knowledge never regretted her move and her choice. When I knew them after some forty years of marriage they were still in love, with all the fierce clinging to their differences that creates such beautiful sparks in a long-term love. That struggle for truth that lay between them.

● ● ● ● ●

As I went into the kitchen this morning to make some tea, I saw through the (intentionally?) open crack in her door, my beautiful young daughter in the arms of a beautiful young Black skateboarder, who had evidently spent the night (skateboard propped against the wall in front of her door, like an insignia). As I went tranquilly into the kitchen and called out to ask them if they wanted tea or coffee, I thought with deep gratitude of some of the women I met when I first left home at the age of eighteen: those beautiful, soft and strong women of middle age with their young daughters who made me welcome in their various homes, where I could observe on a given morning mom coming out of her bedroom with a lover, male or female, and joining daughter and *her* lover at the table for breakfast in naturalness and camaraderie. These women, by now mostly dead I suppose, were great pioneers. They are nameless to me, nameless and brief friends I encountered along the way who showed me something else was possible besides what I had seen at home. Some trust and mutual joy in transient or long-term mates possible between parents and kids. (So that a mom myself, I have always felt the house is blessed by young love: the bliss and softness it radiates to all corners of my flat: discovery and tenderness, like a new spring morning. Trust.)

I think, too, of those other women who taught me other ways, when I was much younger. They had the same strength but not always the same softness. They were the "art teachers" and music teachers I encountered in school, or the women of the arts who sometimes found their way into my parents' home, to be spoken unkindly of later. They usually wore what my mother considered too much make-up. They mostly had sad eyes, but they were sensitive and alert to—well, to me among other things. They were single women and that in itself was considered an anomaly. Single women who had given themselves to the arts—though in fact none of them had achieved great recognition in her loved field. They taught, and wore large jewelry, did not hide behind aprons, were considered more than slightly non-respectable. They showed me a way, and I loved the lines under their eyes their make-up accented rather than hid.

As I loved my cousin Liz, who would show up sometimes, cutting classes. Her cropped hair, and soft, slightly chunky figure. Her intelligence, and spirit. There was a rare day I was home from school when she came by, and we sat together; I was eight, she almost ten years my senior, and she recited poetry to me. "If" by Rudyard Kipling was her favorite, and I soon got it by heart. Liz was unique in my world. No one sat with me, in that way, simply to share feeling. Some early communion of spirit I had found with my grandparents, but with no one else. Years later, my mother hinted that Liz might be gay. She was gone by then, far from family judgments, living in Florida. And I had grown my own agenda, my own ideas of human freedom, so that news made her something of a hero.

These styles, these possibilities of being, and being a woman, being alive as a woman, have stayed with me. As I write now I see how each is still with me, in the form I make for myself, my way of being in the world.

● ● ● ● ●

My grandfather and I had our secrets—as when we listened to Italian opera together. Opera was forbidden Domenico because he had a bad heart—and so moved was he by the vicissitudes and sorrows of Verdi's heroes and heroines that the doctor felt it to be a danger. We would slip away together to listen—I was three or four—and he would explain all the events extraordinaire that filled that world. All that madness seemed as natural as anything else to my young mind. The madness in the air around me, I felt, was no different.

We would share forbidden cups of espresso, heavily sweetened. Drops of the substance, like an elixir of life, were slipped into my small mouth on a tiny silver spoon, while the eggshell china with its blue and gold border gleamed iridescent in the lamplight. I remember that his hand shook slightly. It was the world of the child—full of struggles larger than life, huge shadows cast by the lamp, circumventing the grownups. It was a world of enchantment, and passion.

But then, he told me stories. Terrifying stories, fables whose morals seemed to point to the horror of social custom, of emulation. Or he read me Dante, or we would practice my bit of Italian together. Italian which was forbidden me in my parents' house, and which I quickly forgot when we were finally separated. Italy was a part of that world of enchantment. Domenico would describe the olive groves of the south, till I saw them blowing silver-green in the wind. When I was seven he promised to take me there "after the war", but he died before the war was over. I grew up nostalgic for a land I'd never seen.

● ● ● ● ●

He read me Dante. Told me the book had gone around the world. A world I saw much like the Bronx: tall apartment houses side by side. Marble and potted plants in the lobbies. Linked hands of housewives, passing my grandfather's book from window to window. They would read that one copy and pass it along. That's why it looked so worn: crumbling cover, thumbprints, and dog-eared corners.

● ● ● ● ●

Struggle for truth bonded Domenico and Antoinette. Her rosary, his Giordano Bruno. Fierce, luminous, and coexistent. As how much else my child's heart could only guess at. And in that struggle for truth my grandmother had the last word.

Domenico died when I was eleven, of that same great heart they had tried to protect him from. Antoinette survived him by eleven years. During that time she lived with her various daughters: my aunts and my mother, and much to their annoyance she conversed nightly with her husband. I still remember her in her room at our Brooklyn brownstone, in her cotton and lace nightgown, her luxuriant grey hair brushed and ready for bed, talking to my grandfather's picture, telling him all the varied events of the day in the dim light. Her soft voice would go from indignation to laughter or grief, as the story changed. She told him everything.

Those years must have been hard and sad for her, but I don't remember that she ever complained. She threw herself into the life of whatever household: mending our clothes, teaching me embroidery and linen working, rolling our endless batches of egg noodles.

When Antoinette was on her deathbed, I was no longer living at home, and hence barred from family life. The story of her passing came to me secondhand from one of my aunts—one of the few who didn't consider me too much of an outlaw to speak to:

When Antoinette knew she was dying, she had a last request. She had all these eleven years worn only black, worn mourning for Domenico, though he himself "didn't believe in" wearing mourning. But now she was dying, and she wanted to make sure that she was buried in a bright-colored dress. It was a matter of deep concern; she was restless and distressed till she was certain it was understood, and promises were extracted. "Because", she said, "when I meet your father in the next world" (which world, of course, Domenico the atheist adamantly insisted did not exist) "I don't want him to scold me for wearing mourning".

Certain she was right—how could there not be an afterlife?—and fierce in her love and her right to mourn her husband to the end, but not wanting him to scold her. Like the rosary she slipped in and out of her apron all those years. She was buried in light blue.

● ● ● ● ●

He told me stories. There were many, and I remember that there were some that made me joyous, but the one that has stayed with me all these years went something like this:

Once in a village far away, there was to be a feast. The people of the town picked out a very fine animal, and led it to the center of the square. And they decked it out with a wreath of flowers around its neck, and praised it highly. And they played music, and danced around it and killed it with great rejoicing. And the next day the children of the village got together to play. They picked one of their number, and put a wreath of flowers around his neck and another wreath on his head. And they played their flutes, and danced around him and killed him, rejoicing.

It's hard to say now what I made of this then. Only that a sense of foreboding, and of a huge responsibility of knowledge lay on me, age four or five. *That this was the nature of the world, and we shared this knowledge.* If that was how it was I was willing to accept it, only I wanted him not to suffer for it. How often I wanted to comfort him—old man and child sharing an existential bewilderment. A willingness to peer into darkness. Struggle for Truth.

● ● ● ● ●

I stood beside him as he sat at his desk. He only half-looked at me as he spoke. This was unusual, in the story times I always sat on his lap. Sat in a bentwood chair, sometimes *facing the wall* together as if to shut out distractions. A Zen austerity. Or were there only certain corners we could go to for these exchanges, where the grownups would not see us and swoop down—"Leave the child alone. . . . Come on, Diane, your mother (or whoever) wants you. . . . Pop is a little crazy" (an aside, an undertone). If Pop was crazy, I well knew by then that I was crazy with him. They were too late, with their attempts to save me for themselves. The conspiracy between us ran too deep.

I stood beside him at his desk, and his eyes were not on me. Only, I could feel the stuff of his shirtsleeve against my cheek, the smell of bluing, of starch. He said, "Someday you are going to go out at night and look at the stars and you will wonder how they got there. Then you'll study like I studied, and you'll suffer like I suffered, and *in the end you'll find nothing*". I was not very old but I didn't flinch at that "nothing". Only I knew with my full child's certitude that it wasn't true. Or anyway the despair that accompanied the word had no truth, however much he felt it. I had no words to argue, only the desire to comfort. I may have put my hand on his starched shirtsleeve.

I was being recruited, initiated, and I knew it. With my full consent, entering a world larger than life. I knew there was no turning back, and in fact, yearned only to go forward. To go forward, with him, into the darkness. The struggle for Truth. Only, for me, the darkness held no despair. *Not nothing, Grandpa.* It was someone other than a child who longed to say that.

Not nothing, Grandpa. It was a promise, a vow. I, Diane, age four or five, would make meaning in the world. Make meaning for him, for myself. The dark was luminous, of that I was certain. That much I *knew.*

With that exchange we achieved the full status of lovers. Without further touch or words, we shaped the prototype, the pattern for all my deepest loves to come. Always this despair, this hope, this luminous dark. The conspiracy between us was complete.

● ● ● ● ●

Complete, a world in itself, but it couldn't protect me from my parents.

"Pull up your skirt and pull down your pants". This was a little me, five and under. This was mom, and she would send me for the hairbrush first, myself and then make me get myself ready for the beating. In some ways she was much harder to take than my dad because there was a crazy meanness to her, she hurt you even when she wasn't mad: dressing, washing, everything was painful. She was a methodical hurter, he was driven by rage and weird perversion.

Being sent to my room by my mother, to wait for my father to come home to beat me for something. (This person was a teenager, or close to teens. After dad beat me he was sexually aroused. Would sit me on his lap with a hard-on to "comfort" me—or worse, I don't remember, only sense.)

He would always say "Be-Jesus", before he swung at me with his hand (this was different from formal beatings with the belt, he would just lash out and start slapping you across the face, and if you tried to protect yourself you were "raising your hand to him" and your nose would usually start bleeding, and if you fell down he would keep hitting across your shoulders, and neck, and in some ways it was scarier than formal beatings, because you didn't know what part of you would be hurt, and with the belt it was usually, but not always, your ass, or your back and ass, or your legs—thighs, where it wouldn't show, and the front of you was mostly protected).

"Be-Jesus, I'll kill you", he would say and you believed him, and
then mom or Aunt Ella would come when it was over and try to
stop the nosebleed, and sometimes it would go on for a couple of
hours, and my mother would say over and over to me, "Your fa-
ther is a very gentle man, (or a very patient man), but when he
loses his temper he has a heavy hand". Or "but when you try him,
he loses his temper". And I would be only half-conscious really, it
seems now, looking back, as they put ice on the back of my neck to
stop the nosebleed, and I would wonder what "try him" meant.
And after a while I knew just how long his arms were, and never
got that close if I could help it.

My grandparents' house, my parents' house—the two worlds parallel, but
never meeting.

●   ●   ●   ●   ●

I don't remember my father's mother at all. In the few pictures I have she
is a very young bride—almost a child—weighed down by the requisite
elaborate lace, or she is holding my father, her firstborn, a round, large-
headed baby in a long white dress. She has the soft face and large, round
eyes of an Arab woman.

Rosa Di Prima died when I was two, quite suddenly, from what I always
heard at home was "diabetes". It hit and carried her off in two or three
weeks, whatever it was. There was no diagnosis (no doctor?) and certainly
no autopsy. My mother always described her as a "saint"—which seemed
to mean she had endless patience for menial tasks and the rudeness of her
children.

It was 1975, six years after my father died, when my mother came to visit
me in a northern California country town, and told me with great trepidation a story of those early days, a story which filled in the picture of my father's family somewhat. It seems that in the first years of my life, during
the Depression, my father's father was not earning enough to support his
wife and his other five children who were still at home. He was a baker by
trade and had had his own store in Brooklyn at some point, but perhaps he
had lost it. In any case, my mother and father, who had been married just
a few years, felt it incumbent on them to help out, and did so by the simple expediency of giving Rosa their grocery money, or most of it. We all

three ate at her table every night. I suppose my mother would take me and meet my father there when he came home from work.

Now this sane and eminently practical solution to hard times was told me amidst the cedar and wild hollyhock, the free clams and leopard shark, the wild pot and wilder music, of that 1970s north country culture, in hushed and shameful tones. My mother had never told anyone in her family. I am not sure if even her sister Ella knew. She read it as a disgrace, somehow, that she, a married woman, had not been able to keep her own table. That my father, a beginning lawyer making seven to fifteen dollars a week, had not been able to support the two households separately.

I remember nothing of those early dinners, and though my father's family lived there for some years, I remember almost nothing of their house on Butler Street. I know that my mother would say in such a tone as to indicate that what we were doing wasn't quite desirable, "We're going over to Butler Street". It meant we were slumming, were going to visit the poorer side of the family. Although I am sure she never said anything that my father could quite pin down.

What is a puzzle to me still is who would have found those dinners disgraceful. Certainly not Domenico, who brought home entire squalling families of would-be union organizers; nor Antoinette, with her welcoming frugal abundance. I can only think that some imagination of my father's as to the status and parameters of the provider-role; or some projection of my mother's as to what a husband is, or should be—some preconceived idea about what it meant to be American, perhaps—hung over the simple problem, and kept all ten of us from the enjoyment of its solution.

● ● ● ●

MEMORY SHARDS:

We are in my grandmother's apartment, and she is standing at the sink. The sink is a slate grey, made of grey slate in fact, with flat, slanting sides, and the dishwater is greasy from Sunday dinner: tomato sauce and roast. My mother and one of her sisters are arguing with my grandmother. She is small, soft, the skin on her arms hangs loose, her grey hair is drawn back into a bun. My grandmother is soft-spoken, but she stands her ground. I am on her side, I stand at her side, wordless. Children are not to speak at times like this. They are persistent, angry, my mother and the aunts. I know only that my grandmother holds her ground and I am afraid for her.

● ● ● ● ●

I am in the park with my grandfather, and it is night. I have almost never been out of the house at night, and I love it. I love the city at night, the lights, the noises. It smells of mystery. In the park, Bronx River Park, the stars come clear. They are very bright, they burn. There is some kind of meeting. A "rally" is the word. My grandfather has taken me with him, and I know somehow it is without my parents' permission. They are anyway not there to object, I have been visiting my grandparents without them.

There is a rally in the park—I am not sure now what sort of rally. Was there in fact a particular occasion—perhaps a protest against the coming war? (This would have been the late 1930s.) Was it routine, an anarchist meeting? I don't know that word then, of course, only that there are many people, most of them men, and most of them are not young. Grey hair and white predominates. The smell of the old men of my childhood: cigars, and a particular kind of soap. The low, hoarse voices of Italian men, gravelly, the pitch set by tobacco and wine. There are women, too, in the crowd, not as many, but they are fierce and earnest. Perhaps I am the only child. I do not at any rate remember any other children.

At one point my grandfather begins to speak. Everyone is still to listen. This has been going on for some time, people speak and the others listen, but this time I listen too—it is my Grandpa. I am not sure what he is saying, and then, at the end I am sure. At the end he is talking about love. He talks for long time about love. He is saying that we must love each other or die. I understand this part, I seem to know it in my bones. He means that we'll all die, the people of the world. He is saying that we must love, and it seems it is more than we must love one another. There is a love to learn that is generic, that is just love, and it doesn't need an object. I know this then, I understand it as he speaks, though there is no way I could find the words for it. It is as if he is saying we must learn HOW to love. And it is very clear: if we do not, we will die: all the people of the world will die.

This time I don't want to comfort him, he doesn't need comfort. This time there is no answer to his "nothing", it is not nothing, it is an invitation to love. The stars shine down on us, the leaves glow in the electric lights of the park. I am proud of him, and afraid, but mostly amazed. His words have awakened my full acknowledgment, consent. I hear what he says as truth, and it seems I have always known it. I feel old, self-contained, passionate with the pure passion of a child. In my child's way I remember this kind of love.

Perhaps he is the last speaker, or perhaps we leave after he speaks. Perhaps not, but this is all I remember. And the rough cloth of his coat under my cheek as he carried me home.

● ● ● ● ●

I have been out with my Aunt Evelyn, whom I love best of all my mother's sisters, because she always sings. Heart full of joy, like a bird. We are in Bronx River Park, and Aunt Evelyn has introduced me to rolling down hills. It's a sport I deeply love, the first joyful physical activity I remember. No joy in walking or running in my mother's house. I never tire of rolling down hills, in spite of stones and dog shit, but after a while my aunt tires of following me, and she sits down on a bench. I have a pail and shovel and I start to dig. I know better than to dig up the grass, so I'm digging on the dirt path, the ground is hard, but I am making headway. I am busy, and quite determined. A man in a uniform approaches my aunt, and whatever he says makes her very angry. And it is later endlessly discussed at home. Aunt Evelyn was "given a ticket", "fined" because I was digging a hole. She is furious, seems to think the ground was made for kids to dig in. Says so. But at home when my mother talks I am not so sure. Is it the ground was made for kids to dig holes in, or is it I've somehow gotten my aunt in trouble?

After this when we go to the park with pail and shovel, Aunt Evelyn spreads her skirts, and I somehow squunch behind them, behind the park benches, and dig. It is still fun, but scary. Especially scary remembering how mad she could get.

● ● ● ● ●

I am older, maybe six, and we are outside. It is night again, stars over the apartment houses of the Bronx, paler because of the lights. My parents and grandparents are walking a little ahead. I am looking up at the buildings, and the sky and I am very sad. Knowing this is the last time I'll see this street, my grandparents are moving. It is the first time I know that "this is the last time" for something and I can hardly bear it. (I'm not much better at it today.) I have somehow some paper with me is how I remember it, but maybe I make it up then and write it down later. For years I had the copy in my first-grade Catholic-school hand: the poem I made to comfort myself that night, to "remember forever" the stars over those tall white apartment houses. My first poem and it worked, still works, I still remember that sky. Poem as the gift of memory. Mnemosyne. Mother.

My grandparents are moving, and I walk behind them torn by the knowledge that this is the last time for something. Beginnings of dying, for me, for them. I am sad too because I sense that they don't want to go. This is a defeat for them, some kind of defeat. Their children want them to move, their place is too far away. No more the river, Bronx River Park, no more this particular light. As we return I passionately love their building, its lobby, huge and white marble. The polished stone, the urns in the entry hall. Brass work over the elevator. The cool space and the silence.

● ● ● ● ●

We are visiting my grandfather at "the pharmacy" (this is distinctly earlier, before the move). Corner store, with blue marble tile at the entrance, one of those posts marking the corner, you can cut a diagonal across the en-tranceway to turn the corner. Or go round the post in circles, looking at the blue tiles. He is not a pharmacist, but somehow he works here a lot. My mother's sister Barbara has married a pharmacist and my grandfather assists in the shop. I love to go behind the counter with him. The back room, filled with jars of roots, and dried leaves, all with those peculiar domed glass tops, the kind that end in a knob. The scales, and small weights. Colored powders.

Child and old man are equals here, in the light of recognition. Here we are both at home. This place more familiar to me than my child's body. These smells of herbs. Polished wooden tables where things are mixed. Is it we have been alchemists together? We are so still. High windows in the back, with stained glass on the borders. We meet each other, timeless, in this light.

● ● ● ● ●

DREAM (AUTUMN 1987):

I am in an ancient church in Sicily. In the dream I think that it is "like a mosque"—it is actually bare stone, hung with incredibly rich cloths: deep colors of red, gold, green—satins and brocades. The light is the light of sun on grey stone, but filtered through all these colors. There are pews without seats—we can stand or kneel only, and I am jammed in with members of the family, to attend a funeral. My Uncle Joe has died, and my Aunt Mary is up in front with the coffin, more or less conducting the event.

The funeral service is going on, and it is mainly music, incredibly beautiful vocal music, Arabic in its modulations, but polyphonic, with one voice joining another. In the dream, it is very important for me to understand how "Arabic" my people are (the Sicilian side of the family). It will help me to understand my life.

People are crowding in beside me, there is a lot of jockeying for position by various (female) relatives—the aunts and my oldest daughter—and I am pushed to the outside of the pew, close to the aisle. I decide to move up one row: closer to the altar, which is just the coffin and these incredible hangings. There is more room there, for some reason the next "pew" is half empty.

I start to move, and then out of nowhere my father comes and stands beside me, blocking the way out. I feel as I always felt when confronted with my father's physical presence—claustrophobic and repelled. But I am mostly taken by the ambiance: the music, and the light of that place. Intensity of grief, the melody line of a dirge. Without looking at me, or otherwise acknowledging my presence, my father puts a hand on the back of my neck, just where my neck joins my shoulders. The gesture is humble in a way—even apologetic—and yet it presses on me. It is heavy, demanding: "You're going to have to deal with me somehow". I am aware of the nexus of nerves in that place in my body, the chronic pain of my shoulders and arms.

I don't turn or look at him, but in the light and the passion of the "Arabic" music, I begin to pray. I am not used to praying and I reach for the words, forming them very slowly in the dream-time:

> "LET ME FIND IT IN ME
> TO FORGIVE THIS MAN."

In my dream I repeat this over and over. And I wake forming the words with my lips, an enormous sense of physical release in my body, and a real sense that the work is to find it in me—in my very flesh, the release point for this past.

chapter TWO

I am standing in the kitchen of my parents' house. It is still daylight, I am aware of the light. It is still daylight, but my father is home, so perhaps it is summer. There is that feeling about the light. I am looking at the kitchen floor: black and white squares of linoleum in a checkered pattern. Perhaps there is light on them that cuts across the pattern making other patterns. The squares of linoleum are quite close; I am very short. Perhaps I am three years old.

My parents are sitting in the center of the room, at the kitchen table. It is a brown table, with a brown "enamel" top, very popular to have these table tops, considered more efficient, though I didn't know that yet. Some of the aunts who are poorer have them in plain white, but this one is mottled brown and tan, with a solid brown edge, repeated where there are "leaves" to open it up to seat more folks. I suspect my line of sight is no higher than these edges. I remember that dirt or food drippings would catch there sometimes, between the two layers of table. I would be fascinated by it, by the slight mess, there was so little irregular in the outward trappings of my world, so few places to study the effects of drips, or the drifting of dust.

They are sitting at the table and they have been talking for some time. They are unaware of my presence, perhaps they think I am playing, that I am not in the room. I know they think that I can't or won't understand the conversation. They make this assumption often and I don't correct them. I am perhaps three, not much more, and I stare at the linoleum, and am very still and careful not to make noise, so they won't see me and send me away. Though I am right in their line of sight if they care to notice.

The conversation is heavy. They are talking about the War. They have been talking about the War for as long as I can remember, sometimes in English, often in Italian. I am forbidden to speak Italian, but I understand when they speak it. They do not know this, it is another secret. They have been talking about the War for as long as I can remember, it is the fact, the condition of existence. I am perhaps three years old, this is 1937 or 1938, and the War is everywhere. For me it is everywhere: the War between my parents, the War between myself and the entity they are, the War between all the family and what I have gathered is a hostile world. My father goes out into it and returns discouraged. There is War upon War in my world, and they are all muted, hushed—my parents never argue.

There is also some vast global entity called the War which keeps coming closer. I understand vaguely that it threatens the homeland, the same land my grandfather speaks of with such love. The land of olive trees and battered books. Everyone is afraid of it, everyone wonders what they will do when it happens. In my child's mind they are all one, these Wars: a sense of blackness and of desolation which sits often in my house, in my parents' house.

That blackness hangs over the kitchen table as they speak. I can feel it make the air heavy, it is hard for me to move. I look past the edge of my starched dress, the ruffles standing out, away from my body, to the squares of linoleum, black and white, the white meticulously clean, and I listen. My father says, "We can't get out of it now", and my mother mutters something assenting, almost a whimper of agreement, not even a sad attempt at consolation in it, only agreement and fear.

I stand in the corner by the kitchen sink, as far from them as I can be and still be in the room, and I hear the helplessness and the fear in my father's voice. For the first time, it comes home to me, he is afraid. They are afraid, and helpless, they don't know what to do. It comes clear to me with vehemence and terror: *We can't get out of it now.* My parents are scared, and powerless, and I am in their power. On some deep level I already sense a truth: if things got heavy they wouldn't know how to survive. For a moment I am paralyzed with terror.

And then something else takes over, a fury fills my child's body, almost burns out the circuits: I am in their hands, and they are helpless, cowed people. Anger pours through me, I feel my face flush, and my body becomes stronger, straighter, buys a strength beyond its years with a kind of rigidity. They don't know how to survive: it is up to me to figure it out for myself. For them, too, if I can: it seems to me that I have to take them along. I am still too young to conceive of survival without them. I feel contempt, and impatience; an unchildlike sense of pity too, and the first stirrings of the scheming, manipulating part of the mind. I will have to *think* to trick them into keeping alive. Into keeping me alive. I don't quite know how to think yet, not in that way, and my head feels tight from the effort.

That sense of confidence I feel with my grandparents, never returns with my parents. They are bowed: sad, intimidated people, and, I suspect even then, somewhat stupid. I'm on my own from here on out.

● ● ● ● ●

It seems to me it is spring, and I am playing on "the roof". The Brooklyn brownstone we lived in till I was seven, the first one I remember, was an anomaly: gables and jutting roofs instead of the flat "row house" shape I came to know as typical. One of the windows opened on a flat tar roof, over a florist's shop on the ground floor with the huge, more than man-sized Chinese vase in the window. I remember asking later about that vase, strange to me; it filled the window but there was nothing in it. And my father, or an uncle, telling me that it was full of dollar bills. For years I tried to figure out how much money it would hold.

But that was later. Now my legs are very short, I am very close to the kitten who is on the roof with me and my mother. My mother is playing with me. It is the only time I remember us playing together. There is something about the randomness of the play that stays with me. The randomness of the kitten, its furry warmth. That we toddled here and there together *with no purpose.* There is very little I can remember doing then without a purpose. Running about in the sun and laughing with my mother. She still young and looking very happy. I knew even then the moment was poignant, unusual. I felt some other thing coming. The laughter was so full, with an edge of sobs.

I didn't want to come in, didn't want it to end. Soon after, the kitten was gone; no pet we had was tolerated more than two weeks. No furry, warm-blooded moving pet, at any rate. They were, I was told, "too messy". They moved about at random, left fur about. Were unpredictable. Goldfish we had, and turtles. I got the message.

I didn't know that then. Only knew the edge of sadness in the laughter. It was, she said, time to come in. We played on the floor, me longing for the sun. For my mother's laughter, her belly under her apron. Was she carrying my brother? I remember my parents' long discussions, in Italian, and in my presence, about the bugbear of my predicted jealousy. How to avoid it when the baby came. The child psychology of that time. There was no kitten when the baby came. That gentle being would have been seen as dangerous.

And when my mother came home with my round pale brother, she taught me this song:

> *I am the sister of him*
> *and he is my brother*
> *he is too little for us*
> *to talk to each other*
>
> *so every morning*
> *I show him my doll and my book*
> *and every morning*
> *he still is too little to look.*

He still is too little to look. The child psychology of the day insisted that newborns didn't see anything for at least three weeks. Would have been sure that neither I nor the kitten knew that spring day was our last day together. And I never told my parents that I understood Italian.

● ● ● ● ●

We have gone down to the boat to see them off. "They" are another part of the family, I understand this much, though I don't know any of them well, hardly at all, and by now the names are gone. My father's father was Pietro, and he had a brother, Giuseppe. The War had come closer by this time. My father's father and his brother had come to America together years before. Pietro had baked bread, and Giuseppe pastries, and they had worked together for others, and then for themselves. Now the War was very close, and Giuseppe had decided to "go home", to return to Sicily. He was leaving with all his family. The word that was used was that the family was being "divided".

We went down to the boat, and I was full of excitement. The smells of the water and the dock, and bustle of hundreds of people. It seems to me we seldom went out even then, me and my parents. Later it became obsessive: my father would never even eat in a restaurant.

But now Giuseppe was leaving with all his tribe, and Pietro's tribe had gone down to see them off. It seemed there were hundreds of us, hundreds of Di Primas. The air was rich with the soft sound of Sicilian.

I was full of excitement, but I knew better than to express it. The air was heavy with tragedy; this was a ritual we had all engaged in many times before. Or so it seems to me now. A Mediterranean, or North African ritual, the splitting of a tribe. Pietro, my mother said, had "chosen to stay in America". Cousins wept, and wondered if they would next see each other across battle lines.

(It was not clear at that point, not clear at all what part we Italian Americans would play. How we would fare in the war. Following the rules of some other nation, some other era, my father and his brothers would later argue in the kitchen, offering to take each other's place in the draft: "They might as well take me, I am not married. I am not even engaged. The rest of you have responsibilities". The counterargument: "They should take me. You are the youngest one. It would kill Papa if anything happened to you". There was the fear they would have to fight "their own people".)

A Mediterranean ritual, the makings of Greek tragedy. I know that now, but then I wondered at the grownups' insistence on tears. For me the wonder was the sun, the open space, the smell of the docks, the size of that boat. It seemed to me that it needn't sail at all. As long as it was, Giuseppe's family could *walk* to Europe. A kind of floating bridge, black, and trimmed with an orange red. The prow so high and black, the curve of it, so right, made me feel full. Inexplicable the grief the grownups lived with; the light poured down, we sat on suitcases. We broke bread together one last time. A man I barely remember held me on his knee.

• • • • •

When does fear enter, and how does it "feel"? Or does it, as I sometimes think, not *feel* at all in its beginnings—a shock of terror without emotional affect?

I am about two, I am still sleeping in a crib, its white bars pulled high around me to prevent my "falling out"—climbing out? The crib is in the middle of the room, not against any wall; it is open, exposed on all four sides. Behind me is a door, with a rectangular glass pane. There is a light beyond the door, the pane is a bright yellow and very fearsome. I know this though I don't feel it.

What is clear to me is that "tigers" can come through this door and approach me from behind. They can and will eat, devour, any part of me that is exposed. Wherever bare skin shows. The trick is to lie with my face completely submerged in the pillow; with my hands tucked under the pillow, and the blanket coming just up to the place where they disappear. *To lie very still* so the blankets won't be disturbed; so no ankle, or toe peeks out. I slept like this for years, till the time—was I seven or eight—when all these elaborate protections weren't enough.

● ● ● ● ●

It is hard now to reconcile that sinister piece of yellow light with the warmth and strength I felt when hanging out with my grandparents, Antoinette and Domenico. That they were happening at the same time; same period of my life. A schizophrenia of sorts. Two worlds so different that even at this distance they don't seem to be part of the same life.

● ● ● ● ●

In the last years before her death my mother told me for the first time that I had spent the first sixteen days of my life in the hospital nursery. She herself too sick to go home. Though from the time I was very small I had heard from her various sisters that she had "nearly died" having me: what a long labor it was, how she had hemorrhaged afterwards, somehow I had telescoped all that into the usual five-day hospital stay. Two and a half weeks of electric light day and night, of whatever weird nursery beds they used in 1934, of being brought to my mother to nurse and then taken away.

As we talked of this I asked what her sickness had been, and she told me that after my birth an ovarian cyst had "filled up with fluid" and had to be drained. It was with vast relief I exclaimed "Oh, then it was something you already had. My birth didn't 'cause' it"! only to have this eighty-one-year-old woman turn on me in fury.

"It *was* because of the birth that I got sick. That is what *brought it on*".

● ● ● ● ●

After the hospital we went to my mother's family in the Bronx, and it was in Antoinette's arms that I first tasted safety. The smell of her body even then was the smell of home. Antoinette and Domenico cared for me and for my mother Emma, their frail daughter. My father quite probably came up to visit. Quite probably he stayed with his family, I never asked. But he didn't cook, or clean, or care for himself, so he would have had to stay somewhere.

My memory of nursing is painful and double, the breast held out like a weapon, a shield or wall between us. The breast held out, the body withdrawn and rigid. What was the source of her terror? From where did it emerge? Into her brittle life.

● ● ● ● ●

I have frequently argued theories of infant care with my mother to no avail. It is as a result of these "discussions" that a picture emerges of the next few months of my life. Up to her death Emma totally subscribed to the theory that children should be cared for "by the clock". Again and again she warned me not to respond to my children's cries, not to feed them "on demand". Her own pattern with me she held up as the best of all: ten minutes of nursing on each breast; burp 'em; and put them back down in the crib. Never go in if they cry, never linger over the feeding. Pick them up again in four hours exactly. If they are asleep, wake them up and feed them; and if they are hungry in between, ignore it. She died convinced that my rambunctious crew would never make it: they would be enormously fat and self-indulgent.

Working now with the image/information, I find a root/radix so deep that to dig it up feels like I'm digging up my very self, my identity. A kind of axiom, familiar as the feel of gravity on my body: *that human need and the Order of the World are at odds.* Are basically incompatible. There is the smell and feel of Romanticism in this conviction. And I flash on my first peyote trip, Lower East Side 1959, where I wept for the soft and vulnerable flesh things of the world in a universe that seemed metal and precise as clockwork. Armored as beetles, and moving with blind precision, I could almost hear the clicks of the machine.

● ● ● ● ●

It was probably mid-September when we went home to my father. It must have been a shock. It seems like too many changes for too few weeks. The shortening days, the anxiety in the air. My mother and father strangers to each other. Frightened off by the birth and her subsequent retreat.

● ● ● ● ●

Each year in September when the days begin to shorten perceptibly I experience a rather odd reaction. As the shadows grow long, and the light golden and full, just before sunset, I am caught each evening by chills and flushed cheeks. It's best if I can lie down. I feel as if my power is draining from me; an overwhelming sadness and horror of the coming time (the short days, the cold) possesses me. This has gone on as long as I can remember; by mid-October it is usually gone.

It is only within the last year that I have come to see this as a remembrance. Remembrance of coming into that house. My mother's sickness, and my father's anger. The anxiety of their lives and that vicious, bright yellow glass.

● ● ● ● ●

About six months after my mother died I had a dream. The focus or perspective of the dream kept shifting: at times I was seeing it through my own eyes, and at times through hers. She was at a bridge at the end of a city, and it was snowing. Wind was blowing and there was ice underfoot. In some ways the bridge was like the bridge over the Arno in Florence. It was certainly steady enough, but through her eyes it too seemed shifty, as if it might be swaying in this treacherous wintry wind.

Through all the last years of her life my mother, like so many very old people, had been afraid of losing her footing, and in the dream she was afraid of this. She called for me, her daughter, called by name for Diane, somewhat peremptory, as if she needed help in the kitchen and wanted to know why I wasn't just there—as for the first fifteen years of my life—at her beck and call. And I was, at any rate I came to her side at once, and stood with her in the wind and the snow whilst she fastened with that terribly strong grip of the very old—a death grip—onto my arm. We were both wearing cloth winter coats, I remember.

She was terribly afraid of losing her footing, and yet somehow we had to go on, had to make it across the bridge. Or *she* did, anyway, had no choice but to cross, I was just there as accessory, accomplice, something to hold onto, to keep her from losing her balance. We set out, crossing, Emma hanging onto the concrete rail and to my arm, peering down at her own feet she could scarcely see through the snow, through her glaucoma. As if by looking at them she could keep them from slipping.

We set out. There were shadowy other personages; they seemed to come over the bridge and over the water, indiscriminately. They seemed to walk, or float. They wore black and were backlit, somewhat faceless but not unkind. Not threatening.

There was a row of houses along the water on the far side of the river. Simple, elegant, facing the water as if on some fine marina. I admired the houses, and wondered how to get one. Would love to live there. Was told by dreamvoice in my head: They are the houses of those (dark personages) who help people making the crossing. Or they receive those who have crossed. Their only "job". They never leave this place, this bridge and far-side, and they receive those who have crossed. You can have one of these houses, but that is the gig, that is the price you pay.

We were slowly crossing, progress like worm or snail. My mother always feared and hated the cold. And ice. Called winter "treacherous". I was supporting her weight. We were crossing slowly, in a naturalistic landscape: bridge, river, houses, but something loomed ahead. An enormous figure, ten or twenty times human height and proportions. It was standing on the bridge, or it transected the bridge. The bridge disappeared into that huge female figure, dressed like old Italian women in a black cotton housedress. The bridge disappeared into her, and we walked the bridge. When we entered the figure, like a plane entering a cloud, we disappeared into her. Or rather there was no more bridge, no houses, no figures or landscape. Only this vastness, and yet our feet kept walking. A little more confident perhaps in this empty space. No ice here. We passed through her and came out on the other side. Still on the bridge, still in the storm, and the figure loomed once more ahead. I recognized it. It was Antoinette, my mother's mother. But huge.

Over and over, as we went on, we entered the figure of my grandmother, as if to disappear into her to become a part of that huge ancestral presence in a long black dress. Over and over we found ourselves back on the bridge.

My mother's fatal illness was sudden and swift. She had not been sick. It was a Sunday afternoon, and she had just put a batch of stuffed peppers into the oven to bake. The timer was on and would turn the oven off. She must have been having a headache—she rarely took medicine, and there were several uncapped aspirin bottles around the house when she was found. She apparently attempted to call my brother, who lived in the next town, failed to dial, left the receiver dangling off the hook and fell on the rug a few feet from the phone. A constant busy signal alerted my sister-in-law Weezie, and when she and my brother Frank arrived they found Emma on the rug, speaking in Italian. My brother thought he heard her speak to her mother. She didn't appear to recognize anyone, but once they got there, she must have understood that help had arrived, and allowed herself to lose consciousness. She never came to again. She was eighty-three.

How like a winter storm the *bardo* must seem, to one who hates winter and storms, is afraid of falling. How the last light in the brain might well light a portion of childhood: her speaking to "mom" in soft Neapolitan. I knew that months later I had dreamed her death, how it had been for her: the terror of the icy crossing, the melting into the vast ancestral form, alternating as she clung, or let go. And that I had been with her that night as she died; she had summoned me.

Privilege of oldest child, and only daughter. To be there, whether I would or no through all of mom's endless terrors. Death grip I felt since my earliest memories. Hysterical strength of those fingers. Incredible weight on my thin arm, and with it reiterated denial: this wasn't so bad. I can recall helping with the cooking when I was barely tall enough to reach the pan on the stove, being burned by some spattered oil, and being told:

That *Women had to learn to bear more pain than men. That was just how they were made.* Women, mom went on to tell my puzzled little self, had periods, had babies; even in cooking and cleaning they got hurt more. I would, she assured me, get used to it. My fingers would get callused, and pots and fire wouldn't hurt as they did now. I looked forward to this armor as a good thing; she described it as a blessing.

My Aunt Evelyn, my mother's sister, sang at her work, she had a beautiful low vanity table with cut glass bottles full of perfumes and oils. Her eyes sparkled; she didn't talk of pain, or "getting through the day somehow". When I was allowed to visit, I followed her from room to room just to see her smile. To bask in the light that came out of her. I didn't know then what I drank in in her house. Some lack of fear, some joy in her daily life; the love between her and her husband. Two lives not ruled by *ananke,* necessity. Not filled with the dark.

I write this book to try to understand what messages I got about being a woman. What that is. How to do it. Or get through it. Or bear it. Or sparkle like ice underfoot.

One time, about eight years old, I took the train to Flushing to be met by Uncle Arthur, Evelyn's husband, and taken out to Bayside for a visit. Instead of proceeding immediately to the bus, Uncle Arthur detoured into a small dark shop—probably mostly a tobacco and magazine store, but there were toys. Many toys on a high shelf overhead, behind the counter. And Arthur directed me to pick a toy, pick anything I wanted, to take with me to Bayside. It was, I was certain, not my birthday, nor was it Christmas. It took me a while to get over my confusion, and pick a toy. It was the first time I encountered the notion of grace, as something outside of karma, outside of what we "deserve".

A *man's work,* mom would say, and I'm sure we've all heard it, all of us close to my age and generation, heard it many times,

> *A man's work is from sun to sun*
> *A woman's work is never done.*

In Emma's world, women never lay down while the sun was up. I was close on fifty before I was able to lie down in the daytime, to take a nap in the light. But a toy in Bayside, three beveled mirrors at a "vanity" table, pointed to some other way.

● ● ● ● ●

My mother's life was one of determined cheerfulness. Neatness. On entering her apartment with Weezie the day after she died, that was what struck me: how *cheerful* it all was. And impeccably clean. The few clouded glasses, dusty corners, a sure sign that she had been slipping those last weeks. "Not herself". As also the index card where she'd written a word over and over, trying to remember its spelling.

Her youngest sister, my Aunt Ella, characterized this in a letter she wrote me right after my mother's death. Emma, she said, had always been "a lady". Dark undertones she was unconscious of.

It was often a cheerfulness bought at the expense of much of what was real, what was deep in Emma's life. And in most of our own. The day of Emma's funeral I returned with my two brothers to my brother Frank's house in New Jersey, and the three of us talked for the first time in our lives of some of the darker stuff. *It was as if a vast weight had lifted. A net that had fallen on us before we could see, hampering our movements and impeding our vision of each other.* We learned, for one thing, that each of us thought himself/herself the black sheep of the family. The major disappointment in Emma's life. We exchanged information that we'd each kept secret: a pending divorce, a chronic illness in one of our children. Information we'd kept to ourselves to avoid breaching the cheerfulness, the determined perfection of our lives. Our perpetual fear: "That it would get back to mom".

It is clear to me now that that cheerfulness was a form of terrorism; a device of the totalitarian state. A form of black magick that constellated a world by willpower and froze it into place with fear. This magick has invaded every cell of my body; to this day I am fighting to get clear.

It was not till a year before her death that Emma told me about her "breakdown": an event of the shadowy past, an occurrence of at least sixty years before. The occasion of this disclosure was her last visit to the West Coast; she was installed half a block from my flat in a room at the Zen Center Guest House: genteel, quiet, cheerful, and very clean. It was a perfect place for her, as she could not manage my stairs. It saved our having to deal with the fact that there was no way I could accommodate her in my home: it was neither clean, nor cheerful, nor genteel.

Mom loved the Guest House. She loved the flower arrangements and the girl who came to change them and the well-appointed kitchen. She and I were going full out in our own ways; meeting for hours to tape family history. It was during the taping that several discrepancies came to light.

The first was a relatively minor one, but telling. She mentioned when asked that she was born in 1902, my father in 1904. Now, all the while that I was growing up it was known, well known amongst all the aunts and other relations that Emma was three years younger than Dick. It turns out that this fiction was perpetrated for a simple, and to Emma an obvious, reason: in her world, the woman in a marriage was supposed to be younger than the man. Younger, and shorter. Both of these were important. It emphasized that the man was the leader in the partnership. I remember her saying cheerfully and often, "I'm three years younger and two inches shorter", as if it were a litany. Which in fact, it was.

So Emma went through life being three years younger than Dick, five years younger than her age. Always vague about how old she was when asked, but that, too, was accepted: in her day no "lady" told her age.

The second discrepancy was a bit more complex. Remains in my life a bottomless pit, a endless sequence of question marks. As we talked in her neat and cheerful room with our pot of Zen Center tea between us, and the tape machine grinding away, I made a few notes in my ever-present journal. I did a small bit of arithmetic. It showed my mother graduating from college at the age of twenty-five. No big deal, but with her penchant for punctuality, for not "falling behind" at anything—especially not at school—it made no sense at all. I did the arithmetic again. It came out the same.

"So you graduated from NYU", I asked carefully (the flow of information could turn off at any moment) "when you were twenty-five"?

"That's right".

"How come? Isn't that a little older than normal"? *In my world we go back to school when we please, mom, for whatever weird subject draws us: Sumerian, ikebana, vector analysis. But in your world there was "normal".*

The careful wording paid off. She answered.

"First there was the Spanish influenza. After the War". (For her the War was always World War I, as for me it has been World War II.) "And then I had my breakdown".

"What breakdown"? *Treading on eggs here, careful.*

Emma looked vague. "I guess I went out of my head and said strange things. One day I said things that weren't right, that didn't make any sense and the next day I woke up in a darkened room with the curtains drawn".

One day, the next day? But we are talking about three years. Or, even if the influenza epidemic accounted for a year—unlikely but possible—we're talking about two years.

"I don't know, Diane. I don't remember any more about it".

The curtain was drawn again, and there was no penetrating it. Arcanum. The backstage of that bright and cheerful life. We drank our Zen tea; we went out to dinner.

It was on that same trip that my mother gave me a gift: gift of herself; of myself. We had returned for the third time to the conservatory in Golden Gate Park; it was her favorite place, we spent hours there, talking and taking pictures in the towering greenery. We had returned for the third time; I had helped her with curbs and steps; and we were on the threshold of a room full of tropical growth. We swung the door open, warm mist and the smell of loam enveloped us, and my mother turned to me with fierceness in her eyes—eyes made ridiculously large, like a baby's, by her thick bifocals.

"Isn't it a shame", she said fiercely "that we leave this earth without seeing everything there is to see on it"?

It was then, in that eighty-two-year-old woman, that I recognized something of myself. Something that would not rest "without seeing everything there is to see". Fierce hunger, a glimpse out of her own father's eyes. I saw mom standing on a peak of the Himalayas, peering at plants in Amazonian jungles, rounding the Cape (whatever Cape) in a skiff. My heart jumped.

"Of course", she added, coming to her senses. To her neat and cheerful world. "Of course I don't really want to see anything but you and the children".

We walked into that tropical, glassed-in place. We closed the door.

● ● ● ● ●

There are these moments I treasure; moments of truth close on the death of a parent. No matter what our lives have been, however horrendous and painful the interaction over decades. There is mom in the doorway of a room full of tropical plants, her hunger for the world blazing from behind her thick glasses; there is dad in the car on the way to our country house.

That house is interesting, in retrospect, because it is the only one in which I feel no secrets, no secret rooms. It was perhaps too flimsy, and its design too open for the kind of strange nighttime occurrence that filled my childhood. It was, too, that I was sixteen or older when the family acquired it, and by then all but simple overt violence had stopped. I was fifteen when we first went to Greenwood Lake and older than that when the family finally bought the house.

In my mind the "house at the Lake" lies open, simple, patent, each room explorable and possible. It is the only glimpse I have of what growing up, living as a child in that kind of open world might have been like. It is not that I wish for it; just that I can't quite conceive of it. It remains on the edge of mind, an almost-grasped possibility; like some equation in quantum physics.

In the time I was thinking of, I had long since left home. Had had by then, in various styles and ways incomprehensible to the family, three children. I had come back for a visit, and we were driving to the Lake. Me and my father, and others. I don't really remember who shared that front seat with him. Perhaps it was one of my brothers. I think that on this particular occasion mom was already at the Lake. I have the feeling this conversation would never have happened if she was there.

I was, I remember sitting in the back of the car, the Dodge Dart my father was so proud of, and we were well out of the city, driving through sparse New Jersey countryside, when he asked me about Zen. It was a well-known and somewhat puzzling fact to my friends and relatives that I had left New York for the West Coast to study Zen with one Shunryu Suzuki. This being, at any rate, the most accessible reason I could give them for my defection from all they held dear. All they saw as a Way of Life.

He asked me about Zen; he had to turn around in the car to do it. What was it, what did it teach? More or less, what did I believe at this point was the hidden question though I didn't see that then. What was Zen about?

Thick, white, phlegmatic body, thinned reddish hair, turned to me with worry, with his usual oppressed and preoccupied expression as he drove, and I wished he would keep his eyes on the road, knowing him to be a terrible driver, not trusting this turning around business. What was Zen about?

I don't know what I answered, bumbling about in what was then my "understanding" (as Suzuki called it) for words that would make sense to him, bridge somewhat the gap. Wary, but I flashed on a book called *Yoga for Businessmen* or some such that I had seen at the Brooklyn house the day before. Don't know what I expounded, what belief system, half understood, I offered, but I do remember how his face lit up.

"I see what you're saying. In other words, no matter what you do, you can never make a mistake". The vast relief, yes, *liberation,* in that voice. The sudden feeling of space and openness in that small car. Amazement, too, that we had communicated, some energy or vision had passed between us.

I was to think of this years afterward as his absolution. (This was our last real visit before his death.) But at the time I had no memory, only the dimmest sense of what there was to absolve. Remembered only dimly the most recent beatings in the years before I left home, the terrible trauma and price of the day of my leaving, but nothing of the previous horror. It was to be years before I won back even fragments of that. I win them back now, piece by piece, and partly through this writing.

But that day in that red Dodge Dart on the way to the Lake the sunlight shifted and moved itself inside the car; or there was a space we had never met in before. Space of no-judgment, what a Zen master might call *ken-sho*, a small *satori*, passed from my mind to his. *No matter what you do, you can never make a mistake.*

In the fury and inscrutable karma of our lives together, I am infinitely glad that we shared that moment of peace. Safely separated by car seats, by the countryside, from the pathos of his life of rage and terror. An answer so simple—subtle and direct at once. "The way out is through the door, dad". But those words were only in my mind. It was he who said it, who put it out there, Zen-style.

No matter what you do, you can never make a mistake.

chapter THREE

There are these awkwardnesses I've never quite identified, skills I've never learned. How to dress, wear make-up, present oneself to the world. To know what one looks like, even. I've never known. The body is pain. Is known from the inside out, has no exterior. Is pain, grief, discomfort, imploded anger. Containable or not, is the defining characteristic. Can it be borne?

Most of my early memory of touch, all of my memory of my mother's touch, is pain. How she scrubbed me in the bath till my skin was raw. The dresses stiff with starch that rubbed holes into my neck, my waist. Things that dug into the flesh: underwear elastic, the too-high backs of patent leather shoes. What could be borne.

When told you "looked nice" there was nothing intrinsic about it, it had nothing to do with your body, your face, your hair. As who you were had nothing to do with your mind, your perceptions. You Look Nice meant that somehow the right things had been done to you to effect a certain image (which you, yourself, could never quite perceive, and therefore could never duplicate). At issue was, how long you could hold it all in place: the sock cuffs, the locks of hair. How much you could breathe or move and still contain it.

Thus body image, or the lack of it. Mom undressing for bed in a closet every night of her married life, getting into bed in her nightgown. Her idea or my father's? Photos of her and her sisters, sensuous bathing beauties of the 1920s with their long hair and well-placed legs, make me think the idea was my father's. Mind-blowing. Perhaps they never looked at each other naked. How would I know what a body was, my body?

I knew only that it hurt. Hurt to be washed, scrubbed: soap in the eyes, shampoo, rough digging into the ears, the ass, soap on the cunt. Daily grooming as torture. Mom would boast of how many combs she *broke on my hair,* trying to get the tangles out. Great heavy combs with "unbreak-able" stamped across the top in gold. She'd pull them straight through my hair, pulling handfuls out daily. My thick, ultra-curly red hair that was my special and particular torture, beyond the more common tortures of bath shared by the brothers. *They* got to have short hair. Mine was groomed daily into "Shirley Temple curls" at the cost of exquisite agony. Was my mother's pride and joy.

I soon couldn't see how it looked, even when I looked in the mirror. Could only feel it, the constant pain of hair pulled too tight, held into place with hairpins, the aching scalp. Headaches, they said, from "the weight of the hair", but didn't offer to cut it. I learned the better it looked the more it hurt. An equation.

"How nice you look" mom called to us out of the window one blustery Easter Sunday. It was too cold for the clothes we were wearing, the "spring coats", the skimpy dress, my brother Frank's short pants. She had stayed home, I think now, so that she could see us from the window, see us walking down Court Street with my dad. (How ill they could afford in those days these trappings from the Brooklyn department stores! I wonder now what pressure the extra expense was, and how that fed into his temper, the beatings.) We strolled all three of us slowly down the block, so she could see us from the corner window. Past the florist from whom we never bought a flower.

"How nice you look", and how desperately she needed that image: her two "nicely dressed" Americanly dressed (or so she thought) children with the background of this street, located here in place and time acceptable. It anchored us all to America, to Brooklyn-before-the-War. We knew who and what we were because the picture made sense.

But I could never see it, any of it. Couldn't and didn't see that picture at all. Couldn't see my body, only feel it as pain. So that years later, when the beatings had stopped, I took for a while in shame and trembling to hit-ting myself with a belt to know I was real, was there.

I sit here in make-up. It is Mother's Day. My kids are about to take me out to dinner. I am actually enjoying my hair (cut shoulder-length, loose, easy

to care for), my skin, the feel of my clothes against it. I am actually enjoy-
ing learning to paint my face. Playful disguises if and when I want them.
It has taken all these years.

The first time I attempted make-up I was thirteen, I was going to a
school dance with a girlfriend. When my mother came to pick me up, she
took one look at me and began to cry. "How could you do this to me"? She
cried all the way home and for sometime after, and made a point of not
telling my father.

The message stopped me dead in my tracks. I got the sense I wasn't
supposed to grow up. I wasn't supposed to shift the balance in the house.
That I was a whore for rearranging my hair, a painted woman for painting
my lips. That what I had done was somehow directly threatening to my
mother, and that I should have known. I who could hardly see my face or
feel my body, wrote them off as forbidden.

I went to college with my face scrubbed clean, and in the clothes
my mother picked for me. Effectively withdrew from concerns of this
order.

Years later, an even profounder message, coming as it did into my (I
thought) free and independent life, set the seal on a lot of these memories,
made me understand the transmission from my mother was simply that
body was commodity, not person. Treat it as you will, as you must, to serve
other ends: placate a man, bring in money, whatever. Let it hurt.

It was the 1960s, and I was living precariously in Manhattan with my
husband Alan and three kids. We were doing far from well financially, but
getting by and basically joyous in a rollicking life full of friends, running
theatres and presses. Art and intensity at a high point of the city's history,
and of our own.

My mother phoned one day to offer a way for me to make some money.
She was doing it too. All we had to do was test some cosmetics for a week
to make one hundred dollars. I of course agreed, and found myself applying two creams to the inside of my upper arms, one for the right arm, one
for the left. Apply them daily for a week, and then go in to be tested: it
seemed simple enough.

On the day of the testing I went in all innocence to the lab and something jelled for me, some horror that I have never lost. At the lab a small
round *deep* piece of flesh was cut from each arm. I could not believe it:
that I was selling my flesh, my actual substance, for one hundred dollars.
That my mother should have so casually set me up to do this, that she
thought so little of it, thought so little of her own body that she was doing

this herself. Lower than slave flesh, to be bartered for so little. To *acqui-esce* in being degraded so.

I still have the scars on my arms. I never talked to her about this shame-ful "work", her horrible certainty that I would be glad of the money.

Writing about this now, I see that for my mother to sell off my flesh so cheaply and openly when I was a grown woman speaks also of unspeakable barters made in the dark when I was a child. That my father's wrath be ap-peased, that my mother be left in peace with her griefs, her "breakdowns". Barters made by her own denial, her acquiescence.

● ● ● ● ●

This nonseeing, not knowing how I look. Contract between the visible world and the invisible worlds of the mind. Not seeing the face in the mir-ror, not ever sure. What is acceptable or not. And the perception is cut off before it can be formed. I had lost my face before I could focus to see it in the mirror. I never saw it at all.

There was this ambivalence: one wanted to "look nice", but the cost was so high. There was the pain: prettier = more painful. And, too, if one looked *too* nice one called attention. Unwanted caresses, demands, the in-evitable beating. The fear you might be taken for "uppity". Never knowing what it would be that would please, what would bring the blow. And the whole process was external to yourself; it was not *you* who looked nice, but some external armor. Descended on you from the skies, or through the agency of your mother and her sisters. Like Heracles' shirt, it killed.

Better forget it. Better not see who you are. My houses have always had a paucity of mirrors. Better not to see at all.

My whole life I have been nearsighted, a child in pink plastic-framed glasses, an adult whose love of landscape (was it transferred from the love of the human figure?) made her long to see farther. One day in the 1970s, I was living in northern California, and I dreamed that I was closeted in a very small room with a huge and vague figure who was very dangerous. Very perilous, that you might accidentally brush up against this figure as it flailed heavily about the space. The figure was murderous, capable of terrible rage. The space small and bare, no place to hide, and you had to stay out of its way. Then that small cowering person took a psychic turn, and I woke up on the fervent words "I will see it", repeated over and over.

For the next two weeks I walked through the world with the gift of perfect sight. My eyes alive and awake as they've never been. Each distant hill in focus. My vision slowly faded, but to this day I can bring more seeing by repeating that dream phrase.

So perhaps there was more that I would not, could not see, but the hardest is not to see one's own face and body. "The sequence of exchange starts with oneself" says a Buddhist text.

Perhaps that is why I spent years of my life working as a model. Letting the aging painters of New York paint me over and over. I can "see" art. I was looking for myself in it.

The sequence of exchange begins with oneself, but it moves out, into the world. And brings blessing, as well as confusion. In nursery school when I was two, what I remember is the airplanes in posters on the walls. Above the low, red-enameled tables we sat at. I sat with a boy who told me the planes were real. Would soon fly into the rooms, and might in fact kill us. I wasn't so worried, thought I could probably duck. Perhaps I already had experience ducking. But as for the reality of those images, those airplanes, I held no doubt.

Not strange at two, but it persisted. In kindergarten the pictures in our books, usually Christ and disciples—this was St. Stephen's on First Place, two blocks from my home—these pictures, too, were real. These characters in robes might walk at any moment into the room. Invade one's life.

The persistence of the invisible worlds, past the developmental point where we learn to distinguish. Up to this very day. How often is my dream an event I am sure transpired in the waking world? How much more clearly do I find myself in ancient rooms, as I read of the Templars or Alexandria? More clear than the street outside.

There are goodies, rewards for the subtle demotion of consensus reality, as well as present confusions. But it began I am sure in a subtle shift of attention: away from the body, from the very flesh I inhabit. It was too painful to dwell in. I seek now, like how many others?, to reclaim the body. Without losing my passport to transcendent worlds. Without forgetting the map of the passages.

The secret gnosticism of Dante, of my grandfather, who so claimed the here and now in his politics, passed through the hysteria and grief of my mother, and arrived as the message "this world is intolerable". Translated

by me, age two or three, to "This world is not real. Does not take prece-
dence". Skill at astral travel, at "seeing" other worlds, not separate from
the inability to see my own face.

This world is intolerable. She made it so. With the best will in the world.
Distorted the acts of everyday life into agony. My skin the interface was always red. From scrubbing, from battering, from starch, from shame.

In kindergarten I couldn't see my classmates. Perceptions distorted, I
was pinned in fear on the teacher. Whoever she might have been. Only, I
saw she was big enough to hurt. To do damage. The damage was already
done, but I didn't know that. I learned to read early, never sure when the
pictures in the books would come alive. What their intentions might be.

Nursery school lasted only a couple of weeks. There were tall black iron
gates and a lawn. Mom took me there. A decompression chamber, some
sense of light, of pressure briefly off. Free-er to "be" myself. Whoever that
might be. In spite of my desk companions, the airplanes. Some peers, and
a breathing space.

(Though it was told of me there that when the teacher picked me up
to give me a hug, so unused was I to this straightforward human behavior
that I warned her not to wrinkle my dress. *My dress of a semitranslucent*
cotton, dyed lavender, light blue and pink, so that they almost ran together.
Colors that set me dreaming of other worlds. My mother was very proud
of me for this prissy behavior, the response of a child for whom touch, affection, was already *too much*.)

Mom had taken me to nursery school with trepidation. With the suspicion and mistrust with which both my parents always met the world. The
immigrant syndrome turned to paranoia. And so it was with relief I suspect, with something like relief—I felt it even then—that she took me out
again, and permanently after two weeks. The excuse was whooping cough.

After that, I didn't see a peer till kindergarten. A few youngsters arrived
in my world: my brother, my cousin Chickie. But no peers, these were
younger, I was supposed to tend them. Change diapers, hold bottles.
Mainly there were the grownups, my parents' friends. And the preparation for war.

● ● ● ● ●

The years that follow are a pitiable kind of siege. Lost battle. No clear
memories between eight years old and twelve. Between seven and twelve.

No sequences, nothing that holds still. Conjectures, dark, raised like spectres from the depths of my mind (depths of space). Raised deliberately, with much labor. And questionable.

I was eight when we moved from the apartment on First Place, to our house two blocks away. Our "own" house bought by the parents with much worry. A narrow brownstone, rooms spread over four stories. Two rooms to a floor. A house in which so much was done in secret, done on another floor, in another room. House of terror, and terrifying entities, real and imagined.

The actual "war" had begun in the "old house", the small living room with its green carpet, large wood radio. On which we heard the first warnings of would-be air raids. False alarms that brought my mother to the verge of madness, sent me scurrying home from school, dismissed at midday, no plan for what to do with the children, how to deal with such contingencies.

The war had begun in the old house but it was in the "new house" on Third Place that the War was truly waged. Waged worldwide and in my home. It seemed the external world existed as assault.

Over years I barely remember I watched my friends at school stricken with polio. Or met kids for the first time with metal braces already on their legs, crutches under their arms. Kids in wheelchairs. Little difference in my mind, the assault of disease and the assaults of the grownups. Only, that we kids were vulnerable, we hurt, we were easily broken. These kids had taken the brunt of something, and it was natural, almost a relief, that they could show it. Were expected to show it.

At home these years I was taking the brunt of something. Of something more than I know, even now can guess. Voices in my head invited me to die, the house was haunted. Unspeakable entities lurked in my father's office. And on the stairs each night as I went to bed. Terror of bedtime, not terror of the dark.

The assault was external, and it was all-inclusive. Like bombs falling out of the sky, indiscriminate and deadly. There was polio, and there was the war. There were the gangs on the block, or one block down. There were the kids, my "friends" who waited for me after school. To taunt me or beat me up. I never told any of this at home, what good would it have done? There, too, I was taunted and beaten. Or, as I thought then, I "didn't want to worry them".

The kids would wait outside to call me names. To pull on my corkscrew curls, punch me in the stomach. Somehow it was my fault, and I was ashamed. My main concern, how to get my brother through it without anyone hurting him. How to get home before mom noticed I was late.

For several years I had to come home twice a day. In an excess of zeal my mother prepared hot lunches, usually obnoxious Campbell's soups, and Frankie and I had to run home, eat scalding soup without spilling it on our school clothes, and run back without being late. Dodging my "friends" the while.

I suppose I was really an odd critter to them, and they did the only thing they knew how to do with alienness, the only thing they had been taught. With my curls, and my strange vocabulary (I was reading day and night, to avoid the rest of my home life). My stare that infuriated my parents, probably infuriated my peers. I see it in the photos of that period: utterly clear and fixed, trying to see through, to the motives behind the acts. I see it in the photos of me as an infant.

"Don't look at me that way"! my parents would say, and swing out.

The assault was external, and utterly terrifying. There was at my house a blackout on the news: early in 1942 my parents decided that since we were Italian we were on both sides of the war, and there could be no good news. The children, at least, were to be shielded from it. During the war years I never saw a paper; never heard the news on the radio. My parents listened in the middle of the night. I came to believe that what we might hear would be more horrible than *The Shadow* or *Inner Sanctum,* radio programs we were also forbidden. In a sense I was right.

The assault was external and it was ceaseless. At home there was blind unpredictable wrath, hysteria, and grief. In the streets, the boys from the next block—a dead-end block and therefore with some irrefutable and mysterious logic a "bad" block—would, if they caught you alone, drag you down to the closed-off street where the subway came out of the ground with a terrible roar, and try to feel you up, or pull off your clothes. At school, the nuns were prone to melancholy: hysteria and unpredictable wrath, which I came to believe was the inherent state of all "grownups". And after school your friends waited to hit you. When you went to bed you were most vulnerable of all, anything could happen to you and sometimes did.

School was the safest. It was possible, by being desperately good, desperately vigilant, and desperately intelligent, to carve out an oasis of time in which the nuns were on your side, and everyone else was controlled. A period of relative safety from at least the most physical terror. Of course you paid for this later with the hatred of your peers (you were a "goody-goody" and they would get you for it), I was aware even at eight of the trade-off. But: *it was the only safe time I experienced, and no price was too great.* As we hear today of the tortured accepting anything, trading anything, for a period of respite. Time of recuperation for the soul, even if the body is too far gone to recover.

Most of the diseases of my life have been diseases of stress, results of living in a universal siege: allergies, hives, gastritis, ulcers, muscle spasms, arthritis. The diseases of terror and the attempt to control.

Part of the bind was/is that it is "wrong" for women to control. To try to control, though the instinct is biological. To get a little peace. "Don't be teacher-etical" my parents would say. "You want everything your way". When I got older, what I heard from lovers, was that I was a controlling or castrating bitch. But—the assault was universal and ceaseless. You would have had to be dead not to try to stop it for a minute.

You could stop it sometimes with reading. My mother would stop it for me: "She's studying" she'd say, and leave me alone. Years later, when I had walked out on the madness at home, mom would blame herself: she had spoiled me, she believed, by letting me read instead of making me work.

There were gradations of respect given to reading, gradations of respite. Doing actual homework or studying for school came closest to being sacrosanct. Then reading for pleasure, or for whatever reasons. Last and lowliest was writing. It was, I was taught, imperative to make sure every chore was done before you wrote a poem. Though that didn't become an issue till my teen years. To this day, I have trouble spending money on myself for clothes, or to fix my teeth, but no guilt at all in spending hundreds of dollars on books: the only permitted escape.

The only one. With the sole exception of an abysmal Shirley Temple movie that I hated even at my young age, and even through my awe and amazement at the moving images on the screen, we as children saw no movies but Walt Disney and *The Wizard of Oz.* Somehow, in my parents' minds, Walt was the keeper of kids' morals and intelligence. Many of my early nightmares clothed themselves in Disney images. In spite of the rundown neighborhood "cinema" full of squealing Saturday afternoon kids and the most promising-looking posters, we never ventured into that incredible black and white world of the 30s and 40s. Were not allowed.

In addition to the lack of newspapers there were no comics. No marvels of newsprint and four-color printing crossed our threshold. No feats of magic, instant dialogues. Comics were for lowlifes, we were given to understand. For lower-class children who never really learned how to read. Instead my world was filled with the equally improbable adventures of various codependent Victorians. Child heroines who saved the family through plague, famine, and war. Who *strained to survive,* as I was always straining. Although they rarely seemed to get hit and the assault in general seemed softer. Less like continual invasion, rape.

● ● ● ● ●

Assault was the model of the world, the world around me. The world as my parents understood it. Anything could happen to you anytime, and mostly it wouldn't be good. Hence my mother's real hysteria if we were late coming home, if my father came late from the office. A kind of immigrant fear I carry to this day. Will I wake at night and hear "them" outside my door, arresting, killing my returning love?

The night before I get on an airplane, I am frozen in terror. Not, as one might think, of the flight, which might reasonably crash. Not of where I am going. But simply of the mistakes I might make along the way. Miss the plane. Go to the wrong place. Terror of crowds of people who all know what they are doing better than I do. On my return I dream endlessly of timetables which I don't quite understand, of railroad stations where there is no place to sit down. No place to come in from the cold.

This is a terror I extend to paperwork, to the most innocuous forms. Filling out a medical insurance claim, I fight inertia: will I do it wrong?

There was a story told in the family about my grandmother, Antoinette Mallozzi. For twenty years she had shopped and done her errands in the same Bronx neighborhood, but one day she went out and didn't come back for hours. It turned out there was—or had been—a sign, a woman's boot, that had hung out over the street to signal the existence of a cobbler shop. For Antoinette, it also signaled the place where she had to turn to get home. On this particular day, for whatever reason, the sign was gone: perhaps the shoemaker had retired or died, perhaps the sign was simply being cleaned. In any case—no boot, no turn. Antoinette wandered for hours, till Domenico finally found her, not all that far from her house.

I sometimes think I walk the world like this. Not noting the obvious, sure I won't understand it. Not opening the door to the census taker. Saved from the culture of daily life by immigrant fear.

Threat of poverty was omnipresent, but I saw through that. It was clear to me that the poorest of the great-aunts lived better than we did. Were more loved and loving, lived in more beautiful homes (their altars, and pictures). Saved from this one fear, I have been free to be an artist.

And disease was the very model of assault. The simplest childhood illness would leave my mother frozen with terror. Would subject me, in bed with "the grippe", to tales of her cousins who had died of influenza; to gory descriptions of diphtheria which "closes your throat" so that you die of thirst; pneumonias where you drown. These were the spectres of her Bronx tenement childhood, the stuff of ghosts she sought to pass down to another generation.

When I was two, I had the whooping cough. I still remember Emma shouting hysterically for my father, screaming for towels, trembling and crying as I threw up. That moment hurled me into a vivid consciousness beyond my years. I was doing something awful to my mother. And the proof of it was that after that illness I didn't return to nursery school with its high black iron gates. I lost the lawn, and the vivid airplanes on the walls.

To this day I cannot vomit easily when I need to; could barely spit up phlegm when I had pneumonia. Not wanting to upset Emma, gone these many years.

Disease was/is assault: that is the model we're given. The germ, cancer, virus invades (rapes) us and we are helpless before it. Unknown forces protect us or they don't. God, or immune system, it is all the same. And the cure for assault is assault. Medicines as deadly as they are helpful, invading, destroying our bodies as they "heal". Ourselves, again, as helpless battleground. Neither the illness nor the cure our own. Belying our self-will. Self-generation.

The cure for assault was assault: enemas, "wonder drugs". Toxic stain of red liquid "sulfa drugs" on the bedspread. Being woken all night long from healing sleep. Even then the sense that one was being poisoned.

My mother's love of enemas and laxatives. What horror of the body was she expressing? As she and my father, or her sisters, would hold us down, crying and struggling? And the weekly laxatives: "Clean you out" was the phrase, the phrase for that weekly purge delivered "by mouth". Her love and need of invading our young bodies.

The curing of disease as invasion, assault. And the curing of disease as punishment: quarantine. A single room becomes a fort, a world, in which you are finally safe. Alone. No one crosses the threshold except, illogically, one predictable nurse (usually my mother, who also cooked and cleaned for all the rest of the family). You are, for a moment sacrosanct, no brothers, no father. Blessed silence, and light through the hand-crocheted curtains.

In quarantine you are finally safe enough. It is finally quiet. You hope you'll be sick for years. Folks who can't come into your room: aunts and uncles, your father even, bring presents to your door: books and toys on their way home from work. You are free to dream all day, to tell yourself stories. It's probably as good as it gets. Then comes the punishment: when you are better, the books, the new toys and nightgown, the pictures you colored, *are taken away and burned.* It is as if this respite never existed. Or that the record of it must be wiped from the earth.

Disease as assault, medicine as invasion. And health as return to the unspeakable. The horror of daily life. I prayed that "quarantine" would never end. The methods of the oppressors (Ellis Island) adopted by the oppressed and used against their children.

"Sin" as assault, as taught in school. And the healing of sin, confession, as invasion. What privacy we had, again assaulted. The double bind is: I am expected to go to confession, but I am not expected to believe in God. This was another puzzle my parents set me: Catholic school, where they sent me for the sake of "the education", but where I was, ages five to thirteen, supposed to *have my own mind,* which in their terms meant to have my parents' mind. Not to believe in anything: a kind of fanaticism, religion of the Depression generation.

This, then, was the model. World as battleground. Or more like: the individual as fortress under siege. Invaded by germs, by organisms, sins. Invaded by beliefs. Battered by parents, siblings, friends, and occasionally teachers. And "rescued" only by invading armies at least as destructive as the ones they fought. The medicine, the priest was coming to save you. The enema, the parent, the doctor. You were clearly an ingrate if you resisted, and liable to be battered.

● ● ● ● ●

Of all the wars of those early days, one of the most pernicious, most hidden and far-reaching in its effect on my life, was the war between the Mallozzis and the Di Primas. Between my mother's and my father's families. The battleground of that war was my psyche, that soft and delicate juncture of body and spirit; the dwelling place of the Word. Now wounds to the psyche are invisible, and even harder to find forty or fifty years later than wounds to the flesh or spirit. They dwell out of the light in tiny crevices, the deeply hidden assumptions of our lives.

The problem is compounded when, within the cosmology in which the wounds are inflicted, there is no such thing as the psyche *or* the spirit. Then you search for the invisible in the invisible.

In my childhood home there was no room for the soul. Though lip service was paid to Dante in some begrudging homage to Emma's father, neither soul nor spirit dwelt in the universe. Or so I was given to understand. The world, you see, was packed so close with matter, every crevice filled, that nothing else would fit, neither soul nor spirit, no angels or saints filled my evenings with prayers, no god looked down from the sky. For my grandfather there was the heroic quest for truth, but my parents were two children abandoned at the bottom of a well.

The world was packed so close, every cupboard filled. "Knickknacks" on every shelf. Drawers filled to overflowing with pins, with twine, embroidery thread, bushels of unused corny greeting cards.

Time was filled that way, too: no free ruminating moments. Only the next task: dinner, dishes, sweeping. The laundry, ironing, continual stairwashing. Gardening, canning, sewing, mending. If all else is done you can always plan ahead: fill the freezer with casseroles, crochet a throw for the couch. Never to take a walk with an empty head. Lest something come upon you from the skies.

I remember that when I heard *A Christmas Carol* on holiday radio for the first time, complete with sound effects (I was five or six), I went to bed and hid deep under the covers. Afraid to sleep for the hint of invisible worlds. Ghost of Christmas Past. Ghost of the Past. Afraid to sleep, and needing some reassurance. "No such thing" my mother told me then, "as a spirit". Spirits more palpable in the room than she was. Crowding, filling that air. Dad, a dark spot among ghosts and saints, spirits and angels, upheld her. They left, and I watched the dark.

The Mallozzis, I was given to understand, were everything desirable. (These matters were discussed only by my mother and her sisters, and usually in Neapolitan.) Mallozzis were smarter, thinner, more ambitious. "Upwardly mobile" we might say but there wasn't that term then. All the Mallozzi women had gone to college. The one male Mallozzi sibling had rebelled and refused: but of course, that is different from not being able to, because of lack of money or of brains. Each of the kids in the family was often under discussion: was s/he a Mallozzi or a Di Prima? (I am sure it extended out to my cousins: was s/he a Mallozzi or a Biondi? Mallozzi or a Fregosi? Mallozzi or—oh hated idea! —a Troisi? Rossi?!)

I felt it as a moral imperative. Mallozzi or bust. They were more "northern", too, the Italian snobbery. "Pop"—what the "Mallozzi girls" always called their father, even unto their own deathbeds at eighty or ninety—Pop's blue eyes were often mentioned and with great pride. I remember them for their fierceness myself, a bit like my own stare, but more angry, less distanced and contemptuous than I. Com-passion he had, a fellow feeling I had walled off. In my young life, it probably would have been deadly.

Di Primas, I learned very young, were "like children". (Not a compliment, and frequently used in our hearing.) Except for my father, of course, they were uneducated, got lower-class jobs. Pietro, my father's father, believed in God! Told us stories about Mary and the Baby. They were fat and loud, and going to their houses was like slumming, or so my mother's voice conveyed as we got ready. They tended to be what mom called "laborers": upholsterers, waiters, factory workers.

Di Primas were always being rescued by my father. From something or other, I never knew from what. Probably they needed money, maybe they got into trouble with the Law. He was the oldest son, and seemed to think it natural, as did they. "Frank will take care of it".

Being a Di Prima meant you would come to no particular good, would definitely let mom down. You'd wind up redhaired, with freckles (ugh!) and very white skin. You'd probably be round and not very smart. You might work in a candy factory or a bank. It was almost a threat: If you're not good, you'll turn into a Di Prima! Invitation to unlawful use of the Will. Only ingredient besides Matter in that world.

Oh built-in Manicheanism, very stuff of the Tao! Of Yin and Yang, though I can't say which was which. All dichotomies in the world were laid out for me, and before my birth: Mallozzis and Di Primas. Cosmology.

I learned I was a Mallozzi early on. My brothers were the Di Primas. But it would change. Frankie remained a Di Prima, but Richie? Was Richie not a Mallozzi after all? Polymorphous creature—could he possibly have "a little of both"?

There was this catch, this small detail that warped the heart. This invisible wound I find today woven throughout the fabric of my life, so that to correct this mistake would be to take my life apart, even unto dissolution. The hands that reach to do this work are formed by these same dichotomies. The secret places of my soul.

There was, I was saying, this catch:

The Di Primas, whoever they were, were loving beings. In their loud and rundown houses you were safe and welcome. As nowhere in all that fine Mallozzi world.

In a Di Prima household (there were six besides ours), the children were valued. *I criaturi.* (The creatures. Were we fauns? satyrs?) We might run wild, knock over a vase, eat things out of the refrigerator, even raise our voices in play. Someone would be overlooking us with a beam of love coming out of each eye. We were the kids.

I grew up thinking the price for this love was poverty, low-class life, the contempt of mom. Maybe more than I could pay. Love was not for me. But thinking it secretly, unbeknown to myself.

To give up schooling and maybe be loud and fat. The price for a lap to sit on was to give up ambition. I paid the price, but didn't take the prize. Thinking perhaps to keep my Mallozzi pride.

Mallozzis had precious things on glass-topped tables. You didn't talk loud or move fast in their houses. A couple of them would hold you on their laps. But it was more tentative, certainly not unconditional. It helped if you looked nice, if you had been "good".

Mallozzis knew what you should look like and what you should want. They knew how you should get it, too, if you'd only listen. Straight A's and neatness were the important things. And with these came a rigid self-respect.

The pleasing of Emma, the destruction of Frank. Though these things were seldom spoken in front of him, and always then in a pseudo-impartial tone: "Does s/he take after his/her *father* or *mother*"? etc. But everyone knew Sicilians were outré. Still, an impossible position, and surely a part of his rage.

Codependent, we say now, but that doesn't say it all. To be apologist and rescuer of his father; his brothers and sisters. To feel them a handicap, and care for them as duty. Straining to please his wife and her sisters. Caught between.

His genes not okay. I feel that still.

And find, in the hidden corners, a child's suspicion: Maybe Di Primas were bad *because* they loved us kids? We being after all, not all that lovable. Family love, Mallozzis knew, was something you earned. A corollary of respect, not a thing in itself. Not your right, nor the ambiance you grew in.

Division in yourSelf: between your mind and your hair. Eyes, skin, emotions, nose, voice, all part of the battle. Were your feet too wide? Could you change all this by Will? First use of the Magickal Will against yourself. Against the very tissue of your genes.

● ● ● ● ●

All through this time, the war raged, internal and external. Raged in Europe as far back as I can remember, a presence in my life from the beginning. Raged in America under a blanket of silence.

At school the nuns had us pray every morning for the children. All the children in the world, they said. The children, they told us, on both sides of the war: did they not have souls? Did they not all belong to God? It was the closest I came to hearing the war news spoken, and I was hungry for speech, for open speech.

At home, the war news in Southern Italian: Neapolitan, Sicilian, sometimes Calabrese, when friends of the family came over. It was assumed that none of us kids understood. I schooled myself not to respond by word or expression. Lived in stealth. A discipline.

War news was mostly worry and despair. What they heard or did not hear from the relatives overseas. Or earlier portents: Mussolini's overtures rebuffed by Roosevelt. Or so I heard. "Italians are good for nothing but a stab in the back", is what they repeated, what they said Roosevelt said. That one phrase in English amid passionate Italian. Roosevelt's refusal to see Mussolini, if that's what in fact it was, felt fiercely as personal insult by one and all. Left him, they said, no choice, but to turn to Hitler.

And 1991, standing outside the corner store, speaking with two Arab grocers, I heard the same words, heard the dilemma from the 1930s. "Hussein", said the older man, "wants to talk. He said he wants to talk. But a man can't talk while he's being insulted". The immigrant's impasse, pain of American arrogance I knew, growing up. Felt again the mute despair "Can't get out of it now". Unbroken bitterness and desperation. Mute pride, fifty years late, the same Mediterranean pride. Arab, Sicilian.

Late war news on the radio. Long after we were in bed. Did I sometimes creep half down the winding stairs, where I could watch, or listen, hidden? As I often did when the air in the house grew tense, to check out the coming storms. My interest in weather forecasts holds to this day.

Or sometimes, a bit of the news on Aunt Ella's lips. Her husband, my Uncle Hugo, stationed in Panama, sending home silver filigree bracelets, long letters with words or paragraphs blacked out. Sometimes she spoke despite my parents' prohibitions. Sharing her fears when she came to share my bed. Her warm, pregnant body beside me in the dark. That was later, after war was "declared".

In Catholic school we learned the United States sank the *Maine* on purpose, started the Spanish American War all on its own. Made it easy to wonder about Pearl Harbor. Made it easy, especially if you were Italian.

If you were Italian, growing up in my house, your father handed you Machiavelli to read. To help you understand history, he told you. One of the only books he had besides Shakespeare and the encyclopedia. He read you *Julius Caesar* to show how Mark Anthony manipulated the crowd. What propaganda was. You never forgot.

The actual War began when I was seven. Amid tears and hysteria, my mother hanging onto us as if we were about to disappear. No school that day. That first day the large wooden radio was never turned off. A few days later, a false air raid alarm led the school to dismiss us, send us all home. Through what my mother imagined as an air-raid. Kindergartners through eighth graders wandered the Brooklyn streets, wending their ways to homes where someone or no one was waiting. Where they could or couldn't get in. And then at my house the real blackout began: the war news ceased to exist.

There were blackouts in the "real world" too: the black shades drawn, a single lamp or candle. Civil defense personnel rapping at our door: there was a pinhole in our shade, the light was showing through. We played cards by flashlight, did homework, all gathered at one table. My parents angry at the intrusion of the war.

Everything was carefully monitored. None of us kids had a radio in their room, the only phonograph, a windup, was in the living room.

Scratchy 78s: "I sit alone in my cozy morris chair / playing solitaire / so un-happy there". Made no sense at all, then or now. No newspapers, no comics, no movies, books chosen by mom. Though I had the wild freedom of the library. Where I found out about Leibniz, but not about what was happening right then. Right under my nose. It's where I'm still at, in some ways: can tell you more about Proclus than about TV. Trained to look away, I do so still.

It was into this silence that the Bomb exploded.

It was 1945, my eleventh birthday. August 6, 1945, and we were waiting the celebration for my father. Inane party hats I disliked even then, cake and melting ice cream. My brothers were noisy and annoying, my mom was excited with a fake excitement I hated. Dad was working late. Or whatever he did in the evenings in those years.

He came in finally with a newspaper in his hand, and I saw that the headlines were huge, more than half the page. I can remember stealing a look at them, something I did on the sly sometimes, but cannot remember what the words were. His face was louring, gloomy, it often was. He often exploded, and no one could say why. He still had his hat on though he was in the house. Something he never did. I noticed that.

My brothers stopped giggling and shoving, and the room grew silent. The cake sat on the table, candles unlit. My mom's apprehensive "What's the matter, dear"? her apotropaic formula, was missing. My father threw the paper, still folded, on a coffee table. He who inveighed against drama was being dramatic.

He said *Well, we lost,* and all hell broke loose. The bitterness in his voice. Everyone spoke at once: How could we lose? What had happened? Was the war over? Mom's hysteria breaking the surface of her voice.

It was the Bomb, though none of us knew what that was. It was Hi-roshima, though none of us knew where that was. He said, *Whatever we do now, we've lost.* Breaking the cool of his conservative posture. We had no answer.

We ate melted ice cream, I got stupid dolls. My party proceeded, al-most as if nothing had happened.

And two weeks later, I sat with my mother and aunt, tearing up newspa-pers, tearing up old phone books. Making, they told me, "confetti", hear-ing the news. Boxes of torn paper beside us, on the floor. Radio on all the time now, suddenly. Awaiting the moment of peace, whatever that was.

It turned out to be as warlike as the rest. On Brooklyn sidewalks, kids ran by with dolls' heads on broomsticks. Beheaded dolls with slanted eyes painted on. Norwegian kids, Italian kids, ran screaming, Japanese heads on sticks, or hung on the fences. I stood quiet inside our wrought iron gate and watched. Afraid to step into it.

Confetti we made for days, poured out in an instant. Cars jamming the streets, overflowing, the horns blaring. Whatever cars still ran in that neighborhood. People on the running boards, on the hoods. On the dead-end side of the block, a life-size doll hung in effigy from a street lamp. Hirohito, they said. Flames licked at the feet, the legs. The figure slowly caught fire, it burned, the people screamed. My neighbors, screaming in hate, not in relief. Laughing and crying in anger. Italians, war victims, screaming against "the Japs". Peace where? My world moved from furtive to insane.

chapter FOUR

The men with soft voices flooded our nighttime house. Cigar smoke in the air. They are doing the cooking. This in itself was enough to wake me every time, to bring me in sleepy amazement into the kitchen—am I five? The men are talking and cooking, my mother sits idle on the sidelines. They have stuffed a huge fish and it is in the oven. There is homemade wine on the table.

They are neighborhood men, respected men of business: the florist, the pharmacist, the undertaker. They are men of business, and they are the lesser criminals. There is no distinction. There is only continuum; they have come together to take care of neighborhood business. I come out of my bedroom softly, in my pajamas with feet. I know I am safe, dad is on his best behavior. The men all greet me, I am held on laps. I am passed from knee to knee in clouds of cigar smoke. Mom doesn't order me to go back to bed.

When the fish is done we eat, there are sips of wine. They have come together to take care of neighborhood business. Territorial. Who sells what on what block. What to do with Aunt Gracie's husband who is a drunk. What job to give him, to keep up appearances. To keep up the family, myth of male support. What the "boss" wants and what dues are owed at "the ward". What rewards will be divided up. Politics and crime, business and thievery: a continuum as they actually and constantly are. And cloaked in the grace of the family, of family life. I am petted, I have my power in this world.

·

When I was older I heard it said, and with pride, repeated with pride by my mother, that the meetings were held at our house because it was "safe" there. It was a safe place to meet she said, my father kept his mouth shut and they knew it. *Omertà*. A definition of integrity. His integrity was, I learned, he kept his mouth shut. And for the most part, that he wanted nothing. At home he had power, unrestrained. Outside he moved bowed and with fear through the subways, the streets.

She told the story again and again, that dad had resigned from politics the year I was born. There was some petty preferment he had been offered, and he turned it down and resigned from "the club". My mother had it he'd discovered something not quite above-board in the ward dealings, and wanted no part, no further part of it. It was told he'd made a resignation speech, in which he held that he knew no one *whose hands were clean enough* to hold office, except his three-month-old daughter, and he nominated me for the post.

He was a man obsessed with clean hands. He washed and manicured his own hands endlessly. Never played in the dirt, my mom would tell us, and again there was that tone of admiration. Never played in the dirt when he was little, so as not to get dirty. Loved Lady Macbeth's speech, too: *All the perfumes of Arabia . . .*

As woman, as daughter, holding the rage at bay—the men's, our own. Keeping joy in the air. Joy of Italian family life, the men feeling me up as we tangoed, the women pulling at my breasts on the pretext of praising my "development".

Only one uncle put it out there, as words in the air. I was eighteen and I had recently left home. We were driving together somewhere in Queens for some reason I've long forgotten and he said: "There's a motel here" (some tacky postwar plaster, fake-stucco thing). "There's a motel here, would you like to stop"? The only open expression of what went on, what had gone on, in the pecking order, all my life. Would I like to stop? I said "No", and we drove on. Never spoke of it again, but I was grateful. Am grateful to this day for the forthright proposal. That I wasn't making it up. Weird sexual innuendoes always in the air. What I bought, what I lost, with my body.

That twelve-year-old girl stood in Red Hook kitchen, drying the supper dishes. There was a huge, iron bread knife in her hand. The bomb had been dropped. Some other bombs, too, since the war's end. Domenico Mal-

lozzi was dead. Aunt Ella gone to her new home, no protector now in the bedroom. Some bomb had detonated there, and recently.

I am drying dishes in the February kitchen. The world is full of dopey Valentines. Love in red hearts, cut from books of same, with the brothers. The bread knife is weighty and ample, and the father's back is turned. The moment is eternal, the decision hangs on a hair. *That I am here, and not eternally in prison. Not given electric shock, or surrendered to death through the filthy portals of psychiatric medicine.* Grace of what god?

My father never knew how close to death he came. I dried the knife and put it in the drawer. Wept for two weeks, madder than they could dream. My Brooklyn parents, mother brainwashed blind.

For two weeks could sit at no table with knife, or fork. For fear of piercing flesh, mine, or theirs. To kill the father, to Wake Up the mother. As if either of those acts was possible. For two weeks, feared to sleep: would I walk, asleep, to these acts? My fantasy was: that I would carve filthy words into my body, throw myself naked from public Brooklyn rooftop. Flat roof of our brownstone house, "tar beach" of that ghetto. So They Would Know.

Know what, I never said, never formulated. But I bought my memory back with that undone act. Fact: continuous memory of my life begins with my "breakdown" at twelve. Fact: almost no memory from twelve to seven. Or earlier, to five. No continuous memory of the War. The war inside and out.

War ended with a "breakdown" that they were forced to acknowledge. To take me at least to the family pediatrician. Almost as public as the roof, though I never said, didn't know, what had happened, what was happening. After I held the knife my father never touched me. I longed to be a boy: pirate, bandit, outcast. Recognized myself three years later, in Cocteau's urchins in the snow.

● ● ● ● ●

LETTERS TO MY MOTHER, AUTUMN 1984 (NEVER SENT)

(1)

Dear Mom

I am sitting here copying notes from our talks into my journal and the first of the questions for you to answer on your tape machine rushes into mind. (I *hope* Weezie will show you how to run it! It's really pretty simple.)

1) What year did your dad and mom come to America? You said they were here before your oldest sister Mary was born—what year was that?
2) Do you know what year they eloped? What their anniversary was?
3) Do you know the names of Grandma Mallozzi's brothers (besides Silvio?) The name of the one who died while in college? Was he the oldest? What did the rest of them do?
4) Do you know the names of your dad's brothers and sisters? I have Caminuccio and Eliseo. Were they the only two? Which one died as a baby? *What were the sisters' names?*
5) Do you know your dad's mother's maiden name? Or your mom's mother's name?
6) What are the dates of your mom's and dad's deaths?
7) Was Grandpa Mallozzi 76 or 77 when he died?

There's a lot more, but this should start things off. Here's a couple of blank tapes for starters. I'll send more later.

Hope you got the pictures okay at Aunt Evelyn's. I marked what I wanted. Of course, I also want some of those you had in your little purse—of you and me and Aunt Ella in the Conservatory of Flowers in Golden Gate Park amongst the dahlias—or were they zinnias?

Will write soon.

Please excuse this yellow pad—It's all I have with me.

Love,
Diane

P.S. —Hope you had a wonderful time—I did.

(2)

Dear Mom—

A second batch of questions for you—most of these are about Daddy's family.

1) You said you had Grandpa Di Prima's birth date at home. What is it? Do you know the year?
2) Do you know Grandma Di Prima's birthday at all? Was she Rose or Rosa?
3) Do you remember the actual dates of their deaths?
4) Did they meet here or in Italy?
5) What town was Grandma Di Prima from?
6) Did they get married here or in Italy? What year did they come to America?
7) Did Grandma Di Prima have brothers and sisters? How many? What names?
8) Did Grandpa Di Prima have just sister Angelina and brother Giuseppe, or were there others?
9) Do you know the family name of his mother? Of Rose Sabatino's mother?
10) How does the great-aunt "A-Zia" fit into all this? Was she Dad's great-aunt? Or mine?

(3)

Dear Mom—

How can we know so little about each other? how is it possible to have lived a life here and never have spoken of where we are from, never tasted the names and villages on our tongues? what kind of insanity keeps us from our lives?

(4)

Dear Mom—

Who are we, really? Where is the rage for your cousins working in cotton mills at the age of eight? What happened to you between the time Frankie was born and the time Richie was born that took the light from your eyes, and brought a permanent look of fear to your face? When are you going to tell me what was stolen from you? When will you name your oppressor?

(5)

Dear Mom—

I keep dreaming about you in tears. Your crazy, punishing face looming above mine. The walls of the room are whirling as you shake me, hurl me. What is the source of your madness? What do your sisters whisper in the dark?

• • • • •

It is power I am talking about now, no right and wrong. No cloudy issues of "neglect" or passion. Simply, who held the power in our lives? How did we speak with them, how did they treat us? A pluralism. There are bonds and groupings of power, within each group a kind of hierarchy, never spoken but fully acknowledged. And then there were different groupings, separate and more or less equal. Ward politics. The Church. City Hall. The cops. International relations I learned in the kitchen.

A few years back I sat down with my "Uncle Bill". My genuine godfather, onetime higher-up in Tammany Hall. Met him downtown near Wall Street in one of those discreet, literally underground restaurants with lugubrious waiters in black. We ate softshell crabs and told each other stories.

It had been years since we met, but we met in familiarity and dropped immediately into a kind of ancient intimacy. There were, there are, these things we "know" about each other, about each other's eyes, ways of seeing the world.

Bill was around a good deal when I was very small. Age three and four, two and three, I don't know, there were summers at the ocean. Long Beach, Long Island. Cottages and a magic life we shared. The popular song was *"Bei mir bist du schoen"*, my head was not quite as high as the dining room table. I remember one summer, the table was round and white. Cream colored, perhaps.

There are these photographs of me in a wizard's outfit. Moons and stars on my "beach robe". My hair impeccably curled in that tortuous style, one curl over my forehead. But what matters, what I remember, is being dragged through the waves, lifted high by Uncle Bill, his one "bad hand" curled immobile against my side, long days on the sand. Electric currents of sexuality crackling in the air: my mother and her sisters, Bill, and "the boys", other friends of Bill's and my father's.

There are these photographs of the women in the awkward bathing suits of the period, hair flowing below their waists, their legs suggestively angled, the laughing invitation in their eyes. Where did it go, then, in the next few years? The crackling come-on in the dark-haired men, their melting black eyes, my father heavier and lighter skinned than the others. There was a community of hedonism and I was the one youngster yet born to this group, the only child in those pictures.

There was *"Bei mir bist du schoen"*, pre-war German pop, there was playfulness and the beach, and there was a crackling like small lightning in the air. There were, too, some kind of storm clouds. Unexpressed and undeveloped tensions between the adults, that turned into schisms in the years to come. Years later I heard that Emma had first been "going out with" Bill, that she had been Bill's girl until he introduced her to my father. Some unfinished business drew dark lines on the sand, left sentences incomplete in the summer nights.

The person on the beach was more like the Emma who wrote my father before they were married, the only letter I found after her death: all about a two-tone "roadster" her cousins had in Rhode Island, the train she'd taken there for the weekend. An Emma whose flapper playfulness already had an edge to it, whose taste of the 20s' "speakeasies" gave her such pleasure. This was not yet the Emma broken and hidden in housedresses, hidden behind glasses, who never stopped cleaning, never laughed, never paused for love or grief, never spoke of disappointment. Though even in Long Beach the harshness was already beginning. It showed itself in the way she combed my hair.

Bill was close to us, and then inexplicably he wasn't. Omnipresent, but no longer close. He was, after all, my father's "law partner", whatever that might actually mean, he couldn't very well disappear from our world. He had, as I learned later, power, and power in our lives. No one could afford to leave him out. But there came a day when no one spoke of him much. Emma turned her anger on him, dad was silent. Bill was my "godfather", a serious relationship, taken seriously. It meant he had "stood up for me" at baptism, would act as a parent should anything happen to mine. I felt the tie, but I almost never saw him.

His bad hand was the most impressive thing about him when I was small. Remained distinctive, always. One of his hands crumpled, immobile, hidden in a black knit glove. There was a story of a fight in a summer ghetto when he was a teenager, fourteen or so. His hand had been broken, badly restored by an incompetent doctor, probably free or cheap at a ghetto clinic, at any rate, he had "lost the use of it" somehow. As they told it he had been destined for great things: had had a scholarship to Rome for the coming fall to study the violin. The loss of his hand of course put an end to his music, no one said how he took it, how he became reconciled. Only that later he "took up law". In my child's eyes, that bent, stiff hand in its eternal knit black glove was something inevitable, sinister and familiar. A badge of suffering worn for once in the open. Worn where it could be seen.

There's a note of disappointment in this tale. Romantic disappointment, almost, a Byronic quality. Bill's (perhaps) hidden love for my mother, his lost career. Disappointment or loss marked the men of that world. And silence; one simply didn't talk about it.

Disappointment and silence marked the women too. But there the silence lay deeper. No tales were told about them. They did not turn from one career to another, "take up the law", but buried the work of their hearts in the basement, burned their poems and stories, lost the thread of their dreams.

The rest of what I remember of Long Beach is my first adventuring, my first venturing out. It was after bedtime one night, the moon was full, I could see it from my window. The moon was full and bright, the sea only blocks away and I slipped out of the house through an unlocked door. Perhaps the first and last time I had that simple a relationship with a door. Slight thrill, no strong sense of what was or wasn't forbidden, I *just went out,* filled only with longing to see the sea in the moonlight. To see the night world, but especially the moon on the water. I don't think I knew at all what it would look like.

There were no real "streets" to cross, and I wended my way to the sand. Surprised, I was, at first, that there were people there, many grownups on that warm August night, lying about and digging the moon. Drinking probably, and talking. I found myself in conversation with a rather large man, I remember his belly as he lay on the sand was almost as high as my head, to my astonishment, and we were in conversation about the night, about the moon and how I had come out alone, when my father found me and brought me back to the house. To his credit, for once he wasn't angry. He simply brought me home, and I imagine that he and mom told me at great length not to go out alone, or at night, or to the beach, or under the moon. So I would guess, but I really don't remember. All I remember is the full moon over the water, and the matter-of-fact feeling of talking on equal terms with that bulky grownup.

Years later, and with great resonance, I read in Ezra Pound's translation of *Confucius:* **"The way out is through the door. How is it that no one** *will use this method"*? *And read it as he wrote it and probably meant it, i.e., it's all so obvious how come nobody does it?*

Now I see that the obvious thing is how we are conditioned *out of going through the door. Lose the ability to "use this method". Not that we* **will** *not but that we* **can** *not, perhaps can't even find the door. "How is it that no one will use this method"? How is this method lost? Who takes it from us?*

Over the next years I saw little of Uncle Bill. He was a presence, a kind of guardian. I suspect his machinations helped keep my father in work. My father, unambitious and not much of a businessman. Perhaps my parents' resentment was, we owed him too much.

Later, when I had left home and found myself cut off from family, Bill was my friend and remained so, some times closer than others, as I proceeded to break the rules of that Italianate familial world, one by one. I could I felt count on his unflappableness. As he on mine. We swapped tales from our separate worlds. Nothing either of us said could shock the other.

After, that is, we got the boundaries drawn. I remember at eighteen, going down to my father's (and Bill's) office to type at night, something I often did. I owned no electric typewriter, and it was down on Wall Street near Trinity Church in the dead of night that I typed my early poems, wrote letters, stories. Sometimes all night long.

That night when I arrived, Bill was still there, and got me somehow onto one of those huge burgundy leather couches, the mark of the luxurious law firms of the 40s, still there in the 50s. Suddenly he put his arms around me, tried suddenly to make out with me—not, I must say, to my surprise. I had felt it coming. Experienced beyond my years in the subtleties of Italian familial passion. We didn't call it incest. Tough, self-assured, not surprised but not willing, I found myself reaching for the way to stop this thing. As I had so many others by then.

"Bill", I said, "I'm not Emma". Remembering the early gossip spoken in Neapolitan in various kitchens by my mom and her sisters, Bill and my mother's affair, or whatever it was.

Bill let go of me immediately. "Diane", he said "That's not fair. That's just not fair".

He never touched me again and we never spoke of this.

Unflappable, we both were, and tough. We had tested each other.

• • • • •

*It is power I am talking about now, no right and wrong. No cloudy issues
of neglect or passion. Simply who held the power in our lives? How did we
speak with them, how did they treat us. A pluralism. There are bonds and
groupings of power, within each group a kind of hierarchy, never spoken
but fully acknowledged.*

*A few years back I sat down with my "Uncle Bill". My genuine godfa-
ther, onetime higher-up in Tammany Hall. Met him downtown near Wall
Street in one of those discreet, literally underground restaurants with
lugubrious waiters in black. We ate softshell crabs and told each other stories.*

It was well past lunch and we were the only people in the restaurant. We
had our crabs and salad, a good, light house wine, and we had all day. Or
so it seemed. Bill opened the conversation: "How does your brother", he
asked me, "like his new job"? (My brother had just become head of the
legal department for a well-known company.) I answered that he seemed
to like it very much.

Bill took a sip of wine, leaning forward to hide a kind of grin in his eyes,
his bad hand in its black glove lying on the tablecloth. "I'll tell you how that
happened, Di", he said, out of the blue, and watching me keenly (he used
often to watch and openly relish my responses as we talked). "You see, the
banks own _____ [the notorious owner/boss of my brother's new com-
pany] and they needed somebody in there who they knew they could
trust".

Long pauses between clauses, the keen, sparkling eyes watching me, to
see if I was "getting it"—what I was "getting". As for me, I was translating,
expressionless, listening and translating. Though with Bill I was never sure
how much was true. What he was making up. One makes these guesses in
silence, computer-quick, and never misses a word, an inflection, glance or
nuance. And never lets on, or changes expression.

". . . needed somebody in there they knew they could trust". Probably
means someone who will be responsive to them (the banks) rather than
the "owned" boss. But might only mean someone with no hidden agendas
of his own. The pause extended for a moment, while the black-clad, black-
tie waiter refilled our white porcelain coffee cups.

". . . knew they could trust". (Pause. The waiter discreetly disappears again. Voice now slightly more portentous, some emphasis there that might be going by me.) "Now, your father's name is a very good name". (Does this mean my father was simply honest, and kept his mouth shut, or that he always did what he was told?) "So when I suggested your brother, it was very well received.

"He doesn't know anything about this, of course. He thinks the job came to him in the usual way. As a matter of fact, I suggested he apply for it". (Pause. Maybe I nod, maybe just wait.) "I'm happy to hear he likes it, Di. Maybe it's best you don't say anything to him".

It is power I am talking about, the use and abuse of power. Power and secrecy, and deals made in the dark. The coils of the unsaid winding through our lives, tangling them, tripping us, holding the fabric together.

We tackle the crabs.

I am myself then moved to tell Bill a story. It rambles more, comes to the point more slowly, and I'm not quite sure at first what it is I want him to know.

I say, "I was in Ostia last summer, Bill, doing an international poetry festival with a whole bunch of writers, and it was a very interesting scene.

"They had billed this thing as the 'Woodstock of Poetry', it was very big in all the Roman papers, and about twenty-five thousand people had gathered on the beach. Ginsberg was coming, and Burroughs, Baraka, all the stars.

"About twenty-five thousand people were on the beach, but there were no facilities for them. No shade. Almost no bathrooms or water. Little food. Nothing like the state of the art be-ins I'm used to on the West Coast: paramedics, food stands, counselors, what-have-you. Italians don't think like that.

"When I arrived it was the second evening, and apparently it wasn't going very well. The first night had been devoted to Italian poets, and they had been booed off the stage. The second night was to be European poets in general, and the crowd was in a frenzy, screaming 'Minestrone'! and hurling everything in sight at the performers. They were clearly there for the stars and only the stars—that was us, the Americans, or anyway some of us.

"The physical situation itself was ridiculous. The Italians had built a huge rock-concert-style stage on the sandy beach, backed up against the water. It consisted of a whole lot of metal scaffolding and some wooden planks, two or three inches thick. It was way more stage than anybody needed, and it was way more stage than the performers could hold. The audience was all over it, shouting and grabbing the microphones to make communist, anarchist, fascist or you-name-it speeches".

(I am trying to sound casual, even amusing, but there had been nothing casual about the force, the power of that crowd, the stage backed up against the surf, the crowd's expectations beyond all reason: for a word, for salvation. It is power I am talking about, the limits of power.)

"Things were pretty nuts, it seemed like a riot could break out any minute. Me and Baraka and a New York Puerto Rican poet held a meeting that second night, to try and figure out how to get through the reading. We sketched out a plan, a way of holding at least the front of the stage, and getting the mike from person to person *fast*. Fast enough so that hopefully no one from the audience could grab it for other uses.

"But the next morning, our plan dissolved: the Russians had sent a letter to Allen Ginsberg, requesting permission to read with us (they had been too chicken to perform as scheduled on 'European night' amidst the raining of objects and imprecations). The Russians are a slow-spoken and deliberate lot; they could certainly not be counted on to 'hold' their parts of the stage, or to pass a microphone with alacrity and perhaps even sleight-of-hand.

"We became a house divided. Those of us who wanted to get this thing done and get out in one piece voted No Russians: let them go home without reading, they had blown their chance. Allen G., as ever the good guy, saw this as a chance to be friendly, to play international politics, Buddhist style, so he voted Yes. The debate threatened to take up the whole glorious Italian summer day, and I left the meeting to go to the beach, and swim for the first time in the Mediterranean. Allen's party won the day, and some valiant American poets set out to try to brief the Russians on stage tactics.

"Around this time a contingent of Black Americans who lived in Rome arrived at our hotel, breathless and paranoid. To say they had inside word that somebody was going to try to kill Baraka during the evening's festivities. They vowed to protect him, and waved around these exotic forged-iron musical instruments from Africa. This made no one less jumpy, but at least the notion and word 'death' was now out in the open. Someone seemed to be deliberately playing with the crowd and with us. But who, and why?

"Later most of us were taking a pre-performance nap, resigned to a certain amount of chaos, when our Roman producers came round to wake us for yet another meeting. They had, they told us, been negotiating with 'the beach people' (whoever they might have been) and had come to an agreement with them. There would be one 'beach person' alternating with each one of us at the reading tonight.

"It was then that it really started to look like a setup. It was now seven-thirty, we were already due to start, we had no idea of who might be reading with us: a 'beach person' or whoever, saying the wrong thing could set off that volatile crowd. Anything could happen, and anybody could find themselves hurt or dead. We started to look at who exactly would be the most likely targets.

"Each of us reacted according to type. Bill Burroughs thought it was a good time to go back to Rome and forget about reading. Baraka—like a good Marxist—refused to leave because 'the People were expecting him'. Allen Ginsberg—like a good Buddhist—was sure we were all nuts, and that there was nothing to fear. And I made a speech in unintelligible Italian to the gathered journalists and producers stating that I hoped the proposed 'Woodstock of poetry' wouldn't turn into the Altamont of poetry.

"It was a cold moment, right then. I saw how one could see it coming, and yet be powerless to stop it. I wondered if we were powerless. Then I went with the others to that ridiculous stage".

We got through it somehow, I added, and we didn't "share" with the beach people. The mike was taken from us only once. The Black musicians from Rome stood behind Baraka shaking their iron percussion instruments throughout the show. My lover Sheppard stood behind me like a martial artist, brandishing our small metal tape machine like a formidable weapon. The crowd wandered up periodically during the performance to shake the stage till we all bounced up and down. (The boards were only laid on the pipes, not fastened down.) No one was shot, no one so far as I know was crushed in the crowd. Burroughs, Ginsberg, Baraka, and the others went home alive.

At the end of the last piece, though—Allen Ginsberg and Peter Orlovsky were singing—the mob surged forward as one, and the stage collapsed: the boards just slipped off the pipes. The tall scaffolding counterweight swayed, but didn't come down on the crowd.

Sheppard and I were already heading toward the back of the stage, away from the crowd as we had previously planned. We found ourselves suddenly scrambling *up* the boards which were jutting into the air. We jumped off into the sand and walked along the edge of the water together, skirting the crowd.

It is power and the recognition of power. What works in secrecy behind the scenes. Not what you see on the surface. This is how things actually happen, how the world gets changed, or doesn't. How families rise and fall. How assassination happens, or it doesn't.

Two Italians exchanging tales; the coffee by now cold, even these immovable waiters impatient to close. It is power we are talking about and the workings of power. *How the world works, how it actually operates. Not what you see on the surface.* We understood each other.

I stood with Bill on the sidewalk saying goodbye, him grinning down at me again, those eyes. He so old now, maybe our last lunch. He took his good hand and laid it briefly alongside my cheek. "Funny-face", he said, and turned quickly to walk away, but not before I could see that he was crying.

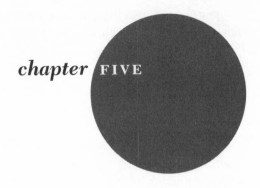

chapter FIVE

It is a spring evening in Brooklyn and I am thirteen years old. The magnolia tree in the Larsens' front yard is in bloom, and the air is sweet. Across the street, they have unwrapped the fig trees—the branches have spread out again and the leaves are coming through like green fire.

I have got past what I will always think of as my "breakdown". I have pulled myself out of it, out of all of it, by promising myself it will be different in high school. It is a kind of internal reorganization, and I have worked at it with enormous attention and precision. In high school I will create another persona (though I don't know the word), I will be someone else. Someone with the power to appear as she chooses to appear. Truly a precocious undertaking. For the moment I am wholeheartedly engaged in finishing grammar school, dispensing with St. Mary Star of the Sea, its manners and mores. Tentatively testing out methods of "fitting in".

There is a school dance tonight, and I am going. The dance itself is a momentous occasion, occurs no more than once a year. At St. Mary's from the beginning, the first grade, the boys and girls live in different worlds, have different classrooms, teachers, playgrounds. There is no concourse, except the concourse of the streets: dark evenings in dead-end alleys, uncertain threats. Knife fights I witnessed from the fourth grade up: girls fighting with knives for the "love" of indifferent Irish altar boys. Chill greetings, snide and all-knowing, a hideous, childish sophistication.

"Don't ever sit", a classmate told me once, "with your back to an open window". An open, ground-floor window was what she meant. "My brother was sitting with his back to a window and somebody pulled him out and beat him up. He's in the hospital, he's lucky he isn't dead". It was years later I realized her last name was one of the gangland names of the neighborhood and she came from one of the fiercer streets: Luqueer or Nelson.

So I sat and still sit with my back to the wall. Facing the door, and as far from it as I could get. Home, restaurant, school yard, even church if I could. A writer in Village coffee houses, a mother in the playgrounds. Cover your back, and keep your eyes open. Be still, invisible if possible and *watch*.

But tonight it is spring, and I am going to a dance, I have somehow got permission. My first and only time. Permission comes easier since I had my "breakdown", perhaps they are scared, but I don't think of that then. Years later I learned they had had me watched. That some of the endless parade of men we had to dinner (we always had boring men to dinner, Italian and in their suits, sometimes with their wives, sometimes alone—they were always "friends of your father") some of the men who came to dinner were there to check me out, to see if I was "normal". Whatever that meant at the period in that culture. As if I could have been normal, in that mad household. Normal as any other Italian girlchild. Vito, Umberto, Gerry— what did they see? All of them doctors, neurologists at best. Never a psych-anything among them. The study of the soul was taboo in that lost, agnostic world.

Was it these men who advised that I should go to the dance? When I ask questions even today I am told only—*how perfect it was*—the perfect, aspiring family. Roses out back (we no longer needed to grow our victory-garden tomatoes), a perfect lawn in front. Floor you could eat off, perfect aspiring children. "Smart" was a virtue, and we were virtuous. All three of us, with a perfect mom and dad. How much was hidden, what had they overcome? As they later gave up smoking. What monster cruelty, repression, madness still lurked in the redecorated "basement floor": kitchen and dining room with a plateglass sliding door looking out on the roses?

I have somehow arranged to go to the dance with a friend: Eileen Schmidt, a good friend from school, though my parents don't approve. The block Eileen comes from is poorer than ours, her apartment is crowded with brothers and sisters. This, I gather, from their secret conversations is a part of the problem.

To be poorer than we are—though we never admit that we are poor at all—is to be somehow unworthy, a little dirty, unless you are part of our family (a great-aunt, or one of my father's siblings). To be non-Italian is suspect, but there is a ranking, a hierarchy: better to be Norwegian than Swedish, Swedish than Irish. To be, as Eileen is, a *mixture,* is in itself a bit disgraceful. A mix of Irish and German distinctly low.

I like Eileen, feel welcome in her house. It is one of the few places where I am at ease. My strange, bookish English, self-conscious pronouncements, habit of quoting verbatim from what I am reading; my odd clothing and hairdo are no problem here. Eileen's mother is warm, if busy and overworked. Her dad is not an overwhelming presence. When he is home, he sits to one side, no one particularly waits on him or notices. He is gentle and silent.

I get dressed at home while Eileen waits downstairs. My striped taffeta skirt is full, but not full enough. Nothing I own is full enough for the current style: a "flare" skirt that stands straight out, perpendicular to your body, when you spin around. Something I suspect came from some Rita Hayworth movie. Gypsy dancer beside some black and white fire. When I spin, my skirt flares out, but not "all the way". I wear a white peasant blouse, with what we called a "scoop neck", and feel good in my stockings and flat black shoes.

At Eileen's I add the finishing touches with her help. Tuck my hair in a net and curl the ends under to fake the fashionable "pageboy" effect, and with trepidation put on a bit of her lipstick. This is strictly out of bounds. My mom wears no makeup, never has, scrubs her face and her hair with Ivory soap. No creams, lotions, shampoos come near our bathroom. No color options grace her dresser top. No extra mirrors anywhere, no vanity tables.

But Eileen has lipstick and I put some on. I've practiced once or twice before at her house, scrubbing it off before I went home, and she helps me now. I get the bright red on without smudging, and blot it on a napkin, feeling very grown-up. Her mother tells us how nice we look and we walk to the school together in the spring twilight.

The dance in the church basement was nothing much. Bright lights, nuns and monks (our teachers) standing in corners. 78s on a phonograph, a few kids actually trying to dance together. I'd been told so often I was clumsy I didn't try it.

It was enough to be there, late afternoon becoming evening, to sit on the hard bench along the wall in that big bare room, or go for a soda pop at the folding table. To actually talk to boys my age without a threat. Here no one would drag me into a corner and feel me up. I felt I was in a pool of light, a center called truce. A place where I had nothing to explain or defend.

It is ten o'clock; has turned dark, and suddenly Emma is standing in front of me. Had I forgotten she was going to pick me up? That was no doubt the arrangement. Emma is trembling with emotion: rage or grief. There is something close to hysteria in her eyes. Familiar and hideous—I hope against hope she won't have a "nervous fit". Not here. A sense once again that the bottom is dropping out, I've done something awful, and I don't know why, or what. I get my coat and follow her out of the room.

In the hall she turns on me, she is furious, she is weeping. How could I do this? How could I do this to her? She slaps me, but I don't feel it, I am too bewildered. What have I done? Apparently I have worn make-up, "put up" my hair. (She pulls at the "auburn" net, and it comes loose. A few hairpins fall to the cement floor.) I am working hard to piece this whole thing together. This hair net, this daub of lipstick are treason, betrayal. I never knew it before, but now I do.

I know it, but don't understand it in the least. Is it betrayal to "grow up", wear make-up? Betrayal to celebrate (our house is so dark)? Betrayal to become a sexual being? Or merely a social one? How had I hurt my mother by "looking nice"? We do not speak, Emma cries all the way home.

Thus the mysteries of pleasure joined the mysteries of play. They are all, apparently, evil.

There was a time when I was little, my five- or six-year-old self filled with desperate yearning, when I would have done anything to protect Emma. To keep her from hysteria, bewilderment, fear. To keep from seeing the mechanisms of denial working behind her eyes deconstructing the structures of her Self.

But now I walk home in silence, and it is not for Emma I give up, but to keep the peace. Hard won, precarious peace bought by near-madness. Mine, not hers. Breakdown shining like a jewel in my memory.

After that night I hid my sexuality from myself. My changing body became the enemy, I hated it with a passion. Spent innumerable hours staring at my breasts, trying to keep them from growing any bigger. Imagining myself flat-chested, tall and lean. A boy's girl-body. No breasts, and narrow hips, tight ass, but no penis either. I wanted all protuberances gone. Anything that stuck out seemed so vulnerable. Like the parts of myself uncovered in the crib. Exposed to the tiger.

This girl-man I longed to grow into had straight black hair. It hung to her shoulders, smooth, no curls, no frizzy places. No freckles either, pale, flat, white skin and green eyes. A look many of us tried to emulate later, in the 50s. In how many fantasies was it already growing?

It was never that I wanted to be a man. I held men for the most part in contempt and dread. But to be a girl in a flat and streamlined body. The opposite of my thick red hair, my Italian figure. Over and over the image of cutting off my breasts, getting rid of them somehow, would come to mind. Breasts that had gotten me battered, simply by growing.

As for what had transpired at the dance, I took that into myself, internalized it. Could not afford my mother as adversary, so took her oft-repeated tenets as my own. *No need for make-up. Plenty of time to date later.* Repeated these axioms through high school and on into college. Only not to see her cry again. Not to be sexual, when she would not.

Later she would cry about what I wore, but never because it was sexy. It never was. And she cried about what I read and what I thought. But somehow my woman self was hers, not mine.

My sexual life became an inner life. Though I seldom masturbated. Touched myself warily, if at all. My fantasies turned toward dark Byronic heroes. Read *Jane Eyre* all the summer I turned thirteen, just before high school. And wept for Schopenhauer, his fear and his hatred of women. Sure I could have saved him, saved all the Romantics.

Later there was the summer that my friend Pia and I discovered Nietzsche: first *Thus Spake Zarathustra,* and then the Modern Library Giant. This was heady stuff and we loved it, but Emma, when she caught a glimpse of what I was reading—Emma, avowed agnostic and daughter of an anarchist—wept and called Pia's parents. The mothers decided between them that we should talk to a priest.

We went to Pia's parish. The poor man we saw was not up for our eager, reasoned polemic, and wound up shouting at us "Don't think! Don't think! It will spoil your faith". We barely managed to hide our amusement till we got out of there, and "Don't think!" was added to our growing list of ridiculous quotes from the grownups that we would shout with great glee when the occasion required.

In the midst of these battles, fantasies, nightmares, storms of self-hatred, I was bracing myself for high school, determined it would be different from everything I knew. A time and place to re-invent myself. I experimented a little, and chose *funny*. I would be funny, and no one would have the space to make fun of me. I put it on like a dress, another face. Internal realignment, fierce season of preparation.

There was, of course, which high school? Eternal question. Eternal tests: the Regents, entrance exams. Competitions for religious scholarships, though no one in the family believed in God. And most of all, the test for Hunter High School.

Hunter College High School was a mecca, of sorts. Was the place the parents most wanted me to go. And I too, I wanted most to go there. At least it was not Catholic. Was not in Brooklyn. Academically the best, was what my parents cared about. The struggle for survival defined as Education. Another all-girls school, but I had given up sexual curiosity at that point. Or—never since kindergarten having been in a classroom with boys—didn't feel the need for it, now.

The test to get into Hunter was in English and math. I took it, and felt okay about it. There was the waiting, of course.

It was during the waiting I found out my father had "reached out". Reaching out was the euphemism used in Brooklyn for pulling strings, using influence to get something illegal or questionable taken care of. You would reach out to someone you knew at City Hall. Or in the IRS. It was protection and a way to get ahead.

Dad, who never expected anything to go right, had reached out in case I scored too low, to make sure I could still go to Hunter. Perhaps I heard them talking about it in Italian. Or perhaps they let it slip, maybe even intentionally—to them it would have been further proof of how much they cared about me. To me it meant they didn't think I could make it. It took all the joy out of testing, out of trying at all.

The test results were published in the paper, New York was still small-town enough for that. And it turned out that I had come in first in the city. Fair and square, no reaching out could have made that happen; it would instead have slipped me in inconspicuously under the wire. There in print, in those narrow columns of type—my name, and I was first. But the thing I was left with was: they didn't trust me. Didn't think I could do it.

(The week I was leaving for college my father turned to me, somber, to deliver his deepest message. Summation of his truth, what he had learned. Held me by the shoulders, or with his eyes:

"Now don't expect too much. I want you to always remember that you're Italian".

Not that we weren't as good, but however good we were, we would be held down. Or back. An underclass.)

When I flew out of my parents' world like a bat out of hell, it was to prove I could make it on my own. No reaching out could reach me where I landed.

Hunter was darker and lighter, at once, than anything I had experienced. Dark locker rooms, dark slate stairs. Institutional halls. High windows with small square panes. Light of the mind and light of a little space. Stepping out of that Brooklyn culture, I scrambled to fill up whatever space there was, like one of those crystals that shapes itself to the opening that's available.

Never again would I be the one to be laughed at. Of that I was determined. Never the one who spoke strangely, wore weird clothes. (Though neither my speech nor my wardrobe had changed at that point.) In the lunchroom I looked around for an opening.

And found it, in a large, sad beautiful girl. Carol Swidorski, Polish and odder than I was. Large, and slow-spoken, and blonde. I could make her laugh. I was smoother than she was, she became my "best friend".

It seems I spent the first year there learning the ropes. Learning what we now call social skills. Could I hold my own, could I keep the others amused. My wit went from clown to biting, but it was a while before I let on what I thought. Let anyone into my maverick inner world. Thoughts and opinions. And I never let anyone in on the facts of my home, effectively forgot them myself.

My life was probably no stranger than anyone else's—that was quite a gathering. There was Sylvia, who later left, age fourteen, for Israel, the new land of freedom (or so it seemed for a minute) to live on a kibbutz with her lover. There was Gloria, whose father (she told us) was a murderer from Spain. He had had to leave quickly (was it the Civil War?). We visited him sometimes, where he, suave, tended bar in the Village, Gloria always wistful for his notice. Wanting to *be* him—outlaw and smooth, she lived with her mother and grandma in Washington Heights in her muscular woman's body. At her insistence, we called her Mephistopheles—"Mephi" for short. There was Susan who also came from a one-parent home. Day after day, she came to school with tales of being terrorized or beaten. There was Gaby from Berlin, whose stepfather, a Freudian analyst, called me Lady Hamilton late one night in his house, when I had gotten up to go to the bathroom, nothing on but a raincoat. His hands all over me. I was hard put to wriggle away. There was Bobi, skinny, Lithuanian and poor, with a kind of fierce slum energy and Renée, an Armenian who cried almost all the time. And there was always Audre Lorde—who was later to become a poet of note—Black and fierce, and in those days often unreadable. She kept us guessing with her eyes and her silence. A kind of knowing and a kind of contempt.

There were meetings of the Young Progressives I never went to and socialist songs in the halls. The war was over, and all the world was astir.

Some of the teachers were the best of all at this all-women's school. Women teachers of all kinds modeled a plethora of ways of being women. And still being smart and saying what they knew. A whole spectrum of possibility.

I remember walking that first term into my first science classroom ever, the world of microphotography just opening up dimension: huge blowups, black and white prints on the walls, and stamens, stems, cells were so beautiful! Shapely—another order. Ruth Lilienthal, our biology teacher, a small woman on a high stool, who later went to Japan to study Zen.

Or the dark intensities of our English classes. Miriam Burstein, beautiful as her name. Her thick, dark hair. Allie Lewis, the actress turned Shakespeare teacher. She had us performing the plays day after day. Our rage, our lust, our fear, our greed for power. We owned it shamelessly in her class.

Or Mrs. Robbins, our history teacher, who sent us by ones and twos into the libraries and progressive research institutions. Vast caves lined in dark wood. Institute for Pacific Relations where I learned about Mao. The struggle for power still in progress in China as I read.

O, there were the ancient teachers, too, the dullards, the almost-dead. We ignored them; we went blithely on our way.

Or they didn't matter, no matter how dull they couldn't obscure the beauty of what they taught. Latin was like that for me. For it was the life of the mind that was opening here. Delight in the trip of the tongues, the shift of ideas. Though I couldn't have named it then.

All this was exploding in the pressure cooker of our adolescence: hormones, justice, passion. Passion for truth. Loyalties "as never before", as Pound might say. Fierce love of comrades, mutualities of Cause. Although the cause was less than half defined.

What we knew, most of us, was we came from a maddened people. (In nearly every case this was literally so.) Our parents, destroyed by depression, war, fear, greed. By being immigrants in a land of conformity. Turned on us daily, we had only each other. In this dark period between World War II and the Korean War, we clung to the safety we made together within the circle of our mutual sight.

That first year was tentative, I felt things out. I had the excuse of homework, lots of homework, and spent my time in my room, doing as I pleased. A new freedom—now Emma seldom called me peremptorily to help her.

At school at some point I ventured to speak from my heart. Only the tiniest hint, but found I wasn't cut down. By my second year I dropped the Comedienne, though she still crops up, and sometimes she's an ally.

In our second year at Hunter we were sorted out, by the language we would study: French, German, or Spanish. Italian, too low class, wasn't offered. And nothing exotic or Eastern, of course.

I chose French. It had always been assumed I would choose French, by Emma at least. To her, French was the universal tongue. Language of the aristocracy, she used to say. I had been named, after all, Diane, not Diana. And her mother was Antoinette. French was okay with me. but it was Latin I was in love with. In spite of my ancient, crumbling, old-fashioned teacher. Structure and fluidity at once, like biology and physics coming together. And quirky surprises. I didn't know to call it linguistics. Light of the mind.

That first year, with only Latin, we were sorted by IQ. A not-quite-spoken but well known fact was that many of us in the A class of freshmen had IQs that were "off the chart", couldn't be measured accurately. Over 165, they said or was it 180. But not to be measured. This was somehow important, whispered about or importantly ignored. I had been taking tests since I was so little, there had been so much discussion of this subject, that tucked in there with other young maverick women all of them "off the chart" for the first time it was safe, it was all right. Not dangerous, as it had always seemed at home. Not a bargaining chip for my parents to play against me. Nor an unwieldy, endless, dangerous obligation.

In the summer of my freshman year, I was sent by a determined Emma to typing school. Over my protests; I of course wanted my time: hallowed time of summer vacation immemorially mine (except for the household chores, eternal stairs to scrub). Free in between to read. To visit my happy Aunt Evelyn in Bayside where it was okay to lie on the earth and look at the sky through the trees. To try again to dog paddle or swim, to fail once more to learn how to ride a bike. To read *Penguin Island* or *Cyrano de Bergerac* with Uncle Arthur. Or fall in love with one of his fencing students. To make up strange secret fantasies of slavery and escape with my young cousins, acting them out for weeks in the backyards of Queens.

But no, this year it was typing school. Emma said: No matter what you think you might want to do, you'd better know how to type. At a loss to consider what I might be up to. My pat kid-answers of my younger years: "I'll be a teacher, a doctor, whatever" had given way to another sort of career. "I'll be a pirate" I'd answered recently when a relative had asked once too often. Emma wept. "If", she said, "you'd started as a pirate and now you wanted to be a teacher I'd be all right. But not this other way around". She had a point.

I can't say how she imagined a typing pirate, but anyway there I was, and here I am. It turned out I loved it. All my physical dexterity and skill, never given a chance to work itself out in my body, came into focus in my fingers. I was good, I was fast.

I loved the mindless concentration, three hours each morning at the blue typing book, at a desk in an office building near Borough Hall. All the huge black iron "standard" typewriters bolted to the desks, and all of us in rows, making little movements. Over and over again. People all ages, earnest, poking the keys. I loved going out of the house in the morning as if to school and yet free-er—that early summer light, light of the brick and brownstone, and the nearby harbor. All the trees green, the birds, the greengrocer setting up. My own person, taking the trolley downtown. The morning to myself, not even intense teen friendships, or mind-boggling classes. Just FRF-FTF-FGF-FVF-FBF, over and over, and the thoughts in my head. Or lack of them. Finally a moment of peace, uninterrupted.

I came away typing fast and never stopped.

The second summer things got complicated. Now, it seemed, it was time for summer school. My parents had been laying their plans.

In the distant world of college admissions, the winds of change were blowing. Schools were tailoring themselves to the postwar influx—GI Bill. I had entered Hunter High School in a February term, but it was rumored that soon colleges would have only September admissions. It might even happen by the time I applied. And since my parents were ambitious, to put it mildly, they were sure it could only help things if I "saved" half a year.

Now, my being in a February class in the first place was, in fact, the result of a half year we'd previously "saved", back when I was in the third grade. There had been what I remembered as a frantic push on Emma's part, Dick backing her up. They had assured each other (and everyone else who would listen) that I was bored, I was "too smart" for the class I was in—and then, too, wouldn't it help me later on if I got a head start? A jump on everyone else my age. Same immigrant vision. After much preparation, they moved their campaign to St. Mary's and took it up with Father Reilly. To my embarrassment and ultimate confusion, I found myself moved ahead, skipping "3B".

Now my relations with my schoolmates at St. Mary's had been none too good to begin with—I had been to three Brooklyn Catholic schools in my first four years, counting kindergarten—and this was the last straw. The only kids I knew were left behind; and at eight I found myself in a new crowd in the midst of immense resentment. Of "who does she think she is"? —always strong in Brooklyn. Strong in the family, as well as outside of it, and so this new version coming from my peers had plenty of room to sink in. I had heard it all before—had already been primed for it.

Who did they—whoever they were: friends, relatives, neighbors—think they were anyway? It was a refrain at our house.

From the time I "skipped a grade" at St. Mary's I had never again found my footing there. Had been the odd one, fat one, highfalutin. Grades too good. Weird corkscrew curls. Goody-goody, too. Talked funny. Quoted books. Plaid pleated skirts and stiff white blouses, no bobby socks, no sloppy-joe sweaters, no hip gangster talk, no penny loafers, didn't know anyone in Williamsburg either, no knife fights over boys—only flying home as fast as I could without seeming to run, trying not to get hurt too much by the girls who waited for me after school. And herding my brothers before me half the time. I had never again found an easy fit. Not, at least, till I found myself at Hunter.

At home it would be "Who do you think you are—Sarah Bernhardt"? whenever I "got dramatic" as my parents put it—took myself seriously in any way. Or "We're not gonna have any Isadora Duncans in *this* house"— often accompanied by a slap. So that for years I thought Isadora flighty and pretentious—maybe even an airhead—till I stopped to read her for myself.

As I was taught by Emma and Dick to think Eleanor Roosevelt the lowest of women—a kind of gutter-slut, not quite as good as a gun moll—she was ugly, buck-toothed, vulgar. What was *that* all about? Was it Emma's power turned against herself, turned against every powerful woman? As it had, therefore, no choice but to turn against me.

It is a spring evening and I am standing in the backyard in Brooklyn. I have discovered the poets this year, the English Romantics, have been taken and taken over by their vision. Dream of the early nineteenth century. Most recently I have been reading Keats—his letters. I have claimed and reclaimed poetry for myself, me and my tribe of friends do it day and night. Come early to school so we can read our new work to each other before class.

I came to Keats by way of Somerset Maugham, "hack novelist" as Miriam Burstein called him in an English class. Maugham had quoted Keats: "Beauty is truth, truth beauty"—was it in *Razor's Edge*?—and I had followed like a hound on the scent, to the poetry section of the Brooklyn public library, 821-point-whatever. There I stayed, hovering like a hummingbird, or coming back over and over for the same flowers. Vibes.

Keats, Shelley, Byron, mostly. Shakespeare's sonnets. Later Millay's "Renascence" and a few of the British women. A tone of passionate urgency I craved.

But now it is gloaming, late afternoon, there are small clouds in rows, striations across Brooklyn, I am looking at the sky and seeing I don't know what. Seeing Keats. Seeing possibility.

"If poetry come not as easily as the leaves to the tree, it had better not come at all".

Seeing the liquid structure language is, like liquid crystal, the depth and possibility of that. Seeing a life of striving, possibility of living within a Vision. Seeing the light pink touches on the clouds. Feeling the house, my family at my back. Behind me, as it were, as I look at this particular sky. But this moment is special, and no one will interrupt me. I sense that though I scarcely notice it.

I am thinking of the striving of Keats, his early death. Passionate urgency. I am thinking of my grandfather's words, his legacy. *"Study like I studied, struggle like I struggled"*. And something is stirring in me, something like power. Like sex, or love, like *kundalini* or vision. Something fills my belly and rises to my throat. It is the taste of possibility.

Poems I've been writing, yes, and poems I will write. But this is more than the poems, is the shape of a Life. Mine. Life lived in the Vision of art to be achieved. Lived in possibility. Rise to it. Yes. No reason it should not be me. Myself as I stand here. Take up the challenge. The knowing: no matter what I will be poet. Be great, whatever that means. Fulfill the dream.

This is Vision, but it is not hope, I can taste the struggles. The things I now leave behind (I am fourteen). Simple comforts of the regular human world, sentimentalized for a moment into a worth, a worthiness they didn't usually have for me even then. But now I am leaving them behind, never having had them. Now I am leaving them, perhaps for good. Leaving the quiet unquestioned living and dying, the simple one-love-and-marriage, children, material pleasures, easy securities. I am leaving the houses I will never own. Dishwashers. Carpets. Dull respect of dull neighbors. None of this matters really, I have already seen it all for the prison it is, but for that one moment it matters tremendously.

Looking at that sky, I know I will be poet, and knowing that know what I will lose. Have only the dimmest sense of what I will gain. What I step into now. What might be mine. Embrace this new thing, my Will. Fierce, silent love of Self, my angel. Where She leads. Keats said it:

I am certain of nothing, but the Holiness of the Heart's Affections and the Truth of the Imagination.

The sky changes, is changing, we are going now from gloaming to twilight—dusk. There is to be a sunset, it seems—less subtle, realer. Vivid reds and purples. Almost lurid. The evening breeze. It was that other, softer, tinted sky I vowed to. Spoke aloud did I? To Keats or to the heavens? I hold a Vow in my heart.

What the Imagination seizes as Beauty must be True, even if it never existed before.

"Nulla dies sine linea" I will write on the covers of my notebooks. No day without a line. A new commitment. Purpose.

It was as if I remembered why I had come here. Fallen to earth. All the day's minutes focused toward an end, and the end was: to sit quietly with my notebook somewhere. Watch words fill out the lines, as the pen moved. Mind moved and heart. And lips. Strings of my voice.

●

●

●

I passed two summers at Washington Irving High School, "making up" a semester according to the Plan. It was a change that came at the right time. Another place to explore. Closer to downtown, to the Village, and Union Square. To the heart of what I thought of as New York.

Classes were easy, and there was plenty of time I didn't have to account for. I found little parks to read in, to write in, places to walk. Cheap luncheonettes for bacon and tomato sandwiches. A special, secret, downstairs and off-the-street stationery store for notebooks and more notebooks, new kinds of pens.

Those summers were dominated by poetry. And what I thought of as freedom. Languor, and heat rising off the sidewalks. Dusty green leaves, and the local greasy spoon. They run together, these summers, though I think it was on the first of them, soon after my Vow, that I had the temerity to bring a poem to class.

Something in free verse, and rather simple-minded, it nevertheless caught the attention of Dr. Serota, a loud and earnest English teacher, perhaps my first male teacher ever. I didn't know what to expect or make of him, but he must have somehow gotten around my suspicion and fear, because I actually did bring him a poem. He took it home and the next day had me read it aloud to the class. This was quite a different matter, I discovered, from reading the work of the day before to my friends and fellow poets at Hunter in the early morning. Somehow this mattered—was it because these folks were, in fact, not poets? How they heard it—that mattered too. It was about how they heard and received myself.

Nothing prepared me for what followed. All summer Dr. Serota looked at my poetry, all summer he wrote comments in the margins. Mainly he searched out the concrete images. The startling. Shone a delighted spotlight on the wayward turns and windings, the dark corners and alleys of my spirit. My already quirky mind. Mainly he tried to excise the abstractions which abounded—grew like weeds through the cracks and lacunae in my thought. Grew as ground cover for what I did not know, and for what I already would not and could not remember.

Sometimes I heard him, but mostly I resisted. I kept what I loved in my poems, however klutzy. But a part of me began to see with new eyes. To hear what sang off the page, and into the heart.

Mainly, he was a witness, a reader. From another world than that of my Hunter friends and brilliant women teachers. More like the Brooklyn folk I came from, my uncles, my neighbors: upholsterers, longshoremen. More down to earth, so his interest touched me deeply. He bore witness that something I was saying reached farther than the closed world at Hunter. I learned I needn't leave *everyone* behind. Though I would forget this again and again on my outward journey.

I wrote daily, I copied the poems out, I labored. And I made a new friend. That was the summer of me and Pia Maria.

It was the same Dr. Serota who made certain that Pia and I met. She was in his other English class, in summer school from her high school in Brooklyn, and our paths would never have crossed but for his insistence. His sense we had something special to say to each other.

It is a summer afternoon in July, and I am in the subway. Riding a train I never ride, a different "line" even—is it the BMT? —so the cars are different, differently configured. There are small compartments at each end of the cars that fit two or four people, and we are in one of these. We are riding above ground deep into Brooklyn, the backs of houses, lines full of laundry, brick walls, odd twisted trees, church spires, are flying past. I am sitting with Pia Maria and we are talking, we cannot stop talking or take our eyes from each other. We are fervently holding hands, our slightly sticky palms are glued together.

She is in love with the poets, as am I. She is in love with music, speaks of opera I haven't heard or thought about since I stopped seeing Domenico, my grandfather. She is in love, is passionately in love with life. She over-flows with emotion, and it is not bogus. Her being is made of it, is "moist" as Heracleitus would say. She is sweet, and passionate, and tender. She mir-rors some part of me I had long mislaid. Some part that is not, and cannot be, mirrored at Hunter.

Among my many maverick woman friends at Hunter—the "Branded" as we loved to call ourselves—not one of the others was Italian. Gloria, with her romanticized Spanish background, bilingual home life, came the clos-est. The others were Irish, English, German, Polish, Black. Not given, any of them, to passionate outbursts, language of feeling was saved for the poems.

And there were those things that, even at Hunter, didn't make it. Didn't fit in. Those ways of being that I had to hide. My love of the romantic, overflowing emotion. Imagination watered with torrents of feeling.

I remember reading Thomas Wolfe there, *You Can't Go Home Again* hidden under my desk in some boring economics class, and my sense—no, my certain *knowledge*—that it was off limits. Too wordy, too passionate. *O lost and the windgrieved ghost come back again.* My quick lie, when asked what I was reading: a comic book, I said. A comic was acceptable to my classmates, Thomas Wolfe was not.

Even the Branded didn't go far enough. And in the school generally, my classmates, the ones who remained after the general exodus toward adventure at the beginning of our second year (kibbutzes, lovers, Europe) held Beethoven too emotional, had learned to say that they "preferred Buxtehude to Bach". At that time I didn't recognize "good taste" for what it was: cultural oppression—a kind of racism, in fact—but simply knew I was "too much" for the general climate, and tried more or less unsuccessfully to tone down.

But now it is a summer afternoon in July, and I have nothing to tone down or hide. We have walked from the subway to Pia Maria's, a ramshackle wooden house in Sheepshead Bay. Where we are greeted by her mother, offered sandwiches. Egg salad. Eternal egg salad of Mrs. Volpe, I was now meeting for the first time. Eggs of the goddess we ate all summer long.

Pia is smaller than me, shorter, more buxom. Her hair is as thick as mine, is as unmanageable (frizzy), but it is very black. And I, who have always been the shortest and roundest person among my friends at Hunter, can now tower over someone. Her hands are tiny and soft, they move incessantly. Her large brown melting eyes.

We are welcome in Pia's house. We lie on the floor, listen to opera after opera while she tells me the plots. Read Keats and Shelley aloud to each other for hours, or walk the ends of Brooklyn, far-flung abandoned streets smelling of salt, small marina with its boats, the tar and creosote by the water's edge. Boulders we balance on, with the sea before us. Lost gardens sporting bronze statues turning green. Green bust of Byron in some old maid's front yard. The moon coming up here, over the ends of the earth.

Pia's father played timpani in the City Center orchestra. He was soft-spoken and gentle. The house was full of music, and light, and kindness. There was a slightly grimy feel to the worn linoleum when we lay on it, listening to music. It was the salt and sand the wind brought in. Or which we tracked in from the beach.

There was no mention of chores. No one asked questions, no one was suspicious. We were "the kids" and what we did was okay. And what we did was explore the world of art: music, painting, poetry—romanticism of all sorts—all summer long in that farflung Brooklyn light.

We wept with Mimi, and we died with Tosca. Poured defiance into the room with André Chénier. We danced the Masked Ball, hid and lurked like Rigoletto, were proud as Turandot and alone as Liù. And Pia, well taught by her father, made me music-literate: "Listen to the oboe" she would suddenly say, or explain what it took to sing *mezza voce,* why it was rare. The voices of Tito Schipa, of Caruso, of Albanese and Gigli filled the house.

After that summer, Pia more or less joined the Branded. Though in some ways it was difficult for her. There was a way she remained a stranger always. Vivid Italian gestures. "Non-intellectual" parents. And her far-away home at the end of a long subway ride. And then, we at Hunter were intensely proud of our difference. The specialness of our school and how we got there.

Pia Maria went to an ordinary high school somewhere in Brooklyn. She had no prospect of going to college, and as time went on and we all began making plans that became another divisive factor. But she spent a lot of time at my house, where the Branded were gathering more and more often—my mother having finally learned to leave us alone, probably feeling it was better to have us in sight, to at least know where we were.

So Pia became a part of the Hunter crowd, adopted for her love of poetry, love of music. Her overflowing affection for us and our ways. Often on weekends we would ride the subway to her house, so much more permissive than any of ours. Play her records, or walk to the beach together with our notebooks. Her dad off playing a matinee, her mother beaming. Friendship intense and formal flowered amongst us.

By the next summer we were pirates. We had the run of the city: Sheepshead Bay to the Cloisters. Coney Island. It was all ours, and after classes at Washington Irving we would rearrange ourselves in the girls' bathroom, standing before the tall mirrors they had so kindly provided. Wide belts and jeans. Blouses with wide, flowing sleeves. Then we would set out, wild for the streets. The summer smells.

It was Susan O'Reilley that year went to summer school with me, and with what wonder I would watch her preen, combing her blond hair just so, and flipping it back. Turning from side to side to admire her waist. Her tiny nose. Humming or singing in her full contralto voice. She amazed me so; she seemed to like her body. So that I liked it too, fell in love with it really, a loved object we could both agree on. Never extending the same interest to my own.

We were pirates, we would set out, thinking the world was ours. Never hindered by lack of money, went where we pleased. Perched and watched, from Union Square, from Washington Square. Benches along the duck pond in Central Park. Walked the Brooklyn Bridge, took the ferry to Staten Island. Learning the turf, defining (marking) it. Stopping wherever we pleased for coffee. Notebooks and pens always with us.

And Pia was a part of that summer, though she didn't go back to summer school. Her home defined one of our boundaries, an outpost at one edge of our Empire. As Gloria's apartment in Washington Heights was another.

That second summer at Washington Irving High School, I found Jean Cocteau. *Blood of a Poet* played for a long time in a movie house close by, its inexplicable poster trumpeting at us, challenging us, as we walked by it day after day, till finally we went in one afternoon, Susan and I. Out of the summer sunshine, into the cool darkness. I watched an unprepossessing man at an easel kiss a mouth in the palm of his hand. There were speaking statues, a black angel with improbable insect wings, corridors with locked doors, behind each of which dreams were being played out.

I had seen very few movies, and now this. I was suddenly electrified—wide awake. I saw for the first time that everything was possible. On the canvas, the page. That afternoon at the movies changed my life.

There would be future summers when I was "on my own" living on the Lower East Side when I would spend whole days at the Thalia, New York's main repertory cinema for foreign films, seeing the same Cocteau movie all day long, skipping out to the lobby (if the second feature wasn't by Cocteau) to write in my notebook, to eat the sandwich and fruit I'd brought along, to wait for the movie to begin again. *Eternal Return, The Eagle with Two Heads, Les Enfants Terribles, Les Parents Terribles.* Claustrophobic intensity of Cocteau's mind. At some point I "got" it, a gift straight from him to me: Magick has to do with the relation of light and time. Bending them. Light and time and the movement of the mind. That simple.

It was Magick I had found, in the dark. In the black and white light gleaming off the screen. Some way to play with reality, bend it to your will. Neither space nor time so solid as we had been told.

Magick I sought and found, too, in the poets. Long evenings in my room in Brooklyn, a room newly redecorated by my parents, with huge red roses on blue linoleum, a built-in bookcase. Long evenings with the Branded, spent "calling up" the ghost of Byron—a cross between concentration and Will. (The ghosts, if they came would stand in front of the bookcase.) Trance sessions we invented, a state between sleeping and waking: half-woken, we answered questions for each other. Telepathy experiments we held. "Sending" words or images across the boroughs of New York, at the appointed hour of a weekday night. Checking with each other the next day, before we read our new poems: what had we "gotten"?

Was this the third year? the fourth? Things were flowering for us. Or exploding.

By our last year Hunter couldn't contain us at all.

We were out in the streets by then, were everywhere. Buying opals and seventy-five-cent Caruso records from a tiny antique store a mile or so from my house. "The Court Street Store" we called it. Reigned over by an ancient woman who knew magick. Gaelic quotations and Words of Power fell from her mouth. Menageries of animals cut out of gemstones lurked behind glass in her breakfront.

Or scouring the secondhand bookstores whose stalls lined Fourth Avenue. Ducking in out of the snow to talk to aged book-men, whose potbellied stoves dried our shoes, whose knowledge fed our minds and moistened our souls. Long hours poring over Doré engravings. Over Beardsley's illustrations for Balzac. Long hours with dusty, leather-bound tomes of travel. Flotsam and jetsam of the nineteenth century. Whatever came to hand.

Our questions, endless curiosity the bookmen loved to encounter. To fill and to feed. So that we came away glutted, and hungrier than ever.

Oh, we went to a couple of classes, English was one. This was a Shakespeare year with Allie Lewis. We got to perform the plays together. And I often went to Latin; we were reading Virgil.

But often midmorning would find us walking out in a group, to the amazement of our teachers, who loved us too much to stop us. Wandering down Lexington Avenue to buy smoked rattlesnake in small cans, candied violets and other munchies we thoughtfully nibbled as we wended our way downtown.

One of our entertainments was Union Square. We had discovered this was the park for mad polemics. For politics without ceiling or limit. We loved

it: anarchists, communists, fascists debating, in all seriousness, points that
to our minds seemed only surreal. We joined them sometimes, sometimes
equipped with vegetables we'd picked up at a stand along the way. It was
our pleasure to argue heatedly some abstruse idea we'd make up on the
spot, and in the heat of our feigned fury to pelt each other with carrots and
cabbage leaves as we stood fierce and noisy, tall on the wooden park
benches. Others of course would join in, take sides, more knowledgeable
and serious, others for whom these questions were life and death, and,
after making up a few quotations from Nietzsche or some other hated figure as a clincher, we would escape, laughing, to skip and run, to tumble
further downtown where coffee awaited us in the Village.

The Village coffee shops were the domain of the Italians. They sported
dark wood, bisque or marble statues, loud arias, foreign newspapers, an
occasional pinochle game. But they made us feel welcome, sheltered by
some European understanding of *i studenti*. They were places to warm
up, eat sweets, talk endlessly, read, drink espresso, scribble in our notebooks. We felt safe and at home in this Village that had never yet heard of
poetry readings or beatniks.

The entire city was our stomping ground. Our playground. We were extraordinarily blessed, though we didn't know it.

Meanwhile our homes—my home, at any rate—flickered from haven to
war zone, and back again.

There was no clocking it, no knowing what was safe. Emma, making
the Branded welcome, or wild and hysterical, threatening a fit. Dick
turned to a battering madman at the sight of a low-cut blouse. A dress he
didn't like. A neatly mended tear in a skirt. There would be nights I returned after whatever arbitrary curfew had been set, and would go to bed
bleeding from something Dick threw at me. Or days when Emma would
burst into tears at some book I was reading. Some title she saw on the
table.

I could be gone for days at Pia's or Gloria's, but wasn't allowed to go to
the opera, return at eleven. And boys were out of the question, I'd almost
forgotten about them. Nearly no one at Hunter dated anyway—when they
were ready they took up with lovers or left for foreign parts.

The signals flickered wildly, and through them I could barely see my siblings, my brothers, growing up in the same war-torn landscape. Or was it
the same landscape for them? I couldn't tell.

.

All of my sexual feeling turned toward my friends. O'Reilley's beauty, Gloria's dynamism. The mystery of her affair with an older woman.

We would all "sleep over" together at one of our houses, and sometimes my body would light up, electric tingling in the palms of my hands, in my cunt. But I didn't know, or want to know, what to do about it. It seemed enough to snuggle and go to sleep.

Simpler and safer, in these exploding minefields.

chapter SIX

VIGNETTES OF A COLLEGE CAREER:

It is a late fall day and I am returning to campus from somewhere. There is the acrid smell of burning leaves, a smell I associate with this place. I never smelled it before I came to Swarthmore, but here for months it seems they have been burning leaves. They rake and burn leaves. The smell is sad, as is the smoke which hangs like a mist on what would else be blue sky.

I am walking to the dorm past a tower that is always locked. Scott Tower. It is locked because so many students have jumped from it. I find this eerie. I have an attic-like room with a gable window on the top floor of the dorm. The "gable rooms" are singles and I managed somehow to finagle one—though they are not usually given to freshmen—because I knew even before I got here I didn't want a roommate.

In my gable room I've thrown out the furniture except for the bed. There are orange crates packed with books along the walls, and orange crates packed with clothes, and on top of the crates my various treasures: opal elephant, white bust of Beethoven with his name underneath, white bisque bust of a veiled woman, the veil drawn lightly over her perfect features. I have a high small window and low eaves. From which hang a waxy globe of provolone tied with string with a knife stuck in it, and a dry Italian salami. No one else at Swarthmore has a room like mine, though I don't think about this then. I am pleased with the smell in it, smell of ripened cheese. And with the tiny window looking out on the sweep of lawn and the turning trees.

I frequently shut my door, lock it sometimes, play music, write, and daydream. Sometimes when I open it, I find people waiting outside. Various young women (this is, of course, an all-women's dorm) who babble at me. They always say that they are worried. So unusual is it to lock one's door that sometimes they wonder if I killed myself. I hate it. Feel invaded. Hate being spied on.

Suicide is very far from my thoughts. It is wonderful to be here and be alone. Away from Brooklyn, the family. I am melancholy in a rich, pensive kind of way, but I am not sad or depressed. But none of these folks seems to understand the difference.

I have made new friends at college, but in a way I see them only as extensions of the ones I left behind. The Branded. Or as new additions to our old crew. Part of the same family.

Lee, who is deaf and sad. "Beautiful as Hamlet" is how I think of her. The head thrown back, Dutch profile, handsome and boyish. Not so different from that backlit romantic Hamlet Laurence Olivier created around this time. Made us all dream of.

Tomi, the catalyst, who will change our lives. Unable to change herself. Quick, nervous hands, mobile mouth. The pain in her face. The sharp, dissatisfied intelligence we thought was sophistication. And yearning. The one we longed to assuage, to make well again.

Long, gentle Erin, some of the other women. The various mysteries I saw in them: their faces, their moods, their just-flowering flesh.

And the closeted gay men I would sometimes visit, though theoretically I wasn't allowed in the men's dorms. I'd lie on a white bearskin rug, with white cub skins around it, and listen to veiled talk of their hidden lives.

Everywhere there is beer, and self-conscious dating. There are hidden rules that I know nothing about. Blonde girls in cashmere sweaters, with single strands of pearls, seem to own this place, they know what it is for. How to act in it. I haven't a clue, don't really care to learn. But am grateful for the land and the breathing space.

It is spring and I am romping in the woods. Small spindly east coast woods that are part of campus. I am wearing a red sash, my hair comes to my waist. Red satin ballet slippers, jeans cut off at the knees with a ragged edge. I have my notebook, and a book of poems. Somebody's work I got out of the college library. Probably Chaucer. I had discovered Chaucer in English I. The class marched on. Everybody else was soon reading Milton, or maybe Pope. But for me it was still Chaucer, my way was to read things through.

The teachers were tired, cynical—jaded I thought. They probably thought themselves sophisticated. Played bridge all afternoon in some public lounge. One of them, a bit more interesting than the others, killed himself a year or two after I left. Or so I heard.

I am romping in woods I never had at home. Dressed like nothing they ever saw on this campus. And reading voraciously under various trees. I have my notebook, but it is hard to write. Since I've been in this place, there has only been one poem. This is the only place I have ever been where it is next to impossible to write a poem. I think about this often, puzzle about it.

I am sitting on the floor in one of the parlors, huddled into myself, my head on the edge of a sofa. Listening to Jake Levy play the piano in one of the parlors. He played so well, I thought; I was more than a bit in love with him. His red hair, his intense Jewish looks. Not sure what being in love entailed. In this place it seemed to entail sex. Not sure I was ready for that, at least not here.

Made out with Jake once in an empty football field. But he didn't really turn me on. Not there. Not then. He was anyway in love with a WASP girl, daughter of one of the school administrators. Would come back sad and frustrated from his encounters with her and stormily play the piano and I would listen.

I am in "the meadow", a dreary place, with a dreary young man whose name I have long forgotten. We are drinking beer, which I greatly dislike, and he has an arm around me. In other parts of the meadow sit other couples. We can vaguely hear them, but not see them. It is dark and I am bored out of my mind. The meadow is almost a marsh, and my ass is getting wet through the blanket.

This is my first date, my first real date ever, and in the rest of my time at college I only go on one more. Emma was right, I think. This is not for me.

My second date is a football game at Princeton. With a man named Whittle Johnston. Shy Southerner, very polite. There is a dance, and Whittle dances like a 40s movie. Holding me at arm's length. Whittle doesn't seem to mind if I follow him or not, he has thick glasses, he grins at me often. I sleep in the women's dorm, and he in the men's. This is a matter of course, no problem at all.

The game the next day though is uncomfortable. Cold. And, too, I haven't the faintest notion what football's about. Or why I would want to know. It doesn't look at all like what we played in Brooklyn—any number of kids on each side, two-hand-touch in the streets. This seems a barbaric pastime. Ugly and dull. No idea at all who to root for, or why I would care. The ubiquitous boring beer. After a short time I don't even try to figure it out.

College football games were something I had heard about at length from Emma. Football and speakeasies, the two things she loved about her college years. Maybe it was her first chance ever to holler or giggle. She would mention the games whenever she made one of those archetypal parental speeches: *College is (or will be) the best years of your life.* Partly I went to the game to see what she saw in it. And partly because Whittle was so shy and improbable. There was a kind of whimsy in it all.

My friends from Hunter, the Branded, keep coming to visit. They are by now friends with Tomi, Lee, and the others, the handful of women I run with on campus—all maverick and mostly gay.

At one point I am called to the dean's office to talk about them—these women who are not playing by the rules, who are developing a network of loves among themselves—but I refuse to reveal anything of our lives. It is not exactly *omertà,* though that code of silence might well be part of the picture. Aroused and hungry, not sexually active yet, still I refuse to give up my right to be gay or anything else I or anyone can conceive of, and I explain this fiercely. My right to experience everything possible. Right as human, and again as a poet.

To my surprise, Dean Cobb hears me and agrees. I come away armed with a Latin quote she gives me which I put on my door: *Homo sum, ergo null'aliena mihi est.* My flag of defiance. "I am human, therefore nothing is foreign to me".

Looking back now, I wonder if it was not my teachers at Hunter High School, those strong and improbable women, who prepared me for these encounters with Dean Cobb. No problem for me to speak to a strong-minded woman, as long as she was intelligent and could listen. No fear in such exchanges, simply a mutual respect: what I had learned in the give-and-take at Hunter.

By the second year my friends were dropping out.

Now it is spring and trees are flowering everywhere on campus. I have never seen so many flowering trees. I sit under a pear tree and try to write, but the poem—the only poem I will write at Swarthmore—is weird, stilted; it doesn't sing.

Spring is gorgeous here. The beauty of the Philadelphia Main Line is outrageous—but it is weird to me, cut off from the world. When I go to these mansions to babysit, as I often do, I am always a little sorry for the kids. Mom so dressed up she doesn't want to be touched: no hugs. I have by this time forgotten a lot of my childhood in Brooklyn, forgotten the beatings, but I remember the hugs—or, perhaps the two things run together now in my mind. Slaps and hugs are touch, are knowing you are valued. And I wonder how the kids here manage without them.

When I babysit, they usually show me where the liquor is. A kind of "liberalism" I suppose. I am not interested in drinking, so it doesn't matter. They offer me food, they drive me home, usually the man drives me back to campus, sometimes along the way there is a proposition, but nothing I can't handle—I'm used to this from the uncles, I've been well trained.

Sometimes too there are confidences: men as well as women are given to them. They make me a bit sad. I am beginning to have a sense of the overwhelming loneliness of this land. Brightly lit houses full of unspoken secrets.

I am going to Chester tonight with Bob Janowitz. Perhaps he is gay, I don't know, we don't talk about it. It's okay with me if he is. I have no romantic interest in him. What I need is a fellow pirate, and one with a car.

Chester is mostly Black, a factory town. Scott Paper owns the place and all its poor. As it owns, or anyway has "endowed", the suicide tower on campus. None of this is lost on us.

We go often to Chester, just to get off campus. Go someplace we can think of as "real": a Black jazz club. Circular bar in the middle of the joint, band playing in the center of the doughnut-shaped bar. People who hang out there live in the town. It is easy and familiar. Black whores come and go; Bob and I drink beer and talk to each other.

He is slated to become a doctor of some kind. At least that's the family plan. His own dream is to be a marine biologist, and when he talks about his family his heavyset shoulders stiffen and move in a frozen lump up towards his ears. He knows I'm a writer caught in a physics program. We share our secret inner lives, and our various hopes.

It is spring, it is heartbreakingly beautiful, and I am caught in a lie. Several lies, a bunch of them it seems. I am not what I seem. Neither is nearly anyone else in this place. They mostly take it for granted, but I cannot. Can't write, or study. Sit endlessly under some tree near the library. Trying to finish a bitter, stilted poem.

Last fall on the first day of our first English class, we were all greeted (our goofy high hopes, our blank expectant faces) with: "Some of you may be writers, we're not interested in that. I'm here to teach you to be *good critics*". The English professor was the classic man-in-tweeds, complete with a pipe and leather elbow patches. My confused, seventeen-year-old heart hooted defiance. But it did not have the wherewithal to keep green—keep moist—in such surroundings.

There were years behind me when I had had all of New York to play in. This campus, stodgy town, and desperate nearby Chester, are clearly not enough. Even the woods have shrunk—become as small as they truly are. I can smell the ultimate poverty of spirit. And I am becoming starved, for joy, for honest feeling. My hunger for truth is turning into rage.

But now it is spring, the world is bursting with incredible beauty. I too am bursting with the blooming of my body. It is a symphony of singing hormones, and it is hard to reconcile this turmoil of the flesh with the pretentious, awkward intellectual life, clipped speech, stiff bodies, unimaginative clothes, poor food, frequent alcohol, and deathly mores by which I find myself surrounded. This is much worse than preferring Buxtehude to Bach. I cannot imagine four years in this place; I feel I've been buried alive.

All that semester the Branded come to visit in ones and twos, and life gets complicated bit by bit. O'Reilley, unhappy at William and Mary College, is trying to figure out how to switch to Swarthmore. She and Tomi are falling in love.

Gloria, not in any school, living in Manhattan with her middle-aged

DIANE DI PRIMA ● 93

woman lover, turns the campus into the Garden whenever she gets here. Adventure in Eden; it lasts as long as she stays. We walk the woods, the forbidden railroad tracks. Scour the skimpy town. She makes the place larger somehow, more possible. Everyone is in love with her.

When summer finally comes, I find I've squeaked through somehow, my grades are still okay, though they've dropped a bit. Perhaps the nights in Chester are taking a toll. Or the deadly dullness of this college life.

That summer I worked full-time at an insurance company for $35 a week, a job arranged by my parents. As the summer before I'd been "mail clerk" in a ball-bearing factory.

That, at least, had been fun. Blue-collar and full of play. I'd ridden a truck around the plant, delivering the mail for my $28.50 a week. But now I felt caught. Trapped in a dull world with no choices.

As I was trapped too, by my entanglements. Dark skeins of emotion. Passion, knotted and angry. No way to understand myself, but I longed so to make it okay for everyone around me. Okay for Tomi and O'Reilley who loved each other. Okay for Gloria/Mephi with her older-woman love. Okay for Audre, turning bitter in Stamford; for Lee, whose sorrow seemed endless and whom I desired. Longed to hold in my arms, only guessing what that might entail. Okay for the Branded and all the Swarthmore women. Who somehow or other had added themselves to this soup.

The Swarthmore crowd and the Branded had mingled and tangled, and there was no map, no way through. Thickets of anger and passion I now called daily life.

Nine-to-five was a prison; family was prison. Cold intellect of campus, another prison. And our insistent relatedness—mine and my friends'— another prison, grown from our caring blindly for each other. Impotent to change the smallest detail of our lives. Where heart and instincts pulled one way, mores another.

Once again, I walked by the sea with Pia, but in a torment beyond her comprehension. I didn't try to explain and distance grew between us, began to grow. And all that summer the poems still did not come.

.
.
.

So that the second fall at college I was like to burst. Stir-crazy. We all were. And our lives unfolded from that point. My life.

It seemed there was no way to stay in this place. No way to spend three more years here. Years of lies. But I wasn't used to quitting, had never quit anything. Or so I told myself. I hung on for a while.

I hung on though the place was not, had never been, my *choice*. It had been chosen by chance. By following the guidelines my parents had set, their projection of what my college experience should be. Once I had insisted that I wanted to go away—once I had won that battle, my course was set, and it had led straight to Swarthmore.

There were these rules I had to follow to get out of the house at all:

The first: *I had to get a scholarship,* wherever I went. No matter whether the place was cheap or expensive. The scholarship, it seemed, was a matter of principle. They wanted to make sure that nothing was too easy.

The second requirement was, *it should be a small school.* For some reason it was generally felt that a small school was "better". But for me, who had just come from the anonymity of Manhattan streets, the small-town mores and gossip were just another level of imprisonment.

The third rule was that the school should be *no more than three hundred miles from Brooklyn.* The idea was that I could come home on weekends. Of course, once I settled in I never went home, except for the inevitable holidays.

Not too many places fit all three criteria, and so it was by default I had wound up at Swarthmore. I had been railroaded. I saw that now.

I was at a place in my life where none of my friends could help me. The Romanticism we'd nurtured, I'd nurtured, so long had turned dark, and there were no charts to show where it went from there. No mentors, no grownups to consult with either—the ones we knew, like Gloria's lover, looked to *us* for answers. For inspiration. Or hoped to ride to heaven on our coattails. My grandfather was long dead, my family more distant than some tropical tribe. I had to go it alone, blunder on as best I might.

It is October at Swarthmore, and all hell is breaking loose. In the dorm, the rooms on the top floor, all singles, stand with their doors wide open. Women are bustling back and forth, uncharacteristically animated. And the Brahms Requiem is filling the air, the space of the hall.

Tomi has decided to leave. She is packing. And Lee is going with her, or has already left. Something about being lesbian in this place. Something about not wanting to live without O'Reilley.

There is the feeling of a vast exodus. O'Reilley has left or is leaving William and Mary. It is October, the leaves are turning, leaves are burning again, the stinging smoke seems to signal a fork in the road. Suddenly I find there *are* choices; choices are being made all around me.

Tomi is broken-hearted: she is disappointing her mother. Whom she holds on some pedestal I don't understand. I am helping her pack, I am doing whatever I can. I am a little in love with Tomi, a lot in love with Lee. I am feeling deserted, abandoned in this place, as it threatens to become even more empty and arid. But I plan to stay on in any case, to finish school. They can go, but even now I feel I have no choice.

There are a million calls from the pay phone in the hall. After each call Tomi becomes more desperate. More hungry for the approval, the unconditional love she will never get. Not from her crazed and alcoholic parents. She curls in her armchair, getting smaller and smaller.

At some point I've had enough, I need to find out what I'm feeling, to be alone. To mourn my own losses and not somebody else's. I disappear into the woods, or walk into town. Or go to the library to write in my journal. To read for a while, away from the breaking storm.

When I return, Tomi has already left. She is permanently gone, her room chaotic and empty. There is a note pinned to my door, a pocket knife stuck deep into the wood. It looks ominous, and it is. In Tomi's hand, in pencil, it says merely: *Where the hell are you, DiPrima?* I was not there when she left, and thus in one stroke she denied my right to leave her, take care of myself. My right to take off at will, be my own person.

I don't know this then, all I know is pain. Yearning and guilt. Will I ever see her again? Has she disappeared forever?

A stab through my heart, not just through the wood of my door. That note, accusing. Claiming me for her uses. Without acknowledgment or love, Tomi is refusing me my own path through this jungle. And promises no reward, no eros. No kindness even. The demand: that I attend on her tragedy. As I had attended on the tragedies at home. I swore to myself to be *there*, to be present at the Dark Moment, whatever dark moments. Always.

Many choices over the next years were shaped by that question. *Where the hell are you, DiPrima?*

.
.
.

It is Christmas vacation, and I am again in New York. It is a relief to be here: the energy, the noise of the City. Even the crudeness—loud voices on streets and in restaurants—is a blessing. Nothing here is muffled or polite. It is huge and unruly and jostling for space. I find it exhilarating.

I have somehow again got through the term, I am sitting in a Greenwich Village bar (though we are underage, we have graduated from coffee shops to bars). I am waiting for Tomi and O'Reilley to arrive. They want to talk to me they said, but they are late.

I am supposedly doing my Christmas shopping. That's what I've told them in Brooklyn. It is dark outside, it is mostly dark inside. Everytime the door opens an icy wind blows in. I am nursing a White Russian and trying to look at home. I play the jukebox. I have a table by the window, I study the street.

They come in at last, so beautiful. Displaced persons. Tomi small, dark, intense, her face which shows her every feeling, her dark upperclass clothes. And O'Reilley, long and languid and blonde. Her schoolgirl hair: bangs and a pageboy, her schoolgirl face: turned-up nose, and wide blue eyes. Her soft full mouth.

She is silent, she leaves the talking to Tomi who says they want me to leave school to join them—to set up house with them. O'Reilley's silence is eloquent, the tension is in her hands, in the twist of her mouth as she smokes; it is in her eyes.

Tomi says she doesn't want to go it without me. That neither of them does. They need me along, though neither of them says why and I don't ask. After all, why shouldn't they need me. My staunch, supportive ways, my love and admiration for them both. Now looking back through almost forty years I wonder in hindsight: did Tomi know she needed my earning power? Had they already figured out they needed another check for the rent? But nothing like that occurs to me then—I love them both and they say they need me, will I leave school?

I have no problem with leaving school. It is a hated and unfulfilling place, where I am studying nothing I care about. Where there are no powerful women teachers. No powerful teachers at all. No ideals, intensity of intellectual life. Nothing I'd hoped for. I am more than ready to leave, to get on with my life. Wherever it might take me. Of course I say yes.

I am ready to leave, but they two together are the catalyst. To simply leave on my own would have been quitting. But now I am needed, and by two such friends! They offer adventure, challenge, a use for the heart. For some kind of loyalty, however misguided. For energy and vision, and I am bursting with both. There has been nothing to engage them this past year and a half.

There is a dark doorway I go through. I will go through it once and everything will be changed. I will go through it over and over, for the rest of my life. Replaying these moments, understanding them. All that led up to them, all that comes after.

Not a passageway, it is just a door. It is quick. No corridor. A period of dense, difficult, but foreseeable time. A passable period, not longer than one can handle.

Not a passage, rite of passage in any known sense. A period of violent, impossible time. But over—over almost before it begins. And when it is done with, it will be done for good. This is the last time I will ever be battered. Last time I will be at the mercy of anyone else. "Browbeaten", a word my mother often used.

No way to guess who I will be after this. No way to foresee the changes. Only, I have been asked to join my friends, I am going to join them, I am leaving college behind me. And all it stands for. Striking out for myself. I feel this as inevitable and right. What I've been waiting for.

Christmas is over, I barely noticed it. Now it is one of those limbo-like days between Christmas and the New Year. Today is the day. I'm not sure how I know this, just that I do know it, it feels clear. Today is the day I will tell my parents what I am planning. Tell them, not ask their permission, not plead or suggest.

O'Reilley has come to the house in Brooklyn. We have spent the afternoon in my room. We have listened to records, some of our favorites: Francesca da Rimini. Grieg piano concerto. Beethoven's Ninth. We have scribbled and talked together, but there were long silences. We talked a fair bit less than I would have expected. Less than we would have at Hunter. After a year and a half of exile in alien worlds, the ethos of cool has been built into our bones.

It is late afternoon—the darkness comes so early to Brooklyn in December. We have made our plans; we know where we are to meet. I pack a suitcase: a few clothes and some books. My snapshot camera. A twinge at leaving my records, leaving so many books and the notebooks. Nothing to be done about it now. Except hope that things will eventually work out, I'll be able to come back later and get my stuff.

There is an upstairs doorway in the Brooklyn house. It opens outward onto the stoop with its wrought iron bannister and sandstone steps; opens inward to a foyer on the "parlor floor". O'Reilley will go out this way and hopefully meet no one—we have planned this in advance. She will take my suitcase, my few warm things for the streets. It's a cold December.

We wait till there's no one around except Emma who is cooking downstairs, and O'Reilley slips out. She has never left my house without saying goodbye to the family, but that will be a minor shock compared to the rest of the evening, what I plan to tell them. She walks the four blocks to the subway, makes her way to the Village. We will meet later, after I've spoken my piece.

I never expected it to be easy, never thought it would be this hard. I wait till I hear my father's voice, he is home. The boys are still in their rooms, have not yet come down for dinner, this is my chance. It feels like a déjà vu, feels inevitable, almost matter-of-fact. I can't tell whether the calmness I feel is real, or if I have just gone numb. A matter-of-factness and distance, like a scene in a play.

I am walking into a maelstrom, the kind of maelstrom I have done my utmost all these years to avoid. Given up my childhood and most of my reason. The kind of maelstrom that came down on my head inevitably, time and again—but which I had never deliberately sought out. Not in this hard-headed, step-by-step kind of way. A kind of cold ruthlessness I can feel behind my eyes.

I am in the dining room, talking to both my parents. Explaining that I am going to leave school. That I, in fact, *have* left, at least in my mind. That I plan to take an apartment with my friends somewhere in Manhattan, probably the Village. That I want to write and I don't need college for that.

I am not sure how many sentences I get out before I am on the floor. I am not sure of what happens next at all. What I remember is mom having a "nervous fit"—as she had often done under emotional stress when I was much younger—thrashing about and moaning. But this time my father is throwing me at her feet as he shouts "You're killing your mother" again and again. It is hard to think, to keep the composure I'd planned on. I remember a rain of blows, several rains, my father too angry to stop hitting me long enough to make sure Emma doesn't swallow her tongue. (Our constant fear all these years when she had fits.) I note, even in all that chaos, that she anyway doesn't swallow it. Not this time.

Then there is ominous quiet. They are making an attempt to reason with me. Gentle voices with leashed rage behind them. The words, to my teenage ears, are utterly outrageous: "All I'm asking you for is the next three years of your life".

My indignation and fury are immense. No way I could answer that sanely. No one had the right to a minute of my life, not anymore, not ever again. Unless I wanted to give it. I am clear on that. I am clear in my own anger. Something my family had never seen before.

There is ominous quiet, and my parents withdraw to their bedroom. To talk things over, or weep, or strategize. I don't know what they're up to, but I know that I don't care. *They are not the object of my anxious concern.* As they had been for years. I am only glad not to be being hit anymore.

I become aware of my brothers hovering on the edges of the scene, drawn from their rooms by the racket: mom's moans and my violent thuds. Watching and quiet, not wanting to draw attention to themselves. They look as they so often looked, from the sidelines.

My brothers are still my brothers; they are scared and hungry, and it doesn't look like dinner is going to happen. Mom's too upset, she probably won't come out of her room tonight. I am bruised, but okay. I feel good. For the first time I can see my way out of here.

I check on the supper—it hasn't burnt. Finish seasoning whatever it is, and set the table. Feed my brothers this one last time before I take off. Feel sane and competent. I fool myself into thinking I am calm.

I feed them and talk to them. I want them to know what I am doing, want desperately that they should understand. A futile attempt my father will sabotage in his rage through the years to come. His grief and disappointment driving a wedge between me and my siblings, my aunts and cousins. Between me and my mother.

Frankie and Richard are fed, the dishes done, and still no sound from upstairs. Where our parents are engaged in what rites of revenge or mourning? Both probably, but I hardly think about it.

They will never again be the object of my concern: sinking pain in my heart, in my belly—my wanting to make it right for them, in their claustrophobia, their fear and shame. Their lost disappointment in this New World. The grief I've felt for my mother since I was four is gone or lightened. I have closed some door against it. And I am the free-er for it.

●

I get my winter coat and walk out of the house. Walk out of the house; it will never be "my" house again. Never shelter, imprison, nurture, or torture me. I walk to the subway in the slippery darkness. Riding to meet Susan, and my things, at our rendezvous. Riding to some new life I can hardly imagine.

I am the free-er but not so free as I think. The yearning, the unease walked behind me that night, rode the subway with me out of Brooklyn. Over the years I would find person after person to pin it on, to make the world all right for, or try to against all odds. Anxious concern will dog my path, will haunt my trails across America. Will fill my dreams. Until thirty years later I finally turn in my tracks. Look it in the face at last. "Good morning heartache".

I walk to the subway in the slippery darkness. A kind of hardness riding on my shoulders, in my eyes. A way of cutting through I will use again and again. "Don't look back" no thought for the parents now, no thought for siblings. No thought I can afford, but to cut a swath. Move forward against all odds, toward what I love. An actual stance, a feeling in my flesh.

It turned out nobody would take us in. Or could. No room, or they didn't want to so close to the New Year, in the midst of their celebrations. Gloria's middle-aged lover wanted her privacy. They had a large, but one-room "studio apartment" they shared. And we certainly couldn't go home to O'Reilley's. Her mother had thrown her out with threats of imprisonment because of her "affair" with Tomi. Homosexuality was, after all, illegal.

Our other friends were perhaps afraid; we had dubious legal status, or none at all. That's how it was in the 50s when you were between eighteen and twenty-one. Neither minors, nor adults, we were on some edge. Some limbo. Barely existing.

We took things as they were. Matter-of-fact. We had laid our plans ahead of time. Had scoped out several hallways in the Village that were carpeted and clean and had radiators. So that night when we were done with coffee shops and talking and writing, when we had hung out long enough at our favorite lesbian bar, dark and welcoming and safe, when we had no more thoughts to exchange about our plight, we curled up in our jeans on the soft grey carpet on the hall stairs of a Village apartment house, and went peacefully and angelically to sleep, our purses under our heads, one of my hands on the handle of my suitcase.

chapter SEVEN

When I talk, as I sometimes do, to others about my life, when they ask, or seek to discover what it meant to me to decide back then to be poet and then as it were follow through, act on it, become "A Writer", they often say, "Ah well, no money, of course, but the fame, the early fame must have been a recompense". And I look at them strangely, wondering what they see, how they imagine those early flats, bare rooms, crates for tables and chairs, and eventually a baby in some corner. Fame, I say tentatively, was there fame? I don't know, don't think so.

What I do know is that choosing to be an artist: writer, dancer, painter, musician, actor, photographer, sculptor, you name it, choosing to be any of these things in the world I grew up in, the world of the 40s and early 50s, was choosing as completely as possible for those times the life of the re-nunciant. Life of the wandering sadhu, itinerant saint, outside the con-fines and laws of that particular and peculiar culture.

It was a world in which religion itself was suspect, and with good rea-son. "Religion" as we knew it was limited to the Judeo-Christian mode— "Protestant, Catholic, or Jew"? we would be asked on entering a hospital or a school. And it was a world one could not embrace with good con-science. Not what the agnostic liberals of the 40s and 50s would have liked us to believe, what they had dreamed—a world where Progress was a given and human society somehow a good in itself. We outlaw artist re-nunciants—would-be renunciants—saw no "good" in it at all. In the striv-ing, get-ahead thrust of America 1950, where nothing existed beyond the worlds of the senses, the clearest way to turn from materialism was to turn to the arts.

To be an outcast, outrider was the calling. Not fame, or publication. Keeping one's hands clean, not engaging. By staying on the outside we felt they weren't our wars, our murders, our mistakes.

(I remember a young anarchist immigrant, Francisco from Spain, imprisoned as so many were in those years after World War II, for being in America without papers. Later he was deported to Franco's Spain, where he was quickly killed. While he was in prison in or near New York, the authorities, having found out that Francisco was a baker by trade, tried to set him to work in the kitchen. Francisco staged a one-man sit-down strike. "I will do nothing", he said in his thickly accented English, "to support this house". It was what we all felt—it became a rallying cry. And remained so, long after Francisco was no more.)

I will do nothing to support this house. Not ours the wars, the cruelty, murder, oppression.

Not ours the men and women in madhouses, lobotomized, terrorized, shocked, or drugged to death. Not ours the politics of witch-hunt: the Rosenbergs, Wilhelm Reich, long-gone Sacco and Vanzetti.

Not ours the hideous heavy furniture, even. Overstuffed sofas covered in clear plastic, porcelain dragons / birds bearing lightbulbs in their teeth. The sliding glass doors looking out on decorous gardens.

The narrow and cruel judgments in the name of decency, order. Not ours the brutal marriages, children beaten into mental deficiency, the blind and blinding worship of money / achievement: is he a surgeon? Did she marry a corporate lawyer? The final word of judgment: "She could have done so much better for herself".

Not ours, the women kept home, locked out of sight. Hysterical or crazy—perhaps—but forbidden the use of therapy by their husbands, because the therapist had had the temerity to discuss the marriage, or these women's sex lives. Sacrosanct stuff of most secret domestic coercion. Secrets the men felt they had the right to keep.

To be an outcast, outrider, was to be eternally innocent of the inflicting of pain. Scornful, contemptuous and beyond the concern for appearance. And yet our obsession with innocence remained. It kept us outside of what we saw as the truly criminal—the respectable world around us. Like my father continually washing his manicured hands, we struggled to keep clean. I didn't then see the painful similarity.

I was a *bhikshuni*—though I didn't then know the word—dedicated to art and to the life of art. *Kai to kalon,* we reminded each other, scribbled on our walls, . . . *to kalon, kalon aiei.* The beautiful is beautiful forever. The one absolute. Like Keats' urn. Beauty is Truth. We took refuge in that place, *kalon aiei,* and mapped it inch by inch, explored relentlessly.

To be artist: outcast, outrider, and *explorer.* Pushing the bounds of the mind, of imagination. Of the humanly possible, the shape of a human life. "Continual allegory". Of a woman's life, pushing the limits. Opening endlessly to the image, words. The rhythm or pattern, sound—the vector swiftly drawn in the dark. And fleeting as lightning.

Do you see? It wasn't just the work, though the work was clearly blessed. Nor the rewards, which were none, as far as we knew. *It was the life itself*—a vocation, like being a hermit or a samurai. A calling. The holiest life that was offered in our world: artist. One that required the purest flame, clear lines of demarcation. Renunciation. "Sacrifice everything" we would write on apartment walls. "Sacrifice everything to the clean line". Continual offering of our minds and hearts. Offering impersonally our most personal passion. Most secret vision. What comfort we could give, and give each other. This beauty. Compassion disguised as aesthetics.

It was toward this I went. This was the vision singing in my eighteen-year-old bones as I looked that spring for an apartment / job.

And so, one day in the spring of 1953, I found myself standing in the midst of my precious cartons of books and papers, in a small apartment on the Lower East Side. You entered through the kitchen. One large room, painted grey, with two windows that looked out on the street from three floors up. Fire escape. White trim and ceilings. Small room off the larger one, painted yellow and white. A closet. A bathroom between the two rooms. Tiled floor. A tub and shower.

I had moved in a double bed and a typing table. Some kind of typewriter. Later there would be an upright piano in the smaller room and a ballet barre on the wall. There was already a "hi-fi", boxes of records, and the eternal orange crates full of books.

The block where I found myself was solidly Polish—Fifth Street between Avenues A and B. On the corner a meat-packing plant kept the sidewalk slick with grease, a sickly smell in the air. Men lounged about in the stained aprons of the slaughterhouse and eyed me as I went by. Speaking non-complimentary Polish or Yiddish about me. No woman lived alone in that world—or in my parents' world for that matter—unless she were a whore. Or somebody's mistress, which to these folks came to the same thing. This was a gauntlet I ran on the way to work every morning: the eyes, the comments. Harder to deal with than the straight-out rudeness, crude remarks of the men-about-town, this was more a duplication of my family's style. Snide and degrading. Smug in its cultural mores. I had moved away from Brooklyn at last, but Brooklyn had followed me. Peasant morals I despised.

After a while I learned to ignore it all. Or at least not take it seriously. A kind of contempt, a "Fuck you, I'm doing my thing, and what that is you can't even guess" became my mode, as I pushed my way past raw naked skinned half-cows lined up on racks waiting to be unloaded. Next to the meat-packing plant was the corner bar, also Polish. The smells of meat mingled with the smells of stale alcohol, the brief blast of warm, rank air as I cut through. Neon flickering in the morning light.

I had at first a full-time job in a Wall Street office, filing for a large sugar company. The credit department was run by a short, pushy guy named Ray who wore suits with huge shoulder pads that emphasized his shortness, and talked loud New Yorkese into half a dozen phones, like a caricature. He was always behind my chair, looking over my shoulder. But he was part of the deal—my ticket out of Brooklyn.

That spring was the first time I found myself alone. It took some getting used to. East Fifth Street, spring of 1953 was the first time and place I had ever spent the night alone; no one else in the house or nearby in the dorm—though street lights and street noises somewhat muted the effect: it was never completely dark in my apartment. Or completely still. But it was quiet and empty and I was there by myself. I listened and looked, sorting out the safe, the usual sounds—lights on the ceiling from a passing car—footsteps in the hall (a neighbor coming home)—the cat upstairs racing across the floor—until I fell asleep.

My first lover was a man whom I thought of as very old. He was, after all, thirty-six—twice my age. Longshoreman, small, thin, and muscular. And literate, soft-spoken. He lived alone on West Third Street, in an apartment that cost him sixteen dollars a month. Sixth-floor walk-up, but worth it when you got there. Books, maps, antiques, soft lamps, all tucked into place with the precision of a man who had lived on boats. His only neighbor a Chinese gentleman across the hall who worked all week, smoked opium all weekend. Always the same pale blue cloth (I thought it was an old pair of blue pajamas) stuffed the weekend crack under his door.

It was tasty at Buck's. Small, but well put together. And full of surprises. Buck knew people who knew Hemingway. He told me his wife had left him for an affair with Djuna Barnes and had changed her name to Mike. He always had something to show me, something to teach. Took me out for my first ever Mexican food. Pointed out old flagstones with rain-gutters cut into them, on city streets still laid in stone. Walked by small, gated alleys ("mews") in lamplight in the rain. He made Manhattan seem like a foreign country.

And there was nothing special I had to do or be. Buck liked me the way I was, and seemed to need nothing. No particular rescuing skills of mine. He was in love with me though, and I knew it. His hands would tremble when they reached out to touch me, although they were otherwise steady. And that was somehow the ultimate threatening thing. It was too close to the touch of my father whose hands had also trembled. Though I didn't know, couldn't have said then what bugged me.

I knew only that for some reason it was intolerable to be loved. To be *seen* by a lover. Though I didn't take that as far as some of the dykes I had come to know at the bars where I went to dance: butch women who would not allow their lovers to touch them at all. Still, I felt it was absurd Buck loved me so much. And him an old man, too. It made me mean. Angry and ugly. I finally sent him away. Locked him out of the pad, changed the lock with no explanation. And began to look around for younger playmates. Folks who wouldn't see me so clearly, people I could take care of. Give my salary to, my space, my desperate longing. Who *needed something*.

But I remember Buck, naked and sad, cooking lamb chops for me at my stove. After our first lovemaking, my blood still on his cock. Or him making me record cabinets with many uprights, to keep my records from falling over sideways, keep them from warping. That care, precision, in his face, his hands. Or his look sometimes of simple appreciation, in the dim light, faux-tiffany lamps of his flat. And oddly, irrelevantly, wish now I could apologize and thank him.

He came for his stuff by arrangement. I let him in in silence and went back to bed in the dark. Refusing to talk, to explain anything at all. He carefully packed up his few things—tools, and a handful of clothes, a book or two—and left. Shut the door softly, noiselessly behind him. Leaving me oddly sad in the summer night.

That first summer, Tomi was around most of the time. (Once I left school, she and O'Reilley had decided not to move in with me.) Tomi supposedly had a factory job in Stamford making artificial flowers, but she almost never went to it and finally she quit. She had to work with wire there, and claimed it was bad for her hands, would make it impossible to draw or play the piano. Showed me a cut in the thick muscle of her thumb.

No one in her family knew Tomi wasn't working—I shared my salary with her so they wouldn't find out. She came into town on the train almost every afternoon, and hung out in my place while I worked at the sugar company. She played my records, played the piano, drew, and slept. She was always napping. Her warm, rosy alabaster-colored flesh in her stark white slip shone in the summer light on my bed when I came home.

We were friends, but never lovers, though once we tried. She impatient as I groped blindly, seeking her pleasure. Totally inexperienced and voiceless. I finally burst into tears and hid in the bathroom.

● ● ● ● ●

JOURNAL ENTRY, JUNE 29, 1993:

It is almost as if an error has been committed. I have arrived at last at the place where the writing can really be done and there is no one to read it.

This is the situation in my dream: I am assessing, should I go on writing? There is nothing particularly heavy about this question. Just: the world is dark and I am crossing a street in the rain. In this dreamspace I consider what I might write: maybe a book, a series of letters to Peter Hartman, my long-time friend and lover—Peter, composer, performer, poet, patron, impresario. And Peter in his grave now these five years. Small hole on a stony mountain.

There was a story we all loved in those days. A piece of Hindu mythology we'd found in Heinrich Zimmer's Philosophies of

India. *In it there was the image of Indra, the king of the gods,
and the vast, indeed infinite net in which he sat. In every juncture of the net there was knotted a mirror, and every mirror reflected all other parts of the net.*

*Now the jewels, my peers and fellows, have fallen from the net.
From Indra's net, in which we mirrored each other. Or it is dark
and I am crossing a street in the rain. There may be other skies,
other nets with their stars or jewels. But that is, after all, not certain. And they are not mine.*

*I do not recognize these new youngsters with burning eyes.
(They flicker on and off in the dream, as if to remind me.) Not
anyway as the stuff of saints or heroes. Though they may be.
When we encounter each other in waking life they speak to me
about their lack of a surround. Community. Or continuity.*

*Without which there cannot be resonance. Reverberation—
Indra's net.*

Reading one of the 50s poets, his preface to an anthology, what he inadvertently lays bare, I realize that there truly was this determinedly male
community of writers around me in the 50s. This thing I am constantly
questioned about, as in: "How did you survive it? Where were the
women"? There truly was this male cabal: self-satisfied, competitive,
glorying in small acclaims. Stance of "A Man Is What He Does" (Charles
Olson). Or "There's a time a man has to do what he has to do" (John
Wayne, etc.) High Noon on the streets of the literary life. But I never saw
it then.

I saw these guys, myself and the others, as artists simply. All the striving
was for and of the Work, and I loved them for it. I loved them at their best
and beyond their best as fellow companions of the Road. My choice: to
overlook their one-upmanship, their eternal need to be *right*. Or I took it
in stride as not important. A minor part of their Act.

Was this denial?

It was truly what I saw and they rose to it. We walked together on the
roads of Art. Roads of our dreaming. And seeing it thus made it possible
for me to walk among these men mostly un-hit-on, generally unscathed.
Made it possible to walk the Dreamtime. Eternal world of the Poem. And
with companions.

There was much they did that puzzled me. At times they were

pompous, self-righteous, but I set that aside. I went for the kernel, for the great poem or line. For the flash of spirit. *"Etonnez-moi"*. Where light came through the page, untouched by ambition or pain. By the desire for comfort. And I loved each of them.

Love them still. Dear friends and companions of the holy art—the sacred task of pushing the container: how far will it go, the language, the form, the mind? the possibilities within the dream? Like bubble theory in physics. How far will it go without breaking, this that we are? How far can we stretch the body, stretch the spirit? With drugs, with art, with vision, sex, or love. With risk for its own sake, beyond rhyme or reason. And the walls getting thinner, like that thin metal box. That holds the ashes of Peter underground.

On the day that I learned of Peter's death I finally understood the role of the artist as Bodhisattva. The comforter. The compassionate one.

It was 1988. I was on retreat at Rocky Mountain Dharma Center and Alan Marlowe came by my trailer to give me the news. We drove together back up to his place, I had with me a tape of Peter's music. Music Peter and I had made some years before, an elegy for another, long-dead friend. We had recorded it in a studio at Mills College, and I had it with me to play at a poetry reading in Boulder.

Alan had sound equipment in that ascetic place. We put the tape on, set the speakers outside, turned up the volume, and listened among the magpies at 8000 feet. Other folks who had known Peter there or elsewhere gathered around. The music brought its own comfort to each of us.

What I saw then was this fairly obvious faculty of art: that it goes on, it lasts a bit longer than our frail human lives—it offers comfort. The vision is more enduring than our persons—it uplifts us past the vicissitudes of time, uplifts till it, too, is done or forgotten: ten years, five hundred years. It is the working of our loving hearts, burrowing out of us into the light of day. Like Bodhisattvas we bring this liberation, this solace to each other when we are simply ambitious: working for fame, as Keats once thought he was doing. Working for money or glory. What we are left with is finally what we leave: this reaching out to touch, to comfort others. To make the world bearable, possible at all.

In the early 1980s, I stood in the Metropolitan Museum, in one of those huge rooms full of old statues: that light, that afternoon light on old marble, anonymous statues stretching as far as the room, I no longer remember if they were Greek or Roman; Greek, Roman, or Egyptian, just the field of broken, yellowed marble. In that moment I saw clearly that there was no calling higher than this: to be an anonymous worker in the ranks, one of the unknown artists who from time immemorial and for all time to come have been making the beauty that is the leavening in our lives. A laborer in the ranks of artists and artisans (there is no difference here, no need to distinguish)—I saw there was no fame worthier than this.

Simply to have lived and made the work, and offered what beauty, what comfort we could to the world. No organization to belong to, no office to hold, no grant or title that was equal to the honor of having been one of these. *This* is the secret society of western mythos, the magickal society we have sought life after life. That Crowley sought, and Gurdjieff. Society of Anonymous Artists of the World.

● ● ● ● ●

Those first years in Manhattan were full of bravado and playfulness. Learning the rules of survival or making them up. Old friends and new came in and out of my house. I went to school. Studied Greek now, as I pleased, and calculus, theory of numbers. Studied Italian and existentialism. Read insatiably, wrote almost every day.

Went to what schools I would, with no special plan. Only to study what I had a mind to. Though I still did it "for credit", with some vague thought of someday pulling it all together. I went to Hunter, to Brooklyn College, to the New School for Social Research. Snuck into graduate math classes at Columbia. Some hunger of the mind.

At Brooklyn College, found myself the only woman in integral calculus class. And was somewhat sneered at until the midterm, when I got a perfect test score—the only one—and the men grew wary. There was fierce competition among them, but they couldn't quite see how to extend it to me. How to talk to me, even. I stuck it out, but felt more and more cut off.

Some hunger of the mind—there was no other reason for spending the day at the office, the night at school. My parents barely spoke to me, would not help. To them, I had lost my one and only chance. A few years later, when I asked them for help so I could study full-time in Manhattan, my father told me he had spent my college tuition the year I dropped out of Swarthmore. Their summer house in the country at Greenwood Lake was bought with that money.

I could feel his sense of vindictive self-satisfaction. A kind of smug but quiet Italian family revenge. His sense of *giustizia*.

Vindictiveness, yes, but they also carried a deep disappointment and wounded pride. For them the struggle for advancement had been so severe, they had felt their low status so keenly, that everything was measured solely in terms of advancement. A special kind of immigrant dysfunction. It marked us all.

When my Aunt Ella, Emma's youngest sister, opted to marry her love just before the War—an electrician, instead of one of the surgeons or other "specialists" who had wooed her (her beauty, her intelligence both ranked high) it was as if she had let the entire family down. Had failed to improve her lot and bring them along. And this very year, at the age of eighty-three, she apologized to me for not being a doctor—for not being able to "provide for us all".

In my way I had let the family down. Nothing I did from then on ever changed their view of my life.

"Could have done", they would say, "so much better for herself". Measuring their climb from Sicily to the Bronx. From Bronx ghetto to the house at Greenwood Lake. From the custom tailor, my grandfather, reading through the night, on a chair set on the kitchen table so he could be closer to the lamp, burn less gas, an English dictionary, Italian dictionary, by his knee. Something I never needed or wanted to climb away from.

One night at Brooklyn College I heard that Dylan Thomas had died. Thomas had been a large presence in the Village: both his actual, physical self at the White Horse Tavern (where I had gone only once to watch him from a distance), and his poetry. It was the first recorded poetry I had heard, and it was in the air everywhere, at my apartment and the apartments of my friends. We listened endlessly to his musical, fiery voice.

I sat that night in the green warm dark of early autumn on a small patch of lawn, I was nineteen by then, and I looked at my life. It was my way of mourning. And I then and there gave up the notion of college degrees, of full-time jobs: the remnants of my family's dream for me. When I left school my plan was to go for it, simply become a poet—why was I waiting?

I wrote Tomi almost immediately afterwards. I burned with excitement as I typed that letter: my loss of interest in what I called the "golden B.A." She was horrified and wrote back immediately to tell me to stay in school. She pointed out that if there was a "golden" anything it was a Ph.D. And if anyone was a writer in our group it was Gloria, not me, and no, not her. "I shall never make", she wrote, "the green gods march".

Well, she might or might not make them march; I thought they marched on the very onionskin she wrote on. She might or might not—but as for me, I had made my choice. They *would* march or dance for me—I would see to that. I never allowed myself the luxury of doubt.

It was then we came to a parting of the ways.

By fall, I had added a roommate to my two-room pad. He was a gay street hustler named Bobi Schwartz, a ballet dancer. Beautiful, and sardonic, he slept in the small room with the piano and the ballet barre. With his acid humor he taught me to cut self-pity, as I already knew to cut regret. I would wake mornings to his loud and obscene renditions of *Guys and Dolls,* or whatever Broadway show was on his mind, a few pirouettes, a peck on the cheek. The easy cattiness of gay street urchins.

Bobi stayed for a while, through the parade of my lovers, and friends, the strays and almost-suicides I shared my bed with. Then he took off again, he was, he said, more comfortable on the streets. Didn't know what to do with himself, he told me almost sadly, when he didn't have to hustle a place to sleep in.

That year, O'Reilley and I decided to celebrate the holidays. We didn't have enough money to get everyone presents, so we decided to concentrate on just one person. After some consideration we chose Bobi.

It was snowy by then; we walked as much as we could on subway grates—for the warm air that came up through them, and to keep our thin shoes drier—and it seemed a bit cold for Bobi to be living nowhere. So we rented a furnished room over the drugstore on the corner of Eighth Street and Sixth Avenue. We figured it was a good, central location for all his endeavors—sex and ballet, mostly—and we paid the rent for two months.

We gleefully took over the space, cleaning and decorating it. Hung colorful cloths on the walls, bought a print cotton bedspread, and some Mexican pottery: crookedly painted dishes and those bubbly irregular blue-green glasses they made by melting soda bottles. At the five-and-dime we found a shiny new pot and a hot plate. Altogether we made the kind of fantasy home we could imagine ourselves enjoying for a while. On Christmas Eve, we met Bobi at a prearranged greasy spoon and brought him up there on some pretext and "gave" him the room.

And Bobi was delighted, or seemed to be; at any rate he nested there till the rent ran out. By then we were too poor ourselves to come up with any more and he went back to working the streets. We told ourselves we had at least bought him a respite for the two worst months: January and February.

●

We took care of each other. When I got thrown out of my pad, a year or more later, I spent the spring in a place that Bobi had in the West Village near a gay bar called Lenny's Hideaway. And later when Bobi got real work as a dancer at Tanglewood for the summer, O'Reilley and I hitchhiked to Massachusetts to see him perform. Set out from under the George Washington Bridge with our bedrolls, and slept on pine needles in the scant New England woods, stealing corn from nearby farms and roasting it.

One of the highlights of those times was the folk concerts in Washington Square. They probably occurred in all seasons, but I remember them in the early fall: the high bright air, slightly crisp, the swirl of leaves, and the music. There were always many of us, we sang along, sang the choruses, and shut up to listen to the pros when the songs got difficult or sophisticated.

We were mostly young, a few of the more aware college kids, side-by-side with the "bohemians": gay boys and dykes, artists and strays. A few of the homeless ("bums" we called them then) and a scattering of older liberals among us, looked ancient to our eyes, with their softly greying hair. They were the ones who sang the Spanish Civil War songs loud and clear. Remembered all the words.

The music spoke of a vast human tapestry in which war, death, hunger, love and betrayal figured large. And into which our own postadolescent drama fit easily: we saw our lives drawn against a larger background and knew for once they would not overwhelm us.

It was a music of human frontiers: the actual frontiers of the West, *the lion still rules the barranca,* and the frontiers of behavior, human spirit, and an underworld of woman spirit. *O hold your tongue, my sovereign liege* stood beside *Wild women don't worry* sung by Ida Cox.

The songs were peopled with outlaws—whores, gamblers, murderers, political rebels, deserting wives—as well as with semi-outlaws: union leaders, lovers who loved outside their class. The songs were about risk, which we were just learning to love, and love for its own sake. Risk which was to become the spice of our lives.

There was even risk in the singing: city ordinances against music in the parks, on the streets, police raids that would suddenly turn into riots. As well as the many risks of heightened emotion: love, or the grief for our own, friends and allies, lost or gone under in our helter-skelter lifestyles:

madhouse, prison, suicide, OD. We sang loud and long together in the bright autumn air.

These folk songs were a huge part of our education. Of our coming to know the world. They gave to city-bound creatures like myself their first taste of the West, of what those spaces might be like, the flavor of life and death under those skies. There were songs of the mines, of factories and farms and of the sea. Songs of immigration, indentured labor, court intrigue and betrayal. The underground railroad, in all its incarnations. Songs of riding the rails. There was many a song of a hanging or a jailbreak.

We drank in the flavor, the images, and thought we knew, we understood these worlds. That the music had made us one with all human life.

By now I was more or less on my own. Tomi had been scared off by my disrespect for academe. She herself had gone back to college to please her mother. It turned out I had deviated too far from her plan for me, just as I had previously blown my family's plans.

O'Reilley still came and went, occasionally threatened with the police by her crazy mother. Audre was in Stamford, working in a library and trying to finish college. Lee was in Boston, living at some student co-op. Gloria I seldom saw—immersed as she was in her love: those intensities and psychodramas. And Pia Maria, dear first close companion and confidante, was about to marry some German guy who forbade her to move her hands when she talked, and thought he was "civilizing" her.

In the midst of all this, I was making new friends. Finding them in newly opened coffee shops and ancient bars, on park benches in the rain. At the library, various schools, or ballet classes. At a museum, movie house, or restaurant. Dance Players Studio. Paperbook Gallery. 4 A.M. luncheonettes. It was easy to talk then, the air was full of excitement. Ideas not quite formed buzzed around us like summer flies.

I took nearly everyone at first with a grain of salt. But when I found friendship, I quickly trusted it. Utterly trusted my instinct for the real. The friends of those years were more than family to me.

My house was abuzz with all forms of humanity. Haunted and drinking dykes, thieves, hustlers, confidence men in trench coats, runaways from the suburbs, dancers, musicians. A hundred kinds of crumpled, flamboyant persons. Wearing their scars like tattoos, their tattoos like banners. Tearing into the bread, the wine, the conversation. Leaving ashes on my painted floors.

It was only a step from the artist-as-outlaw to the outlaws themselves. The bikers, junkies, burglars, professional book thieves. I was immediately at home in this ambiance, this underworld of childlike men and women— their flash, their dreams. They made my self-identity as maverick, out- rider, seem natural and easy. And after Brooklyn nothing really seemed that strange or unlikely. I had come away with no clear sense of right and wrong. Just a feel for the facts and how to work them. I was hard to rattle.

Through it all I wrote constantly: notebook, typewriter, letters. Wrote every day once again as I had in high school. With joy and abandon found the poet again, the vision from which I started. "I am certain of nothing, but the Holiness of the Heart's Affections, and the Truth of the Imagina- tion".

I had happily left the world of the full-time job, and never again com- pletely returned to it. I found myself working for a while at Columbia in the Electronic Research Lab. Part-time hours and free classes at the Uni- versity. I smoked my first pot with the scientists there, as we sat for hours watching electrons in an oscilloscope. Took a class in tensor analysis. And had my first taste of printing on their multilith press. Like a bee tasting a hundred kinds of flowers.

● ● ● ● ●

It was about this time I made what I thought of as my decision not to be beautiful. Actually, I had no idea what I looked like. Too many years of grueling programming at the hands of Dick, of Emma, had left me blind to myself in the mirror. I simply couldn't *see* what was there. But what I did know was I got a response from folks, mostly from men, whether I wanted one or not.

I had the requisite large bust and small waist, good hips a bit fuller than the fashion, flaming red hair, and a symmetrical, if too Italian, face (big nose). I decided to make it all less than obvious—downplay it somehow. And never to trade on it; the price was too high.

And so I began to clunk and barge through the world. My image of "cutting a swath" gave me the outlook for this. To be flat-out and forth- right, no shimmer, no finesse.

I had watched the burden that beauty was for the women and girls around me. Watched how they watched themselves, caught in a hall of mirrors where it was hard to get to the heart of things, to own their passion. Caught by a kind of self-love. Watched how they *were* watched, both by friends and lovers, so that they were not *seen,* not truly presences, but the painting, movie, statue of someone's dreams. A piece of the furnishings.

I am not talking here simply of objectification, though that was certainly a part of it. Not just the "I am not a sex-object" we've heard so much about in the past ten or twenty years. But there was something else: a gauze veil, a veneer, between the truly beautiful women and men in my world, between them and the world itself. It formed a barrier between them and the events of their lives. Their feelings. The rawness of friendship or love. There was some stance they never threw away.

And, too, no matter how truly they were loved, they were truly never loved. Or so it seemed to me. Perhaps it was my blindness. My need to disown whatever part of myself had led my father, uncles, the men in my family to behave as they did. My need to disown whatever had made Emma cry when I put on that first lipstick. Perhaps what I saw in the lives of these women was nothing but projection, my own neurosis, but to this day I sense some truth in it. *No matter how much they were loved, they were never loved.*

And so, standing alone in my Fifth Street apartment one day, I put it to myself and that simply: that I "chose not to be beautiful".

Once the choice was made, it was easy enough. I opened the door and let my rough-and-tumble self out. Let the tomboy out who had never had room at home. Let the forthright, cruel truthsayer out of the shadows— the same one who would later stride through literary cocktail parties disguised as "witty". I met halfway the one who had never given a damn: about clothes, appearance, walking gracefully. Who had been told, and told again, she would never dance. Couldn't carry a tune. Whose choices in clothing had been laughed at, or beaten out of her. "Clumsy as an ox", I clumped through the streets of the Village in my sneakers.

I imagine it was also a kind of test. Of the men and women who were my would-be lovers. Could they see through the disguise? Were they that acute? Or did they want something that looked good? (Those ones left fast.)

I cut my long red hair down to a crewcut. I took to men's shirts and jeans as my disguise. Costume. Liked best those corduroy men's shirts that were popular at the time. I preferred dark green. Or plain white cotton dress shirts, extra large. Hanging outside of my jeans and hiding most of my body. My eyes became the eyes of some untamed cat: wary and looking sidelong at the street.

What I meant to do was never rely on beauty. No easy commerce between myself and love. Myself and sex. I *wanted* the thorn hedge, the rocky ride. Though I was most often the one who hacked her way in to the prince or princess trapped inside the castle. Rode the small boat through the storm to the Other's side.

And I tromped through the city as some strange hybrid: neither gay nor straight, neither butch nor femme. I cleared some kind of path, cut a swath. I was rarely stopped, or hassled.

Reading my short stories from those early years, a friend asked me recently how I did it. "They seem so *masculine*", she said, "your adventures". She could not imagine them. Could not imagine that I did not open more than that, open my heart.

But I truly didn't. Walked the Village, stalking, looking. The East Side streets. Walked the halls of my heart.

Set out as in a sailing ship to explore. Flesh and minds of the creatures I frequently came to bed with. But without passion, and curiously without love. Adventure, I called it to myself, those nights with calypso drums on the crowded streets, or leaving a bar with a painter I just met, going to his studio with him, going to bed and coming back to the bar for the last set. To drink, and perhaps go home with someone else. It was years before I was overtaken by something like feeling.

And the very beauty I eschewed in myself, I often sought in others. A kind of artiste-explorer at the ends of my fingers. Or riding the beams of my eyes.

This would have been no problem if I were a boy, the pirate I had always longed to be. Most natural thing in the world. But somehow reprehensible—my friend seems to say—somehow *wrong* in a woman, this lack of feeling.

Of all the places I have lived, this first small apartment is still special to me: self-contained, it held in its tiny space all the elements of my world. The typewriter, phonograph, piano, ballet barre. Oddly, no art supplies (drawing was Emma's province).

And so, no art supplies for me yet. But a record always on, good food in the frig, prints on the walls, good light, my time my own. Dance class and languages: Greek, Italian. And the poems I once again worked on every day. Bach Two-Part Inventions I played. Without these studies I would not have been whole. Somehow not validated, not really there.

"The time", Emma used to say, loud and clear during my last years at home. "The time of the Renaissance man is over". She was waiting then for me to "specialize", to choose some one field of study. Preferably, of course, something professional and lucrative.

"Did you ever tell her", a friend asked me recently when I told her this tale. "Did you ever tell her that the time of the Renaissance *woman* was just beginning"?

One night in that first spring—it was soon after I moved in—I was striding through the Village alone, feeling very much my own person, out in the twilight, watching the street. The weekend crowds. Feeling anonymous. A writer. Invisible and free observer of the world. Anything, I felt, could happen. I was on some brink.

When out of the shadows, out of the doorway of Mona's, a lesbian bar I rarely went to—it was too uptown and expensive, the women there too chic—stepped a large Italian man, one of the several Mafia bouncers who were stationed in all these places, to keep an eye on things. He stepped in front of me, stopped me in my tracks. He regarded me benignly from above his stomach.

"You're the Di Prima kid ain'tcha"? he inquired mildly.

I mutely indicated that's who I was.

He grunted satisfaction at his own astuteness. "We heard you wuz in the Village". Paused for a drag on the requisite cigar.

Whereupon, regarding me even more intently, he intoned: "You ever get in any trouble, come in here and ask for Tommy". Indicating the bar behind us, blue awning, a few steps, neon sign in its window, jazz pouring out.

As fast as he had appeared, he was gone again.

I continued on my way, somewhat bemused. Not sure, in fact, if I was pleased or annoyed. "The Di Prima kid". Was my family in fact that well known? Had Bill "reached out"? That would have been okay somehow. Almost okay. It felt kinda good to think someone might be concerned. Might actually care what happened to me. Or was it my parents, worrying again? Should I feel safer, or just spied upon?

All my much-loved and hard-won anonymity, New York invisibility, was shattered—gone. The long arm of the ancestral tribe had reached out and touched me.

Weighed against that I had a new talisman "Tommy at Mona's" and though in the years ahead I never used it, still, it felt good. A secret dubious protection. Like wearing your lady's garter on your sleeve.

● ● ● ● ●

AUGUST 29, 1993

I am sitting at the Great American Music Hall in San Francisco, it is a performance night for me and my friends, Michael McClure, Ray Manzarek, and Robert Hunter, and I'm sitting and looking at my two sons and their girlfriends/wives. They have all come to hear us, to see the show. They are four profiles in a row, utterly unselfconscious for the moment, listening to Robert Hunter read his poems, and I am caught up in watching them, knowing there is another kind of beauty here. Not the "deciding to be beautiful, deciding not to be beautiful" of my youthful struggles, but simple presence. It seems to me that this simple unselfconscious presence abounded in the world of the 1950s. Incisive burning lines, a shining energy. We reveled in it. I did. Never for a moment thought of setting *that* kind of beauty aside, or cutting it out of my life.

I revel in it, still. Celebrate it here, tonight.

But the thing is, I note somewhat sadly (the performance goes on, they sit still)—the thing is, that one of the hardest lessons I have had to learn as a mother, is: *just because they look pretty together don't mean it's going to work.*

Hard to learn about ourselves, too. Think about it: the ones you were sure you'd be with forever just because of how the two of you looked: the line of your hip along his, or your two profiles at a nightclub table. Maybe it was one of those sneak photos a friend took turned you on to it, or you caught a glimpse in the mirror as you both stood naked, or dressed to the hilt for the Street. Or you cultivated the mirror, maybe on the ceiling, maybe behind the bed, just so, because you did, you looked just so, classical sculpture even when you were fucking. Especially when you were fucking.

The color of your hair on his shoulder, his arm brown along your olive one, while "Willow Weep for Me" led your mouth over his nipples, down the long torso to the sex.

But not the sex, it wasn't that, however great—it was how you two *looked together* made you sure it would last. And then when it came apart you felt betrayed: by art, by aesthetics, the mirrors, your friend's camera.

Betrayed by the promise: *What's beautiful lasts, is immortal.* Like in Greece. *Kalon aiei.*

And still and again I find I do it about my kids and others. I see them, usually they are young, and I see them on the street, out on the beach, walking the Golden Gate Bridge in the fog and I think *They must be happy; they look so beautiful together.*

Ah, pet, if beauty was a guarantee of anything the Bolinas mesa would still be a redwood forest, the lagoon deep enough for whales, the earth— Helen would still lean over the parapet and smile into Achilles' cool grey eyes and would they, wouldn't they just

LOOK GOOD TOGETHER.

But alas, and you know it too, even beautiful women leave and are left, even perfect profiles go their several ways, and betrayal beyond betrayal— all chins sag! Oh, don't they just.

Back then there was real beauty, don't all us old ones say it. Beauty past anything you see now, I am tempted to add. But know it isn't true. Beauty *different from* anything you see now, for sure. Something more self-contained and lonely in it. Tragic flaws all over the place. And the sexual revolution just a gleam in Wilhelm Reich's third eye.

Bill Aubrey, well-loved dancer, with the scarred imperfect face. Perfectly beautiful, buckling a fine leather belt. Checking himself in a mirror.

The high cheekbones, incredible angular faces. Pale skin with its own light, incandescent: Nicky, Freddie, almost caricatures of themselves. The bodies a bit *too* lean, we loved them for it, the asses *too* tight, beautiful hollows in the buns when fucking. I curved my palms into.

In women we favored the high style, a touch of swashbuckle in it. Taller than they should be. Like Mary Travers, 1953, a hint of butch in her collar, scarf around her neck, her head held just a bit too high, and her large dog, entering a MacDougal Street restaurant, breathless, looking around from the doorway. Her quick exit. As if whatever she wanted wasn't there.

Or the sad, slim tailored dykes from the uptown scene, the too-black hair swept back, the too-white skin. A touch of particular sadness.

One perquisite of beauty then was the Secret. To look somehow as if you carried a secret. A sorrow you could not tell. Or forbidden desire. To look at eighteen or twenty as if your past weighed on you. Sometimes it did, sometimes more than we knew. Like Freddie.

● ● ● ● ●

I bonded with Freddie Herko because of our pasts. Our battering parents, though I never talked about mine, hardly remembered. He told of being beaten with a strap by his father, night after night when he came home late from a date. I listened, not knowing why my sympathy ran so high. My indignation, yes and some desire. As if by loving him I could make it go away. As I never could for my brothers.

I first met Freddie in 1954, on a bench in the rain, Washington Square Park. He was sitting on a bench on the south side of the park, not far from the chess players. And crying because autumn always made him sad. Or so he said. I invited him for coffee. We walked to Rienzi's and sat talking, looking out on the rainy street.

He was a pianist, he looked a little bit spoiled. Still lived at home in Ossining with his family, was studying at Juilliard on a scholarship. Dancing, and sex, and unrequited love had not yet honed his face to the fine fire it would later be.

After a bit he didn't always go back to Ossining at night, but would stay in town at my pad or with a lover. He had taken the single dance class required at Juilliard and had gotten caught by it. He switched his major. Gave up the piano he had trained for since boyhood. Dropped out of Juilliard and began to take two and three ballet classes a day.

He was the first dancer I'd met who knew other arts, and knew them well. Gertrude Stein, Matisse, Scriabin, Messiaen. Ionesco, Genet. He was as likely to bring me a new record to listen to as I was to put a new poet into his hands. A different breed from my street friends, the hustlers and runaways like Bobi Schwartz. Freddie was the first who made it clear that I could seek and find new friends who would touch me as deeply as the Branded had. And who would go even further with me. Further into the arts, and the life of the arts.

Freddie had a wit at once childlike and sardonic, a sense of play lightly colored over with a streetwise bitterness. We soon had a language and viewpoint all our own.

"Treat it", he would say of something we'd do better to leave alone. "Treat it with ignortion".

He was my brother, closer than any lover, and remained so for ten years. We bonded rapidly and utterly.

● ● ● ● ●

JOURNAL: SEPTEMBER 24, 1993

Walking out on the street tonight from Jean Claude van Itallie's apartment, out into the West Village, a balmy Friday night—I am struck for a moment by what has not changed. Cobblestoned street, partly covered over with asphalt; the way the streetlights catch in the tree leaves amidst the brick and brownstone; the un-mistakable charge in the air of something about to happen: "You can make anything happen"; and in spite of the many folks all vocal in a way they never are in the West, it is silent—so silent and charged. A kind of eternal present.

It is thirty years since I spent any time in the West Village— and with the hindsight of further travel I see that part of what I read out, always read out as timeless here is the European flavor. It could be Paris. Plugs into my DNA in some special way. Did so while I was growing up. How I was caught by that: the memories almost at the tip of my tongue but not—the tantalizing near-glimpses of an ancient Europe, like the sound of a language I almost remembered.

This New York doesn't sleep. The fax stores, botanicas, record shops, boutiques are lit, the doors open. It is after ten, people stroll in pairs and groups clustered by age or sexual preference, there is no song on the streets as in Amsterdam, or Italy, but the town is awake. People carry their plastic shopping bags full of melons and spaghetti home to their various apartments at mid-night.

I hold these almost-memories lightly, afraid to crush them, afraid they'll fly away. Somewhere nearby, Gloria and her lover. Was it Bank Street? Across the street, the White Horse Tavern, unchanged since 1953. Same dreary white tile floors, those small

hexagonal tiles, so tawdry, noisy. Is that tiny island truly Abing-
don Square?

It all belonged to me then. The charge just equal to my own, I
rode it, and danced.

Danced nights at the Swing Rendezvous in my long red hair I
whipped around me and later in my crew cut. White men's shirts
and grey flannel slacks. Ballet slippers for quick turns. A mixture
of Martha Graham and The Fish, later The Twist, to Dinah
Washington, Joni James. Danced on the loading platforms, cob-
blestone streets of West Broadway, Lafayette Street. Danced at
28 Cornelia Street though I couldn't keep up with the boys, they
were so good, pranced, strutted, and did The Freeze. Danced in
Washington Square to the bongos, the folk guitars, in Central
Park to the rhythm of the wind.

It was as if my body had come alive (it had). After years of sitting in-
doors it stretched out, claimed all the space of the city as its own.

JOURNAL: SEPTEMBER 26, 1993

Now sitting at Cornelia Street Cafe, which was once, I think, the
Cafe Cino—or was that the building next door, 31 Cornelia
Street? Where Charles Stanley played Medea so brilliantly,
screaming beyond any acting as he put her babies in the laun-
dromat dryer. Where Joe Cino killed himself, and covered the
walls with his blood.

A short block, for many years the heart of my Village. Phoenix
Bookstore: 18 Cornelia Street. The restaurant next door, still Mo-
roccan, where Larry Wallrich and I would order dinner, and the
owner would bring it to the bookstore in his best dishes: lamb
cooked with cherries, desserts made of yogurt, honey, and roses.
We'd scarf it in the back of the Phoenix, working late, smoking
hash.

Johnny Dodd's where I stayed in the 1970s, whenever I re-
turned from the West: 5 Cornelia Street. Where I began writing
Loba 1971 the day Suzuki Roshi died in San Francisco.

The 28 Club, 28 Cornelia Street, where the "boys" danced—

*Claudia with a black streak in his blond hair. You entered a pool
of sweat, a large sauna, reeking of beer.*

*Apartment building—next door was it?—where Charles Mal-
ley, bedridden defrocked priest, performed the gay marriages of
the 1950s. It seems to me I went to services there more than once.
The smell of the place, and Charles propped up in bed.*

*The storefront across the street from where now I sit eating
buckwheat pancakes held the Aardvark Press, of the late 1950s,
small offset shop where they offered to publish my first book,
1957, me carrying Jeanne. They finally did do the printing,
though I wound up publishing it myself.* This Kind of Bird Flies
Backward. *Indeed.*

*All this on a tiny block that runs at an angle off of West Fourth
Street and Sixth Avenue, runs down to Bleecker Street, and
comes to an end. So much of my life encompassed by this place.*

Last night I dreamed of Johnny Dodd, now dead of AIDS. He had come
back for prayers and healing—for magick. But secretive as always didn't
want it known. Wearing *elekes* and an Indian shirt and blending with the
crowd. It was some kind of (clothed) gathering at a new age resort.

In the dream when I introduced him to the others, I tried to tell them
about the murals on his walls at 5 Cornelia Street. Johnny had painted
them. On the lower walls against an earth-brown background, Indians on
horses stood forever at attention. The upper walls and the ceilings fell to
blues, angels, a kind of fantasy world. They were both Johnny, who was
part Indian. Who came, in fact from Indianapolis.

Remembered on waking his fine intensity. That chiseled face. Beauty of
himself and his lover Russell shooting up. "Brown sugar" or china white in
the light of dawn in that Renaissance apartment.

And when I woke and went out, I found myself walking, without plan or
intent, from the far West Village to this small cafe. To the block where
Johnny lived for as long as I knew him.

And where in the late 50s I would walk to work, to the Phoenix Bookstore, 18 Cornelia Street, pushing months-old Jeanne in her stroller.

chapter EIGHT

It is the fall of 1955, and I am in a new apartment, a place that will later epitomize for me all that was wonderful about New York life in the 1950s. It is a railroad flat on the edge of what was then still called "Hell's Kitchen": 59th Street and Amsterdam Avenue. The street slopes down from our corner to the Hudson, there is a clear view, clean wind, and smokestacks. Gulls fly overhead, and people walk to the edge of the city to fish for eels off the piers.

I am perched on the second floor of an old tenement building in what we still called a cold-water flat. The toilet was in the hall and was shared by the tenants in the other apartments on my floor. The front room had windows that looked out past a fire escape to a shoe factory across the street. And a frequent view of the moon. The whole block across the street was this one huge, purported shoe factory. We sometimes speculated on what else might be going on there. Smuggling maybe. The lights were on day and night; we seldom saw workers coming and going.

The flat had come into my possession through Nicky Thatcher, a beautiful blond junkie folk musician I had the hots for. Nicky had had the place before me and had nearly burned it down by dropping a burning log on the floor near the fireplace and forgetting to pick it up. He was rather proud of this exploit. Some key money changed hands: I "bought" some old furniture from him, a beautiful scarred-up drawing table and some broken chairs for a hundred dollars and moved in. The rent was thirty-three dollars a month, and no questions were ever asked by the landlord as to who I was or how I got there.

It was good to be somewhere again, after six months of crashing with friends and sleeping in the park. I gathered up my odd boxes of stuff from Bobi Schwartz's West Village pad, from my parents' basement, and put up the requisite bricks and boards for the books. The place was four rooms arranged in a line, going from the street halfway to the back of the deep, narrow building. There was an identical apartment in the front of the building and two more in back.

I had a front room with a working fireplace, and it functioned at various times as a sitting/living room, study, or general gathering place. It was there I put my desk and typewriter. There I wrote, studied, tended the necessary fire for half of the year (I had no other heat source except the kitchen stove). There extra people stayed: Bobi when he was crashing with me, and later Freddie Herko when he more or less moved in. On both sides of the fireplace bookshelves were precariously balanced. The phonograph, when I finally got one, sat directly on the floor, with records strewn and stacked around it helter-skelter.

The front room opened directly onto the middle room which was my bedroom. The double bed from the Fifth Street apartment had followed me here. There was room there for more bookcases, an orange-crate night table and little else. Once in bed I faced a door, barred and bolted and set at a diagonal into the opposite wall. I built a bookcase in front of it. The pad had been broken into soon after I moved in, when a lover of Susan O'Reilley's came looking for her, and the way in had been through this very bedroom door. That, I figured, was reason enough to disqualify it as an entryway: too easy to get in.

Beyond the bedroom, a much smaller room I called the "woodshed"— using Mezz Mezzrow's word from *Really the Blues*—functioned as a kind of catchall closet. It had a dresser, a metal file drawer (found on the street, and now used to hold all my writings arrayed in labeled folders), and an ever-varying stash of wood: boards, chunks, beams, and odd-shaped pieces, gleaned from wherever. That wood together with a handsaw was my insurance against the cold. And there was a dresser, scrounged from somewhere, whose drawers were filled to overflowing. The file drawer usually perched on top of it.

Perhaps there was a real closet somewhere in the place, but I don't remember it. All the clothes I remember having were in the woodshed. Mine and everyone else's. And most other stray supplies: big paper for drawing, bags of plaster, should we be inclined to sculpt, new empty notebooks.

The woodshed was smaller than the other rooms because the outside hall and stairwell cut into its space, but beyond it the place opened out again for the kitchen, which boasted a more or less authentic window and a full gas stove on legs, dating from around 1920—one of those stoves with the oven high up and to one side of the burners, not underneath. A stove in green and ivory enamel. The bathtub was beside the kitchen sink. Top of the bathtub, a large enamel cover, also served as the dish-drainer and the counter for chopping vegetables. This lid lifted off entire, to reveal a huge tub with ancient brass fixtures. We availed ourselves unabashedly of the tub whenever we had the need, with absolutely no shyness or concern. Large conferences might go on in the kitchen with one of us in the tub, others stirring the soup or making coffee.

As we availed ourselves unabashedly of the couch, the bed. No telling how many of us would pile in together, especially in the winter. Or shared the cash, whose-ever it was, the food, whatever it might be. People brought wood, or bread, or coffee, stayed to eat the eternal stews, crash anywhere. We sat in front of the fire on benches stolen from construction sites, until the wood ran short and we burned the benches. Then we sat on the floor.

I had come into my own in a way. Had found a large extended family, many loves. Friends who were painters, actors, dancers, musicians. Occasional writers. Friends who just dug the scene. I lived here almost two years, digging into the heart of the city. Not the Village, not the Lower East Side, but a midtown world of museums, libraries, movies. Of coffee at cafeterias where ancient journalists hobnobbed with method actors. Of the Art Students League, the Actors Studio, and the Ballet Theatre school. Gossip from the New York City Ballet. Whole series of movies at the Museum of Modern Art, where for three dollars a year you could get an "Artist's Pass" that made everything free except the sandwiches and coffee.

It was here that I came of age; from here that I set out to visit Ezra Pound in St. Elizabeths. Living here, I found my early style and wrote my first two books. I loved the windy streets, the light off the river. There was a rawness, a harshness, to the life that suited me, fit my high energy and spirits, as I matched myself against various privations: the cold, the dirt, the bugs, the poverty.

I had come into poverty as into an inheritance. It was how I bought my time, days at the Donnell Library, or at the Museum watching von Stroheim classics. Scribbling in notebooks in the museum garden. Endless cups of bitter coffee at Longley's cafeteria, raving and rehashing politics or aesthetics. All the refills free, and likely to poison anyone older than us.

Long hours in Central Park, where one of the huge boulders on the southwest edge carried for years after the colors of oil paint, having been used as an outdoor palette by one of my friends. Boulder I gravitated to, alone in the mornings after an english muffin at Bigelow's to read whatever I was then reading. An hour or two of study, perhaps some dance exercises or stretches to keep from freezing, then a brisk walk home to predictable soup and a fire, and the typewriter all afternoon.

Unless there was a movie. MOMA was doing series in those days: all the movies of Dietrich, of Garbo, of Carl Dreyer. I sat in the dark and watched the world of light I had discovered in high school through Cocteau extend ever further, cut mind into structured crystals. Light and time, the real dance, the essence of illusion. I learned things in that small theatre that I could never name, never put words to, though I used them later when I went home to write.

And I bought this luxury, freedom to pass my days as I pleased, exploring, researching whatever came to mind, writing in front of ancient oils at the Metropolitan, walking Manhattan from end to end, talking everywhere to strangers—bought this freedom with dire poverty and I knew it. Though I never saw it as sad or hard to take. Just as the terms of the deal I'd managed to cut. I thought myself lucky.

By this time my working hours were down to a mere twenty a month. At three-fifty an hour for modeling for the Soyer brothers or their friends, that came to seventy dollars a month. Rent was thirty-three. And by living on oatmeal for breakfast, various forms of rice and beans for dinner, whatever vegetables were cheapest, chicken gizzards at nineteen cents a pound, occasional eggs, the perpetual soup or stew made of all the leftovers, and free wood for fuel; by having no phone, and minimal light bills, sometimes pirating the electric from the hall; by stealing toilet paper from public bathrooms, having friends who came to dinner bring the coffee, or wine if there was to be any, fresh bread, and whatever sweets we scored, by limiting eating out to twenty-cent cream-cheese-on-datenut-bread sandwiches at Chock Full O'Nuts, and coffee at MOMA or Longley's, scamming art books from mail-order book clubs and trading them in for whatever books or records we couldn't otherwise score, seventy dollars a month was quite enough, thank you.

There was always the odd extra job, the friend who worked who invited one to dinner or a play, the Christmas check from home shared amongst us. And Bobi Schwartz would occasionally show up after a good night of hustling and take us out for a real breakfast: eggs and bacon, maybe fresh orange juice.

• • • • •

Roommates were various and ever-shifting, but what I came to think of as the core household consisted of me, and Susan O'Reilley (old enough finally to associate with me without fear of her mother's calling the police and back from Spokane after a failed love affair with a dyke named Brandy); and Freddie Herko (now dancing full-time, taking two or three classes a day, mostly at the Ballet Theatre School, a few blocks from the house, getting summer stock jobs in what we thought of as the wilds of Connecticut); and Bret Rohmer. Bret was a slightly newer friend, a child actor who had grown up to become a painter. He studied now at the Art Students League and painted in the evenings in front of the fire.

He covered our walls with unicorns and strange, Matisse-like maidens, plastered huge pieces of masonite with polka-dotted or striped monsters in oils or acrylic, clambering awkwardly over paisley hills under purple moons. The inside of his head was like that. We watched fascinated as the aliens piled up in the woodshed and along the walls.

In addition to this core, many folks came and went, stayed for a while. Ben Carruthers, a gorgeous haunted-looking mulatto actor, became a lover of O'Reilley's and moved in with all his jazz records. He filled the pad with his brooding vibes and nervous drumming. He was making a movie with John Cassavetes and we would all troop out sometimes to watch them shoot *Shadows* on the nighttime streets of Manhattan. It was a pirate operation, since Cassavetes had gotten no permits, and watches were posted during the shoots to warn him if the heat was coming by.

Ben had various folks in love with him, and justifiably so. He carried that mark of beauty on his face, in his eyes: hidden, secret worlds, and lots of folks went for it. He would bring home steak and brandy and other goodies from the freezers of Broadway producers, or from staying overnight at Montgomery Clift's pad. The way he told it these folks never minded at all; they were real glad to help feed us. I remember one time he had Wally Cox's apartment in the West Fifties for a few months, whilst Cox was working someplace, and I went there to visit him and have a little taste of luxury, see what that was like. There was lots of light blue satin, as I recall. Draperies and fringed thingies on the big bed. Picture windows with some kind of view. I kept my cool. Never let on anywhere in those days that I was impressed. Or felt out of place. Unflappable everywhere I hoped. I kept my cool.

Bobi Schwartz dropped in and stayed for a week or two now and then when things got tough for him, as did many other dancers, painters, actors, writers. Friends of Bret's or mine or Freddie's, out of work. In transit between apartments, or hiding out from the heat or the FBI. Or nursing a broken heart.

Aside from the transient residents who made a bed where they could, left blanket rolls of dubious cleanliness rolled up in the corners, the pad never lacked for regular visitors either.

Freddie at this point began rehearsing several dances he had made, with an eye to a performance somewhere, sometime soon. The work was intense, and balletic, and heavily symbolic. The dancers availed themselves of thick exotic eye make-up and spectacular, pyrotechnic jumps. It was all very earnest and emotional, and the whole cast would come by afterwards to unwind. Talk by the fire, eat soup, mend their tights.

Bret's friends were from the Art Students League, a bunch of non-verbal angry abstract painters, and a stray woman painter or two who would bake us bread or cookies on occasion. The angriest painter was a big fan of Ayn Rand, and Bret moved out for a few months once to go live with him, share a "real painter's pad", which it turned out was really just a large furnished room with a hot plate. There was one double bed which they shared (we all seemed to share beds as needed with or without sex or sexual overtones), and Bret had to give up on this latest experiment with the artist's life after the night when the Ayn Rand fan brought a huge wet oil painting to bed with both of them.

Bret also had a modicum of friends at Actors Studio. He had attended Performing Arts High School in New York, which was a clique, a whole world of its own, with its own friends and rules as much as Hunter High School ever was. On festive nights like New Year's Eve, and other odd times, the grey construction benches in front of our fire might hold Marty Landau in his trench coat with the collar turned up (it was too cold in the pad to take it off), Billy Gunn, whom we would later go see in Joseph Papp's Shakespeare Theater in the park, Lou Gossett, quiet and funny, the observer, and Billy James, who had once been the "Boy with Green Hair", with his puckish face and body, his quick eyes. They would have brought the requisite wood for the fire, or long loaves of French bread. There would be Method Acting Jokes (a variety unto themselves, of which a sub-species of course was Marlon Brando Jokes) and anecdotes about Lee Strasberg, Stella Adler, about the blacklisting that was so much in the fore-ground of our minds. Our lives.

It was never clear how that hit, or whom it would strike. My firsthand ac-quaintance with the Cold War madness came early on in my second apart-ment, when the FBI came to my door looking for a lover of O'Reilley's, a young writer whom we knew as Mike Strong. That was his alias anyway. Mike was from Yugoslavia, had been left in America when his dad, who had been here as some kind of cultural attaché, was recalled to Yugoslavia by Tito. (The various factions of Eastern European communism were be-yond my comprehension, but I had basic peasant wisdom: *all governments were up to no good.*)

Anyway, Mike was left in Los Angeles with an aunt and no papers when he was about fourteen, and he had wandered eastward, ending up in New York, where he met O'Reilley and me. At some point his existence was dis-covered by what I was later told was a "routine" FBI check of the local em-ployment agencies. (Made me wonder back then, 1955, about the level of surveillance we were all being subjected to, but that is another story.) At any rate, Mike was determined by the FBI to be a fearsome menace to the safety and order of our American way of life. Their valiant search for him led them somehow to Freddie Herko, innocently filing away at some tem-porary office job, and Freddie was startled into giving them my address.

I stood my ground, stood literally in the doorway, wouldn't let them in-side my pad without a warrant, and refused to tell them anything, but it *was* traumatic. My first close-up glimpse of the Big Reality that had un-done so much of Hollywood, of New York. Had killed the Rosenbergs and was even then gunning for Wilhelm Reich (whose books Mike Strong had incidentally introduced me to).

It was a while before I felt okay about Freddie after that. I struggled with the fact that someone I loved so much, and whose intentions were so pure, was not necessarily completely trustworthy. Might suddenly give my address to the FBI. I finally made my peace with it, as I did with almost everything else, by lowering my expectations. I made myself accept that those around me, no matter how correct their views, might turn out to be wimps when push came to shove. I decided that in friendship, as in love, the risk was all mine, and it was pointless to fret about it.

The FBI came back a second time, a year later, to tell me that Mike had now achieved the status of "Federal Fugitive", and if I gave him "Shelter or Comfort" I would myself be committing a federal offense. At that point some atavistic conditioning kicked in, some story my grandfather told long ago in the Bronx, and I flipped into genuine rage. I backed those two guys down the hallway and down the stairs, while I yelled at them that the laws of hospitality were older than the laws of the United States of America, and that by God, if *anyone* came to my door seeking shelter or comfort, they would certainly get it.

But Mike remained a fugitive, first here and then in Canada, hiding for years in an attic apartment in Toronto without going out, until he finally lost it, became paranoid and crazy. Last I heard of him, I was told he was in a loony bin near Buffalo, another casualty of the American Way.

My friends were various, from all walks of life. I usually found them when I was drinking coffee somewhere. There was Noah, a street person we would say now, who had been a dancer, a "Eurhythmics instructor" he liked to explain to us, and had once shared a studio with the sculptor Malvina Hoffman.

Noah waved his long hands when he talked, and he talked a lot. We fed him whenever he showed, terribly thin, elegant in his long black coat, and dirty from sleeping on the sidewalk. One day he never showed again, and after a while we heard that he had died.

Another ancient being I met at this time called herself Cassandra Lee, and claimed to be a journalist. She could be found at all hours of the day and night at a table in Longley's cafeteria. She had patchily dyed red-and-yellow hair and an odd assortment of clothes, with which she always wore the same long brown overcoat and any of a variety of little hats. She also had a pronounced limp and a cane. She was, I suppose, close to being a bag lady; I believe she had a furnished room somewhere in the sleazy West Forties.

She opened a conversation with me and O'Reilley one evening when we were sitting in Longley's with our notebooks, alternately scribbling and chatting, as we watched the November rain threaten to become snow. After determining that we were writers and relatively unorthodox, she apparently felt free to confide in us. She launched on what must have been her favorite subject, her own private conspiracy theory.

Cassandra Lee claimed vehemently that she had been a reporter. A reporter for whom or what she didn't say, and we never asked. Simply took her at her word, as we tended to do with nearly everyone. It was a kind of politesse, and a kind of cool, and anyhow we didn't distinguish between those two. In her work as a reporter, she informed us, she was privy to information that proved that FDR had in fact been murdered by his wife.

The story included a young couple who were friends with Eleanor and who had gone down to see Roosevelt just before he died. The fact that they were well-known to him, were family friends, accounted for why he took no special precautions. Cassandra Lee drew the layout of the room on paper napkins: Where the young couple had entered, how one had come in front of the president's wheelchair to greet him, while the other had gone around behind him and stuck a pin in his neck. This, Cassandra assured us, caused a massive and unsightly hemorrhage, which was why there was a closed coffin at the funeral.

She went on to detail (foreshadowing all the conspiracy theories I have heard since) how the two left the country, where they went, how they were paid and where they were now living. As for a motive: it seemed that Eleanor learned that Franklin had decided to reveal the terms of the Yalta agreement, and feared he might repudiate our secret ties to Russia. As a "communist" she, Eleanor, could not permit that. His death was the only way to stop this betrayal of the Revolution.

Cassandra Lee further informed us that at a recent conference in Geneva to which she had gone as a journalist, someone had tried to kill her by pushing her into an open construction pit. She had broken her hip, and this was the cause of her limp.

There was, of course, much more. We listened bemused. Not that any of it was that credible to us (we knew almost nothing, for example, about the Yalta agreement) but that *anything* was and could be credible. Like our family homes the world was full of secrets. Plots within plots, violence and cruelty. It brought me back to the Machiavelli I'd read as a child.

We knew that probably none of this was true; probably Cassandra Lee was a mad old woman. But there was always the possibility that it *might* be true, given the insanity of the world. And that was enough to hold us and make us listen.

We filed it away with all the other stories we'd heard, or dreamed, been told, made up, believed, wished were true or not true, hoped for, kept secret or wrote in large grey notebooks in the November snow.

● ● ● ● ●

We had these rounds we made: the new Donnell Library, clean and warm with rugs and tables in the windows to write at, luxurious, really good bathrooms for washing up; the Museum of Modern Art to eat little sandwiches with tea or coffee, see the old movies, hang out with a painting or sculpture and write (the Brancusi room was a favorite—its space, and light); Longley's cafeteria to run into friends as the day turned into evening. In between were the schools: Art Students League, where I wrote the "Thirteen Nightmares", my first-to-be-published "beat" piece, in half an hour on the steps there while I waited for Bret to clean his brushes and come out to lunch; Ballet Theater and the Chock Full O'Nuts across the street from it, where the dancers would all come to chow down; sometimes Downey's, an actors' bar, or the Actors Studio—though I for one never went in till Jimmy Waring a few years later performed a monologue there I'd written for him, and Lee Strasberg told me it was a shame, I could be such a good writer if I would only "do realism". But that was later. I'm not sure why I never went into the Studio, maybe it felt more formal than the dance schools or painting schools and it made me self-conscious, or maybe there was even then a mythos or glamour that hung over the place, that would have been enough to put me off.

There was another "leg" to the rounds, one that swung more to the east, took us into Central Park, the lake on the south end with the ducks and garbage swimming together, the big rocks in the southwest with the oil paint on them, sometimes as far north as the zoo, or up to the Metropolitan Museum for old times' sake. That leg of the route took us to Bigelow's, the cafeteria just off the park where day and night neon burned in the window and the waitresses were tired and wise like at a truck stop in the West, and they served english muffins swimming in butter, and had a great jukebox.

I had another, northern route, but I usually did that one alone. About six blocks from the pad, on Broadway and 67th Street, there was a large, majestic old building called the Lincoln Arcade. It was there that most of the painters I worked for had their studios among many others of their ilk.

The Lincoln Arcade had shops on the street level, people selling flowers on the sidewalk in front, and then inside these elevators. The cages of wrought iron, and too the doors, so that you could see them coming as you waited, look out of them as you rode and watch the cables sway. I rode. Up several floors to the long hall with many doors, behind each of which a solitary individual labored in a world of his own making, surrounded by the images of his mind. His nightmares, or his genius, or both. The doors all looked alike, that was their magic. What was behind each door was utterly different.

I mostly came here alone, and mostly to work for Rafael Soyer. Rafael and I had become fast friends. He seemed to know when he should work in silence, leave me to my reveries, and when we could chatter easily, nothing special on my mind. Sometimes he drew me out with what he probably thought were skillful questions, about my life and doings, my roommates and lovers. Or about the family I'd left behind and their feelings.

Rafael could get away with most anything, any question however clumsy or impertinent, stuff that I would have met with a cutting silence, or an angry, curt remark in most other places I'd answer for him, because I knew that somewhere under the persistent inordinate curiosity, there was a lot of caring. Compassion and fellow-feeling.

He was infinitely and unendingly curious. About the life I lived with my many friends, about art and what I thought it might be, and why I wanted to do it. About the cold-water flat and how we took care of ourselves. Of each other. Occasionally he'd ask me to bring O'Reilley to pose with me. We'd work together for a few drawing sessions; or he'd get caught up in an idea, and do a whole painting of her, or her and me. O'Reilley was actually his perfect model, her face could be anything, and he used her as much as he could. But that never cut into my time. I only wanted twenty hours a month, after all. And got that easily.

Rafael had come up through the difficult 30s. He had been a part of the WPA art projects, the group dubbed the "ashcan school" because of their love of the poor and the streets as subjects for the paintings. Later the art critics called them "social realists". He retained that careful, Jewish socialism; respect for the model as Worker was part of it. It was always warm enough in his studios, and the modeling breaks came punctually every twenty minutes.

Sometimes there'd be a little extra: sandwiches Rebecca had made for him to share with his model. Hot coffee, or brandy on a snowy day. He liked his liquor, liked to drink and work. And play the radio. Some afternoons it would be the radio I heard, rather than conversation or the inside of my head.

There was this magic spell that was cast by the place. First, the walk up Broadway in the inevitable wind; then the Arcade: the whirl of shops, of color, flowers, and smells. Then that strange, art-deco elevator cage. The long silent hall, where I'd listen for the sounds that told what each one was up to. Joseph Floch had a class of German housewives—their noisy conversation broke the silence. Or Hans Boehler was having a party, or his mistress was practicing her violin.

Then Rafael's door: I'd knock, he'd open. There was at once this rush of impressions: the light muted, the shades pulled up from the bottom of the windows to keep the shadows from being too strong. The eave-skylights also with shades, light pouring in from the open sky. The smells I loved and love to this day: linseed oil, turpentine, the various smells of oil paint. Mingled perhaps with alcohol and coffee. The rush of warm air inviting me inside. And Rafael himself, in his shirtsleeves, he would have taken off his jacket to work, but almost always wore a regular man's shirt, so neat he was at the easel, so precise. It was his smallness I would notice each time. No matter how often I encountered him, I was always surprised to realize I was the taller. Rafael would embrace me, lead me in, walking with dignity, not quite five feet high.

We'd have been working on a painting for a while. I'd have worn the shirt again as he asked me to, not washing it till he was done. Or we'd be seeking an idea for something new. Short, different poses, dressed, half-dressed, undressed. The "studio couch" with its various draperies. I could see how it literally got its name. The news on the radio, early winter dark. Sometimes I'd stay while Rafael closed up the place; washed his brushes in the filthy sink, turned off the lights and the electric heater, and we'd take that strange elevator together back to the street. Where the winter dusk was full of sadness. A wistfulness or grief, made somehow stronger when seen through Rafael's eyes. His sense of the essential tragedy of things. Of human life.

His paintings were full of women sewing. Holding babies. Worn women ironing, or leaning against a wall. A door jamb. As if the grief he felt, saw everywhere, could only be expressed by the female form. The eyes of the women who modeled for him: angry, sad, at bay, exhausted, kind. A few times he painted me fierce.

The times I liked best were when he recited Pushkin in Russian, as he could by the hour, painting away the while. Stopping occasionally to hesitantly translate. To tell me the bare meaning, "but I cannot really say what it means, you know". I knew.

He photographed me and O'Reilley lying naked together like lovers. He painted us both life-size, standing unclothed, holding hands and staring straight ahead, a messy bed behind us. I loved that painting, it was fierce and powerful. Years later, when I visited Rafael in his studio on 77th Street, he gave me a small head of myself from 1955 or thereabouts. It was, he told me, cut out of that same large painting. "I destroyed it", he said. "I thought it was compromising". There was that struggle in him between what he saw and what was permissible, what could be said. Or painted. We never talked about it.

Returning from the Lincoln Arcade to the pad on Amsterdam Avenue was easy; I remained in a continuum, Rafael's time to mine. His way of seeing the world and mine, which I thought of as so much harder. So tough. Compared to his gentleness, soft-spoken hesitant accented English. But there was this continuum of aim, of style. The artist's life, in two of its many guises.

I learned habits of work from him. Or they were anyway confirmed in me. He was always at his easel at the same time in the morning, always painted for the same length of time, stopped for lunch, perhaps with a friend. The afternoon session too was punctual and predictable. He had two models a day. Only in the last years of his life when I went to see him would he sometimes paint only a single session, often only a morning. Parkinson's disease made his legs tired, and he limped pronouncedly when we went to lunch.

It was from him, and from Moses, his brother, from Nick Cikovsky and Taubes, from Joseph Floch and Hans Boehler, workers all with a socialist mentality toward art, that I learned that you did the work come rain or shine. Whether or not there was inspiration for it. You did it, and didn't judge it, and did some more. Industrious, painstaking, careful, the routine itself was the support. What you built on. What sustained you.

I would leave Lincoln Arcade renewed, and ready to return to the notebooks, the typing. In those days I revised painstakingly and carefully, shaping the words to my Will, learning what that was. Each line change meant retyping the entire poem, so I could "see" what it looked like, how it worked on the page.

At home there was the phonograph, instead of the radio. The good smell of wood fire. Smell of oil paint from Bret and his friends. The smells of sweat from dance clothes thrown in a heap, smells of the catbox, the stew. Still, it was a continuum, and I could and did continue.

I would get up in the morning and go out first thing. The corner of Amsterdam Avenue and 59th Street is high ground: you look downward toward the river. There were two smokestacks marking the edge of the land, sometimes smoking, more often not, yellow brick with black, flaring tops, and I would stand on the corner and look at the day, the sky over the Hudson, the feel of the light and the land. Sometimes someone (probably from Hell's Kitchen) would be walking up from the river with a catch, usually eels, sometimes with a pigeon held firmly in one hand. The pigeons I learned were used in some forms of magick: you baptized the poor beast with the name of your enemy and then you slowly starved it; sometimes they were just eaten I surmised, I sure hoped so. I would stand and see what was coming up the block, a kind of oracle, how the clouds lay or didn't, the feel of the wind, would stand with my red crew cut, in my motorcycle jacket and black engineer's boots, and then I would head down the hill dragging my shopping cart behind me, heading for the shop in the middle of the block where they crated automobiles for shipping overseas.

There were usually a few boxes of scrap lumber out front, all of it at least two inches thick, some of it hard woods, long-burning, and sometimes there were others, old ladies mostly, a few men, picking through the wood, taking what they could carry back to their various tenements. I had the shopping cart and I lived nearby, so I had the advantage. I'd fill the cart, lug it the half block back up the hill to our flat, unload and come back again. I often made five or six trips in the morning, to make sure we had enough lumber for the day. There wasn't that much wood outside in the boxes of scrap, but when that ran out the men in the shop would usually cut some for me, they liked me, liked to joke with me, and we'd talk and semi-flirt as the smell of wood sap and electric saw filled the shop, and I'd let them know when it was enough. I needed more for the weekends.

None of the others who lived in the house made serious wood runs like this but I didn't really mind. I liked the physical labor, liked to use my body and feel how strong it was, liked the wind and the light of early morning (the place opened before eight). I was usually the first one up, it was natural that I would be the one most concerned about having a fire. By the time the others were awake, I usually had some kind of breakfast made: oatmeal most of the time, on affluent occasions eggs (they were about twenty-nine cents a dozen). When all the wood was in, and organized into soft and hard wood piles, when the fire was made and the breakfast, and the oatmeal was threatening to get cold, I'd wake everybody one way or another. Either by shouting, declaiming some verse, or by putting some invigorating rhythm-and-blues on the phonograph.

The phonograph was our prize, our pride and joy. I'd gotten it one night late, by walking into Sam Goody's with a couple of my cronies and accosting the young man behind the counter.

"I need a box, man", I said doing my best method acting imitation. "How much for a box"?

I was duly informed that the cheapest "box" came to fourteen dollars and change, with the tax.

"I got twelve dollars, man", I went on. I was really getting into it. "I only got twelve dollars. But I gotta have a box, man—gotta have a box tonight".

Needless to say, we walked out of there with a phonograph. It might have been of questionable quality (this was before "high fidelity" had caught on, at least in my set) but it could definitely play records, and play them in all three speeds. I still had a ton of 78s from my high school days—some of my favorite classical stuff was on 78, but all the newer stuff we were acquiring—jazz and modern classics most especially—were on LP. A lot of ten-inch LPs, and a few larger ones.

We carried that phonograph home unwrapped—the guy didn't see fit to also give us a bag for our twelve dollars—taking turns lugging it from Seventh Avenue in the low Fifties back to our pad where it became our treasure, our prize possession. The house was almost never without music after that. From the moment the majority of us opened our eyes, till the last of us bedded down for the night Messiaen, Scriabin, Miles Davis, the MJQ, Stravinsky, Stan Getz, Dave Brubeck, Bessie Smith, Sara Martin, filled our space. Our ears and our heads.

● ● ● ● ●

We had these routes, these stopping points through the city, the midtown city, and it was inevitable since so many of us took them that we would run into each along the way or at various hangouts. We would sometimes go out, just go out with no particular aim, set out with the thought of maybe writing for a while at the Library, and go where our instinct, our telepathy, our inclinations took us. We would find each other in various ways, have various adventures without preplanning, without telephones. We called this Swinging.

In our own private lingo, Swinging was being at the right place at the right time to run into the right people for the right adventure, or when all the people you were wishing could see it wound up at the Garbo flick at MOMA together. Swinging was setting out with a dime and running into the person you loaned five dollars to last year, and that person has money now and has been wondering where to find you. On the days when nothing worked like that, you would tend to go home early and hole up, figuring either you were out of sync or the world was.

There was an element of being psychic in Swinging, but we never made too much of that part of it. A bit afraid of that level of things perhaps, or else it was one of those understood things you felt you didn't have to talk about, couldn't talk about without being uncool.

The psychic dimension was of course something O'Reilley and I shared, from our days with the Branded. Though there were now no séances, no telepathy experiments in our lives; we had put all that aside, or it was subsumed into our notion of Art.

There was, though, one way she and I still traded on that stuff in getting basic information about our lives. It was a kind of routine we played out. I would "get a feeling" that something was wrong—something was "up" was how I would put it—and on the basis of this feeling I would alert or question O'Reilley. Sometimes even wake her up in the middle of the night. "What's Up"? I would ask her (not wanting to prejudice her reply by asking "What's Wrong"?). "What's Up"? and O'Reilley, half awake, or startled from her reading or reverie by the fireplace, or in the midst of watching a movie, would tell me. "Bobi's just been busted. He's in the Tombs".

"But he knows", I would argue, "not to cruise Lenny's just now. He knows it's hot".

"It wasn't at Lenny's", O'Reilley would answer patiently, "it was in Central Park".

And sure enough, two days later, Bobi would show up with most of his hair cut off, and tell us he'd been in the Tombs for cruising a plainclothesman in Central Park.

O'Reilley never did this stuff on her own, never "read" what was going on unless questioned by someone else. And only Freddie and I ever knew to question her like that.

There was a night we were out Swinging soon after we'd moved in, walking around midtown, O'Reilley and me, and we wondered why we felt so weird, what was wrong. We stopped for a long time under a movie marquee, looking at a big colored poster for *Rebel Without a Cause,* we hadn't seen it yet, debated going in and didn't, and then, still feeling weird, we wended homeward. We decided to go to bed early. O'Reilley and I were sharing the big bed in the middle room, where the barred door was covered by a bookcase. She got into bed and I went to the bathroom.

The bathroom was in the hall, and when I came back into the pad, there was O'Reilley freaked out of her mind, sitting bolt upright in bed in the dark. She'd had a vision, didn't call it that exactly, I don't know now what she did call it, but she "saw" the bolted door fly open and a figure, a young man silhouetted against the hall light, stood in the doorway panting as if he'd been running very far. We tossed this around matter-of-factly, wondered who was hurt or in trouble, and then went to sleep.

To be wakened an hour later by Freddie coming in, had we heard the news? We hadn't. Jimmy Dean had died.

It made sense then, the feeling weird, the lingering under the poster, even O'Reilley's "vision", her way of reading the news in the dark. Then others came by, and none of us slept till dawn.

There were these figures, luminous in our lives. In my life. Live or dead, known or not, they were never far from my life, never remote.

I had no diffidence, no extraneous shyness. I had taken my cue from the *Cantos* when I first read them in my Fifth Street pad: *But to have gathered from the air a live tradition / or from a fine old eye the unconquered flame/ This is not vanity. / Here error is all in the not done, / all in the diffidence that faltered . . .*

I'd written to Pound back then, sent him some poems I was working on. He was easy to reach, incarcerated as he was at the madhouse in St. Elizabeths Hospital in D.C. He wrote back, a short note in blue ink. Large scrawl, almost a drawing on the page.

> *They* SEEM *to me to be well-written, BUT—*
> *NO ONE EVER MUCH USE*
> *AS CRITIC OF*
> *YOUNGER GENERATION.*

That observation certainly stayed with me, I found myself quoting it this year, almost forty years later, to my poetry students at Naropa Institute.

Correspondence between me and Pound continued sporadically for the next year or two, and due in part at least to his constant urging, culminated in our going to visit him at "St. Liz" as he called it.

It was spring of 1956 when me and O'Reilley got on a Greyhound bus. I had saved the extraordinary sum of fifty-five dollars, and she had a similar amount. I'd written ahead to the warden at the hospital, made arrangements. We would be allowed to visit Mr. Pound every day during our visit since we were coming from out-of-town.

We'd also arranged a place to stay: during the previous years I'd met a painter, an extraordinarily beautiful woman named Sheri Martinelli, at a tiny bookstore in the Village, called Make It New. The bookstore was run by John Kaspar, a really unpleasant fascist who was to achieve some notoriety for his perverse behavior during the civil-rights movement. But that was all later.

All I knew then was he ran this small shop where one could buy hard-to-find books Pound had mentioned in his writings. I'd even gotten a Latin-only Oxford edition of Propertius—which I later had to give up on, as Propertius' syntax was too complex for my high school Latin. Eventually we stopped going to Kaspar's bookstore, because he got a crush on O'Reilley (this was back when she was in love with Brandy the Dyke) and when she wouldn't go to bed with him, he took his revenge by writing to her parents and mine and telling them that we were lesbians. But that is another story.

During the months that I frequented Make It New, I did meet Sheri Martinelli, and found out she was a very close friend or lover of Mr. Pound (I was too courteous or cool to determine which). Later, when she moved down to Washington to be closer to "Grandpa", as they all called Pound, she gave me her address, and invited me to visit.

So Susan and I set out in our jeans and holey sneakers, with a modicum of clean underwear and socks, and the thirty or so dollars each that was left after buying our round-trip tickets, and we went to Washington on the bus.

Sheri went with us the first day we went to St. Elizabeths. We'd settled into her pad where she was living with a Chinese-American composer named Gilbert Lee, whom Pound had decided she should marry (he liked to arrange the lives of his close disciples). Sheri was not too inclined to this arrangement, she was irritable at any rate, the rumor was she was recently off smack, and Gilbert and she had frequent and loud fights which took place around and through the room where we slept.

Sheri went with us, and I for one was glad. I'd been in a madhouse once or twice before, once to help spring someone from Bellevue. The other time I was just a visitor. But I certainly didn't feel comfortable going there.

Madhouses to my mind were not friendly places. I'd already lost a couple of friends to them, and all their stories and adventures were in my mind when I set out with Sheri and O'Reilley for St. Elizabeths. There it all was. The high brick walls. Locked doors. The waiting at each huge door while some staff person unlocked it.

We finally found ourselves in a kind of dayroom, where various men were wandering about. A television blaring in the corner. A bunch of run-down chairs. But there was an alcove, a kind of ell on one side of the room; as I recall it actually had a piano. It was there that Mr. Pound held court on visiting days. Mrs. Dorothy Pound was there, serving tea and handing around cheese. Folding chairs had been brought in from the lawn outside; they were somewhat more comfortable than anything else around. Visitors had already gathered, and O'Reilley and I joined them.

Pound, an extremely handsome man, rose up when we got there, bowed ceremoniously over our hands. He was wearing shorts, his legs were muscular and beautiful I noted, though he was seventy and more or less imprisoned. He greeted Sheri intimately and with great affection. We felt she was indeed "mistress" in that situation, as Dorothy was wife. Then he turned his attention, his keen eyes on each of us in turn, sizing us up, reading what we were up to. The conversation that afternoon was genteel and cultured, but general.

The next day was not a regular visitors' day, but since we had come far we had a special letter of permission. Mr. Pound was in his room, and we waited for him in the dayroom with some trepidation, eyed as we were by various unseemly men. Drooling, or talking to themselves as I remember it, though it might not have been that bad.

When he came out of his room, Pound told us he had been working on his translation of the Chinese Odes. (Some of this had been published as *The Classic Anthology Defined by Confucius.*) I felt awkward and apologized for taking his time, interrupting his work. Naively, I suppose. I hadn't yet known enough folk who had been incarcerated to understand that he had more time than he needed. He set me at ease by waving all that aside.

He wanted to know what we were up to, every detail. What life in New York was like now, though he assured us we had missed its golden age: "When the Flatiron was the tallest building in Manhattan, and mister cummings discovered Patchin Place".

He drew us out about how we earned our livings, what we were reading, what our vision was of our art. (At that time, O'Reilley, too, aspired to write.) He had all kinds of plans for us: what we could do. How we could improve the cultural tone of the age.

The previous fall, I had sent him a program from a performance I'd attended of the Pro Musica Antiqua. I just thought he'd like to see it, since they'd printed the words—Latin, medieval French, etc.—of the songs they were performing. Now I found Ezra thought *I* should be the one to get the Pro Musica on television! I who had never owned a television or lived in a house with one. I said nothing at that point, just listened.

The next day was also not a visitors' day. Ezra Pound was waiting for us with a brown paper bag. In it, carefully packed, were cold cooked sausages, a jar of canned fruit salad, and some dubious muffins. Stuff he had taken off the hospital dining table, and wanted us to take back to Sheri's for the four of us. "Line those stomachs" he told us. "Poets have to eat". We settled in for a chat. I had tons of questions.

We passed about a week and a half like this. On visitors' days the conversation would tend to be general, there would be a motley and constantly changing crew. I met all sorts of folks in that little alcove. I remember especially a student of Chinese who drove a cab for a living, and worked at the Library of Congress for hours copying by hand old music that had never been published. He had, at Pound's behest, married a painter. I visited them both and posed for her. I had tons of spare time.

One other thing I remember about Washington was the rampant racism. Not that there wasn't racism in Manhattan, there certainly was. I had seen plenty of it in the Village of 1953-4, when the Italians would swarm up MacDougal Street en masse from below Bleecker to threaten or wipe out a Black man for coming to the Village with a white woman. The outcome of such encounters, if any of us was foolhardy enough to call the police, was that the Black man was arrested (after he'd already been beaten up) and the local hoodlums went home.

That had been ugly and scary enough, and it was something that I knew better than to talk to Tommy at Mona's about. But this stuff in Washington was something else.

We had come down there with what seemed like a bit of money to us in those days, and we wanted to contribute to the house, to Sheri and Gilbert's cupboard and refrigerator, knowing from our own pad how important that was. And so one night I found myself on line with a small cart of groceries at some Washington supermarket. The Black man in front of me stepped back to give me his place, and I said, as I would have said anywhere, "No, thanks, that's okay, I'm not in a hurry".

The tension in the store was immediate and palpable. At that moment, I realized that Washington was the South—the fabled South of rigid segregation that we in New York avoided and feared. I held my ground behind that anonymous Black man in that supermarket line. I held my ground and he held his, and we faced down the anger around us. We didn't look at or speak to each other again, but we were a team for that moment and we both knew it.

The whole visit was a very intensive schooling. Ezra Pound's generosity, his unique perspective. The social order, if one could call it that, in the madhouse. How he would walk us courteously to the door, as in a Victorian manor house, and we would all three wait together, chatting, till the warden unlocked the door and let two of us out. The social order, or lack of it, in the streets.

At Sheri's, too, between her fights with Gilbert, there was so much to learn. Gilbert held forth to us on various five-tone scales: Chinese and Greek. Played them for us on a wooden flute. Spoke of old and new forms of musical notation.

Sheri brought out her exquisite paintings, on wood, on stone. Small tile works she'd made, intensely beautiful. A medieval compression of space, of line. She told how she'd needed the formula for faience, the ancient Egyptian blue glaze, to use on a batch of miniature heads she had sculpted. It had been lost—at least to artists—for centuries, but "Grandpa" had managed to get it for her, by writing to some Egyptian scholar he knew. She showed us the heads.

In all this there was a purpose, an urgency. The question of what could be saved, as civilization went down.

Ezra told us of copying Vivaldi scores in the library of the Dresden Museum, copying them for Olga Rudge, his love. When the Museum was destroyed in the bombing of Dresden, they were the only copies of those scores that remained. They were being transcribed even as we spoke about them.

Stories like this made a deep impression on me. They made me realize that what is saved, the shards we call civilization, is saved by a few. By people photographing, or copying by hand. Today as I sit here writing at my computer, I think of the library I've put together since then, the alchemy books old and new I've xeroxed for students. Stuff I've copied out by hand. How much of that came out of the Vivaldi story.

●　●　●　●　●

Apart from the music and the friendships, the most important thing that was happening to me at this time was the theatre. The theatre in all its forms was burgeoning in the mid-50s; it, like the jazz clubs, was where you went to have your mind blown on a regular basis.

When I walked out of Swarthmore one day in 1952 to play hooky with Tomi in Manhattan, one of the things we found on our very first evening was the Living Theatre. They were at the Cherry Lane Theater, a space at the end of a small cul-de-sac, performing a play by Picasso, called *Desire Caught by the Tail*. The play was full of weird choreography on a crowded stage, of people playing animals and inanimate objects, and the whole event made me totally, unreasonably happy. Joyous.

And I remember another night a year or two later, when they performed uptown. That night they presented the theatre version of Cocteau's *Orpheus*. There was a talking horse in a wooden stall—instead of the car radio Cocteau used in the film—giving out with poetry for Orpheus. That night, at the end of the show in whatever narrow hall that was, Julian Beck stood on the stage and invited the entire audience to his house. We all went.

And so from the start the theatre was the place where almost anything could happen, where the most unlikely events could be made solid, made flesh, and taken to their amazing conclusions. From the very first, I was caught.

Those were the years when Jean Genet's work first came to Manhattan, and the first thing to come was the plays. I remember seeing Julie Bovasso in *The Maids* in a theatre on St. Marks Place—a woman playing a boy dressed as a woman: feint-within-feint.

A storefront theatre on Sullivan Street did Ionesco's *Jack,* and later *Rhinoceros.* There was a special, secret pleasure in walking off the street into an ordinary store, a sheet hung over the store window and folding chairs set in rows. A few lights and a rudimentary stage. On which stood a man with three noses.

In that makeshift theatre we could have been anywhere, it could have been any time in history, any era. And no one knew we were there, no one knew what was going on. Or so it felt. I'm sure in actual fact there was probably a sign in the store window, the plays were probably reviewed someplace or other. But—while we were there, while the play was going on, we were outside of space and time, in a world which transcended natural law.

There was in the early 50s a bar on West Broadway called the Open Door. I first heard of it one of the times I fled college, and was spending time hanging out in Manhattan. I'd gotten into a downstairs joint on West Fourth Street called Louis' (pronounced Louie's) Tavern and encountered the unforgettable phenomenon of Charlie Parker, standing indefatigable in the midst of the crowded barroom, handing out flyers for his next performance. Which performance, the flyer announced, was to be at the Open Door.

I went there to hear Bird—the music vast and heartbreaking—and often thereafter. Even on nights with no performance, even as a bar, the place was interesting. Sawdust on the floor. A large open space in the center of the room for dancing. All kinds of dancing. I once spent the night watching some Portuguese sailors engaged in some kind of male dance ritual that ended with a hop, a small jump, which landed the dancer on one foot, on just the sole of one foot, on top of a wine glass full of wine set on the floor. The object was to accomplish this maneuver without breaking the glass or spilling the wine. And to hold your position atop the glass, balanced on the sole of one foot, your arms in the air.

The Open Door also became a theatre-in-the-round on occasion. The large space in the center of the room became the playing area, and the audience sat round it, drinking and watching. I saw a performance of Genet's *Deathwatch* there, with a beautiful mulatto actor named Harold Scott. *Deathwatch* in 1954 or thereabouts was the embodiment of the zeitgeist, the way we all felt. That trapped, that paranoid, that senselessly guilty. The play was dark and powerful in that setting.

Thus I learned that theatre could happen anywhere, that all kinds of things were theatre. A manipulation of space and bodies in space. That led to a vast opening of the space of the mind. Enactment of a mystery rite. Embodiment of the most subtle and fleeting movements of the heart. Or shaking the rafters, cracking the walls, with vast epics of despair.

A certain closing down happened later with Beckett. I remember going to see *Godot* when it first happened. It was great but classical—old form. There were no surprises, not in that all-out sense—*"étonnez-moi"*—Diaghilev's challenge to Cocteau.

For me there was something especially dangerous and rich when the risks, the adventures, took place in a tiny space. Condensed. Took place in the mind.

There were great performances in those years, too. Great single forms sculpted by actress, dancer, musician, singer.

There was Geraldine Page in *Summer and Smoke* playing the Circle in the Square like some kind of flickering flame. Pale as foxfire, but long—glimmering wisps of light as she played to all sides at once and showed us what theatre-in-the-round could be. What it really was.

As a few years later I saw Cecil Taylor in "The Circle", as we called it—an audience all around him—him and his piano in the middle of that. His own piano he brought to all his gigs back then. Later I'd hear the same piano in some upstairs club on Bleecker Street.

So much of what I remember was the music. Miles at the Cafe Bohemia playing one note that seemed to go on forever, then walking out when people giggled, nervous or afraid. Monk at the Five Spot in his funny hat walking around and around the piano, playing a few notes whenever he went by the keyboard. It seemed to me that first there was music, then theatre, and then there was dance. Or music and dance together. That poetry, all word-forms followed; they happened later.

Occasionally Harry Belafonte stalked West Fourth Street or showed up unexpectedly in some club. (The Montmartre on Fourth Street for one, already full of drumming. Full of congas and bongos carried in by young men with berets. With flying hands.)

Belafonte, singing for free in that small Village club. Haunted by his own beauty, or by some vision of a world that could be. That coexisted—parallel universe—in his mind's eye. He cast a shadow of it on the room where he sang. It glinted its own colors off the smoke, the neon.

We were all like that. We carried a world in our hearts. In our mind's eye. And cast a glimmer of it, half visible, on the streets around us. Where these worlds overlapped and pooled their light, we stood sometimes as if in a follow-spot. Avoiding blinking, lest the whole thing disappear. We watched our hearts' glow flicker on and off.

It was watching the performers that I learned the strength, the power of the game. What art really was. That it did for a moment change the world around us. Was more than interior.

It was through the theatre and the music that we caught a glimpse of the power of what we were doing. That it existed beyond the studio, the typewriter, the apartment. Cast a new light on these streets. That it—even briefly—changed the world.

"I am certain of nothing", said Keats, "but the holiness of the heart's affection and the truth of the imagination. What the imagination seizes as beauty must be true, even if it never existed before".

A sultry dawn on the islands transferred to Manhattan
Stars opening beyond stars in a smoky bar
The paisley beings walking on striped hills
Or Monos, my totem harlequin, facing off history in small poems
Songs of old China coming back to life in a dingy room in a madhouse

At first we thought we were studying technique. What "worked" in the various arts: how to make it happen. How to translate those "tricks" from form to form. From one medium to another.

Lord knows it was fascinating watching Rafael Soyer lay one color next to another. How a single brush stroke could change the whole canvas. Or reading Eisenstein's *Film Form,* applying montage straightforwardly to the poem. Or the smallest gesture in a Bogart flick.

But there was more: the heart, the raw power inherent in art. Power generated out of discipline. Out of doing the same thing, day after day at the typewriter. In the studio. At the piano.

I remember in the 70s, hearing an interview with Pablo Casals on the radio. It had been done shortly before he died. The interviewer, a young reporter, none too bright, asked "Mr. Casals, to what do you attribute your extraordinary success"? Or some such. And Pablo Casals answered in his careful, particular English: "Every day, since I was twelve, I play all my major and minor scales". The young reporter evidently didn't find this too interesting, was going on in his brisk way to the next question, when Pablo Casals cut him short, interrupted him in the middle of a word:

"Did you hear me young man?—Every day, since I was twelve, I play all my major and minor scales".

Something he earnestly wanted to get across before he died. To whoever could hear it.

But the evening that marked me most deeply, aligned my fibers, brought me most sharply awake and for all time, was the night Billie Holiday sang at Carnegie Hall. She was already for many of us the supreme artist, the one with no equal, and we had all followed the horrible heartbreaking course of her fight with the New York City Police Department as if the battle were taking place in our own living rooms (it was).

She was the Lady, the one who made fire out of the most tired lyric, who turned our ears and our hearts for all time to come to the subtlest inflection, syncopation. Accent of the genuine in a breaking voice. What we later sought in the poem.

And, too, in a universe where "big" meant impersonal as in Government or God, we clung to sexual love as the only real value. Only thing we could—maybe—trust. That and friendship, one-on-one and *private,* for God's sake, private. Billie was quintessentially the singer of the one-on-one.

(I remember the poet Joel Oppenheimer telling me breathlessly in that last year of her life that he had met her. Someone had burst into his apartment and said, "Joel, Billie Holiday's downstairs"! and he had run down. She was in the back of a convertible, and he was introduced to her. He took her hand. He said he kept bowing and bowing over it, mumbling brokenly "Thank you. Thank you". Over and over again till her car drove away.)

When Billie was coming to Carnegie Hall there was no way I could have gone. No way to afford it. But I had a friend, a kind of acquaintance on the fringe of my scene, a woman named Joan McCarthy who liked us all very much and would invite us over to eat steak and talk. She was a woman who was not like any of us at all, she held a straight job, had no imagination, nothing in her mind or conversation flew, and we were always fondly exasperated or outright angry when we left her house. I think she was glamorized, fascinated by us all.

Miraculously, Joan McCarthy invited me to go with her to hear Billie Holiday; she had two tickets. Never before or after do I remember being invited, or going, anywhere with Joan. Just this one miracle.

Naturally I said yes.

We sat high up, looking down on the stage, and it should have been hard to see, but somehow it wasn't—everything on the stage was crystal clear, luminous. Existed, as Michael McClure likes to say, in eternity. There was that edge to it.

I had always loved the late, 50s voice of Billie's beyond anything she'd done in her younger days. The raw quality of it, cutting through all lies. But tonight she went still deeper, into a whole other dimension, and took us with her.

I knew from the first I was hearing one of the great concerts of all time, that there had never been anything quite like this, and certainly not at Carnegie Hall. I drank in every inflection, every intonation, every subtlety of timing. Almost not daring to breathe.

Pain, the heartache of our time, our cruel culture, was laid out, golden and crystal before our eyes. Nothing held back. A power and dignity that can only grow in the depths.

And when she sang "I love you Porgy, don't let him take me . . ." I saw death standing beside her on the stage. Almost as luminous as the Lady herself.

chapter NINE

It was at one of those theatre events, somewhere midtown, that I met James Waring, a man who was to be mentor and friend for the next twenty years. I don't remember what we had gone to see that night, I was with Freddie and we were a little late, slipping awkwardly into our seats over legs and laps, when Freddie spotted Jimmy in the row in front of us. Still balanced over chair-backs, he introduced me to Jimmy. In the dimming light Jimmy scanned my face, while he continued to hold my hand tight in his tiny one.

"Oh", he said. "Oh. Oh". There was surprise and some pleasure in his voice.

We all sat down. We watched whatever it was.

I remember thinking that he had the oddest face. Small, thin, and pointed, like a bird. A remarkably long thin nose. And those penetrating eyes, the kind that held your gaze, that seemed to see through you, and yet remained slightly veiled. A veil of sorrow, of sadness I thought.

At intermission we exchanged addresses. Jimmy was living somewhere in the West Fifties. He was a dancer and a choreographer. He and Freddie knew each other well.

Jimmy came frequently to my house after that. Or I went to his dance classes, held here and there in various West Side dance studios.

I had an engagement with dance that had started when I was fifteen. In one of those "windows" that sometimes opened in those years, I had found my way to the New Dance Group on East 59th Street, just off Central

Park. There a whole bunch of stuff I had known only through reading suddenly became clear, became flesh and part of my life.

Through years of staying home and reading, I had found books on what was then called "modern dance". I learned that there were at least three "schools", self-described as such, and named after their founders: Martha Graham, Hanya Holm and Jose Limón. I had already memorized lineages of dancers when I came upon the name and address of the New Dance Group, and wended my way one early evening to my very first class.

I was terrified, and with reason. I had sat so still so long that at fifteen I couldn't straighten my knees in front of me when I sat on the floor. Dance class was painful, intense work, but I kept coming back, much as I later came back again and again to the *zendo*. There was something there for me, and from the beginning I knew it.

Class was hard, and sometimes humiliating. There were so many things I couldn't do, that it seemed *everyone* could do. So many moves I couldn't make at all. But I stuck with it as much as I was allowed. There were Saturday daytime classes, for instance, and I could be home from those before dark.

Some of the instructors took an interest in me. Maybe because I was so stubborn. One young woman, after trying all sorts of exercises to help me flex my lower back, decided that I must have been born with fused vertebrae. She was wrong, but thirty-five years later I learned that I was indeed born with spinal stenosis. An extreme narrowness of the spinal canal that has left me with scarred ligaments, fiery nerves, and a limited range of movement.

At that time though, I was sure that nothing was wrong. Like most of my generation, I believed I had been "born perfect", and that any subsequent defects were my own fault, something I had done wrong.

I told myself I was "just tight" and I would get over it. But since I could not curve my back, not do the "contract and release" on which all Graham dance is based, I tried another "school", one that did not require I flex my spine so much.

I began to study with Mary Anthony. Her classes were some of the toughest, but in an odd way some of the most encouraging. Mary Anthony was meticulous: her students worked very hard and progressed very slowly. It gave me a sense that change was possible.

And so I moved for the first time into a conscious relationship with my body. I learned I had limits that I could work with. And my body was grateful; it liked to move. I would bound up the stairs to the New Dance

Group, change into leotard and tights, energetic and eager. An excitement was in the air.

An excitement was in the air. Not just my excitement. It was as if all the city of New York, all the nation, was discovering movement. Was learning to move all at once.

My childhood years had been marked by the fear of polio: ten-year-old school friends in braces, trailing withered legs. A president in a wheelchair. As well as the paralyzing realities of war. And now in the aftermath of the war, in the bright clear air of Manhattan, we were discovering, or rediscovering, movement.

The dance classes were packed. The theatres, rehearsal studios. We were discovering together the life of the body.

With movement came an inevitable interest in sex. As the years went by I returned again and again to the New Dance Group. Returned between high school and college, on college breaks. I found my way often to the classes on 59th Street.

And from there sometimes to some Central Park South apartment. Where some wistful older man would offer me chocolate, brandy, various tidbits of sexual experience. It would go only as far as I wanted, and then I would say stop, thank you, and goodbye. I was lucky, or I had good intuition. I was perfectly sure I could tell how a man would be. Whether he would accede to my wishes.

These various men served my unconscious intent: they helped me to begin to wake up my body. They showed me ancient African statues, played me new jazz. Fed me exotic foods, and talked about interesting things: art and travel. Probably there were only two or three of them. I remember walking away one day, down Central Park South and thinking how glad I was to be free—out of that stuffy house and in the bright, clear air. I knew it was the last time I would go home like that with anyone.

After I left Swarthmore, and moved to the Lower East Side, I continued to go uptown to the New Dance Group. I also tried various other teachers, recommended by one friend or another. A sadistic Italian ballet master whose studio was above Carnegie Hall; a wonderful and delicate Russian woman who gave private lessons only, and who would inquire in a sad, accented voice when O'Reilley and I tied ourselves into particularly awkward knots: "What / arrrrre you trrrrying / to ack komm plisch?" Alas, we had no answer.

There were crowded classes too: at Ballet Theatre, and other, less famous schools, where sweat ran down the mirrors, and no one would have dreamed of opening a window, for fear that a sudden draft might tighten some muscle on which we were lavishing endless effort and pain. Where we performed infinitely complicated patterns, on the diagonal, across the floor, or pirouetted again and again to practice "spotting".

For many years I kept wanting to be a dancer. Believed I could be one by the sheer power of my Will. But I started too late, or I was battling too many obstacles: a short torso and my eternally swayed back. More weight than was fashionable in ballet. And a stiffness and fragility that were more than physical. That had come about through pain and battering, through holding myself at the ready to do more than I could. The stiffness of an overtaxed organism.

I didn't know that then, none of us did. Would never have recognized ourselves in that description. Freddie whose scars had left his flesh but not his mind. Or his heart either, questing in a kind of eternal pain.

We each of us carried our pain with a certain rigidity. Pride, or some kind of ego-encasement that helped us go on. That made all our movements particular to ourselves. A kind of stamp of our individual histories. Some of these ways worked better for dance than others.

But then I knew nothing of the stories our muscles carry, the histories articulated by our nerves and joints. Knew only: I loved to dance, loved dance, and there had been up to this point nothing I couldn't do by willing it. So I kept on for ten or twelve years, kept pushing my body into and past its limits. Broke my ankle once doing *tours jetés* across a slick floor, taking a dance class an hour after I sold a pint of blood to pay for it.

It would be many years before I came to know there was anything I could not do. Beyond my ability to will a world into being.

The first four or five years on my own I never used birth control. I felt I could "feel" it if I was going to become pregnant. And that I could will the child away if I had to, any child.

It was a tricky edge, because at the same time I felt that when I went to bed with anyone it should be someone whose child I wouldn't mind bearing. And in my world, where doctors, together with cops and psychiatrists, were people you almost never called on, bearing a child, I was acutely aware, might mean losing my life. So every chance sexual encounter was weighed: was it worth, ultimately, dying for, if it came to that? And the an-

*swer was usually yes. Partly because my Will, and my close connection to
my body—its reproductive part at any rate—loaded the dice in my favor.*

*It was not that I held my life so cheap, but held experience, the savoring
of life so dear. Experience itself was good, the ultimate good.*

There was one time I was sure I was pregnant, my period was weeks late,
I hadn't given much thought to who might be the father, but knew I didn't
want this child, not at all. My Will connected by some hotline to my womb,
and I talked to no one about it, feeling that words might solidify that tiny
embryo.

There was a summer day right then that I went for a walk with a wild
friend, Ed Fitzgerald, crazy red-headed nomad, we walked briskly along
West Street in the heat, me silently directing whatever was in my womb to
be on its way. Somewhere along the edge of Manhattan Island, we connected with a ferry to the Jersey shore. Decided to take it, go wherever it
went, have an adventure.

The ferry took us to what the man who collected our fares (twenty-five
cents each) assured us was Jersey City. We went down a ramp and into another time. Quiet streets of 1950s small-town America. Wooden houses
with front yards, swing sets. And some of those postwar shacks we called
"tract housing". Brand new and nondescript. On some corner we found a
neighborhood grocer, bought sandwiches and something to wash them
down with, and then continued ambling, looking for a place where we
could sit down and eat.

What we finally found was a graveyard, graceful trees, a bit of green
between the tombstones. (It crossed my mind that the proximity of
death might help to hasten the demise of whatever it was I carried. If
I carried anything at all.) I found a low white mossy stone to sit on, Ed
sat on the ground nearby. We ate our sandwiches. For some reason we
found ourselves reciting Keats—was it the "Ode on Melancholy"? A large,
dirty-white dog came quietly by and stayed for a long time, with its head in
my lap.

When we got up to go I knew I was bleeding. Took care of this somehow—was it a gas station restroom? I know we stopped more than once to
ask our way. The dog came with us to the edge of the graveyard but no further. Everything was clear, but it wasn't. The town not quite how we remembered, but not really different. But they told us there was no
ferryboat.

We asked repeatedly, there was no ferryboat. There used to be, they
said, but there had not been for some years. We knew to keep quiet, keep

our story to ourselves. After some time spent searching, we took the Hudson tube back to Manhattan Island.

Where in the night whatever it was I had carried flowed copiously out of me with no fanfare.

I never made sense of this incident, filed it away with the things I'd never explained, not too surprised. But the miscarriage, if that's what it was, the restoration of my blood cycle, gave me once more the sense that one navigated, if one navigated at all, by Will.

There were many instances. Accidents foreseen in a dream, and thereby prevented. Around the next bend, said O'Reilley quietly, there will be a stalled car. We were hitchhiking. The driver slowed down, navigated matter-of-factly around the stopped vehicle and went on. The pragmatic and the magickal were so interwoven in our lives, in my life, that I would have been hard put to untangle the threads.

This hard-bit practical magick was my power (though I never thought of it that way), and my protection. It carried me forward, and I, with my Will—I ever-so-little changed the course of the stream. I lived under a kind of protection, but at the cost of great vigilance.

And so for years I continued to take dance class, and not just simply for the pleasure of it. There was this piece of me that was determined to be a dancer. A piece that would not, could not, take no for an answer. Hurled itself incessantly against the limits of the flesh. Of my particular tough and sturdy flesh. After a while I left the ballet behind, and studied with Jimmy Waring or with his students. I danced through three pregnancies, returned after three births.

It was part of our language, how we spoke to each other.

It was part of our language, how we read the world. There was the City Center Company, unequalled in those years. Maria Tallchief dancing *The Firebird Suite,* a vision of controlled wildness. Or Tanaquil LeClerq in *Afternoon of a Faun,* a svelte, fey quality, a kind of nineteenth-century paganism that was yet at home here in New York. (Oh, we had "read" the photos of Nijinsky, and knew we had not seen that animal flavor of embodiedness, combined with the flare of spirit. Not near. I did one day see something close in Vasiliev. But that was many years later.)

·

·

I sat in the dark, night after night, in theatre after theatre. Reading the movements, the music, sometimes the words. I hungered, I strained after meaning, seeking to make some sense of our lives, our deaths. Dance was a ritual religion I had found. I held on tight with my eyes, sought to memorize each movement, keep it forever.

As with my first poem I had once sought to hold on forever to the stars as they shone over my grandpa's apartment in the Bronx.

Now I reach back inside myself to find that girl. To feel her energies, her passion. Who was awakening, what was being summoned? Dance, more than any lover, gave me to myself in those days. Gave me to the life of the body.

I learned to *see* dance, by knowing it in my body: the subtleties of movement, ineffable tiny embellishments of line, the reaching like flame.

And feeling the dance and the dancer, the small adorable increments of movement, the almost-invisible surrenderings to the breath, to a breeze of emotion passing over the dancer, I learned also to feel myself. To come for the first time to encounter my flesh.

My body stirred in its fullness. It had its own agenda. Built-in design and plan. I had just turned twenty-two, and the autumn came on quickly as it often did after my birthday, the first sharp tastes of it in the full richness of the August air. Sharp smell of autumn, the season so full of sadness, so beautiful in the still-crystalline New York of those years, a city of spires and light, reminding one always that there was no time to waste, not even a moment of the summer sun.

I went halfway to meet the urgency, to hear what it was my body wanted from me. It met me with new demands. I heard and I understood, not quite prepared. Not surprised either. Reaching back today, my flesh that of a woman of sixty, I try to remember, to reconstruct the feeling. What I do remember are the words in my mind: That if I didn't have a baby I was going to get sick.

I knew that with certainty, no question at all. My physical being had come to the place where it wanted to flower, to put out fruit and seed. As I knew with certainty that if I foiled it I would not and could not live happily and long.

Years later I would come to know that the body has a vegetable mind, like a plant. It has its own agenda and intent, separate from the mind, the heart, the Will, and if you want to go your own way in spite of the body some negotiation is necessary. But in those days I knew nothing of negotiation. I had honored my body through these first four years of loving, and it had rewarded me with no unwanted pregnancies, no disease. Now I recognized that it was changing, that its *intent* was other, in bed and out.

There was a feeling of fullness in me, a fullness almost to bursting, as if there was more of me than I needed or could use in myself. That needed to grow into another. I sensed this then, though I didn't know how to put it into words.

I was certainly not surprised. Since I was twelve, all my fantasies of life on my own had included children. Usually many children. It seems I had always known that sooner or later this playful fulfilling life of poetry and study, of theatre and friends, would include an infant, probably several infants. I just didn't know how any of that would work. But then, I figured I didn't know how any of what I had now would work, and it had. Here I was, writing, learning, robust and joyful (in spite of political and social ugliness around me), in a life I certainly couldn't have imagined at Swarthmore. I was thoroughly of the opinion that the only way to find out if angels would bear you up was to make the leap.

But this one wasn't so simple, wasn't as simple as I liked my leaps to be. For one thing it required a partner, a second person, to go along with the plan. Not that I for one minute thought of including a man in my life, in my home. That was out of the question. I had seen enough in Brooklyn in my growing years to rule out the possibility of living with a man. Someone probably stupider than oneself who wanted control. Who thought he knew how things should be done, how money should be spent, even worse, how children should be raised. As far as I could see, all they were was trouble.

No one, I vowed from the first, would ever tell me how to raise my children. No one would ever be angry or violent in my space. No one owns me in any way, my body, my love. No one by "providing" (I scorned the very notion) would buy the right to tell me what to do.

I didn't question for a moment that the child I bore would be mine and mine alone. The man was obviously an incidental and unimportant adjunct to the process. No man could ever "have" a child, they simply did not know how, did not know what it meant. In those days, and in that time, I was sadly right.

I went about the business of looking for a father. Someone who would like to have a kid of his kicking about in the world, but wouldn't bother me too much. Wouldn't, as I put it, "get in the way". In the world I was moving in, such fathers were hard to find.

The most likely candidate was Freddie, and I asked him first. He was brilliant, and beautiful, and gay. We had never been lovers, but had been, and were, closer to each other than either of us was to any of our lovers. Our friendship was tough enough to survive a lot. And I was certain we could get it on if we wanted to, if we had, so to speak, an extracurricular reason. But Freddie recoiled, literally and physically, recoiled in horror, perhaps disgust, when I asked him.

Then I tried asking certain of my lovers. (Certain others didn't seem fit for the job.) Some of them hooted with laughter, some reacted with fright. I learned a lot about these guys I was hanging with. What was most infuriating was their fear of being "caught". As if anyone would *want* to live with them!

This whole process took several months—most of the fall and winter. Meanwhile the world around me was falling apart. The cozy, smooth-running albeit impoverished household I'd put together, which had functioned so well for so many of us, was coming apart at the seams. There were many signs, all different, all pointing to the same end.

O'Reilley had had an abortion the previous winter, one of those illegal procedures we went to so matter-of-factly in those days when we had to. It was part of the picture. Woman business. Women took risks every time they made love. We knew that from the get-go and toughed it out.

But O'Reilley's abortion hadn't gone well, by any standards. She never quite stopped spotting. She grew slowly more weak, spent days lying on the couch, reading gloomy books and smoking. Her teeth started to decay; they looked yellowish-grey. Her usually pale but luminous skin turned greenish. It had, even to our eyes, an unhealthy glow. And she started to cough.

All we knew for certain was that we didn't trust doctors, and had no money to spend on them in any case. And abortions were illegal, and Little Mike, the ex-baby's dad, was wanted by the FBI. Under the circumstances we did nothing at all. O'Reilley revived a bit in the spring and summer, but started to decline again as autumn came on.

One day she announced that she was moving out. Was moving in with one of the Branded from the old Hunter gang, who had an apartment on Madison Avenue and a good-paying job. O'Reilley said she was going to try to get well. Would get some money from her mother and go to the doctor, the dentist. Maybe get one of those good-paying jobs herself. Nobody was surprised, and nobody blamed her. We all had very strong feelings about "selling out", a topic we discussed at length for many years, but even we could see that there was a moral difference between selling out and trying to stay alive.

The next problem was a mechanical one: the building next door to us had technically been abandoned for years before we moved in, but it had actually housed a huge population of rats and an occasional transient human. It was torn down that summer and the rat population did the logical thing. It moved into the nearest edifice: ours. We were suddenly overrun and terrorized by very large and very loud rats. They stayed for the most part in the kitchen, where there was plenty for them to do and to eat, but it was an uncomfortable situation to say the least. Whole loaves of bread were being dragged across the floor while we slept.

The neighborhood, too, had taken a turn for the worse, and now that all our side-windows were suddenly exposed to the street, the hoods expressed their disapproval of our lifestyle by tossing bricks through the glass. It began to get chilly in the middle rooms.

To top it all off, a Puerto Rican family moved in on our floor, complete with livestock: roosters and rabbits. They had a little girl who seemed mildly deranged: we caught her one day in our communal bathroom trying to set fire to her dress (which she had, fortunately, at least removed). Her reasoning, near as we could make out through the language barrier, was that she was burning her dress so her mother wouldn't find out she had torn it.

Now, none of this was too delightful, but we stuck it out—those of us who were still around. Thirty-three-dollar rents were no longer easy to come by. And we had a certain attachment to the place.

But the changes kept coming. Freddie found a roommate, and announced he was moving into a delightful loft on Prince Street. It was a big step. His part of the rent there would be fifty dollars a month, which meant he would have to temp more and dance less, but the chance to live in a large space with a gay roommate, decorate it, live out a lifestyle that was still then being defined—this was something he didn't want to pass up.

Freddie's loft on Prince Street became our new toehold in the downtown world, the Village and the East Side which I had abandoned without a second thought a few years back. It came in handy on various occasions; we camped there when need or fancy took us.

•

And then, that autumn Bret got very ill.

On the particular night he got sick I had stayed out overnight with some lover or friend, and he was the only one home. Theoretically, this wasn't a problem. Although Bret and I had been casual lovers, the unspoken rules of the tribe made it clear that this relation left neither of us with a claim on the other.

Of course I didn't call since we didn't have a phone, but Bret chose for some reason to wait up for me. And though it was cold, he never made a fire. I came home in the morning to a freezing, disheveled pad. And Bret, upset and ill.

He was running a fever, shivering under some blankets on the couch. I built a fire, got him into bed. I cleaned up the pad, made soup. Nothing worked. He was sick and he stayed sick for quite some time.

I felt angry and outraged to my core. Wasn't it just like a man, I thought to myself. To fall apart on you, make you take care of him for weeks, play the martyr like this. Who did he think we were to each other, anyway?

I had never been close to Bret as I was to Freddie, but there was a real friendship, a camaraderie between us. I loved to lie in bed and watch him paint. Watch the magic as colors and space shifted on the canvas. The board or plywood. Whatever he'd laid his hands on. I had an affinity with his impish, whimsical mind. His otherworldly figures, ancient scroll paintings. He was like a brother. We played well together.

On the other hand, I would never have dreamed of asking him to father my baby. It simply didn't "feel right". There was this matter of "fishing for genes" that I slowly became aware of. An unconscious and semiconscious scanning of each male. His physicality—how would it blend with mine? His mind, his humor, emotions. Which of his flaws could I easily overcome in an offspring? Which might be serious or permanent? Which could be simply the result of his upbringing and therefore erasable.

It was not as cold and calculating as it sounds. But it was certainly there, a consideration. A filter that colored how I saw everyone, at least everyone male, for almost two decades. There was no way around it. From the morning I woke with the desire for a baby, till the point when I knew for certain I wanted no more children, I was at the mercy of this thing. This way of seeing. I was no longer simply with a man for himself, but for what kind of children he might make. And whether he'd leave me alone to raise them as I wished. This point of view intensified whenever my body demanded another child. But it was continuous, and never far in the background.

●

It was only when I was past the need for having more children and there-fore free of this "fishing for genes", that I found my own choices and wishes were very different. I was suddenly free to be with a playmate again, as I had not been since the summer I turned twenty-two. A play-mate as in the old days—but with a difference. In the interim I'd learned something of how to love. And I'd left my Cool behind me along the way.

● ● ● ● ●

Bret stayed sick for a long time. I nursed him gently, never letting on to the anger or guilt I was feeling. My concern was real, but so was my claus-trophobia. The feeling of being trapped in a silent battle. And my impa-tience that wanted out at any cost.

And all the while another struggle was going on—momentous, inside of me. For the first time a part of myself was at war with my art. With the guardians of my art.

I had enjoyed, since I first met myself head-on in my mother's garden and decided to be a poet, a kind of at-one-ness, a kind of peace with myself. I knew what I was, and what I was going to do. That knowledge made it pos-sible to leave home and school behind. It was the fuel that had carried me this far: I was a poet, I had a work to do. It has carried me all the years since, but with many differences at different times. And seldom with the one-pointed certitude of those first years.

I was a poet, I had a work to do. And that work included an old resolve that I had expressed to Dean Cobb at Swarthmore, and that she had given me back as a Latin proverb. *I am human, therefore nothing is foreign to me.* It came to me still as a resolve, a vow: There was nothing that I could possibly experience, as a human in a female body, that I would not experi-ence. Nothing I would try to avoid. No part of human life I would turn my back on. To me this was obviously just part of the job, part of what one as a writer set out to do.

(Oh, certainly there are many things I've left out of the tally: never could shoot up, for one thing, I always hated needles, the invasion, the rape they represented, so certain drug experiences and archetypical haz-ards of my time were completely beyond me. And I'd prefer, if the gods will be so kind, to go to my grave without human blood on my hands.)

But this simple thing that was looming ahead of me, just a little way down the road, this inevitable, as I felt it, next step in my life: to have a baby, to become a mother, this seemed to hold the essence of what I needed now to know. To be. In order to be a woman and a poet. There should, it seemed to me, be no quarrel between these two aims: to have a baby and to be a poet.

But there it was. A conflict held me fast.

Since those teen years when I took the vow of poetry—of poverty, sometimes I hardly knew which—I had held John Keats in my heart as mentor and guide. A kind of touchstone, a point I could refer to to see: was I still on course? There had been the spectacular séances and visions of those teen years, during which I felt I had established communication, a real sense of who this man was, what he stood for. And there had been, would always be, his letters. He held a place in my life, my inner vision.

And of course the life we had lived on Amsterdam Avenue never turned aside from the psychic, the visionary. Had merely and matter-of-factly incorporated it into the daily routine. Our ways of "reaching" each other without a phone, our various revelations and understandings, had often a sense of other worlds in them, at least a contact with the nurturing, friendly dead. The artists who'd gone before.

So it was with real shock, and something like terror, that I felt the John Keats in my heart, in my mind's eye, turn away, condemn what I was doing. What I was planning to do. It was as if the ground was gone from beneath my feet. The road was no longer marked. The danger, as he pointed it out, was clear: *You have said nothing will be as important to you as Poetry. And yet you now plan to have a child, a child who will certainly come first in your heart. In your life. There will be no time, no energy for the work.* He made it clear I was breaking a sacred vow.

I was bewildered and angry. Felt stopped at every turn. There was nothing in my vocabulary of responses to meet this dilemma, to deal with being stopped. Cutting a swath was what I knew how to do. Breaking through, whatever the problem was, and *going on.* Headstrong. But now my clear principles, the two basic values I held and trusted, were set on a collision course, and even I could see that.

Finally Bret, who had continued to grow weaker, agreed to call his parents. The next day he took a cab back to Forest Hills, where the family doctor diagnosed pneumonia.

When he emerged months later he had visibly changed. And while he was sick his huge paintings—stored in the loft of his father's auto-body shop—had been cut up, literally sawed to pieces (they were on masonite) and used to patch the holes in the ceiling, the walls and the floor of his father's place of business. Bret's alien figures no longer walked on polka-dot hills; they lay face down and truncated in a century of grime. New York filth, and motor oil, and paint.

Bret never came back, all the way into himself. A short time later he was drafted.

But when I put him and his suitcase and boxes into that cab to Queens, saw the cab head for the tunnel, I turned back to the pad, went up the flight of stairs, and sat down on the bed. I was in something of a state of shock. For the first time since I'd laid eyes on my apartment over two years before, I was alone there. It was time to take stock of things.

Having the place to myself was wonderful in a way. Oh, I knew it would have to go soon, all the signs were there, but in the meantime it had become a one-person apartment. I rearranged the furniture, put the double bed by the window in the front room near the fire escape. I could look out at night on the moon through various metal steps and wrought iron bars. The moon over the still-suspicious Miles shoe factory across the street. And the fireplace was right there: I could go to bed with a book and watch the flames.

I cleaned the place thoroughly, swept and dusted and scrubbed the floors. Filled it with free wood. Played music whenever I liked as loud as I liked. Sat on the floor in front of the fireplace, and carved chunks of plaster of paris into various shapes. Watching the white motes of plaster dust dance in the air. I was tasting what it might be like to live alone. And about to give that up for the next thirty-odd years.

Folks still came by for dinner, a lot of the old crowd. The same old soup or stew was always ready. We talked as ever about our various work. Some of us were already moving out into the larger world: summer stock jobs had led to jobs in theatres, dancers were working as extras at the opera. And I was putting my first book together, picking out the poems that would go in it.

It was one of the nights of that fall that someone brought by Ginsberg's *Howl.* It stood for me as proof that the work I was doing—had already been doing for some time—could and would be published. And read. O'Reilley had so long contended otherwise, we had struggled so often about this. She vigorously hated the language of the streets.

I promptly began a correspondence with Lawrence Ferlinghetti. Sent him my "Thirteen Nightmares" written the year before on the steps of the

Art Students League, while waiting for Bret to finish class and clean his brushes. Ferlinghetti wrote back. And when Allen Ginsberg, Peter Orlovsky and Jack Kerouac came through that winter on their way to Morocco to visit William Burroughs, it was to this clear, bright apartment, classic cold-water flat of a bygone age, that they came. It was here that we read our poems and peered at each other's notebooks till we tired of that and Allen announced that he wanted to find some lovers.

I took them to Freddie's new pad on Prince Street. Where he and his roommate and the four of us made out and slept fitfully in various combinations.

It was in this last incarnation of the Amsterdam Avenue pad, that I finally confronted John Keats. What I felt was the contract I'd made with poetry. Lying down on the bed, alone in my house, I conjured the presence, the "feel" of him, as it had been for me in high school and ever since. I lay on my side in the afternoon light, facing a shadow-energy Presence beside me.

He told me I was taking a terrible risk. That I might lose Poetry forever by giving another being a claim on my life. He told me if I did this thing, he could no longer promise to come when I summoned him. I told him I had to at least *know*, taste motherhood. I asked for two years of it: and could we talk then?

He told me, as he often had before, that it was hard enough for a woman. That women didn't do it right, the art thing, we wanted too much of the human world besides. That no one had done the thing I wanted to do. At least in hundreds, if not thousands, of years. That I probably wouldn't succeed.

I told him I knew the risks, but I had to try. Not at all sure it would work, sure only that I was putting the one thing I loved most in jeopardy. Because of some urgency I couldn't explain. We said goodbye, me knowing I couldn't be sure when I'd "see" him again. *If* I'd see him again. I simply couldn't be sure I would still be a poet.

But I was damned if I refused to try.

It was shortly after this imaginal encounter, one February afternoon on this same bed, looking out at a winter sky, that I—without broaching the subject with my partner—conceived my first child. This event, so long considered, was only semi-intentional. I used birth control (something I'd ironically just started doing a few months before) but somehow my diaphragm failed me in this instance.

Stefan was a long-time lover, an old friend who was living out of town. He was long-gone by the time I discovered I was pregnant. I didn't say anything about it to him—or to anyone else for a while. I went on with my life as it had been: sustainable and simple. I modeled for money, I wrote, I studied, I saw my friends. I gathered my poems together.

Within these forms, these ways of being I knew so well that I could do them by heart, I began to gather the energy to move on.

•   •   •   •   •

It wasn't only John Keats who was dubious. All of my friends felt pretty much the same. They looked upon my desire to have a baby, and (when I told them about it) my actual pregnancy as a form of insanity.

When we gathered in early spring to pack the apartment, the scene had all the solemnity of a rite. It was hard to leave the place: so much had gone down there so fast. We had, each of us who had lived there for some time, come up against some of our dilemmas, some of the personal *koans* with which we would be struggling for years to come. We had, many of us, grown up there, come into our own as artists.

The very walls bore the marks of some of our struggles, some of the aesthetic and political battles we'd fought with each other and with ourselves. They read: SACRIFICE EVERYTHING FOR THE CLEAN LINE (an aesthetic ideal some of us were already growing beyond). They read: THE UNICORNS WILL INHERIT THE EARTH, and, simply: SWINGING (a reminder to stay psychic, and flexible, mobile, and yes, Cool).

The walls held many marks of tape and thumbtack, from the hundreds of pictures we'd put up at various times: Lord Byron next to Marlon Brando in *The Wild One*, Miles and William Blake and Greta Garbo as Mata Hari. Nijinsky and Jean Marais. Ezra Pound, Marlene Dietrich, Salvatore Giuliano, Gertrude Stein and Jean Cocteau. At times the wall in the front room opposite the fireplace had been solid with black and white imagery. Photos, and pictures torn from magazines and books. Record covers.

There had been one night in the past year when aesthetic disagreement had led us to tear all the pictures off the walls. Each of us declaring passionately from her own perspective that the others, because of their obviously wrong views of art, had forfeited the privilege of being in such company. When the walls were stripped we proceeded, as I recall, to break the dishes.

The walls showed dents and drawings in charcoal: a unicorn of Bret's and innumerable inscrutable female faces. More faces were drawn in orange paint on the black-painted floor.

We used the fireplace a lot while we packed. There were more drawings than anyone could carry away, unusable chairs and oddments of poems and letters. There were half-finished lumpy sculptures, and notations for choreographies long abandoned. The ubiquitous not-very-good guitar we kept around, for whoever might want to play it after dinner. Finally we were finished, books and records stacked and tied up (we didn't have enough boxes). Clothes and dishes sorted, some packed, most discarded.

Two cars were loaded, one going to Brooklyn, to my parents' house, with stuff I would look for later when I had a new place. The other to O'Reilley's, where I'd keep the things I'd be needing every day: clothes, notebooks and the like. When everyone left, I walked through one last time.

chapter TEN

I was standing on a ladder painting the middle room of my new apartment when the water broke. It was about midnight and my friend Jo was with me. She was helping with the painting and generally being around as I waited for the baby, who was by then more than a few days late.

I climbed down rather gingerly and threw a few things together while Jo used the phone (I had a phone by this time) to call the poor man's taxi: an ambulance, to take me to Gouverneur, one of the city hospitals for the indigent at the edge of town. I had already packed most of my stuff a week ago, and there was really not a whole lot to do but wait till they got there.

Jo came along for moral support. I kept insisting I felt perfectly all right, but the paramedics put me in a wheelchair anyway. I sat in it, feeling ridiculous, while I answered questions for Admissions. Hoping I remembered my story, and could keep it all straight. I had figured out well in advance that I had better say I was married, in order to keep the vultures away: all those well-meaning social workers and their ilk who had already, in whatever brief but truthful contact I'd had with them, tried to persuade me that what I really wanted was to give my child up for adoption. (It had been explained to me, at one point, that although there was no shortage of babies for folks to adopt, there was a shortage of *white* babies, and many people would be most eager to relieve me of my burden.)

It wasn't only that I didn't want to go through all that again, felt that I'd have enough to do after childbirth just recovering without being subjected to unwanted pressure and moralizing—but also because I was paranoid enough by then to be afraid they might take the baby away from me against my will—declare me "unfit" or something, so that some adoption agency could have its way.

What I figured out to do was to give my own real name and give Stefan's by-then-long-unused nom de plume as the name of the father. I had gotten all this worked out because my paranoia extended into the future; and I realized I didn't want anybody bothering the "real father" for child support later. To my mind this was total bullshit. The poor real father had had no say in this matter, having a child had been entirely my desire and my choice, and even at that very moment he had no idea it was happening. I saw no reason why the unsuspecting man should be penalized for my lifestyle.

I got that part all right, but some of the other questions threatened to trip me up. For instance: what was my religion? The only choices they gave in those days were: Catholic, Protestant, or Jewish. I forget what I said, but I knew that it was dangerous to be Catholic, since Catholics believed that in case of trouble one should save the baby at the expense of the mother. I felt like I was navigating rapids on some unmapped river.

Of course with a little forethought I might have gotten some of this stuff out of the way ahead of time, by preregistering somewhere. But no. My strategy in those years for dealing with the world of officialdom, which included doctors and hospitals, as well as the IRS, FBI, the police and a whole raft of more innocuous types, was simply to avoid doing anything at all until it was absolutely necessary. Consequently, I hadn't seen any doctors while I was pregnant—I frankly hadn't seen any need to: pregnancy wasn't an illness.

There might have been just a touch of female macho in my stance. After all, my mother's favorite image of childbirth, and one that she held up to me all through my childhood, was the one from *The Good Earth*, where the woman has her baby in the field and goes right back to ploughing. Mom thought this was just terrific. It wasn't till some twenty-five years after my own first labor, that she finally told me she stayed sixteen days in the hospital when I was born. Such an image of weakness would have been detrimental to the notion of womanhood she sought to instill in me. We had to learn to bear more pain than men. And we were well-nigh invincible.

I was invincible all right, and more than a little arrogant and impatient with this whole admitting process. But when I was finally whisked away in my wheelchair (Jo having been dismissed) when I was finally wheeled into an elevator and shoveled onto a cot in a "labor room"—where I was surrounded by six or eight screaming, moaning, or semi-unconscious women—I have to admit I did lose some of my bravado.

The scene was weirder than anything I could have imagined. Weirder than anything my paranoia could have come up with. Various women of all sizes and colors, in various stages of labor, wept and groaned and screamed in the dim light. They were each alone, since no mates or friends were allowed in the "labor room" in those days—though occasionally nurses walked among us. Hell, it was weirder than anything in Dante.

As so often in the past few months, my impatience and contempt saw me through. I simply couldn't believe any of it, so I didn't. Lay down where I was put—I was hurting by then—and told an unbelieving nurse that I didn't want any pain medication.

I had given long and earnest thought to being conscious through the labor and the birth. Being present. Had read what few books then existed in paperback about "natural" childbirth. That's all: I'd practiced nothing, taken no classes. There were such, but only in expensive "uptown" hospitals. It seemed to my logical mind that just as pregnancy was not an illness, so too labor and childbirth were meant to be taken straight. As they happened. Undiluted. I figured I could handle the pain. (I had already handled so much of it, went the subtext, one of the invisible sources of my female macho. But I remembered nothing about that.)

When I had asked my mother about "natural childbirth" she was horrified. No, she said, *of course* she didn't remember any of our births. She had been unconscious. She was quite self-righteous about it. Why, she wanted to know, would anybody want to experience all that? "They put me to sleep, and when I woke up, you were there". To her, as to many women of her generation, pain-free birthing was one of the marvels of modern medicine. When I told her that I wanted to be awake, to see and feel my baby come out of me, she looked at me as if I was quite demented and not a little perverse.

The nurses at Gouverneur evidently felt much the same way. They came by regularly to measure my dilation and see if I'd changed my mind. I was something of a problem to them, as I was in a lot of pain and cursing vividly. Now, shrieks, cries and groans were all A-OK here, but evidently obscenity was not. And colorful, elaborate obscenity was what I was most devotedly given to at that point. They tried now and then to hush me, fearful probably that I was offending other would-be moms, but there was really little or nothing they could do about it.

It was getting light when a new nurse came on, one who was genuinely curious about my motivation in refusing to be medicated. When she caught on that I wanted to be conscious and present, she offered me a shot of demerol, which she assured me would not make a dent in my wakefulness. I accepted, as I was getting quite worn out by then.

Unfortunately it also didn't make a dent in my pain, but things did pick up now that it was morning, and finally they decided that I had dilated enough. I found myself being transferred onto a gurney and wheeled into the "delivery room". There to my horror, various medieval degradations occurred. I had already gone through the required enema and shaving of my pubic hair (all routine in those primitive times), and hadn't really thought the process could get much worse.

But now I found myself strapped onto the delivery table, my hands and arms strapped down, and my body in the most unlikely position possible for producing a child: my pelvis and legs way higher than my stomach, my legs tied onto the stirrups of this contraption. Nevertheless, I was still with it, paying attention, and that in itself in this place seemed something of a triumph.

Even that was taken from me. As Jeanne crowned and just as I was about to push her out, an invisible demonic being standing somewhere behind my head forced a gas mask over my mouth. I twisted my head as far as I could to get it off, I held my breath (all the while still trying to produce this infant). But to no avail. I finally *did* have to breathe, and the mask being over my face, I *did* pass out. At that crucial moment I was not allowed to be Witness.

I felt it as the ultimate violation. When, a short time later, I came to and they held my baby near my head (I was still strapped down), all I could do was turn away and say bitterly, "I hope you're going to give that poor thing a bath".

The rage and the sense of violation remained with me throughout my five days at Gouverneur Hospital. Perhaps in a way they sustained me. Jeanne was born around 11:30, and by the time they got me back to the ward, lunch was already over. I, however, was ravenously hungry (they don't call it "labor" for nothing). It took a fair bit of growling and general heavy-handedness to get something to eat, but they finally came up with some soup. Even as I ate it, I watched pieces of the ceiling fall onto the foot of my bed.

The folks on the ward were some of the New York's poorest. I learned a great deal about just how poor that was, and how hard and scary things can actually get.

There was one huge Black woman, Janelle, who had just had the tiniest baby girl. Probably no more than five pounds. She nursed her tenderly, but the baby seemed to just disappear next to her tit. I sensed her largeness was due to an illness but had no way of knowing. I don't think anyone there, nurse or doctor, tried to find out.

Janelle had numerous other kids, how many I'm not quite sure. Every day after school a solemn young boy of about ten would show up on the ward. She would give him some change: a quarter, sometimes a bit more, and tell him what to buy, what to do with the house. "Cook up some beans, and feed those children good", she would say, day after day in the late afternoon.

There was Juana, a tiny Puerto Rican woman, a slip of a girl, who spoke not a word of English and would not eat the hospital food. Juana wanted, clearly and passionately, to go home. I think, like me, she thought pregnancy wasn't an illness, and now that the baby had safely arrived she couldn't see why these people sought to detain her. Why they took the child away and brought it back at regular intervals. I think she saw the hospital as some kind of prison, might have feared she would be there forever.

Juana never stopped crying, or talking softly to herself in Spanish. Only sometimes at night everything would suddenly change. There was a Puerto Rican janitor on our floor, and he would let her husband in after hours. A dark, gentle man, almost a boy himself, he would come bearing food. Juana would stop crying. She'd eat; she'd talk. They would talk earnestly and intensely for what seemed like hours. Then Jorge would climb into bed with her and hold her till the janitor came to tell him he had to leave.

We—all eight of us in the ward—never told of these night visits. We were emphatically on the side of these two children. But during the day when Juana cried, I regretted my lack of Spanish and longed to reassure her in her native tongue.

Juana had given birth a few days ahead of me and I was there to see her go home. It was a moment of triumph such as I have rarely witnessed. I think the young couple felt that solely by their love and constancy and insistence they had managed to spring her—to free mother and child from this place.

●

As for me, I set myself to endure, to do the time. I had brought a scarf I was knitting for Freddie: solid black and already seven feet long, and I would sit propped up in the hospital bed, knitting for hours, the tail end of the thing cascading over the side of the bed to the floor.

I had also brought Proust, and I read a great deal of it in between nursing Jeanne. (From the very beginning we called her "Jeannie" and still do.) There were these brief and bright intervals when they brought her to me, when we could be together and plot or talk about our eventual escape. I knew that she desired it as much as I did. Possibly even more. And then she would be whisked away again to a fluorescent, glaring room with rows of small plastic beds. I knew it couldn't be comfortable at all.

The younger of the two doctors who made infrequent rounds was, I think, intrigued. Wanted to know more about this person who knitted black, seldom spoke, glared at everyone and read a large book. This person whom no husband or boyfriend visited in the evening. He was kindly and amused. But I kept him at bay, sure that any information that I unadvertently let slip would be used against me. I was holding out for the ultimate: my freedom, with the babe in my arms.

Jo came to see me once or twice. Freddie came one afternoon, and peered at Jeanne through the nursery glass while someone held her up. They thought he was the father and I didn't disabuse them.

Mom came up hastily one afternoon, I think it was a clandestine visit. If so it was one of the only things of the sort that she'd ever attempted. She brought with her several bags of Italian food, which I was very glad to get. It was all she could do to keep from bursting into tears.

It was Jo who picked me up when it was time to go home. Who carried Jeanne out of the hospital on one arm, my bag of possessions in her other hand. It was strange to be out again in the light, in the air. Close to the edge of the river.

Jo hailed a taxi and put us all in it. We wended our way back to my Houston Street apartment, where Jeanne and I went immediately to bed.

● ● ● ● ●

The six months before the birth had been filled with various forms of madness. Once I had determined that I was actually pregnant, I put the whole thing on ice for a while. Didn't tell anyone about it, not even my closest

friends. It was my secret, and besides, I was afraid. Afraid of the histrion-
ics I knew would inevitably ensue. Afraid I might even be talked into an
abortion in spite of myself. The best thing, I thought, at least for starters,
is to let this one grow in secret. I passed a few months in a blissful state of
tranquility.

When about three months had gone by, I told a few friends. Mostly,
they took it very badly, as if I had done something to affront them person-
ally. To threaten their lifestyles. Most of them came around after a while
and we went on being friends, more or less as we had been. Though in
many cases we were never close again.

Telling my friends brought a scary fact to the foreground: that I had to,
sooner or later, tell my parents. But tell them what? That was the question.
I was more than a little terrified of their reaction.

I had seen, in my first years in the Village, a woman friend, a painter,
killed by her perhaps-well-meaning but definitely stupid parents, when
they took custody of her illegitimate baby and committed her to an insti-
tution in Pennsylvania. Shock treatment wasn't yet regulated in that state,
and this particular place promised to restore your loved ones to their
senses in a month. Three weeks later my friend was dead, and her parents
had the child—who was, as they saw it, "another chance". A chance to do
right with their grandchild all that they felt they had done wrong with their
daughter. And—not the least of their concerns—a chance to save the baby
from her mother.

Not that I thought my parents were capable of that, exactly. But—I
wasn't sure. I was aware that I really knew nothing about them. I had no
clue as to the nature of their true feelings. The depth of their disappointment with me. I wanted to step carefully.

My first plan was to tell them that I was married. I asked Freddie if he'd
pretend to be my husband, at least for my parents. He said yes, and it was
very emotional for both of us. We designed two beautiful but inexpensive
silver bands and had a jeweler friend make them for us. We then took
them one spring day to the Brancusi room at the Museum of Modern Art,
one of our favorite and most sacred spaces, and put them on each other. I
don't remember what we said if anything, but I know the feeling was that
we would help each other out, try to take care of each other in the craziness of our lives. Wherever they went.

My parents received the announcement of my wedded state with astonishment and some joy, and invited the two of us over for dinner. The
evening went well enough, but I think it showed us that our pretense was

untenable. In any case, within a couple of days Freddie came to tell me that he couldn't carry it off. I secretly knew by then I couldn't either, but I allowed myself to feel abandoned and betrayed, and to cast him as the villain for backing down. Part of our Code was, of course, that you never backed down. Stood your ground no matter what, once you gave your word. (I was getting a lot of intimations by then that our Code didn't work, but I managed to ignore them for many more years.)

Time was moving on and I was starting to "show". I would soon have to tell my parents something. At this point it seemed just as easy to do the whole thing at once: tell them Freddie and I had lied about the marriage and that I was pregnant.

I had delayed as long as I possibly could because I wanted to be past the point in my pregnancy where abortion could be considered an option. I felt I needed to rule out all possibility of being coerced either emotionally or physically into having one against my will. Given the technology of that time, the point of no return was somewhere in the fourth month—a point I was now approaching.

As a first step I went to see a family friend: Dr. Veccali, who was a prominent neurologist in Manhattan, and who, I knew, had been to visit us in Brooklyn numerous times in the years before and after my "breakdown"—ostensibly to have dinner with the family, but in reality to "observe" me for my parents.

He received me in his office and listened carefully with an air of assumed detachment. Of course, he said, I knew who the father was. I certainly wasn't *that* promiscuous.

I was taken aback. I did know who the father was, but only by a fluke. Usually, I reflected, I would have had several possibilities. Did that make me *"that promiscuous"?* And what is *that promiscuous?* Does *that promiscuous* mean more than one lover between any two menstruations? I ran all this through my head while I grunted assent. Yes, I knew who the father was.

I had no intention of telling him and I didn't. If that was the ploy it didn't work but he agreed to be present when I told my parents, and we made a date to meet at the house in Brooklyn.

It may be that Doctor Veccali's presence was the only thing that came between me and physical violence. It may be that it was for the well-being of me and the fetus that he agreed to be present. I was grateful for that then, and I am still. However, the violence that my father did manage at that meeting hasn't healed to this day.

For, having been informed—nay assured—by the doctor, his good friend, that there was no way I could safely have an abortion, that given the stage of pregnancy I was in, *there was at least a fifty percent chance that I would die if abortion was attempted,* my father insisted that I should have one anyway. For the first time I saw fully and clearly how little value I had in his eyes compared to his "honor", and what he considered to be the reputation of the family. What he always called his "standing in the community".

I shouldn't have been surprised, but I was. When everything else is past and forgotten, there is still that between us. That he would have rather had me dead than himself dishonored. Better to have me dead, than myself and my child thriving outside his code of ethics.

There were a few other surprises, but none commensurate with that one. My family dropped all contact with me after it became clear that I would go my way and have the baby.

And then Susan O'Reilley, my closest woman friend for ten years, cut me out of her life, claiming the coming child as the reason. She soon after broke off her engagement to Bret and disappeared completely from our worlds.

I had stayed with Susan while I worked a temp job in the West Village and scoured the city for an apartment. A bunch of my stuff was at her apartment on East Seventh Street. After she broke off with me, I stayed with Freddie. He had given up on the Prince Street loft, and moved in with Vincent Warren in an apartment on the Lower East Side.

Vinnie was also a dancer, though he inclined more to classical ballet than Freddie did. He would later become the celebrated love of Frank O'Hara, the man to whom Frank would write so many great poems. It was through Vinnie that I met Frank about a year later.

After I finally found a place on Houston Street and moved into it, Freddie came—in about the seventh month of my pregnancy—to stay with me. He had it in his mind that he would help me out. In his very dear, but misguided, way he worried aloud so much and so frequently—fearing among other things that I'd die in childbirth—that I finally had to ask him to go back home. It wasn't good for me, I felt—neither for my resolve nor my convictions—to hear such dark oracles on a daily basis.

I hung in there. The mystery and power of pregnancy itself—all the various emotions and energies my body was going through—outweighed any and all of the vagaries of my friends and relations. The further I got into pregnancy the more I liked it; the more invigorated and positive I felt.

I was working all this time, doing regular office work for a firm in the West Village. Working—except for swollen ankles near the end of my time there, and a general sense of discomfort I always felt when I perched precariously on a high stool at the lunch counter of the only nearby eatery—didn't seem to be a problem.

I had needed to find something that would create a lump of cash faster than my usual modeling work, so that I could plunk it all down on a new apartment. To get the job, I had lied about how far along I was. Like many women carrying their first babies, I looked small, and when I finally quit, a week before Jeanne came, the folks in my office still thought I was six months pregnant.

● ● ● ● ●

It was midmorning, on the day after Jeanne and I got home from the hospital. We were both dozing and Jo was hanging diapers on the clothesline, when a hearty, booming voice from the next building inquired "Well, was it a boy or a girl"?

Both Jo and I were taken aback, to put it mildly. Though I'd been living in the place for several months, none of my neighbors had ever acknowledged me, much less expressed the least interest in my condition. Once they had determined that there was no male in the vicinity who could be awarded the dubious honor of inferred paternity, they saw no reason to notice my existence—as far as they were concerned, I wasn't there at all. No one was living in my flat, no one walked down the stairs, went to work, picked up the mail in the evening. They never so much as grunted.

This didn't surprise me. I was, after all, back on the Lower East Side, and I remembered very well with what non-cordiality I had been greeted, even without an impending offspring, when I had arrived on East Fifth Street a few years back. I had re-arrived in a world where a woman without a man didn't exist at all; a mother without a husband was more than invisible: she was a kind of negative force-field, a bit of antimatter.

And so, to hear this cheerful, welcoming voice inquiring as to the gender of the newly arrived one, and—when Jo managed to haltingly answer that "it" was a girl—to have the voice go on to ask after my health and well-being—loudly, and certainly within the hearing of all my disapproving neighbors—was more than amazing. I frankly didn't know what or how to think of it.

The booming voice and cheerful matter-of-factness belonged, it turned out, to a neighbor who lived one building over and about a half flight above me: a large Hungarian woman named Anna Butula. Anna had a huge and generous heart, two girls, Dolly and Rosemary, and a truck-driver husband named Bucky. It seemed that she had determined, long before I got back from Gouverneur, to make me and Jeanne a part of her sprawling extended family.

All sorts of stuff flew back and forth between our windows: advice, questions, gossip, offers of help, cheerful goodwill, and interest. In no time at all Anna had contrived to visit, and soon after she hooked up a clothesline from my window to hers. And thereafter baby clothes that Rosemary had outgrown, and mason jars of stuffed cabbage and chicken paprikash, came creaking over the clothesline on many an evening.

Anna had been a pediatric nurse, and had in her time been a nanny for many of the richest of the poor little rich kids in New York. She was, additionally, a raconteur of enormous gifts, and we spent many hours in the park, or at her place or mine, keeping an eye on the kids and exchanging tales. Our friendship has lasted from that day to this, through all manner of changes and vicissitudes.

But on those first days at home with the baby, the thing that Anna did was to open our existence up to the neighborhood. She threw her friendship down like a gauntlet, a challenge to all those smug, self-righteous and small-minded women and men who occupied my building and hers—that corner and its enclosed courtyard—and no one dared take up the challenge. By the time Jeanne and I were ready to head out to the store, the park, we had suddenly and miraculously become visible.

But before we became so mobile, something occurred which made me realize how utterly vulnerable we were in this new life; how fragile and breakable.

It was about six days after I was home from the hospital, and Jeanne and I were alone. Jo had stayed as long as she could, but she had to get back to her factory job in Hartford, and to her own life in her parents' house there.

I was already in bed and asleep and Jeanne was sleeping when I was awakened by cramping. I was bleeding very heavily. I knew enough to know this shouldn't be happening, and as it continued I knew I had to do something about it. I made a call or two, but no one was home. So I set out warily, moving slowly, down the steps and out into the street, leaving Jeanne asleep and alone. I knew that I had to get to the hospital, was not sure I could carry her, didn't know what they'd do with her there, and too, I was just confused.

It was almost midnight. My apartment was pretty far over on the East Side, near the corner of Houston Street and Avenue B, and cabs rarely came that way, but that night one miraculously did. I hailed it and got in, hoping to get the help I needed and get home again, all before Jeanne woke up. But when I said "Bellevue Emergency" to the driver, he pulled over and stopped and refused to go anywhere. Perhaps he thought I was having a drug overdose, or—who knows what? Perhaps he thought I'd been shot. The only thing I knew for sure was that, like so many New Yorkers, he didn't want to get involved.

"Get out" was all he would say, and any pleading or explaining I tried only made him more adamant.

I got out—I had to—and began a slow, careful walk toward the streets with more cabs. At Avenue A I did get someone to pick me up, and at Bellevue they gave me a shot to stop the bleeding and told me to stay in bed for three or four days. I got home again before it was light, though whether Jeanne had awakened while I was gone was something I never knew.

This precarious night's adventure left a mark. It made me see how few choices there really are if you are a woman alone with a baby. How easily everything could go wrong: I could have lost consciousness at the house; could have been detained at the hospital. I could have brought her with me and had her taken from me, if they decided I needed hospitalization; or I might not have been able to manage the walk, carrying her.

It gave me pause. When I looked at how the whole thing could have been construed, I realized how far beyond any viable judgment and censure most life is actually lived. Most poor life especially.

The woman who is charged with manslaughter when she leaves her child alone to go to work, to go to the store or the doctor and the house burns down, is doing what she has done a thousand times before, what she has had to do, in a world, a society that leaves her no options. I saw this now.

It was the beginning, for me, of a new kind of radicalization.

Nothing, not even the iniquity of her daughter, could keep Emma away from a baby—especially not her first grandchild. And so my mother and father were soon reconciled to the event in their different ways and to different degrees. I think to Emma the circumstances around Jeanne's birth soon became irrelevant, but to Dick they were, and remained, an open wound.

They came by frequently, were soon familiar figures on East Houston Street, and came to know my friends and neighbors. Emma would have come with him or without him in any case—she rode the subway in the beginning, and occasionally thereafter—and so Dick came perforce: to give her a ride, make sure nothing untoward happened to her in my dubious neighborhood. They came bearing food and baby clothes, and gifts of all kinds. And they came at least once so Emma could give me a lesson in child rearing.

There was a day in December when Jeanne wouldn't stop crying. I had been on the phone to my mother in Brooklyn, not once but many times, as we both tried to figure out what was the matter. Emma would listen judiciously to the sound of the crying, and make some suggestion. I would duly hang up and try it, only to have to call back to say that that, too, hadn't worked. Jeanne was still crying.

It wasn't as if I was inexperienced. I had been changing diapers and burping cousins by the time I was four, and was fairly expert by the time I was seven or eight. Nevertheless, neither my expertise nor my mother's could appease my daughter that day: she cried as if her heart was broken, as if the entire world had entered into a conspiracy to betray her. And in between, she yelled with rage and indignation as only an infant can.

Finally, Emma decided that the only thing to do was to come to the house, and see for herself what might be going on. And as soon as my poor father got in the door from his own workday, Emma was waiting to rush him out again, so that he could drive her on her rescue mission. At that moment my brother Richie, who was then living at home, also came in, and to his astonishment was told by his two discombobulated parents: "We're going to Diane's because the baby is crying". Richie took this in for a minute and then sanely inquired: "What do you want her to do, lie there and laugh"?

Mom was not appeased or pacified by this perspective however, and she and my father were at Houston Street within the next half hour.

My parents and I had entered on a period of wary cordiality, a watchful and uneasy truce.

• • • • •

There followed an idyllic six months or so. I was ensconced with Jeanne in a warm, steam-heated apartment, and for a while there was nothing else I could imagine wanting. Nursing a baby for the first time, I could feel in my flesh how totally absorbing this was, how men and sex, friends and even art lost their importance. It was something I was unprepared for, as I was also unprepared for the actual physical exhaustion that followed childbirth.

Vigorous and energetic up to the moment I went to the hospital, the last thing I expected was to find myself wiped out afterwards. Nothing I had read, nothing anyone had told me, had prepared me for the feeling of utter fatigue, bordering on nausea, with which I would often wake in the night to Jeanne wanting to nurse. Or the mornings, when the only sane thing to do was lie in bed with her, let go of any and all plans I had made for the day.

Not only was I unprepared for this, I was also emotionally and mentally unsuited for it. I had no idea of what it might mean to slow down. Everything I knew about survival was predicated on doing, and doing vigorously and endlessly, the tasks of the day, foremost among which were writing and studying. Everything before the birth had supported my belief that pregnancy was not an illness, that one could do everything one had always done and more, that motherhood only enhanced one's strength, one's creative powers.

Insofar as I knew / acknowledged Womanhood, it was as Mary Shelley I saw myself. Her journals had been models for me of what could be done. And how to accomplish it. Terse and unimpassioned, they recorded even death in a monotone, and then went on in the same entry to say who had visited, what she was reading. Some might call the journals cold.

Reading my own journal for the weeks after Jeanne's birth, I realize how much it sounds like Mary's. These are the entire entries for those particular days:

> *10/28. Jeanne-Athalie born 11:30 A.M. Feel weak & sleep all day. Mom up—evening.*
> *10/29. Start nursing. Get out of bed. Sleep much of day. Fred up. Call Jo—eve.*
> *10/30. Stronger. No one up. Get stir-crazy by eve— Try to reach people but no one home. Sleep badly.*
> *10/31. Feel better. Read Proust. Knit. Start letter to Kitty— Eve Bernice up— but they sent her home without my seeing her.*
> *11/1. Better. Read Proust all day— Knit— Call Jo— Very hungry.*
> *11/2. Home. Dinner Bret.*
>
> *. . . .*
>
> *11/10. Up late writing. Baby to doctor.*
> *11/11. Yvonne. Hemorrhage.*

. . . .

11/17. Jo takes baby to visit Audrey. I go to Museum w/Freddie.

. . . .

11/30. Merce's concert. Order linoleum.

. . . .

12/12. No heat. Goof all day. 12 hrs sleep. . . .

. . . .

12/28. See Freddy— Fledermaus. Dinner w/Bret & Freddy.
Write 20 pomes. . . .

Looking back at this now, I cannot believe that I had these concerns. So little about the immediate impact of the baby. The moving and absorbing experience of nursing. Of being alone with her and looking into her eyes as she drank. As if I had to *prove* I could have the child and keep going. Keep being an artist. Without coming up for so much as a breath of air.

Nevertheless, my life had changed in every way.

When I moved downtown in 1957, a whole network disappeared. A whole way of life, actually. Soon after that, Bret went into the army. Freddie stuck around. Ever since Ginsberg's visit that past winter, there had begun to be a new network of writers in my life: those who lived in New York and those who were passing through. But most of my lovers and many of the friends from our Amsterdam Avenue life didn't come around much. There was a break in the continuity of things.

This break was for me further highlighted by the new demands of my situation. For the first time since I'd left college five years before I found that I wasn't the mistress of my time. It was no longer feasible to stay up all night, writing or talking with friends, when inevitably I'd have to be up all day, feeding and playing with Jeanne.

At first, since she slept and ate around the clock it didn't matter when I slept, and the only real restriction was that I would have to have someone at the house with her, or take her with me, whenever I ventured forth. Since none of my friends had children, or expected to have them in the near future, or in some cases ever, Jeanne was a novelty, something special on the scene, and there was no shortage of willing babysitters for whom a couple of hours with "Chiccups" (as she was soon nicknamed) was the greatest of imaginable delights.

Around this time, my friend Jo and her new lover Pauli took the apartment just above mine, and that circumstance made everything more flexible. From the moment she carried her out of the hospital, Jo had been

Jeanne's devoted surrogate parent, and I could usually bring her upstairs at a moment's notice.

And, as I said, in those first six months or so, there was nothing more interesting, more absorbing, than being the mom: nursing, holding and cuddling, sleeping with Jeanne beside me. We wrapped each other round and made a nest. It was a wonderful way to pass a winter.

Spring burgeoned that year. It came into the world with trumpets and all the trees flowered at once. I found myself suddenly opening windows. New music was playing on my cheap phonograph. Jeanne had a stroller and Freddie was around, and the three of us often found our way to Washington Square Park for an afternoon of talking and reading, while airing and sunning the baby (a prominent New York City pastime, since backyards are so scarce).

At the same time I was working on my first book, *This Kind of Bird Flies Backward.* The work had been long in the making—some of the poems reached back to 1953—but the book itself had come about through the good offices of two young men who owned a print shop on Cornelia Street. I'm not sure what inspired them, but one night in the Village they approached me and said they wanted to be publishers, would like to print a book of my work. They even had a name for themselves—Aardvark Press.

I had tons of poems and had started assembling some of them into a book back on Amsterdam Avenue. I knew they were ready to be out in the world. It didn't take very long for me to put a manuscript together, following my new friends' guidelines. They wanted to print it four-up and explained that printer's concept to me.

The whole thing was an initiation into a craft that I've been involved with ever since. What Aardvark Press offered at first was to do all the photo work and printing and cover all the expenses, in return for which they would be the "publisher". I went down to Cornelia Street, and took a look at their small shop about which I knew nothing. It seemed fine.

I found myself relegated to doing the typesetting—they explained what "camera ready copy" was. I had by then acquired a rather inept and clumsy IBM typewriter, which was the joy of my life, but was very far from being what I needed to do the book. I rapidly figured out how to get around my lack of equipment.

IBM had recently come out with electric typewriters with "proportional spacing", which looked much more like type than any previous typewriter, (and in fact in the next few years ushered in the "cold-type" revolution), but were a bit more complicated to use. In order to encourage people to buy them, they were offering to lend one for two weeks to would-be customers. I called their sales representative and presented myself as a college student whose parents wanted to buy her one of these new-fangled typewriters. I allowed as how I, myself, had my doubts that I could use such a high-tech machine. Within a day or two, one was delivered to my house for a two-week trial period.

Of course I immediately got to work, and whipped out all the copy for my book, typing it on the requisite "coated stock" provided by Aardvark Press. *This Kind of Bird Flies Backward* is quite a small book, and even with proofreading and retyping poems with mistakes, the whole thing was done well within the time limit. (Only one mistake got through, and in the finished books we sat and corrected it by hand.)

Anyway, with absolute meticulousness, I called IBM in plenty of time to tell them I didn't think I would be able to work their machine after all, and would they please come get it. Phase one of the project was completed.

It was about this time that the guys at Aardvark decided not to go through with their publishing venture after all. I never did find out why. However, they offered, if I did all the rest of the work and paid for the paper, to do the press run for nothing. They had themselves a deal. Over the next months I learned such arts as dummying a book for printing four-up, and stripping and opaquing negatives, which I did in the Aardvark shop and at their light table, often with Jeanne along in carriage or stroller.

Freddie did the actual paste-up and did calligraphic brushwork for poem titles and the cover. A bunch of Bret's drawings graced the inner pages. And when Ferlinghetti came through a bit late with a requested introduction, I simply typed it on a different typewriter and didn't worry about it. Consistency of style or of design was not our strong point. We also forgot all about such amenities as a title page or copyright page—the book simply begins.

It was all very exciting. I went exploring in the world of printing machinery and came back with a huge stapler for thirty-five dollars, and a couple of bone folders for almost nothing. The stapler was to grace one end of my drawing table (which doubled as the dining table) for the next few years.

I also found myself paying attention for the first time to the notion of a publishing imprint. Now that Aardvark was not officially "doing" the book (though their name remained on the cover of the first edition), I decided I wanted to have *some* imprint, so as not to be simply self-published.

I had by then just become acquainted with LeRoi Jones—he had appeared at my door one day with his friend, the photographer James Oliver Mitchell. I knew that LeRoi was planning to start publishing as Totem Press, but that he had as yet no books ready to go. I, on the other hand, had a book but no publishing name. In a moment of inspiration I suggested that *This Kind of Bird Flies Backward* be published as the first Totem Press book. We could thus be mutually helpful to each other: Totem Press would have a book out and I would have an imprint. Roi agreed, and the beautiful logo that Fielding Dawson had designed for him was added to the back cover of *This Kind of Bird*, further adding to the confusion of designs and styles.

But I was oblivious. I think we all were. This was, after all, the first actual book that any of us had done. And many of us had actually, hands-on, done it together.

I visited the shop many times over the week or two when the pages were being printed, caught up in the wonder of offset printing. Hooked, though I didn't realize it. And then there was the day when we actually picked up the finished pages and covers, and carted them in a cab back to the apartment. For the next month or so whoever came to visit me wound up folding pages, or collating, or stapling, depending what stage things were at.

This was to become a pattern, a way of having visitors that I maintained for years. "While you're talking to me, would you lick those envelopes"? I'd ask. Or stuff them. Or stick labels on. Or collate, or staple, or . . . I learned that one of the best ways to get to know anyone was to work beside them. It was not till fourteen years later, during the hippie revolution in San Francisco, that some folks indignantly refused to go along with the program.

We would sit in the bedroom / living room / dining room (my middle room was all of these at once: the room beyond belonged to Jeanne and was "the nursery", and the small room off the kitchen was my study, and sacrosanct)—we would sit there, talking, eating, writing together sometimes, and we slowly but inevitably folded, collated and stapled the nine hundred and fifty copies of the book.

And when at last they were ready, we found a car and took the whole lot to a binder to have them trimmed. The final miracle. What had left the house looking like bunches of folded papers came back looking like boxes of books.

I sold them around Manhattan, and they went fast. I'd pile them and Jeanne in the stroller and set out. Leave them on consignment, come back a few weeks later, pick up money, and leave some more. An interesting business. Within a year, the books were gone.

•   •   •   •   •

One day that spring Jeanne's father came to visit. We sat in his car, up at the Cloisters, while I nursed her, and we looked out across the Hudson toward the sunset over the cliffs of New Jersey. He was very tender and kind, and somewhat wistful. I was glad to let him share our lives for an instant, but knew more than ever that my choice to have a baby alone—not have a man around—was a good one. They were, it seemed to me, at best so very easily *overcome* and useless.

I had not told Stefan anything at all while I was pregnant. We had had our afternoon of lovemaking and then he had gone back to what I thought of as his "straight" life: school and teaching, and his marriage. As was usual with him, he didn't try to get in touch: no letter, poem, gift, or gesture ever followed our meetings. That's how it usually was and I never thought much about it, thought of it just as part of the "cool" of our scene.

He didn't get in touch and neither did I. I went through the months of struggle with friends and family, of moving and work and finding a new place, and then sometime after Jeanne and I had settled in on Houston Street, I let him in on the secret. I sent him a Christmas card which read, in part, "By the way, you have a daughter in New York. Come and see us sometime".

I got a phone call almost immediately. Stefan was excited, moved, loving, and angry. Why hadn't I let him know? Because, I answered frankly enough, you wouldn't have wanted me to do it. And, I might have added, because it's essentially nobody's business but my own—I don't want or expect anything from you and don't want you meddling.

He professed himself full of longing to come up and see Jeanne—his first son from his marriage was just a bit older—and a few months later, when he had some legitimate reason to be in New York, we got together and headed up to what had been one of our old stomping grounds: The Cloisters.

I felt gentle, loving. Was willing to concede that all this might be hard for him. (Though secretly I felt it had nothing to do with him in his separate life hundreds of miles away.) Was willing to let myself feel sexual and to share the intimacy of nursing Jeanne with him, as we sat in his car.

When we got back to my place we made love, but when he left it was easy to put Stefan out of my mind. My life was so full, so good. And as far as I knew, or had ever experienced, no good could come to a child from having a father.

● ● ● ● ●

The house was full of this new life: the baby, the book. I had been preparing for them both for so long, but they still brought many surprises. So many new things to do and to learn how to do. And too, I began to find new friends, to fill the void left by the ones I had lost with the move.

There were writers who stopped by on their way through town, sent by Allen Ginsberg, or by Ferlinghetti. Kenneth Rexroth sat on my couch for a couple of days, talking at some length and watching the comings and goings; Edward Dahlberg found his way there, too, and made a general nuisance of himself, coming on to me and various other women like an insistent old lecher. Other writers, mostly poets from the new, fledgling downtown scene, began to visit; we came to be friends a little at a time. Joel Oppenheimer, Max Finstein, Fielding Dawson. LeRoi Jones had found his way to my house early on; it was he who sent some of the others. Fielding, at one point when he was between apartments, left at my house a priceless collection of poetry books from Black Mountain College: early Creeley and Olson texts which I perused, and in some cases copied poem by poem, entire on my electric typewriter. So when I gave them back I would still have a copy for myself.

There were Jimmy Waring's friends, dancers and theatre people: Nick Cernovich, who had also been at Black Mountain and who now worked at Orientalia Books (the only bookstore for Eastern philosophy and religion then extant in New York) and did lights for plays and dances; Remy Charlip, who danced with Merce Cunningham and wrote children's books; Norman Solomon, another Black Mountain person, who made photos and Ray Johnson who did collage. There were, too, the younger dancers who studied and worked with Jimmy. Over the years these included (besides Freddie, and Vincent Warren) Yvonne Rainer, Valda Setterfield, Trisha Brown, Lucinda Childs, Deborah Hay, and many others.

The worlds overlapped in a million ways and places. The art world, the worlds of jazz, of modern classical music, of painting and poetry and dance, were all interconnected. There were endless interweavings; they happened slowly, over several years, and they were the stronger for that slow growth.

By the time Jeanne was two and a half, she found herself bedding down Monday nights backstage at the Living Theatre while I stage-managed a "dark night" series for Jimmy that included Frank O'Hara's *Awake in Spain* and a staged reading of my own play *Murder Cake*.

All this activity didn't go completely unnoticed, though for the most part it was only heeded by the small circle of us who were in the midst of it. *Life* had announced the existence of the Beats and a new wave of young suburban hopefuls began arriving in the Village on the weekends. They all dressed dutifully in black, the girls wore black tights and lots of eye make-up, and most of them went back home to New Jersey on Sunday nights.

Where there had once been one or two coffee shops we all frequented (aside from the ancient Italian ones like the Caffe Reggio, which I had gone to since high school, and were mostly for equally ancient Italian men)—where there had once been just the Rienzi and the Limelight, there were now dozens of cafes opening up all over. Within a year or two they all featured poetry readings. Awful poetry proliferated like crabgrass on Long Island lawns. Mostly, we didn't take any of this seriously, it was a nuisance only on weekends, and only in the Village.

At the same time, I was getting used to a different lifestyle. There were new limits to become accustomed to. By now it was imperative that I sleep at night—Jeanne was a vigorous and active creature by day, and I had to keep up with her. This ruled out—except for the times that she visited my folks—all-night writing, talking, and most gallivanting. The radius of my stomping ground was distinctly diminished: mostly I ranged from the East Side to the Village and back. Everything I had come to know and enjoy above Fourteenth Street became once more a never-never land. I was limited, in large part, to the places I could get to on foot and pushing a stroller, and while these were not inconsiderable, the change took some adjusting to.

Then, too, the seasons became more of a factor than they had ever been before. I began to mind the cold. To bundle oneself up for a romp in the snow in Central Park, ending up at Downey's for a hot rum toddy was one thing; to bundle oneself and one's child up for a much slower and therefore chillier trip was much less desirable. I began to spend a lot more of my time inside.

And inside had also changed. My house had become much more tame:

domestic, I suppose. After the initial camping-out that was still going on when I went to the hospital, furniture and accoutrements had slowly come together. One of the great additions was a couch. A real sofa—wooden platform with screw-in legs, foam rubber mattress, and two bolsters, all covered in the latest 50s-style black-and-white fabric—had been bought for me by my parents and delivered in due course from one of the midtown department stores.

The sofa figured large in the social life of my Houston Street apartment. It was here that Rexroth lounged for days and observed the scene; here that Bret slept whenever he came by on leave from the army; here that various babysitters slept over, various love affairs—mine and others'— were begun. This sofa was the setting and support for many of the dramas of my four and a half years in that apartment.

It changed the tone of things, there was no denying it. The sofa, together with the "nursery" (full as it was of toys, and a crib), the better-equipped kitchen, and the central heating—all announced this apartment as domestic—domesticated. Compared to The Pad on Amsterdam Avenue, the place proclaimed itself homelike, reassuring.

What we did was different there, and how we did it. Instead of ranging the city, we might be found at home, writing a play together, "exquisite corpse" style. Or eating some delivered Chinese food and listening to a new blues anthology on LP. Or perhaps James Mitchell would come by to photograph me nursing Jeanne. Or John Fles would bring over a new jazz record and talk with me about his one-shot journal, *The Trembling Lamb*.

In the second summer, when Jeanne was almost two, she went to my parents' house in the country for a month. I took that time to rediscover one of my lost loves: the movies. Together with my comrades, the poet A.B. Spellman and novelist Hubert Selby (we all called Cubby), we'd smoke some grass and wander 42nd Street together, going to one movie after another all night long. Seeing what there was to be seen. Catching up.

We'd come back to my place at dawn and talk the day in, A.B. worrying about LeRoi: his ambition, his projects, Cubby ranging through worlds with his tough, oddball humor. These were friendships I cherished, and they helped keep me sane. In the exacting close range of most of my life at that time, they helped me keep a wider view. Dance of the mind in the black and white of film. Dance of the images. Outside the possible. The ordinary.

chapter ELEVEN

It was the winter when Jeanne was one and a half. My old friend Jo and her lover Pauli were living upstairs in the apartment just above mine, and it was at a gathering of their friends, a lesbian party, that I first met Bonnie. She was a large woman with intense, penetrating green eyes and the huge shoulders of a construction worker. Her lank, dull brown hair hung straight and she pulled it back out of the way, keeping it off her face. Perhaps her voice was her most memorable feature, breathless, intimate, always urgent, it conveyed a wealth of feeling, depths of knowledge: the inevitable *secrets* we were always on the lookout for—and which were a mark of beauty back then—desire and desirability.

When Bonnie was near you, talking to you, you felt special. You really did. Something about the way her gaze held yours, the way she leaned forward, hunching those huge shoulders, to catch your every word, the way her face changed with every nuance of what you were saying. And that voice. What it said to you it could surely say to no one else. Or that was the feeling.

I had let my hair grow out after Jeanne was born, but I still dressed like a dyke: grey flannel pants with a sharp crease and a man's white suit-shirt were my dress-up gear; otherwise black denims, the tapered kind. "Pegged". And a white sweatshirt, or handwoven Mexican cotton, or—my favorite—green corduroy man's work shirt, breast pocket and all. Now this was, strictly speaking, not the prescribed costume for either butch or femme; but as I was neither, was nothing but myself, it suited me just fine.

Bonnie, I noticed right off, wore her own variant of mixed-message clothes: she affected faded baggy blue jeans and a variety of androgynous shirts: blue or grey / green velour, open at the neck, often with paint stains on them. The whole thing looked offhand and thrown together till you noticed how carefully the colors were chosen. How they brought out her eyes. Their sea-green depths.

I am no longer sure how it was that we first got together, what once memorable but now long-forgotten words, what electricity, drove us into each other's arms and into bed, but I remember how fierce our lovemaking was, how explosive. Giving birth for the first time, delving deeper into my own woman-nature, had left me more open than ever for an affair with a woman. I needed someone to mirror back to me some of the softness— and, yes, the mystery—I was beginning to discover in myself. And to lead me further, teach me secrets of my own sexuality.

This of childbirth, of being opened *from the inside out,* I thought, was how you truly lost your virginity. Torn open so the world could come through. Come through you. Not that semipleasant invasion from a man, excursus from *the outside in.* That in itself, by itself, was merely invitation. Some kind of beginning. Now I felt the joy, the power, of being OPEN. Something unconquerable and deep about it. Place from which I live. Twice-torn.

And I needed my body honored for what it was. What it had become. What I had learned it could be. For the milk it gave, and the comfort. For its status as communal property: it was no longer mine now, a private preserve, but there for the kid to climb on whenever she would. That one fact alone changed me—that I truly did not own my physical self. Changed everything about who I was in the world. What flesh really is. A woman's secret knowledge.

In rather recent times I had a dream: I was a child, in a kitchen with my mother and grandmother Antoinette. We were all three engaged in cooking together. The food being prepared glowed with our attention and care. Our love. We laughed a lot, we tasted things. My mother sang; my grandmother sang. It was on the tip of my tongue in the dream to say "Please, let's shut the door, let's keep the men out". All the men. Who would bring worry lines back to these faces I so loved. Would bring fear and sadness to my heart.

I longed to stay there with those beloved figures, in that world where making and the moment were enough. Realm of the Mothers. Where there was enough to go round.

●
●

For a brief while Bonnie, Jeanne and I shared such a world. A surround that was almost womblike—I think I would say now that we were protected by the Goddess. In Her hands, whatever that might mean.

There were no worries, no differences that mattered. Money demands, the flow of time stood still for a bit. There was Jeanne, breathing in her crib, and Bonnie and I making love in the next room. There were winter mornings in bed. Walks in the park with Nails, Bonnie's boxer, as inexplicable to me as a pet crocodile. There were long Sunday mornings when Jo and Pauli would visit from upstairs, and we'd all have brunch together, waiting for spring.

Bonnie was the first woman I had a real affair with. Maybe the first person of either gender, come to think of it. A love affair, not just some casual adventure. Complete with all the trappings of human love.

And it seemed to me that there was so much more to this of loving a woman than there was, or had been to date at any rate, in my casual affairs with men. For me the miracle was that I had let men in at all. That I could. I had expected nothing special from them and whatever was good had been a bonus. I was grateful.

I had come through a passage of several years where what I wanted and found were playmates: men and boys to romp the city streets with, to share the exuberant and awkward works of our respective apprenticeships as artists. It had been an era where time stretched out: there seemed to be an infinite amount of it: for study, for talking, for making art, for making love. For vast and unwieldy projects that never came to fruition. Nothing was very urgent, and the love I preferred was also "cool". Now I had emerged in a place where time was measured and structured, where my child slept (usually) at night and wanted me awake and lively in the day, and this one fact alone had changed my style. Changed everything in my life.

I was coming for the first time up against the limits of my own energy— how much I could actually do in a given day. I was finding it harder to be available to work and play, to love and friendship, to Jeanne, at any and all hours. There were—for the first time since I left my parents' house behind me—constraints. And with the constraints came the need, nay, even the demand, that everything—love affairs, writings, friendships, escapades—be more intense. Be richer and fuller. Instead of that lovely randomness, cool diversity, rambling quality, of our earliest years. Now I needed to cram a lot into a little space. "Load every rift with ore" was how Keats once put it.

In some sense I had left my apprenticeship behind; had come into the journeyman stage of my poet's training.

And it was at this point that Bonnie's intensity caught and held me. The timing was perfect. When she turned the light of her eyes on and turned those eyes your way, there were few women, straight or gay, who didn't feel *something*. Some melting in desire. Somehow she forced you to see yourself at your most amazing. Most precious. And believe in what you saw. She saw. All obstacles fell into shadow, disappeared, backlit by the blaze of what could be. Potentiality. The possible worlds.

Freddie entered this womb-cave of ours that winter now and again. We let him in for his gentleness, his gayness. He had a kind of broken wistfulness around Jeanne. Of all the folks I'd invited to father my kid, Freddie was the one who remembered. Remembered he'd turned it down. Some way, it haunted him. There had been nights when he'd cried in my arms, wishing he was "Jeanne's father". Wishing he was my lover. Till I finally called him on it, sensing the underlying sentimentality, false emotion, offering to fuck him then and there if he wanted. And of course we did no such thing, just slept till morning, naked in each other's arms. Two waifs with no clue as to what sex between us could actually change. If anything. Ascribing to it powers beyond our knowing.

After a while Freddie's presence—he was spending more time at my place than at his own—and his presence became an integral part of that winter, an attribute of my love affair with Bonnie. Many nights he slept on the couch in my bedroom so that he could hear Jeanne when she woke— babysat, actually—while I wended my way (looking, I hoped, cool, nonchalant, and *tough*), through the freezing slippery dangerous streets of the far East Side, to spend the night at Bonnie's studio.

● ● ● ● ●

I had never been seriously in love with a woman before, though certainly there had been a subtext of girl-love through my life since my teens.

All through high school I'd been in love with O'Reilley, her insouciant beauty and pirate's ways. Her tiny breasts, long waist. Her androgyny. It was really a high school crush, had never worked for us, and years later, when she and I were briefly lovers, when she came back drained and cynical, battered and ill, from hitchhiking across America with an intense and alcoholic "butch", it had taken only one night of loving, and seeking to heal through love, for both of us to put our passion to rest for good.

At Swarthmore, I had gone through agonies of love for Lee, had had a huge infatuation with Tomi—both unrequited. The years after we left college put these and many other fledgling relationships through their natural changes: Lee and I briefly became lovers—there was a period of time when she wanted me as passionately and compulsively as I had wanted her at college. Mostly it just made me sad. That feeling of "what goes around comes around" is supposed to be satisfying but I doubt it ever is. It's just frustrating: the timing—is the timing ever right? Lee would lie on my bed in my Fifth Street pad and stare long and hard at the ceiling, and I would stroke her hair, relish her strong, beautiful woman's profile, the purity of her gaze, and wonder where that desperation, that yearning to connect (only two years before) had gone to.

The one important affair I'd had was with Jo—and actually it was a one-night stand. This one night of sort-of-loving had happened while I was living on Amsterdam Avenue.

Jo was from Hartford. I had met her through Audre Lorde. She was a shy, silent, dark Italian woman, whose gaze unless she knew you well was usually directed at the floor, and whose conversation, except on rare occasions, was almost nonexistent. But a wonderful person gleamed out of those black eyes, if you could catch one of her quick, sidewise glances summing things up, checking out what was really going on. A sharp and yet elfin intelligence, maybe gnomelike would be a better word, but there was something playful about it, too. This elf or gnome, I suppose, was the person who lived in Jo and made things. Wonderful boxes whose satin linings held secret compartments. Whose secret compartments held other compartments, even more hidden.

This was the person who lived in Jo and wrote. Or occasionally drew. Who could fix broken kitchens and floorboards, who could fix broken hearts. Who slept in my bedroom on an army cot when I came home with baby Jeanne to an otherwise empty house.

There was something of *Nightwood* in her, and something of the dark woman in that wonderful Capote story, "Tree of Night". The quality of "secret" carried to another degree. Reshaping the world to conform to a different order.

Jo was precious to many of us. Many women I knew fell in love with her, one time or another. She had been through the classic hard times of our era, had been subjected to shock treatment by her Sicilian family for "schizophrenia", which might have been nothing more than their reaction to her homosexuality. Or her reaction to them. Certainly she was often depressed—but then, I had never known her before the shock.

Jo and I were good friends for many years. We had a special understanding, based on our both having been subjected to a southern Italian upbringing with all the particular neuroses that go along with that. We knew a great deal about each other's vulnerabilities and foibles. A list of hidden "shoulds" that we took for granted, acted as if they were published every morning in the paper, though no one else in the world—it kept turning out—had ever heard of any of them.

There were occasional visits. She fixed the floor in front of our fireplace where the former tenant had burned a large hole, while all the denizens of the Amsterdam Avenue pad looked on admiringly: nothing to trip over when she finished—it was so smooth.

We became lovers one night in 1956 when I stayed over at Audre's apartment on East Seventh Street. Jo was living there at the time. I can't remember what the sleeping arrangements were, but Jo had a bed to herself in the living room and at some point I found myself in it. We were making love. It was silent, dark, and would have been beautiful except for the disconcerting fact that *Jo wouldn't let me touch her.* I found this upsetting, even frightening. Every time one of my hands wandered in natural response towards Jo's body, she took it and held it so that I couldn't (didn't) touch her at all.

In a way it was pleasant enough. Jo made love to me, we slept, and in the morning I got up and went home. But in the night, in the silent struggle between us, something froze in me, and I knew I would never be lovers with Jo again.

But now there was something else going on. Maybe a first serious affair. An affair with feelings—actual emotions—attached. Which had not previously been my way at all. First serious love affair; serious lesbian love affair. It felt good. To care that someone would be there when you got back, would come over at six for supper, would stay the night. Would fly to the door as soon as you rang the bell. That you didn't have to be "cool" and *not* ask her was she coming over, would she stay.

And so, there were many good nights, when "Chiccups" slept in her crib in the nursery and Bonnie and I bedded down in my double bed. A world of women. And safe and loving—manageable—as only a world of women could be. We slept fitfully, waking to make love or to talk all night long, throughout that fall, that winter.

● ● ● ● ●

Bonnie was a wonderful lover. I found myself in her arms, in our various beds, owning a new sensuality and range of response. The slow, unpressured quality of our days and nights, the tucked-in feeling was part of it. It gave me permission to be rather than do. To explore in a rich silence.

She was herself a thoroughly sexual creature, most at home perhaps in the world of the flesh. Though there was a certain desperation about it. As if however often she came, it would never be enough, would never bring her to the point of rest, of peace. We would make love for hours, as much out of this urgency as out of her desire to bring me to new levels of feeling. It was exciting and very absorbing, but it was also, very often, painful.

I would reach some point of satiation long before she did. Some point of longing to emerge from this cocoon of sensation, into the upper air. Or to slip into sleep. Was it, I wondered, simply that I was not sexual enough? This was the big fear of women in my time, exacerbated by Wilhelm Reich, and I often stayed with the lovemaking past any point of interest, just to see if there was something I had missed. Something else that would, at last, surface for me.

Then, too, Bonnie was so often obsessed with making love to me, with giving me some newer, mightier satisfaction, that her very urgency would turn me off, and I was at a loss to communicate this tangle of emotion to her.

Another thing: this was the first time in my life that someone truly gave me the feeling that I was special. That there was concern for what I felt, for how the world treated me, how things were going. That it was not all simply a matter of indifference. Staying cool.

This was such a novelty I really didn't know how to take it. For the most part I tried to ignore Bonnie's interest in my day, my moods, the events of my life. Like Jo, who was not able to let others make love to her, I was simply not equipped, not able to take in the idea, that the pain and pleasure of daily life was something to acknowledge. That someone was willing to talk about these things. It was hard enough to simply let the love in.

My mode had always been to tough it out, a shrug, a "what did I expect, after all"? was how I dealt with loss, betrayal, general unpleasantness. The problem with that was it never discharged anything. Tons of remembered grievances, things I'd "never forgive" even some of my dearest friends for, pain of being let down at the most crucial moments—these cluttered the air, and tended to turn my muscles into a knot.

It was interesting in many ways to share stuff with Bonnie, but I was wary. I knew better than to make it a habit. Was afraid, in fact, to lose any of my toughness. So I took her interest with a grain of salt.

And actually, it would be many years before I again encountered a partner who had the least interest in my life and its effects on my spirit. On the ongoing work. Not Roi, and certainly not Alan. Not Grant either. The years slipped by again in a tougher mode. I took my comfort where I could get it: sometimes from women friends, or the gay men in my various worlds.

The thing that Bonnie mainly was was an artist. It took a while for this to sink in, as probably the fact of my own work, its importance, took a while to come fully home to her. So taken were we with the dance of courtship. Swept up in it for months. But as we came to know each other this fact of our artistry loomed large. It was, for each of us, the root of our power.

Bonnie painted in casein. She had studied at Yale with Josef Albers and he had made her a colorist. Or more likely she was a colorist from the beginning, her own eyes and heart made her so, and Josef Albers had given her the means. Put some tools into her hands.

When I knew her, she mostly painted landscapes: painted, tore paper, collaged, and painted again—forming ten-by-fourteen mat board into the improbable hills and mesas, horizon lines, of the Oklahoma landscapes she had grown up in. She painted landscapes, and often she painted them all night long.

Bonnie had a studio—an apartment actually, but once we got together she only painted there. For "living", she stayed with me and Jeanne on Houston Street.

The studio was even deeper into the East Side, into a war zone, a never-never land. Even most of us acclimated East Siders never ventured past Avenue B if we could avoid it, but Bonnie's studio was on Fifth Street between Avenues C and D—a very cheap first floor apartment in yet another tenement building. It was there, amidst stacked finished pieces all the same size, boxes of materials and potential materials and stacks of mat board and paint, that she fully came alive.

Many were the nights that I went with her, or more often *to* her in the middle of the night, after Freddie got back from whatever he was doing. I would wend my way to Bonnie's studio, lie on her dirty yellow couch and watch her paint till the dawn light came in.

Bonnie's world and life were full of chaos and crisis. It seemed she went from one drama to another and her apartment reflected that: all sorts of objects tossed hither and yon—but her actual work space was something else. She worked in casein and she always had—precisely mixed and ready to go—something like sixty-four colors of paint in little white dixie cups, all lined up in rows in square baking pans. From the palest yellow, through the full range of reds and on to the violets, blues, greens. All the nuances of raw umber, the earth colors, the greys, graduated, laid out so carefully—I could spend my nights just looking at them, relishing the thick, luscious feel of the paint.

There was this tray of paints on a high white table, and her easel, turned to catch the dawn light, should it come in while she was still working. And the peculiar, pinkish and bluish fluorescent tubes overhead—the closest thing to "daylight spectrum" that the technology offered at that time. Pieces in progress were propped around the room on ledges and tables: Bonnie would be waiting for them to dry, for the glue to take, for various magics to happen before she could go on with them. This sense of many pieces happening at once, the plenitude, made me supremely content. I loved to be surrounded by her magic.

Loved it, and yet there was a certain nagging question: there was in this place a desperation, an overflowing of work beyond what could ever go out into the world. What *had* ever gone out. The work itself, the profusion of creativity, was the chaos.

I had seen this kind of chaos before: the overflowing beyond anything that could be sorted out, anything that was called for by the world, and had a sense of the protagonist, the artist, literally *drowning* in it. Had seen it before, but would be hard put to it to say where or when. It seemed to me that I had always feared it for myself.

I found I thought of it as a particularly female syndrome. Great work without outlet, without, also, *articulation* as to its meaning, its actual intent (and it seemed, people needed that verbal underpinning, couldn't or wouldn't look for themselves). I was used to thinking of this creative profusion as a kind of craziness.

But now, for the first time, I saw the chaos in the actual process of manifesting, and I questioned whether indeed it was "crazy" or only a particular part of our dilemma as women artists. If one persisted, what to do with the work? How carve a niche for it, if one doesn't have access to galleries, to publishing houses? How make a place if one doesn't speak the language of the critic?

There is, after all, a natural form to a life in art. Or so it seemed to me then. The work of the early years, much of which is expendable, can be lost or thrown away. Then the work of early maturity begins to pile up. If, in due course, the artist is acknowledged, there begins to be an outlet for the work, the work slowly finds its way into the outer air, evaporates from the studio, and one has the room and resources to make more. One may then have the means, too, to keep the extra pieces, the overwhelming and endless results of one's incessant creativity, in some sort of orderly array. One may actually sell enough paintings or books to hire help: get things catalogued and retrievable.

Modeling for the Soyers and others, I'd actually witnessed stages of this process. But not for women. That is, I had never seen or heard of things happening in quite this way for a woman artist.

Not all of this was conscious then—I would have been hard put to verbalize it, but it was there. And Bonnie was just enough older than me, just enough further along in the process of making a body of work, for me to take her as an example of the problem. I had seen her foundering amidst the papers and accouterments of her art, and known too intimately this dilemma, this feeling that one is perhaps, after all, just crazy. As one goes down amidst half-finished projects.

My understanding at this time, too, was that there was inevitable guilt in being woman and artist, no matter how "clear" one tried to get, and that this guilt alone would bring one down eventually. At any rate make one sick. I knew no older women artists who were not ill. Not in the 1950s.

Bonnie was no exception. She suffered from migraines, terrible indigestion, all manner of skin ailments, other less definable diseases. In between bouts of illness she painted; we made love.

● ● ● ● ●

When I arrived at her studio those nights, she'd open the door immediately. Her place was on the first floor in front, a low "stoop" of only three or four steps raising it above the street. I remember sometimes knocking at the window instead of ringing the bell—the bell didn't always work. I'd signal my presence, one way or the other, and it felt like I was instantly in her arms. Her breathless voice all over me: How *are* you? Come in.

There were these rituals. Her pulling me inside. Into the clutter, and warmth, and passionate struggles of that place. There was instant coffee (the only place I ever drank it). There was a bit of talk about Jeanne, about my work, whatever news seemed urgent, and then there was Bonnie getting back into it while I settled down on the couch. The old yellow couch, not really as dirty as it might have looked. A lot of spills, that couch had seen. A lot of encounters. With coffee. With sleepiness. With paint. With love.

I was supremely content there. For me there have been few pleasures as deep and intense as the pleasure of watching someone paint. Watching a friend paint, as Bret on Amsterdam Avenue in those days that already seemed so far away. Watching one's love paint, even more so. I felt I could sit all night forever and watch as one color was laid beside another, and all the space shifted again, and then again. That mystery.

Dance paled before it. There was nothing like it. Space shifted, took to moving, flowing, or vibrating. I could see it. I watched as the colors changed as dawn came in—and they did change, giving the lie to the "daylight spectrum" bulbs. Watched as lines and exhaustion returned with the morning to the loved one's face.

As Bonnie mixed her meticulous colors, I felt sometimes that I knew paint more intimately than the palms of my hands. Than my baby girl, the streets of my city. More fully than my poems.

I was happy as a clam to be settled on that old couch watching Bonnie work, watching the red and orange hills of Oklahoma march to the foreground, recede again in the distance, become a detail, change from brilliant to grey as a color was laid beside them—while Bonnie worked in silence, stopping occasionally for the two of us to talk or briefly touch.

Sometimes Bonnie would announce that she wanted a break, or I would get hungry, and we would venture out into the highly specialized and isolated nightlife of Avenue C for coffee and english muffins or maybe a BLT on toast. There were two all-night greasy spoons near Bonnie's place, both of them were no doubt open for more dubious forms of traffic, unsavory commercial activity, than our innocent snacks. We didn't ask.

Frankie & Charlie's was the place closest to the studio. It was more "family", with women waitresses complete with world-weary street wit and dyed hair. They dispensed advice like after-dinner mints, loved especially to counsel Bonnie and me, letting us know while they did it that they knew we were lovers and it was okay by them. They called both of us "honey". There were no tables at Frankie & Charlie's, you sat at the counter, so you never really settled in, besides the advice after a while was unnerving, like a country-western record stuck in a groove, so Frankie & Charlie's was where you went for all your shorter trips.

Johnny Longo's was a block or two further south and on the other side of the street. It had tables and a little service bar and maybe they served hard liquor. The personnel were all male and Italian and somber, and you could always find a plate of spaghetti there and a glass of wine. At any hour. If you wanted to really talk, if there was something serious to discuss, or if you just wanted to get away from the studio and read and hang out for an hour, then you went to Johnny Longo's. They asked no questions and never let on what they knew. And they never called *nobody* "honey". All of them looked like bouncers and one of them always was.

These folks were family in a way; they formed a social context for the nightbirds of Avenue C, their lives and problems. They would worry if we didn't show up for a few days.

It was a strange—and very different—night world I found my way back to, after the hiatus of living in the daytime only. This one had none of the easy playfulness of Amsterdam Avenue; now there was always the next time to check in at home, the next babysitter to arrange. I felt like I was living in two places at once: wherever I was, and wherever Jeanne was.

So I took my nights carefully and consciously. Making the most of them, spreading them over the week, the month, trying to figure out when I could nap. And I took dexedrine.

Dexedrine had always been around, had been in my life since college. Early on it was supplied by the family; my mother's sisters who worked in hospitals brought it home to us, so eager were they for our future achievements. Whatever these were to be, it was certain they would raise the status of the tribe. The entire fucking clan. I can remember to this day the bottle of a *thousand* little orange triangles in my brother's study, the gift of one of the aunts. Dexedrine, they said, wasn't a *drug*, not in that *bad* sense. It was an aide, an ally: something to help us get even more things done. Be even smarter, and even more productive. Get organized too, maybe.

I had used amphetamines occasionally and sparingly from college on, and had never made a routine of them, but in the aftermath of Jeanne's birth—when I finally felt "Dammit, enough time's gone by, and I'm still not back on schedule, not really writing as much as I want to, too tired at night by the time she falls asleep, too tired to get up before her in the morning"—then I began to use dexedrine on a regular basis. My myth, like so many addicts', was the myth of control. I figured as long as my use didn't escalate I was doing okay. And nobody ever told me any different.

After a bit of experimenting, with higher and lower doses, I settled down to a "spansule" (timed release capsule) of fifteen milligrams of dexedrine in the morning, and a tablet of five milligrams after Jeanne went to sleep. This plus some coffee kept me working fairly consistently: I could usually get up before Jeanne now, as I had always gotten up before my many roommates, do my stuff, have my silent time, then do the day with her, and hang out with friends at the pad or write after she went to bed. If I was going to Bonnie's for the night, I might take a second "spansule" then, but figure to sleep later the next day. No three-day jags for me. Having a kid just simply didn't allow it.

There is a story circulating—in fact it is told by Creeley in a documentary about the Beats—that gets this point, the addiction to control, exactly ass-backwards. Creeley tells it as a man would tell it, as a man would want to have it happen in fact, and I think it's time I told it like it was.

It happened one night I was visiting Allen Ginsberg's (this was a little after my time with Bonnie, but Jeanne was still quite small). Allen was living around the corner from me on Second Street between Avenues A and B, and I was visiting because I'd gotten a call from someone there that a few of the writers were in town—Philip Whalen was visiting from the West Coast, and Jack Kerouac was in from wherever—and did I want to come over? I did want to, and found a friend who could babysit till 11:30 that night, and went, and had a really good time. It was one of those nights with lots of important intense talk about writing you don't remember later: half of the participants were drunk, and the rest of us no doubt loaded one way or another, and grass was going around.

Jack was lying on the kitchen floor, and pontificating about this and that, and Philip would deftly cut him down in a couple of words, and they would all laugh and go on to something else. Finally I noticed it was past eleven, and time for me to go home and I said so, and of course everyone urged me to stay. Philip and Jack were leaving in the morning. I told them that I had promised my babysitter she could leave at 11:30. Whereupon, Jack Kerouac raised himself up on one elbow on the linoleum and announced in a stentorian voice: "DI PRIMA, UNLESS YOU FORGET ABOUT YOUR BABYSITTER, YOU'RE NEVER GOING TO BE A WRITER".

I considered this carefully, then and later, and allowed that at least part of me thought he was right. But nevertheless I got up and went home. I'd given my word to my friend, and I would keep it. Maybe I was never going to be a writer, but I had to risk it. That was the risk that was hidden (like a Chinese puzzle) inside the other risk of: can I be a single mom and be a poet?

Now, how Bob Creeley tells that story in the movie, is that it was an *orgy* I was invited to stay for (mixing it up no doubt with the orgy at the end of *Memoirs of a Beatnik*, or the eternal Beat Orgy that will live forever in the minds of all guys who were around for the second half of the twentieth century) and that I quickly forgot about the babysitter and stayed for the orgy.

Now what I find so destructive, and so telling, about Creeley's version is: *that if I had, as he put it, so "charmingly" opted to stay for the orgy, there would be no poems.* That is, the person who would have left a friend hanging who had done her a favor, also wouldn't have stuck through thick and thin to the business of making poems. It is the same discipline throughout—what Pound called "a 'man' [read 'woman'] standing by [her] Word".

● ● ● ● ●

It is hard, in our present era of self-righteousness, to even begin to imagine what drugs and the taking of drugs meant to us in the late 1950s. How special and, indeed, precious it was—what promise it held. Hard to imagine where to begin in the telling of it.

Recently, speaking to Jeanne, my oldest daughter, about her early memories, I said "Honey, you see, we all thought *experience itself was good. Any experience.* That it could only be good to experience as much as possible". I don't know if she did "see" but she thanked me for the information.

Consciousness itself was a good. And anything that took us *outside*—that gave us the dimensions of the box we were caught in, an aerial view, as it were—showed us the exact arrangement of the maze we were walking, was a blessing. A small *satori*. Because we knew we were caught, knew beyond a doubt we were at an impasse: where to next, Uncle Whitehead, Daddy Camus? But we had yet to take measure, find out all we could about what held us, kept us "fascinated". In the old sense of that word. Hypnotized. How to circumvent, bypass, or take on the monster.

A recurring dream in my teens: I was, alone or with others, plotting an escape from some kind of prison. Prison camp, it was all outdoors. Barbed wire and guards. After many machinations we escape. We really do. We travel far, through woods, various landscapes, arrive at a house. Where we are given shelter, only to find out that the house is part of the prison. We're still on prison grounds. I usually woke up at that point.

As far as we could see, we had been given no real information that showed drugs to be evil. Sure, some of them were illegal, but given the monstrous behaviors of the lawgivers, the nightmare years of McCarthy, the imprisonment and death of Wilhelm Reich, my personal knowledge of murder and mayhem in the nation's madhouses, the daily pious lies—given all that, there was no reason, per se, to obey the laws of the land. We simply assumed we were being lied to again.

The laws of the land were a hodgepodge of prejudice, fear, and bigotry. That much was clear. Homosexuality was illegal. It was illegal in many states to experiment in your own bed with your own "legal" partner: your own willing husband or wife. Married couples were being arrested for sodomy. Kids were (mostly still are) owned outright by parents. The dance we had all performed to keep parents and the law from ganging up on us when we were teenagers had not been lost on us. Nor had we forgotten the many friends who had disappeared: madhouses, deportation.

I did have it figured back then, though, that none of this madness could possibly last: that it would take only a few years (five or ten at the most) for people to accept homosexuality—and all free joyous sexuality, for that matter—and maybe that many years more for drugs to be legal. Better than that: for junkies to stop being outcasts. They would just be another part of the society, no big deal. Hell, I figured, twenty to thirty years down the road racism, too, would be a thing of the past. Would have to be. It seemed obvious that none of this stupidity could continue. Seemed clear as day.

But getting back to the drugs: Of course, there were "hard" drugs that we considered dangerous, and most of us avoided: heroin was seen as a big problem, mainly if you shot it. Shooting cocaine was also beginning to be questioned, but snorting it was nothing to be concerned about. Hadn't Freud and all his circle done it for years? Needles were the biggest red flag and it was easy for me to stay away from them: they turned me off. They seemed a violation of my person. My physical integrity.

One big myth of that time was: once a junkie, always a junkie. It was pretty universally believed that sure, you could kick for a while, but hardly anybody ever kicked for good. We didn't have too many samples of ex-junkies who had stayed clean roaming around New York as role models, so there was an almost Greek sense of tragic downfall around heroin addiction.

But speed wasn't really considered a hard drug then. We just didn't have that take on it. It was the 60s before we identified speed as dangerous and began to see it was as much of a "hook" as horse.

There had always been marijuana on the scene. It was around all through the 50s, and I remember my confusion in high school when someone's hysterical parents would occasionally accuse us kids of smoking pot when we'd come home late from school. Actually, we'd had no idea then of wanting grass, or where to get it if we did want it, had just been talking over our hot fudge sundaes—another addictive, seemingly innocent substance.

There was some pot at Swarthmore and lots when I moved to Manhattan. It was mild and pleasant, and in no way noteworthy. But an escalation occurred in both quality and quantity somewhere around '56. All of a sudden, there began to be a lot of real strong hallucinatory Jamaican pot on the scene. With that particular, beautiful shaggy jungle look and funky smell that is characteristic of Jamaican weed.

It upped the stakes a little. This kind of grass was like tripping (though I didn't have that to compare it to). I had my first past-life remembrances around '58, sitting in my bedroom / living room, smoking Jamaican grass with Freddie and James Waring.

All of a sudden I found myself standing next to a river, a big tree and a large flat stone we used as an altar. I thought I was in India maybe. And I'm about to sacrifice something—animal or human?—by knocking it out, hitting it on the temple with the large blunt crystal I'm holding in my hand, and then cutting its throat, with some kind of stone knife. It was all enormously familiar.

All the while I was sitting on my couch, and friends were about, and none of this was real, and I knew it—so it wasn't like acid, where none of it might have been real either, but you wouldn't know that while it was happening, wouldn't find out for a while. I dispersed the picture by speaking, as I knew I could. But I believed the memory, took it as data. Who I was, who I once had been.

Another day, when we were all smoking weed together, I remember I found Freddie at the far end of my apartment, weeping madly as he clung to the doorway of my study. "The first thing I've ever loved", he said to me, when I pried him away, half crying and half laughing at himself. "The first thing I've ever loved, and it had to turn out to be a doorjamb".

It was around this time Freddie was hanging out uptown with Doris, a Black girl from his day job on Wall Street. They were both file clerks, had struck up a friendship, and sometimes he'd go up to her place for the weekend, and come back with pot someone had sent down for a present. Freddie said the weekends uptown in this basement apartment went by with grass and lots of couches. Doris favored wigs, all colors, and there were lots of them in her house, and everyone, men and women, would put them on when the mood struck them.

The lights were low, the black and white TV was always on, minus the sound, but with all kinds of colored filters in front of the screen. People would get up occasionally and change the filters, or change the records on the stereo—they played jazz: Miles and Bird and Pres, sometimes Monk—and folks would talk a bit and sometimes dig how the TV was in synch with the music, or how it wasn't. Every now and again somebody would pick up the phone and order Chinese food, and before you knew it, there would be a person standing in the doorway, laden down with bags of egg-rolls and pot-stickers and such, and people would doze off, or come and go, and so it would continue till Sunday night. It sounded terrific. Doris had invited me and I always wanted to go, but between Bonnie and Jeanne I never quite made it.

By the time I was hanging out with Bonnie, straight-up dexedrine had mostly given way to dexamyl, a version in which the harsh effect of speed was softened with miltown, a popular tranquilizer of the time. I wasn't at all sure that I liked my ups better that way. Dexamyl had a way of sneaking up on you, disguising your jitters. It left me more open to excess, 'cause nothing told me when I'd had enough. Bonnie and I had many an erudite discussion around this issue, but basically we took whatever we could get. What came easy.

Sometimes after an extra half a tab, and coffee and english muffin at

Frankie & Charlie's, I'd come back to Bonnie's studio and curl up on the couch to write in my notebook for an hour or two while she went on with her painting. I felt tucked in—warm and fed and reasonably secure.

Until outside the blue-grey light, the birds and the trucks, announced the start of another morning in the "real" world that swirled around us like we were the rocks and it was the stream. Then we would stop whatever we'd been immersed in and worriedly check out the new day: what did we *have* to do today, what could be put off? What time was Freddie's dance class / rehearsal / errand, so I could get back home in time to be there for Jeanne? (There was no telephone at Bonnie's, so everything had to be pre-arranged, of necessity.) Where did we want to sleep—and when—if we slept during the day?

● ● ● ● ●

When things came to an end between Bonnie and me they did it very suddenly.

It was late spring of 1959, and everything had been happening in the same way for months. We wrote, painted, made love, took Jeanne and the dog for walks.

The one break in the routine came when Bonnie had, at one point, rented another, fancier apartment in Gramercy Park. It was a very pretty place with wood-paneled walls and old gaslight-style fixtures. It cost a bunch, and it gave us access to Gramercy Park, a whole new venue for walking Nails the boxer. I liked it a whole lot, but somehow couldn't see it when Bonnie asked me to give up my place on Houston Street and move in with her there. Couldn't bring myself to believe it would work.

Bonnie's family had plenty of money, but as for her getting any part of that, even the part that was legally hers—that was unlikely, to put it mildly. And I knew Bonnie was just crazy enough, and openly lesbian enough, that tangling with her straight Oklahoma family might land her in a heap of trouble.

She told me once about visiting them in the town they mostly owned, somewhere near Tulsa. After a while when she'd had it with family squabbles, she decided to leave and got into her car and set out on the freeway. In a short distance, she was stopped by the sheriff.

"Miss Bonnie", he said to her, almost apologetically, "your daddy tells me you *stole* that car". Bonnie protested that the car was hers, whipped out registration to prove it, but the guy didn't even look at the documents. Didn't bat an eye.

"Miss Bonnie", he repeated, just as softly as before, "your daddy tells me you stole that car. Now you don' want me to have to go and arrest you, so why not be a good girl, and drive that car on back to your daddy's ranch"?

Which Bonnie did, no doubt raging the while.

I couldn't see it. Couldn't see squeezing Chiccups into this smaller though very nice space, couldn't see moving out of something I could afford to something I couldn't pay for by myself if push came to shove. Which I figured it would, sooner or later.

Bonnie was optimistic: it was spring, we were in love, there was the prospect of a gallery. She discovered a renewed interest in fighting the family for what was rightfully hers. She was confident, in fact. Made like she wanted to provide for all three of us. And I can't say it wasn't tempting to think of somebody else worrying about the bills and me just worrying about my kid and my writing. But when it came right down to pulling the books off my shelves and stuffing them in boxes, I couldn't do it. I really couldn't see us living there.

This could have, in some way, marked the beginning of the end. I think Bonnie was put out by my lack of trust. My unwillingness to go out on a limb. Willingness to go out on a limb without a net and with no guarantees was one of the chief ways in that time and culture to prove that you loved someone. Really loved them. If you really loved them, you'd risk everything. Unfortunately I was to buy that myth often in the years to come, but at that particular moment I was blessed with the pragmatism and hardheadedness of a new mother and I just stayed put.

Bonnie held onto the Gramercy Park place for a month or two and I visited her there. She kept her studio on Fifth Street and Avenue C for painting, and when her new apartment went away again she took to spending more and more nights at my house.

There was one night she was supposed to come by and didn't, and it got late and I fell asleep waiting on the couch, pulled an afghan over me and slept in my clothes. She got there in the dawn: I was awakened by the ludicrous sight of Bonnie on her knees by the couch, her arms full of roses, weeping and saying dramatically "Forgive me".

It took me a while to wake up and figure out that I was supposed to forgive her for an infidelity that had occurred on that very night, and that I would have known nothing of if she hadn't brought it up, and that I was not at all sure needed any forgiveness at all. I was very confused, and sleepy.

I finally realized that the *act* might not have needed forgiveness but apparently Bonnie did. She needed more than that: needed to act out and—worse—have me act out with her, this particular unsavory style of romantic drama. She would beg for forgiveness, I would be hurt and upset. I would forgive her and she would weep. We would put the roses into an old milk bottle. Something like that.

Only thing was: I couldn't do it. Every muscle of my spirit rebelled at the very thought. It was uncool for one thing. For another, I didn't believe people needed to be forgiven or given permission to make love. And then her assuming that I could possibly think I had this claim on her made me feel cheap and sleazy. Who did she think we had both been all these months, what did she think we'd been doing? What kind of love was she playing at, or believing, that could possibly include this ludicrous, embarrassing scene? I was affronted and outraged. It was hard not to laugh at her. And too, I suppose the whole thing lacked respect.

I don't know what I said to Bonnie then, what words came to smooth things over for the moment. She had fallen too low too fast in my esteem for me to explain any part of all I was feeling, all this I suddenly understood. For me, at that very instant the affair was over, but Bonnie—Bonnie would never know exactly why.

It was as if there was a flash of lightning or an explosion, and in the aftermath the whole landscape was swept clean.

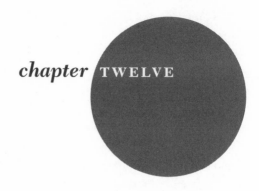

chapter *TWELVE*

One evening in that spring of 1959, my next door neighbor, Randy French, knocked on my door. Randy was very little, and very muscular, and very gay. He had the apartment next to mine—his door was at a right angle to my door and in the same corner of the building and it opened into a very long hall with the rooms on either side.

Randy and I had never been close, but I had visited his place once or twice at his insistence. Mostly he would invite you in to see his murals. Randy did very meticulous and precise trompe l'oeil murals; they tripled the feeling of space in the apartment in a very weird way. You would be sitting in what you knew to be a very tiny room, but the wall you were facing was painted with arches opening on a garden with the effects and perspective so calculated that you might actually try to walk into it. He had painted windows on walls with no windows and had them actually looking out across a street at other windows, complete with wrought iron balconies and climbing, flowering vines. I don't know what Randy actually did for a living but he could have made a fortune doing this stuff.

This particular occasion was a little different. Randy knocked and when I opened my door he inquired casually, would I like to have some peyote?

I said sure.

I had never had any peyote nor known anyone who had—this was after all 1959—but I figured it was a high and therefore probably not that different from grass.

I left Jeanne alone in our apartment—she was already asleep—and propped open Randy's door and mine so that I'd hear her if she cried, and then I joined the others.

There must have been five or six people sitting on the rug in the dim light of Randy's largest room. Preparations had already been going on. There was a large bowl filled with a mushy orange substance which I was informed was stewed dried apricots and a platter with a stack of round green "buttons" a little more than two inches in diameter. They gave off an acrid but interesting smell. Something of the earth came with them, a sense of *ground* rather unusual for a pad on the Lower East Side.

I sat down on the rug with the others. The procedure, I was instructed, was to cut up a button and chew it, slurping it down with a large quantity of apricots. The theory was that the fruit would cut the bitter taste. It didn't. It actually made the bitterness more noticeable: more pronounced and unique.

I soon discovered that I actually didn't mind the taste of the peyote at all, I rather liked it in fact. It reminded me of various bitter greens my grandmother used to cook: strong, and healthy tasting. I went on for some time, alternating between peyote buttons and stewed apricots, and only stopped when someone suggested to me that maybe, just maybe, I'd had enough. I had by then eaten six large fresh buttons.

Nothing was happening as yet (I had the sneaking suspicion that maybe nothing would) so I said goodnight to everyone—they all seemed intent on hanging out together for the duration, however long that might be—and went back to my pad.

They had warned me I might be sick, and indeed I soon was, but that seemed to be no problem. It was one of the only times in my life when it was easy to vomit, and the stuff that came out of me looked so beautiful: dark green and orange, I couldn't help admiring it. All this led me to wonder: was I perhaps getting high? I went back into the living room and sat down on the bed.

It was then I noticed that the floor was curling. Not curling in any way that that word usually implies, it was more that when I looked at the usually horizontal plane under my feet it took some ultra-mathematical curve into another dimension and went straight *up* in a way that seemed to indicate that walking anywhere might be a dubious enterprise. I contemplated this curve for a while with some interest, and then my attention was caught by an object on the straight-backed chair at the drawing table next to the bed.

With little difficulty and no surprise, I determined that there was a horse's skull on my chair and that it was laughing. Now, I had never encountered a horse's skull in "real life", but I had no trouble recognizing this one. Perhaps from the movies, or photographs of the West in those big art books. At any rate, there was definitely a horse's skull on my chair and it was definitely laughing. Not at me, by any means, I am not even sure that it was aware of me at all, but laughing at some vast, cosmic joke. Laughing at the universe itself.

The sound was huge, and awe-inspiring. Not scary exactly; but I got goose bumps. The skull was laughing at the universe, or perhaps it was the universe that was laughing. (I noted with another part of my mind, that the "sound" hadn't wakened Jeanne.)

I am not sure when it was that I lay back on the bed, but I found myself there, lying on top of the blankets, observing the universe. Absolutely pinned to what I saw. The universe I saw that night, on my first "trip" was Newtonian—though I couldn't have called it that then: for me, at that moment, I was seeing absolute truth, seeing it like it is—a universe of absolute precision and mechanical law.

A "metallic" universe I called it in my mind: I could hear the clicks and whirring sounds it made as it did its thing. It seemed to me then that nearly everything in this hard, shiny, deterministic place was built to live there. Most of the creatures throughout the worlds (and I scanned many worlds that night) and most of the creatures on this one were "armored" (as I thought of it). They had hard, protective casings, which enabled them to move with some degree of impunity amongst the gears and engines, the "wheels within wheels". But humans—humans were not only armorless, but even furless. We moved helpless, soft, through this calculated dance, were crushed by this cosmic machine so easily . . . We were so tender, I wept for us.

Many years later, I found that in one of his books, Aleister Crowley lists, as one of the magickal visions achieved by the adept at a certain stage of his/her growth, the "Vision of the Universe as a Machine". I stayed with this vision for a long time that night, watching this vast machine and the beings in it, weeping quietly from time to time for the softness of our flesh, while Jeanne slept softly in her room.

The next thing I remember is finding myself in a huge desert, like the deserts of the American West. I had never been West at this point, never left the East Coast, but the peyote cactus brought the West to me. I found myself looking at a vast expanse of crumbly, tawny sand, punctuated here and there by huge and human-sized cacti of various kinds. Then a zoom lens effect brought me close to one pad of something like a prickly pear. (I knew these 'cause we used to grow them in Brooklyn.)

I stared at it a long time, waiting, and slowly the antennae and then the head of an enormous insect appeared over the top. It seemed to me the insect had climbed up the other side of the pad. It stopped when its head was fully visible and looked long into my eyes. I felt I was drinking in knowledge, a knowledge without words.

I am not sure when, but at some point I must have gotten lonely or afraid or simply wanted someone to share this stuff with, and called Bonnie. Suddenly there she was, in the apartment with me, an over-dramatic and distracting presence. In hindsight I see that she must have been terrified: she kept asking in a distressed voice, "What do you see"? It was very annoying, made it hard to stay with the information that was still coming up. I felt astonished, awed, stretched, yes, but not scared, but when I started to tell her about the horse's skull, or the Machine, she got even more upset.

Though I couldn't have explained it I knew and sensed that there was a beautiful precision to what was happening in my bedroom up to that point. What was unfolding for me. But, confronted with Bonnie's superstitious fear, and her desire to save me from something or other, all that was interrupted. She made me weary with her middle-class solicitude. I wished she would shut up or go home, but I didn't know how to tell her. There was really nothing to do but get her to lie down, and lie down next to her and fall asleep.

I see now it was Bonnie's attitude that night when I was tripping, her fear of the mind and what might be in the mind, as much as the melodrama later that spring, that led to our splitting up. Simply, I had been awestruck, stretched and filled with grief, but not terrified. And there was no way to explain that to my lover. I saw that in spite of her genius she had no sense of adventure. Could never grok exploration for its own sake. Risk which was at the heart of my love for the world. And which would now come to be more and more important to me.

For Bonnie, the adventure was all in the studio, or in bed. Drugs existed merely to enhance the known, to strengthen her grip on the world as she knew it, not to extend the boundaries of that world at some risk. For me, that night with Señor Peyotl in the form of an insect looking into my eyes over the top of a cactus, that night with its magickal Vision of the Universe as Machine, was the beginning of a whole new relationship to things, an invitation to journey amongst familiar impossibilities.

It was also the first time I realized that *creativity does not necessarily come with its own built-in courage*, wisdom. I had always assumed that it did. Sometimes I still forget that in the flush of excitement of meeting a great artist, healer, magician, thinker. I still seek the fearless explorer in every playmate.

● ● ● ● ●

Around this time, I began to work regularly at the Phoenix Bookstore. Every day—four to six times a week, at any rate—I would put Jeanne in her stroller sometime in the late morning, fill the stroller bag with whatever toys and kid's books she indicated, throw in my notebook and a couple of pens, get the whole thing downstairs somehow, and walk across the city from Houston Street and Avenue B to Cornelia Street, Jeanne sometimes toddling alongside me, sometimes being pushed. Cornelia Street is one block long and it connects the cafes and galleries of The Village with the Italian markets: bread stores, fish stores, etc., bridging two worlds.

When I got to 18 Cornelia Street, I would greet Larry Wallrich, my boss, park the stroller by the desk and go to work cataloguing books on little index cards, or typing up mimeograph stencils for the mail-order catalogues that went out regularly to all our customers.

The shop itself was tiny, with a functioning potbelly stove in the center, precarious bookcases all the way to the ceiling, an ancient, rickety library-style ladder and books piled everywhere on tables. There was a large desk where either Larry or I sat facing the door, and behind the desk a private space: a large back room you entered through a curtain, where most of the rarer books were kept, and where there was also a cot, a table, and some rudimentary kitchen equipment (we could make tea, for instance, or soup on a hot plate back there). From this back room, a door let onto the hallway of the building, where there was a toilet we shared with the tenants of the ground-floor apartment. (There were also several apartments upstairs.) Just a toilet—one washed up at a small scruffy sink in that same back room where we napped and made our tea. Soon after I started working at the Phoenix, a Gestetner mimeograph machine also took up residence in that room, on a long table shoved against one wall.

I had worked in bookstores before, usually in some grimy old second-hand shop that I had been drawn to for a time for some specific reason. I usually wound up doing the cataloguing—thanks to that long-gone summer in typing school, I typed fairly fast and didn't mind doing it. I rather liked making sense of things, making order out of interminable piles of ancient texts.

I remember with especial fondness one upstairs store somewhere on Eighth Street, which was more or less a part of the owners' living quarters. It was run by an ancient couple: Leon Kramer and his wife, Celia, who specialized in books on anarchism. The Kramers were white-haired and bent, but full of intellect and fire. They had an only child: a daughter in her thirties. She was ostensibly to inherit their business, but did not hesitate to express her extreme dislike—indeed her hatred—of the place. She certainly had no interest in such details as I was engaged to take care of. Mostly she wanted out and when I was there she left the store as often as she could.

I loved Leon, his keen mind, our impassioned debates. He reminded me in many ways of my grandfather, long dead, but the house was too gloomy, too dark and packed and dusty; the wife was brilliant but sickly and the daughter too grouchy to be around. I learned what I could and left after a few weeks, after buying a few rare pamphlets with most of my salary.

There had been other such jobs, they had woven in and around the modeling, which had been my chief source of cash until Jeanne was born. I still modeled now and then, but not as much. I never quite lost touch with the painters, especially with Rafael and Moses Soyer, they were my fallback when I needed counseling, or extra cash, and Jeanne loved to go there with me, to name the colors of the oil paints in their immutable order on the palette, and to draw on big sheets of paper on the floor while I worked.

But there was something about having a routine, and a more or less predictable amount of money, which felt good with a one-and-a-half-year-old in my house, and so when I was offered the job at the Phoenix, I took it.

Larry Wallrich and I became good friends. For two or three years the

Phoenix Bookstore was the center of my life, the main place where things happened, where I wrote, saw friends, hung out.

The Phoenix specialized in modern first editions, which in those days meant F. Scott Fitzgerald, or Gertrude Stein. Early Pound volumes. Though it also meant the Black Mountain poets, Robert Creeley's first book, and the "little mags" that were beginning to come out of the new writing—our new writing—and flood the city. There was very much a sense that we younger writers were a part of that live tradition, a sense of the continuity of the arc from Yeats to Robert Duncan and beyond. It was perhaps the first "establishment" where we, the writers, didn't feel ourselves to be outsiders. Or even to be in a *tradition of outside*. We *were* the tradition and that felt good.

Felt good to many of us, we gathered there frequently: old scholars and printers and book collectors, old and young writers passed through the place on any given afternoon. Jeanne lorded it over many, playing and coloring, or taking naps in the back room. Sending various willing souls out for ice cream, apples, or yogurt (her favorite foods).

When I got to work in the late morning, Larry would almost always be there before me, puttering, and opening the mail. He was a gentle, kindly soul, with sad eyes and a very warm smile, and he would survey me for a long minute.

"Not high yet"? This was often his opening greeting. "You can't go to work if you're not stoned". Larry would lock the front door, and we would repair to the back of the shop and settle at the table to smoke grass, or a combination of grass and fine shavings of hashish, or sometimes (his favorite) hashish lightly sprinkled with cocaine. Smoking slowly, leisurely, talking about whatever came up, we would finally wend our way to the front of the store, unlock the door, and proceed to the day's business.

All kinds of activity came through the shop in the years I worked there. These were the early years of political stirrings on the Black front, Robert Williams was active in South Carolina, and somewhere during that time Patrice Lumumba was killed in Africa. There was a period of time when the cot in the back of the store was a drop-off for various disassembled armaments. Someone we didn't know would come in and put something—a bunch of miscellaneous hardware—under the mattress, making the cot lumpy and unusable for a while. In a day or two someone else would come by and take the hardware away again in a shopping bag, and that would be that for a week or so. There was one wonderful Black man, an artist, who often came in with the empty shopping bags, and from what I understood he would leave the Phoenix on a zigzag path and eventually get on a train going south. Sometimes he'd change trains a few times along the way. One time he called from somewhere to leave a message, he had been slowed down, we should let his friends know that things looked hot; but I guess he got through all right, because he showed up again a few weeks later, ready to make another run.

Larry was a quiet, gentle man as I have said—and an anarchist and utter radical. With everything that word meant at the cusp of the 1960s. Political exasperation, all the frustration of the 50s, looking for an outlet. And as far as I was concerned: while I held onto my healthy suspicion of all "organizations" as such, I would eagerly do whatever came to hand to help to bring down the established order. Nothing that had happened—from the times when I went with my grandfather to rallies in Bronx River Park, all the way to working here in this bookstore, with my baby beside me—had changed my point of view.

The book trade, certainly, gave one little reason to respect the law. At that period, we were in the throes of an insane, obsessive repression of the written word—you could get arrested for selling Henry Miller, or Jean Genet. *Howl* was on trial, and *The Love Book* by Lenore Kandel.

Both Miller and Genet were being published in France by Olympia Press, and were much sought after in the States. My own first taste of Genet's novels had come while I was carrying Jeanne, when Freddie Herko had stolen *The Thief's Journal* in a limited Olympia edition (beautifully bound in red leather with a Cocteau drawing stamped in gold on the cover) from his "shrink"—ironically, the very "shrink" his parents were paying to "cure" him of his homosexuality. The book had been an instantaneous turn-on: the language, the stylization, the subject matter, had all seemed to me realer than almost anything that was being written. Miller I cared less about, he seemed to me too macho to be interesting, though certainly "The Tropics" as we called them, were much sought after.

And this stuff was only the tip of the iceberg. *Cain's Book*, by Alex Trocchi was outlawed for some reason, and there were the obvious interdictions against Frank Harris, the Marquis de Sade, and so forth. The manifest stupidity of the situation, the fact that I was already breaking the law, whenever I pulled a copy of *Our Lady of the Flowers* out of its hiding place in the lower drawer of the desk and gave it to a Phoenix customer, set us up to *do what we saw fit* in all circumstances. In a sense, the bookstore was a training ground.

The Phoenix had its own underground railroad for books, its own method of importing desired but forbidden literature. Most of it was printed in France by Olympia Press, and book-like packages coming from France to the U.S. would have been suspect—likely to be examined by customs. In the system that Larry Wallrich had worked out, the books went from France to Turkey, where a friend of his lived. In Turkey, they were wrapped in small packages (about three books to a package) and *stamped with the return address of an Episcopalian funeral home in Ankara*. They were then duly labeled as somebody's ashes, and sent to an address (ostensibly a relative of the deceased) in New York City. Each two- or three-book package was sent to a different address of course (Larry had plenty of friends in New York to receive them), and the mailing was spread out over a period of weeks. It seemed that no one at customs felt a strong urge to open packages of Episcopalian bones and ashes—the books got through.

●　　●　　●　　●　　●

One evening in February 1960, I was home alone with Jeanne—writing or puttering—when there was a knock on the door, and when I opened it LeRoi Jones was leaning, drunk or stoned, in the doorway. I felt a sinking inside me, a scared sense of inevitability, almost of doom. I let him in.

LeRoi and I had been doing a dance around each other for some time. The first time I met him, Jeanne was an infant. In '57 or early '58, he and James Oliver Mitchell, the photographer, showed up at my house and introduced themselves. They were newly arrived on the scene. There had been a stint in the army, and one at Howard University, and here they were. Many people showed up at my apartment in those first years after Jeanne's birth, most of them writers or artists come to check me out, check out the scene, so I thought nothing of it. We had coffee, probably, or beer if I had any, and talked for a while, and they went on their ways.

Jimmy Mitchell came back fairly often and we became good friends. He took the only pictures of me nursing Jeanne, of me and Jeanne in the Houston Street apartment, of the apartment itself. In early 1958 he took the picture which came years later to grace the back cover of my book, *Revolutionary Letters*, for twenty or more years. He took that picture and several others, each completely different, all in one sitting. I felt at ease with him, his gentleness, his devotion to his work; I love and have loved Jimmy, all these years.

•

LeRoi was a different matter. I had gotten to know his girl friend, Hettie Cohen. I had worked for her a few times in the subscription department of the *Partisan Review*, and it gave us time to gossip. Hettie was determined to marry LeRoi. She told me she was considering getting deliberately pregnant, which I wasn't sure was such a good idea.

I was all for pregnancy if that was what you wanted, but dubious about its usefulness in making other people to do any particular thing. It also seemed like it was a good way to doom a relationship in advance.

Near as I could make out, in the world we moved in, if you wanted a baby, you had to be willing to have one on your own. Not asking or expecting anything from anybody. To my mind, "father" was a mythic, insubstantial relationship that had nothing to do with anything in the real world.

(Hettie finally did get pregnant, but of course I knew nothing of the circumstances under which that happened. And of course I never asked.)

Sometimes I'd visit Roi and Hettie for dinner. This was always a strange affair, Roi hiding out behind his newspaper, Hettie brightly cheerful, having worked all day, and come home and cooked. We all sat down to Roi's deadly silence. Afterwards we would work together on *Yugen* magazine or one of the early Totem Press books. (At this point I no longer recall which; just the feeling of the importance of the work—the importance of getting it out.) We would type and proof and paste till almost midnight. I learned some of the production skills I later used at Poets Press, while working with Roi and Hettie.

Over those years, Roi had come on to me now and then, but I had thought nothing of it. I figured he came on to everyone. Then too, he was "with" Hettie. I had consciously tried to avoid sleeping with anybody who was part of an actual "couple"; it seemed unnecessarily messy. And Hettie had been a good friend. She had been there for me when I was sick after Jeanne's birth: had come over to the apartment on her lunch breaks to help out when I needed it.

At first I had found LeRoi's flirtation almost funny: it was so transparently opportunistic and unemotional; but after a while something happened, and I began to feel myself drawn in, began to feel very attracted to him. It happened first one night at the San Remo bar, when Roi and Hettie were there, and many of our friends. At one point, glancing at Roi while he wasn't looking, I felt my heart catch: there was something of real suffering in his face, and the honing that suffering brings to a spirit; it was the first hint I had of the possible depths in him, and I knew I could fall for him—or for his pain.

(For many years after this, there had to be that look of suffering, of moving against almost overwhelming odds: pain or exhaustion, for me to find a man interesting at all. Only way I could let myself be touched by them. Some way it evened the odds between us. A man "on top of it" was an ugly thing, a monster to be avoided. Still is, in a way. They were, inevitably, so much on top of it anyway. Any way you looked at it.)

Perhaps, that night I felt safer, more secure in my womanhood, now that I had a child. It was possible to look out from that position of secured power, my own woman-function, and allow myself for the first time to feel love for a man.

My solution at that point had been: to stay away from Roi—so after that night at the San Remo I didn't go often to places where he hung out, I kept my distance. It had worked for a couple of years. When I saw him at all I saw him *en famille;* we worked on a project.

I had by this time developed a studied, casual way with guys that could keep them friendly, but keep them at arm's length. Shiny surface camaraderie that stood me in good stead.

Now, suddenly here was this apparition, none too clear-eyed, leaning against my doorjamb, like a blow in the solar plexus I had known would come sooner or later. I let him in.

Roi was insistent, and I was predisposed to fall for his line. Whatever it was. As I sat on that couch in my front room, his head in my lap, all I could do by way of defense was warn him that whatever we did now, wherever we took it, for me it wouldn't be casual. Couldn't be. For me, we were launching on something monstrous. Huge.

Big enough so that in my mind I called it inevitable, called it destiny, felt I was betraying friend and principles, but had no choice. Accepted this dawn of passion, wherever it would lead. And for me, with my view of the world, it made me an outcast. Increased my outsider-ness, because I felt I had betrayed, or was about to betray, even the rules of my community of mavericks and artists. One did not mess with an established relationship, betray a friend.

I don't really know if Roi heard what I was saying, about the depth of this affair, how far it would take us. Or how much credence he gave any of it. We spent the night together, and it was passionate and very beautiful. And in the morning light, in my kitchen, Fred Herko who lived upstairs now— Jo and Pauli having moved away—saw through my kitchen window, my hand passing a mug of coffee into Roi's black hand, and knew immediately what had happened. Only our two hands, but Freddie was angry at me for days, feeling I had turned our world upside down. Betrayed some important sense of myself. Or who he thought I was.

That very day, Roi and I began the first phase of our affair, which for me was all-absorbing. And clandestine. We took pains to meet "accidentally" at the Cedar Bar, or the Museum of Modern Art; we showed up separately at parties and left separately, only to come together later at my house. I took a bitter-sweet pleasure in still going to his house for dinner, keeping my distance, working on the magazine, or the first Totem Press books with him and Hettie. Hoping, or assuming she knew nothing about it.

At work, Larry Wallrich became my confidant. And Freddie, once he forgave me for what he considered basic stupidity. And soon after, Frank O'Hara. Frank, who had his own crush on Roi, was a loyal friend. And slowly the literary community in New York came to know what was going on; there was no concealing it, though we thought we were being so clever. In later years, Joby Kelly was to write me:

"The first time I ever saw either of you; it was at a party & you were dancing to something of Miles/ I don't even know what any more, & you were wearing white pants looking about 12 years old & both of you looked like a single flame/ there was no black or white, just the two of you & the music & your complete absorption in it & in each other".

I don't know when Hettie caught on, but she and I never talked about it that first year. I stayed out of her way, created a world apart, remained the person Roi might come and visit before he went home.

And when, later that year, there was LeRoi's first political trial, for picketing after the death of Lumumba, I said to Larry I felt I "had no right to be there". That I, like a good mistress, should stay invisible. What ancient Italian / Sicilian / indeed Arabic or West African rules was I playing out, I wonder? Where did I learn this game plan? Larry, bless him, told me I had as much right as anyone to be there, but I stayed away.

Not that it all was so simple as this sounds. From the beginning, LeRoi had other lovers, and I knew it. Over the years we were together there were many of them, both men and women I assumed, and faithful to my belief in our mutual freedom I accepted them all, became (or already was) good friends with some. Nothing was ever spoken, but I knew. As Hettie knew about me, by a kind of psychic osmosis. The taste of another's vibes on the beloved's soul. His aura. Or the etheric energy that rubs off in bed. Gets left on the sheets, somehow.

With all my belief in freedom I was in pain, of course, was wounded again and again in the course of this love. But for me these wounds were a kind of decoration. The scars of intentional battle against deadening rules, against all sense of possession of the Other, against my unruly, starving, clamorous self.

I remember one time in bed I asked Roi to leave all this and run away with me to Mexico or somewhere. He said, "You're the second person who's asked me to do that this month".

I said "Who was the first"?

He said "Frank O'Hara".

I said "You've just had two very good requests. Good offers".

There was this going away party I gave with another of Roi's lovers, a very beautiful mulatto woman, who was concomitantly the mistress of a well-known publisher. It was probably, come to think of it, the publisher who inadvertently paid for the party. We gave it for a wonderful (male) West Coast poet, who we all knew had been attracted to Roi and who was now returning to California.

We held the party upstairs, at Freddie Herko's pad. It was very elegant, and everyone behaved impeccably. At least one other current lover of Roi attended and brought some wonderful gourmet salad. We were all exquisitely dressed and very kind to each other. Not a put-on. Maybe because we each knew how much we hurt. We were united too in a secret glee that the poet was leaving. Somehow we all sensed what I for one knew for sure: how much more threatening this young man potentially was to each of us than we were to each other. How much more absorbing same-sex love could be, if it really clicked. There was no way to compete against it.

● ● ● ● ●

That spring and summer brought with them a burst of poetry. That very first morning after Roi and I "got together", when he left I found my way back to bed, and found a notebook.

> "time and time again the laughter after the footsteps
> in the snow, the moths walk stiffly
> dont palm off yr deaths head on me man . . ."

Wrote all five parts of a long poem, "The Jungle", that morning without stopping, writing under the three bare lightbulbs that lit my room, sitting on my stained and rumpled bed in the dark, chilly February dawn. Finding there, on the page, a world without shame, beyond good and evil. A world where things, in all their intensities, just *were* whatever they were. Where I could be who I was, without pulling punches, where there was room for my cynicism, my bitterness and my strength, as well as for the vision and the passion.

Perhaps I had known this before about poetry, how willing it is to contain all paradoxes, how adept at dancing with all intensities, holding them "like a fly in amber"—but alive, a dancing fly in eternally liquid amber—for all time to come. Perhaps I had already known this, but now, in the first flush of this love affair, this experience of love coemergent with love's end, of joy born with instantaneous regret and bitterness and, yes, nostalgia for what was still here, still warm under my hands, I found the poem in a new way, and it found me.

"The Jungle", "The Ballroom", "The Party", "The Beach", "Lord Jim", "The Yeoman of the Guard", "Blackout"—all of them substantial poems, where long lines sang, and I did not seek to "understand" the images that danced on the pages. Over the next few months this new work astonished me. LeRoi and I began a dialogue—often painful—in our poems that went on for many years, went on past our finally leaving each other. And parts of that dialogue found their way into the issues of *Yugen* we pasted up together.

These new poems of mine, with their longer lines and almost deadly certainty, had already begun before Roi knocked on my door. They had begun with my first peyote trip, and with the vast permission I had found in Jimmy Waring's "composition classes". But now, as my emotional life came to a strong, though temporary, focus—this new work, too, came to a fruition: a powerful voice found its way through me and into the world. The first of many voices that would speak through me, now that I no longer sought to control the poem.

For isn't it not that we "find our voice" as poetry teachers are so fond of saying, but rather that voices find us, and perhaps we welcome them? Is not poetry a dance from possession to possession—"obsession" in the full sense the word had in nineteenth-century magick? We are "ridden" as by the gods.

One of the mistakes I made at that time, and for a long time after, a mistake many artists make to the end of their days, was thinking that surrendering control of the poem was and should be concomitant with surrendering control of my life. From that time onward for many years, I was totally available to the emotional currents of my being: would go where they led me without question. Almost without hesitation. It was, simply, an article of faith in the only religion I knew. Religion of art. Interwoven inextricably now with the religion of passion. Of love.

Who was she, this young woman, so fierce, so certain, so swept away? Who would she then have said she was? Should anyone have thought to ask.

She defined herself as a duo: herself and the child. She defined herself as her work. Aside from this, had no other clear expectations. Stepped into the "love affair" not knowing where it would lead. How she would hold her own, but sure that she would somehow. As years before she had stepped into the work.

Holding her own meant keeping the work going somehow. Not allowing it to be snowed under by the work of her lover. Or his demands. Holding her own meant being there for the child. These two requirements that shaped her life.

Among her peers, her immediate friends, there were no women with her certainty. No women writers who were *artists first,* who held to their work as to their very souls. There were writers and would-be writers among the women, but they held other, alien priorities, assumptions. The assumption that Art (always the capital A) was compatible with comfort, a nice house in the suburbs; all this poverty and struggle was a kind of a trial period, something you passed through on your way to better things. (Like going to medical school.) The assumption that there truly *were* better things.

Those women were present and articulate, and friendship with them was possible, though bewildering. Led to enmeshment in the "eight worldly concerns": gain and loss, pleasure and pain, praise and blame, fame and obscurity. Those eight obsessions could cloud the artist's mind, and though she didn't know them by name, she already knew that about them.

And then there were the women who while throwing themselves utterly into their work threw themselves concomitantly into drugs (heroin usually) and sometimes into prostitution to pay for the drugs. Sirens of the scene, glamorous seductresses who found themselves destitute, sick, discarded and quickly dead, poems scattered on the wind. Or locked up again and again in some Long Island madhouse.

These women, while venturing further in the work than their middle-class sisters, fell prey to the same delusion: that *there was something a man could do for them* that they couldn't do for themselves. And in these ones, too, there was a gnawing uncertainty—"lack of self-esteem" we say today, as if that explained or solved anything at all. They literally threw themselves away for a smile or a song.

In a way she knew she was lucky. There was this fierce determination in her. And too she had waited till she had a child before she ever loved a man. The commitment, then, to Jeanne echoed and doubled the commitment to writing, and while she might have set her own work aside for someone else, she never could or would set her daughter aside. Poetry and Jeanne became inextricably one: her life, self-defined. She held on, carved her own path, with or without role models.

On the periphery of her vision there were the women painters: Grace Hartigan, Joan Mitchell, Helen Frankenthaler, Elaine de Kooning. Who had carved out some kind of precarious independence. Who defined themselves by themselves and by their work. Whatever the struggles of their shaky hearts. She saw herself mirrored in them and took heart, as she saw/heard herself in the women blues singers: Sara Martin, Trixie Smith, Ida Cox.

The lyrics, and then, too, the biographies. And to this day, I am inspired by those blues tales: "Then I stopped singing, worked in the mill for a while. Oh, about twelve, maybe twenty years. Then Mr. Whiteman So-and-So came looking for me and I made another record".

Felt more kinship to this notion of the artist, the writing—still do—than any model propagated in the art world, over the past three hundred years, or so. That the work is a part of the life, and you have leave to stop it, become a hobo, a mother, disappear, get sick, strung out, and you have leave to go back to it, and maybe you'll be as good as you were before. Maybe you'll be even better. Because in one sense, one part of yourself, you never do stop. What you don't control is the spirit, the voices, coming through you.

All through my two and a half years with Roi there was magick, but it seems to me now that the best of it was concentrated in those first two or three months. Before the world stepped in. Before each of us, our programs and agendas, gave the thing a predictable shape.

He would come late, and often come stoned. Sometimes just make it to my house and fall asleep in his clothes across me and the bed. He would come angry and intense, from some encounter. Some confrontation with the straight white world. He would come for the evening with time enough for food, wine, talk, before lovemaking, or would arrive at 3 A.M. and leave at 4. But what was perfect and inviolable about those first months was the feeling, a depth of feeling you can't fake. Later, I would wonder where he was at or what he felt, but then I didn't have to: there was no counterfeiting the energy in the air.

We didn't talk much, didn't have a language of feeling at all, and my few attempts were cut short by Roi, his cool, his contempt for the speech of emotion: "middle-class" he would call it. What we had was gestural language, a kind of metaphor.

"You smell like the sea", he told me once. "Have you come from the bottom of the sea"?

And often he would call me Lady Day.

We often made love to her music, especially the fiercer, sadder pieces, the last records: "Willow Weep for Me" and "Strange Fruit", on an LP that had her on one side only, that I carried with me everywhere for years, till a junkie biker staying at my house, lover of one of my daughters, made off with it.

At that time I was only half aware that the songs carried the bitterness, the dilemma of our "interracial" love, as well as the outsider-ness of our social situation: Roi was, after all, a "married man". I accepted the otherness of our blackness/whiteness without question, amidst the scowls of my neighbors when we kissed in the doorway of my apartment, the blind bigotry of my "block" on the Lower East Side, of all the surrounding blocks, seas of Indo-European ethnicity that washed against the oases where I and my friends lived, worked, drank coffee, danced together. Made love. Learned, or sought to learn, each other's hearts.

Knew only there was no world where it was simply okay for us. Not for our black and whiteness. Not for me, a single woman with a child.

As for me I kept my images of Roi, of the two of us, to myself, except for the poems where I could always disclaim them. Say they were a device—just part of the poem. But I saw us as eternal and archetypal lovers. Myth-making. At least as significant as Mary and Shelley. Outside the law, like Tristan and Isolde.

> "Shiva
> Braiding and unbraiding
> Uma's hair."

Years later, some months after Dominique's birth, we stood naked in the light of the front room, in another apartment on East Fourth Street, and in the light of day, in the piercing heartbreak of "Willow", moved each of us our mouths slowly, all over the other's body, memorizing the sculpture of our separate flesh with tongues, with lips. Saying goodbye, and subliminally knowing it.

●　●　●　●　●

Light dappled as through leaves, through which I catch glimpses of the action, the flavor of that life. To be *available* simply to it, as I was available then.

Available to LeRoi, as I had been for the past two years and more to Jeanne, as I had been for more than ten years to the poem—not my timing but theirs/its. His key in the lock, 2 A.M. or ten in the morning. Her cry in the night, walk in the park with me and Freddie in the afternoon.

And I drop what I am doing, drop even the poem for either of them. As I drop all else for the poem.

Make love, make coffee. Make a painting with my daughter. As also a soup, for the friends who still drop in. Clear the friends out when necessary when Roi wants to come by. And often, wait alone while no one comes. Having sent everyone else away. The rules of the game.

To be available, a woman's art I saw as a discipline, a spiritual path. To be available, but stay on course somehow. Self-defined in the midst of it all: my work, my life.

So that, a few years later, when I was asked to articulate a poetics for some important publication, I could only write: THE REQUIREMENTS OF OUR LIFE IS THE FORM OF OUR ART. *Knowing for certain no one would know what I was talking about, what that meant. Or that the "us" was—the women.*

Much as it was also all of us, artists and makers, caught in the grind of economics, the various ugly requirements of our lives of choice, still it was most and most essentially the women. The writing of modular poems, that could be dropped and picked up, the learning to sketch when you used to work in oils.

THE REQUIREMENTS *(all of them)* OF OUR LIFE *(simply, in many ways it is one and the same life, as the requirements are not plural, but singular, hence:)* IS *(not "are" there are no plurals here, the Require-ments, a monolithic unsorted bundle of demands, formulated for the most part elsewhere, but acceded to blindly, somehow still we manage to make art "do the work" as we say)* THE FORM OF OUR ART.

I didn't expect them to get it and they didn't. It is only now, more than thirty years later, that I can speak this line as a "Poetics" and have an oc-casional friend or student nod in agreement. Get it.

THE REQUIREMENTS OF OUR LIFE **IS** THE FORM OF OUR ART. *No two ways about it.*

As later, my friend Michael Goldberg, the painter who was Frank O'Hara's friend, when asked to write a book on painting, cut it all down to the sentence: ART IS MAGIC.

ART IS MAGIC.
THE REQUIREMENTS OF OUR LIFE IS THE FORM OF OUR ART.
ART IS MAGIC.

Meanwhile I was learning to acquiesce with honor. With what I thought of as honor. To my mind, when you loved someone, you were there for them without question. Without making conditions. It was the simple impera-tive of passion. Old at least as Western civilization. Maybe as old, or older, than the species.

Roi slept around, he lied, he came over drunk or stoned and fell asleep on the bed. He didn't show up when he said he was going to, showed up unexpectedly, treated me like a peer, a queen, a servant. A less than human, don't-have-to-explain-to-her kind of being. Or sought a confidante, a place to weep. To put all the burdens down and with them the roles. All that went without saying, I took it as it came. As it was dealt. The access of feeling that flooded me left no room for hesitation, or doubt.

In *The King and the Corpse* by Heinrich Zimmer, I found an old Grail story, and saw that in a reversal of roles that was usual with me, I was Lancelot to Roi's Guinevere. It was I who had the task *not to hesitate* when he appeared suddenly, as he often did, in a gallows-cart in front of me. Not to hesitate for the barest second, not to miss a step—as Lancelot did in the story—but to leap on the cart beside him, share his fate. Whatever that might be.

I leaped. I was acrobat in life as well as in art. I leaped often enough that it felt like a way of life.

•

Of death. It was barely three months, the spring had not yet turned to summer, when I was caught up in high drama between Roi and Hettie. At her request, and in an effort to make room in their marriage, I talked one night to Roi about a love affair she found herself in, but I only succeeded in making him angry.

I sat out the storm with bravado. Then I uncurled his fist as he sat on my couch, uncurled it finger by finger, and asked, with unconscious hubris:

"Can you be angry in bed"?

No time at such a juncture for contraception, it would have felt like a betrayal of courage, the high drama I was playing out, that was meant to move toward love, toward understanding between us. Between all three of us, and whatever lover Hettie took, had taken. And all the rest of the extended tangle. Princely and dignified. I felt I could afford it. We could. Out of largesse of love, could be generous everywhere. Not to hesitate, not to interrupt this moment. We went to bed.

Hours later, to my chagrin, Roi dressed in the dark still angry, and set out to berate his wife, break dishes. Make the kind of scene I had thought was beneath us. Destroy the dream of openness and freedom. Grace to be loved, and graciousness in loving. All gone awry.

I resolved not to see him again, he had so disappointed me. So broken my image of who we were, who we could be together.

I went away to "the country" to my parents' place at Greenwood Lake, to recuperate. I had Jeanne with me, and the tag end of a book I had to finish. "What I Ate Where" a piece I was writing for *Dinners and Nightmares,* my second book, already overdue at Corinth Books. I wrote and pondered this piece, pondered what I considered the end of my affair: began methodically erasing Roi from my mind: getting out of it—a skill I had mastered way better than staying with it.

And during this process it slowly dawned on me—with growing horror and claustrophobia—that I had skipped my period: I was probably pregnant.

I felt I had seen to the essence of this person, who he was. Who I was. That the Beloved as Godhead was not strange to me. Not rhetoric. We were each to the other the door into boundless space.

Was willing to leave all that rather than watch it become a part of the squabbles, the sordid tug-of-war of domestic life.

I felt the affair had lost the brightness, the wholesomeness and pride, Grail priorities I had wanted for it. Had seen in it. And in this moment without denial I wanted out.

But the fact of this pregnancy pulled me up short. I thought I had cut loose, but there I was. There it was, whatever I did, whatever choice I made, we were bound together by it.

And there was no easy choice, not in those days. And certainly not for me. The primary thing was, I was available. As available to the imperatives of the flesh, as to my art, or my lover. More available, I learned later to my cost. But I didn't know that then.

All I knew was, that I felt the child had a *right* to come through me. To be and dance in the world. Difficult as that might make it for everyone. I had no moral imperatives as such about abortion. Illegal and dangerous as it was, it was our woman-right. But I saw myself as a channel. Through which souls fell to birth and became my guests. My darlings, for a tiny slice of time.

I returned to the city, prose work finished, manuscript in hand, and my self at a stalemate.

●   ●   ●   ●   ●

It was Roi who finally insisted on the abortion, and now, the day before I was to leave to go deep into Western Pennsylvania by myself to have it done, it was Roi who stood beside my bed and said nothing at all. I lay on the bed and cried, and he looked down at me. He had come to bring me money, two hundred dollars to get the job done and whatever more it took for the bus fare, and perhaps he hadn't counted on a scene.

"Lie down with me" I pleaded, through snuffles and sobs. "And hold me". I couldn't have looked very appealing.

But Roi wouldn't lie down, wouldn't look at me. It was as if I was in some way the enemy.

And something in me held me back, would not let me insist even then, demand that we talk about what was happening, how we felt. The sense of cool, of what was expected of me as a "chick", and behind that a kind of "respect": what he couldn't do willingly I would not ask for, force from the situation. Since my return and the ensuing pregnancy test, it had become our way of being together. There was a dividing wall between us that Roi would come to count on. Everytime. It got him off the hook and would continue to do so, as long as we were lovers.

After a short while he said, "Look, I've got to go", and I nodded and turned away, didn't say goodbye, and he went out the door without looking back.

I finished crying, and lay still in bed trying to calm down. I kept thinking it wasn't too late, I didn't have to do this. Then I got up very slowly, and changed my rumpled shirt, and tied my shoes. I had decided to go out and get something to eat—to be among folks, not be alone the night before my journey to Pennsylvania. It took me a while but I finally made it downstairs.

When I got there I was startled by the sight of Roi, standing stock-still on the traffic island in the middle of Houston Street, staring at my building. Staring, it seemed to me, up at my windows. Immobile.

He didn't see me and I didn't speak to him. Just wended my way towards a warm, lighted place, some food and hopefully a few friends. All the time wondering what was in his heart.

Abortions in those days were held to be simply women's business. Something you didn't talk about, didn't "lay on" anyone else, especially not the men. One of the unsung, unspoken, ways women risked their lives. Without making too much of it. Maybe you never used protection, for any number of reasons. Maybe you did and, like me, you didn't bother on that particular occasion, particular night, because you wanted to make a gesture, didn't want to interrupt a delicate situation where emotions ran high. Didn't want to seem to be thinking of yourself at such an important moment.

For me, I had always gone to bed with any lover knowing I could become pregnant, knowing I could die, over the encounter. However casual the immediate feeling. I had often looked at that squarely. I felt it was the only way one could look at love. Could see it clearly as it was, a life-and-death matter. So, I had made it a rule not to make love if I wouldn't have wanted the baby, not to do it if I wasn't willing to die.

Everytime you made love you risked your life. Or risked changing the rest of your life. And here it was.

As for me, I was torn apart. Though intellectually I had always held firmly there was nothing wrong with abortion, as woman I felt myself so much the *channel* of new life, the door into the world; as budding Hindu or Buddhist, I saw all life as so sacred; as the artist I was I felt so deeply that whatever happens has its reasons, and that if you "go with it" everything will be taken care of—that there was no way my having an abortion made sense. And too, as lover, everything in me screamed that I wanted this baby, wanted something of this man to keep, to love and live with.

I had already given up the notion that we would ever "be together"; it was bitterly clear to me that that was not what Roi wanted. Although he was unhappy where he was. I, of course, was sure I could make him happy where Hettie couldn't, where none of his more casual women could. Was sure, as we all were in that innocent time, that *love* could and would make the difference. Make everything okay. Nevertheless I could see clearly enough that that wasn't it, we weren't, simply, going to live together, happily or unhappily. For me it was all the more reason to want this child.

The reason not to have the baby was simple: Roi didn't want it. And though I didn't want or expect anything from him, neither support nor moral backup should I go ahead and have it, still, there was no way I could see myself going against his wishes.

Since Roi didn't want the child, I felt that if I loved him, it was incumbent on me to have an abortion no matter what I was feeling. To show the extent of my love by doing what I felt in fact was wrong. To commit what for me was tantamount to a crime, simply because the man I loved willed it so. And I would take the blame, the consequences, the blood on my hands. And not say anything about it.

It was, after all, the code I had learned, code of the Italian woman: to do what *he* wanted and take the consequences.

Something else was also going on. There was a part of me that was aware that up to that point in my life, though I had done many things that seemed odd, or strange, or even wrong to others, *I had done nothing that felt wrong, to me, myself.* And a part of me I thought was the artist part, sensed—nay, *knew*—that I had to experience being the betrayer of myself, of doing wrong, of doing something I could never justify or feel right about, if I was to understand the humans around me, stay close enough to them to continue to write and be heard.

None of this was something I talked about. Though I told close friends like Freddie that I didn't want the abortion. I would have scorned saying anything that made it seem I was asking for sympathy. Any attempt to explain or excuse myself. Asking for anything that was not freely offered.

In spite of "cool", in spite of all the taboos about abortion being woman's private business, there were those friends, both men and women, who would have willingly traveled with me into Pennsylvania (not Roi). They had offered to keep me company, help me get home afterwards; but the instructions from the abortion doctor's office had explicitly stated that I should come alone.

The bus ride was long and arduous. We drove through the mining country of western Pennsylvania, and I looked long and hard out the window. This was where Freddie had come from, where he grew up; he had been raised in Johnstown, and I tried to grok, to soak in the vibe of these little towns with their dark mountains of slag and waste, to try to know my friend better. Feel him from the inside. What he had had to push against in his maverick growing up.

Actually there was no place I ever traveled to that I didn't look long and hard at. As if to understand, to soak in, the countryside, the landscape, the towns, the rhythms of speech. The sameness and the differences. I do it to this day, though I tell myself now I do it a little less desperately. But then I looked at changing landscape as I listened to music: trying to suck out and keep the essence for myself. I thought of it as part of my job, part of being a writer.

It was late afternoon when I arrived at the designated town, and I walked down the street from the bus station to the small brick house.

I was lucky to be where I was. The man I was going to, the abortionist, was a doctor, a real M.D. it was said, who did the work he did out of the conviction that it was needed. That it was right. He kept his prices low and only worked part of the time, stopping when he got wind that the law was coming too close.

He had actually suspended activity when I first looked for him. Rumor had it that he had stopped for good, was retiring because of the pressure of the police. But then I had miraculously gotten through to his nurse, or receptionist: a kindly woman, who carefully gave me precise and meticulous instructions. I was to come alone. If I was being driven, the car could only go to such-and-such nearby town, and then I would have to get a bus the rest of the way. I should not take a suitcase, put whatever I would need for the night into my purse, plan to stay the night before the surgery, but not the night after, and expect to be out of town that same afternoon. I was to bring the money in cash, of course.

I had heard from others who had gone to see this doctor that he was a humane and kindly man, that the premises were clean (a major consideration), and the rooms where you slept were comfortable. That he was willing to see you again, or talk to you on the phone at least, if anything went wrong. And that no one there laid any trips on you at all—this was important—no blaming, and no guilt.

But I was unprepared for the fact that there would be several of us on the same day: someone else walked down from the bus station almost beside me, and we rang the bell together. There were six of us there in all, and we were given our rooms: two to a room.

That night we were examined one by one. The good doctor used cocaine on my cervix, to numb it, he said. Then I was given a sleeping pill of some sort, we all were, so that we would be well rested in the morning. I fell asleep almost at once on the narrow bed in the tiny room I shared, glad enough not to have to talk to my roommate. Hoping to hold her and the whole thing at arm's length.

● ● ● ● ●

In the dawn they did the procedure with, mercifully, plenty of anesthesia. Sodium pentothal, which I had had before at the dentist's, and liked because it was so mysterious: it erases even the unconscious sense of time, of time passing, that we usually retain even in our dreams. Even when we black out. Eliminates any sense of the event.

But I lay on the table wide awake, feeling like my heart was going to explode. Every nerve in my body screaming. Screaming that it wasn't too late, I didn't have to do this. I could stop it now. Get off the table and go home, why don't you? Just do it.

The first dose of sodium pentothal in the IV did nothing at all, didn't make a dent in my whirling brain. My grief. I was awake all right, eyes staring at the ceiling—staring at the doc and his nurse, staring out of my silence with that fixed glare I can so often muster. Glare that's even in my baby pictures. It's not too late . . .

"We're going to have to give you another dose of anesthesia" somebody said and I nodded and then I was in my room again waking up.

Waking up to groans and sobs I thought were coming from my roommate. From another room. They seemed so far away. They mingled with the sound of somebody's radio. Then slowly and after a while I recognized the sounds as my own. It shocked me somewhat that I had expressed, was expressing so much emotion. So uncool. Unseemly. I found the place in me the sounds were coming from and turned them off. There was a radio playing somewhere, and blood on the sheets.

It was still early morning, but the woman on the next bed was awake— she'd been "seen" before me. She suggested we take a walk around town, go somewhere for breakfast. The bus didn't leave till two. The people at the house encouraged us to be up and about as soon as possible: to help the cramping, and to be sure we'd be okay when we got on the bus. We went for french toast at a greasy spoon on the main drag while she told me the story of her life, and we both had terrible cramps.

Then I was home, I had made it somehow. The trip back had been a fuzzy nightmare of pain and pain pills. Now I was back in my own bed, with plenty of kotex, codeine, and chloral hydrate.

And I was of course alone. It simply hadn't occurred to me to ask anyone to be here when I got back. I had sent Jeanne away for a couple of days and had told almost no one what was happening. Freddie knew, but he wasn't around—maybe working summer stock or something. It was the beginning of summer. Roi hadn't offered to come around and I hadn't mentioned anything.

Pain in my heart far worse than the cramps. I was writing, persistently writing to the child I had killed. Had sent away. I filled page after page, in some kind of wobbly scrawl, written mostly lying down. Some kind of ritual goodbye:

> "Dear fish, I hope you swim
> In some other river . . ."

I had taken a chloral hydrate thinking to sleep, to stop crying (my eyes were sore) but it hadn't worked. I took another, but found I was still awake, still writing and crying. After the fourth I had finished the poem. My body was numb, barely manageable, but my head wouldn't turn off. Wouldn't sleep.

I decided to go out. I got dressed drunkenly, veering about the apartment, bumping into the furniture. I hardly felt it, but later I would find huge blue bruises on my hips, my thighs, from the corner of the drawing table, the knob of the front door.

I got downstairs somehow and made it out of the building, onto the sidewalk, Houston Street, where two days before Roi had stood staring blindly up at my house. Well, he wasn't there now, that was for sure.

The air straightened me up a bit. To be on the safe side, I had donned two huge hospital-style "sanitary napkins"—enough to handle a fair amount of blood. I decided to venture a walk to the Cedar Bar.

Roi was there, deep in conversation with Franz Kline. They were both leaning on the old wooden bar, drinking beer. Roi turned when he sensed me standing behind him.

I don't know what he saw in my face, but what he said was "You're never going to forgive me".

"No", I said, "but it doesn't matter".

Knowing that in one way it mattered more than anything that had happened in my life so far—but that was a place I would never let him into. That deep.

In another way I was telling the truth. It didn't matter.

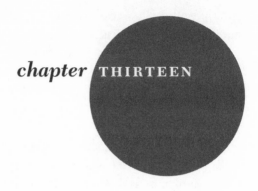

chapter THIRTEEN

Time broke there, along that line. Splintered along the flaw line of the abortion. Those three days. Nothing on the other side of them at all like what had gone before. That day to this—

The truth is: though I had thought I trusted no one and nothing, I had looked to love to be some kind of bulwark. To offer a haven carved out of honor, respect. Even truth. And nothing now held that place in my sight lines—no refuge.

On the surface, I picked up the thread of my life. Things were as they had been. Continued. There was movement of the same kind as ever in my house. Same comings and goings of friends. But if you looked close you saw it was all shot through with darkness. A kind of existential self-reliance. Core of silence, and a bitter taste, as of iron.

Roi and I also came back together, but warily and with a difference. Signalling through the smoke of our separate battles ("I woman, you Black". We are both being broken against something we cannot name.). Sometimes a gesture, a word got through, but not often. We loved the ghosts of each other, who we might have been.

I had been hurt by the fact of who I was, as surely as he had been by his skin, his fierce intelligence. Locked into a woman knowledge I couldn't share, I let him keep his secrets.

Knowing, too, he lied. Lied more often, after the abortion. While for me non-truth could not coexist with love. Was the quintessence of non-love.

Sensing he loved me, but in no terms I could understand or accept, I stuck with our dark affair for two more years. Stuck outwardly close, while my secret self watched, assessed; and the core of me went further and further away—deep inside, where there was only poetry, and secrets.

What could you expect, after all? What could I expect? Hadn't I been forewarned by Antoinette Mallozzi? Men were an indulgence, not to be taken seriously.

What could I expect? Had I ever seen a woman treated well? Treated as she should be? Not in my home, certainly, not among my parents, or their relatives, or their friends. Not among my own friends, in their various modes of coupling. No room to speak truth. For the woman to speak her truth and be heard. And be safe.

Perhaps there could be honor among friends. Among artists and peers. Perhaps. But certainly not between lovers.

I never did forgive him for wanting the death of the babe I had come to think of as my first son. Or for not being able to bear witness for me, before or after. For not lying down beside me while I wept. Sharing the grief. At least that. Sharing the guilt.

I never got to tell him about the bus trip into Pennsylvania. The blood, the eeriness and fear. The long ride home. As he had told me about landlords who wouldn't rent to him, various political betrayals that had come close to costing his life. And I—I didn't know how to make him listen.

But I now know I wanted him to be the one on that table, the one to bleed. Or at least to cover his hands with my blood, smear it on his body. Go to sleep in the smell of it, smell of our murdered child.

After all that, I was uncertain how to proceed.

● ● ● ● ●

There was, that summer, soon after I got back from Pennsylvania, some kind of poetry conference at Wagner College on Staten Island, probably the first conference to involve any of our writing community. Allen Ginsberg spearheaded it, but LeRoi was going too, as were Joel Oppenheimer and a few of the others. I had of course not been asked. I didn't find this strange then, I was often not asked to literary events, though I published with everyone in the usual places, worked side-by-side with the men putting out the magazines and books, read here and there with them on the East Side or in the Village.

As a woman, I was invisible. I took that as a matter of course.

(As I had taken it as a matter of course when Donald Allen stopped in a doorway at a party at Roi's house, to tell me that he wouldn't be including my work in the *New American Poetry* anthology. Though the work I'd given him—"The Jungle", "The Ballroom", "The Party", was certainly strong enough; holds up even now. He had been, he told me in that doorway, requested by Hettie Jones to leave me out. Because of my ongoing affair with LeRoi.

I never did ask Hettie about any of this. I figured it might or might not be true. Donald could have had his own reasons for not wanting me in the book.

At the time, I simply said "Okay". On one level I thought it really didn't matter *what* anthologies my work was in or not. The work was good, I knew, would find its audience anyhow. But, too, there was implicit my ever-present acceptance that I would carry the guilt for the affair: LeRoi's poems could be included, but not mine. He was married, which made me, by implication, the home-breaker, the scarlet woman. It was all very matter-of-course.

I nodded, and I think I shrugged. I didn't see how all that could possibly affect me, my work. I accepted the scapegoat role though in my heart of hearts I felt no shame or guilt. Only pride, defiance, a loyalty I called honor, and some kind of blind integrity: adherence to passion.)

Thus, I was already prepared to be invisible. And I had prepared myself, using some obscure, ancient Sicilian woman's code.

But LeRoi, when he came to see me before leaving for Wagner College, had suggested he'd set up a reading there for several of us—I would read too. He'd call me. I could come out there for a couple of days, and join the conference. Join him. He and I would have some time together away from the constraints of Manhattan and I would be a writer with the rest of the guys.

Of course, Roi never called. I caught myself waiting from time to time for the phone to ring, eyeing its black presence on my wall. Caught myself, and was immediately angry. Didn't I know better? Not to expect anything from anybody, to be utterly self-contained: me and Jeanne and the apartment, ready to join in when invited, ready to welcome what came by, but not expecting anything and thus not disappointed, not in pain. No, never disappointed or in pain. That was simply not an image I could tolerate. It filled me with shame to think I might let that much feeling show.

So the early summer had this quality of being in limbo. Of waiting, but not waiting, for the phone. For the first time, the joy of the weather, of the permission the heat gave in this grey place—New York a suddenly tropical city, with open windows, folks on stoops and all-night music—was not enough to restore the quality of rejoicing, of persistent, almost-embarrassing *élan* to my body. My heart.

"Let Nature Heal Life" says the persistent tee shirt of a large Oriental man who sits in front of me at the meditation center where I've been going for teachings on these summer weekends, thirty-four years later, as I write this chapter. "Let Nature Heal Life". He wears it most of the time. And I wonder if "Let" is necessary. Just "Nature Heals Life" would be enough. It just does.

That, certainly is what happened for me then. It happens so often I have come to count on it, as I once counted on honor or love. A kind of persistent, impossible return of—what? Energy, I could say, or life force, and it is that, but it is something else, something more than that. That "energy" moving in one's flesh brings its own kind of joy. Unconditional. A kind of singing in the blood, the bones.

So that I came after a while to waken again in the mornings with my heart intact. A kind of singing in me. Eager to join in the dance.

And after I stopped waiting for a phone call, the summer was very full: I worked at the Living Theatre for Jimmy Waring, and had my first staged reading of a play there: *Murder Cake* which I wrote one afternoon, part random exercise, part free association.

I had become friends with Frank O'Hara, and hung around his house sometimes in the evenings. Or walked over on Sunday mornings with Jeanne in the stroller and a fresh loaf of Italian bread stuffed in the back. Frank would scramble eggs very slowly in a double boiler while we talked about everything and nothing at all. Sliding from jokes to deadly serious without a hitch. Changing dictions and styles and lives while the coffee brewed.

I sent Jeanne to Greenwood Lake with my parents for a month and hung out with A.B. Spellman and Cubby Selby, two dear friends who were also friends of Roi's, but knew how and when to be silently supportive. We made it to at least a hundred movies on 42nd Street, sometimes wandering from theatre to theatre all night long, in search of the classics, in search of funk and corniness and high style. Grist for our writing.

Or we would sit in my living room / bedroom, smoking weed, or snorting a little coke, and talking or reading our stuff to each other. It was in one of these sessions that A.B. made the remark that "Roi wanted to be the Black Ezra Pound". He felt it was dangerous, did A.B., that that much ambition was dangerous.

About this time, A.B. and I cooked up an idea for a literary magazine we thought to edit together: we were going to call it "The Horse at the Window", and started putting the word out to get manuscripts. They were all to go to A.B.'s house, and we'd take it from there.

The poems and stories started to come in, and everything seemed like it was going along okay till one afternoon A.B. came to my place and told me he'd have to resign. I thought he was joking at first but, no. He had, he said, just read a piece he knew we'd have to reject, and the idea of doing that—of rejecting anybody's work—just didn't sit right with him. He said he wasn't cut out to be an editor. Thus "The Horse at the Window" came to its untimely end. The stack of manuscripts lay dormant at A.B.'s house.

I was writing to Peter Hartman all that summer, addressing letters to Africa, to India. As he moved from place to place on his big world-traveler adventure.

Peter had showed up on my couch about a year earlier, a teenager with melting black eyes, who was in love with Freddie Herko. And whom Freddie had loved, and then dumped, as he so often did. Peter would sit on my couch and weep, and we would talk. Oftentimes while Freddie had a lover in the apartment overhead and the bed upstairs would make my ceiling creak Peter would bewail his unrequited passion.

We had come to be friends. He was an odd one for me: monied—I was always wary of that—and also from that Other Coast. Los Angeles. I had heard nothing good about Los Angeles. But Peter was a composer and a theatre person, full of energy and surprises. A wonderful playmate. He had a beautiful split-level loft full of velvet, with a grand piano, more like a stage set than a real house. Then one day he decided to put it all into storage, and travel. A much-relied-on cure for unhappy love affairs amongst the young men of his class.

He picked himself up, as it were, and dried his tears. He was going, he announced, to India, but was going first to Africa: Egypt and Kenya and the like. He was a bit vague about it, he waved his hand.

This was quite a different matter in 1960 than it is now: there were many places, especially in Africa, where the only way to go was to hire a private car. Peter had a travel agent make all these arrangements, and invited me to come along on the African leg of the journey. He wanted, he said, to be in India alone, so that he could seek truth or a guru, or whatever. He was airily nonchalant about it all.

I indignantly refused. I felt that if I wasn't invited on the whole trip I wouldn't go at all, thank you. I said as much. For me, too, India was the heart of the matter. It was an insult to be left out of that part.

However, once he was gone, well-launched on one of those old ocean liners, the Queen-Something-or-Other appropriately enough (we'd had a champagne party: brioches from the Village, and cases of Dom Pérignon)—once he was gone we somehow became very close, and entered on a vast correspondence full of depth and passion. A truly nineteenth-century correspondence.

Perhaps it was only in my letters to Peter that I told the truth at that time. A large part of it was he was gay, and had just gone through an unhappy affair himself—I felt he could really hear me. And he knew and treasured my work, my peculiar intellect.

And most of all he knew and treasured Jeanne. That was always a test for me of a person's depth. Their perspicacity. And a sure way to my heart.

● ● ● ● ●

Toward the end of summer, while Freddie was still away and I had use of his place as well as my own, I was visited with another trauma—an ethical puzzle from one of the many worlds which touched my own.

I had never lost touch with my lesbian friends, especially the ones around Audre Lorde and Jo, and in that group there was a wondrous creature, a great beauty much lusted after, named Felicia. Fel*lee*, as we called her, was a tiny, delicate-boned mulatto woman with big eyes, a fey, intense intelligence and wild humor. She had been lovers with nearly all the folks in her circle in turn, and the turns came around now and again, again.

Problem was, Felicia had gotten herself strung out on heroin and had become a great nuisance. How to keep her out of trouble with the law, how to keep her alive, had become part of the local pastime. I stayed out of it mostly. I had a healthy fear of heroin and needles in general, and especially didn't want "heavy drugs" around the house with Jeanne in it. But there was the corny and totally predictable fact that I would always do what I was asked to do, especially if it required a kind of idiot courage.

So there came a day when several of the Village dykes came to my door in a clump, bearing a completely limp Fellee in their midst, and asked me where they should put her. She had OD'd, they kindly explained, and needed to be given a salt injection. I took them upstairs and opened Freddie's place, all the while wondering if I'd tell him when he got back. They then dumped Fellee on the bed, administered the salt injection, and prepared to take off, leaving her to my tender care. I didn't like it at all, but I would have died before admitting I was chicken.

"Come upstairs every half hour or so", they advised me, "and see if she's still breathing. If she's not, you could try giving her another shot".

"Walk her around, if you can", added someone who had an aura of experience. "As much as you can".

With that they all split, and I went back down to my place. I checked on Fellee all night long, always wondering as I went up the stairs if I'd find a corpse on the bed.

Felicia made it, though. She came to rather suddenly, and decided to try to come downstairs on her own, threw herself down one short flight of stone steps on the way to my pad, and passed out on the landing. I really don't remember what kindly visitor it was who helped me get her out of there, finally. She was breathing real good by then.

Then the fall came, everyone was back: from the conferences, from summer stock, from wherever they had strayed for a while. Everyone was back, and on the surface everything was the same, but the ante had been quietly upped.

Things picked up speed and intensity, as they always did in New York in the fall. The skies brightened and the wind came up and blew away the miasmas and hopes of summer. The angle of the sun, as it headed south, reminded us all of our mortality. That if we had any hand to play the time was now.

At the Phoenix Bookstore things were particularly intense. The world had become much more political.

Alex Trocchi hid out in the back room of the shop for a while, on his way home to Europe. There was a warrant out for his arrest; he mumbled a garbled story about shooting up with his girlfriend on a street corner—was it in New Haven? He was leaving her behind in prison, and skipping out.

He slept on the cot, or paced the small room stripped to the waist, looking for a viable vein anywhere on his torso. We kept the hanging curtain between him and the store tightly shut, we brought him food from the local restaurants, and for me part of the gig that week was going around town picking up the money various people—patrons of a sort—offered, to help him leave. Larry held onto it till it was enough, bought a plane ticket from Toronto back to England, and finally we both put Alex Trocchi on a train to Toronto.

I had trained myself over the years to be nonjudgmental, was used to impassively taking things as they were, but this tale of the woman abandoned did not sit well with me. At least, I thought, he could have waited long enough to bail her out. To hire a lawyer. But he was gone, and I never heard what happened to her.

Roi came and went from the Phoenix, angry, nervous, sometimes distraught. His first political group, ten in all, had attempted its first action, and somebody—some one of the ten—had talked. Heat was waiting when they arrived at the chosen site. They barely got out, he said, but they did all get out.

I kept my mouth shut: listened and learned. Learned that even in a group of ten there's likely a traitor. Or someone who jabbers like an idiot to his girlfriend, maybe because he's nervous, maybe to impress her. A group of ten, I learned, was nine too many. It jibed with the lessons I had learned in Brooklyn. From Machiavelli, from my father's reading of Shakespeare. From long fish dinners in the dead of night.

In Brooklyn I'd learned, too, not to ask any questions. I'm not sure where, or how, but that was in my bones, as deep as the weird love-stuff from the ancestresses. Whoever they might have been, this was part of their rule-book. Especially the women don't ask questions. They just do the part they are told to do, no more.

I did what I was asked to do and truly didn't want to know the rest of the plan. Left the overview to the men, though they weren't too smart. Would often convene in groups of ten or more.

One day that fall I went in a cab to 42nd Street on the far West Side to an army surplus store. To pick up a case of hand grenade shells for Roi.

I had a Chanel dress Peter Hartman had bought me. A copy I'm sure, but we called it "the Chanel dress". It was precisely tailored, and unobtrusive, and lightly trimmed in soft leather, and it reeked of money. For me it had become a talisman. When I put it on with stockings and make-up, and put up my hair into a smooth chignon, I was sure I was unstoppable. Unapproachable, and at the same time invisible. No one would question me.

I wore the dress for delicate operations. Wore it this time to pick up the case of grenades. Took a taxi to the store and had it wait. Paid the clerk in cash and had him load the case into the cab. Delivered the wooden box to a Village address I'd been given and promptly forgot about it. Walked home in my heels, washed the make-up off my face, and put on my jeans.

Folks came and went from the bookstore; they printed all kinds of stuff on the Gestetner mimeograph in the back. Flyers and political handouts, posters and broadsides, and in between Larry and I turned out the actual catalogues that kept the place running. We worked around whatever else was happening.

Late that fall LeRoi came to my house with a plan, and it, too, involved the Gestetner at the Phoenix. His idea was that he and I would do a literary newsletter together. We would mimeograph it at the bookstore, and mail it out to the people who mattered: in poetry, painting, music, dance, theatre, and such. The people who we thought mattered.

We got together a couple of times, went through our address books and came up with about a hundred and twenty names. For manuscripts, we had for starters everything A.B. Spellman and I had collected for "The Horse at the Window".

We needed a name, and I suggested *The Floating Bear*, which was the name of Pooh's "boat". I think there was something about animal names that year, and too I'd been reading *Winnie the Pooh* to Jeanne. Roi didn't like the name at first, but I explained that The Floating Bear was an upturned umbrella and "sometimes it was a boat, and sometimes it was an accident". I figured our magazine would be like that.

Working on the *Bear* brought Roi and me closer again. In that atmosphere of quasi-trust that is generated when you work on a project with someone. For the time, the personal stuff seems set aside.

Hettie must have felt something of this, because she asked me to drop the project. She said she and Roi were getting along much better, and this would wreck it. I knew it might, but there was no way I would stop. It wasn't as if she was asking me to give up a simple love affair. Anything that had the tag "The Work" attached to it was sacred. I felt it was more important than all our affairs. All our various personal dramas and domestic happiness. Maybe I was kidding myself, but this was passionately how I thought I felt. What I believed I believed.

I told her forget it, the *Bear* was going to happen.

• • • • •

In the midst of all this Peter Hartman had come home from the East with treasures: silk saris woven with ancient patterns in real gold thread; brooches of turquoise or opal with gold so pure it crumbled in your hand; a Tibetan *t'hanka* depicting a tree of demons, and another faded one which was an inexplicable intricate mandala with a skullcap in the center; Nepalese necklaces of bones and teeth interspersed with blood-red coral terrifying to behold.

His hands and steamer trunks overflowing with silk, with jewels and mystery; he asked me to marry him and I said yes.

He returned oblivious with a burden of tales I found karmically horrendous: tales of haggling with Nepalese holy men for magickal objects and paying far less than their worth. He was proud of all this.

The worst was his tale of a trip up the Nile on a small boat with a young and very sick boatman. After sailing the boat all day himself while the boy lay ill—and having a wonderful time by his own account—Peter refused to pay for the boat or the journey. Instead he simply said to the young man: "Surely you don't expect me to pay you, after I've given you such a nice ride". The boy probably just looked at him and coughed.

He continued telling me stories: of ostriches that ran for hours alongside his touring car in the pristine African countryside; of a Kathmandu where even tin cans were works of art that had been hammered out by hand. He told of the looted brocades of the Potala palace on sale in the markets of northern India, swarms of Tibetan refugees on the move. One of the *t'hankas* he brought back had a dark brown stain across it. I was certain it was blood.

Peter returned sure that he was in love with me, and when he asked me to marry him I said yes. There was, to both our minds, nothing odd about my being in love with LeRoi—and continuing to sleep with him—while becoming engaged to Peter. As there was nothing odd about Peter's being in love with both Freddie and me at the same time. People were complex and we knew it.

It seemed to me I could do worse than marry Peter. He had, after all, some flair I appreciated, was constantly surprising me, and he wouldn't interfere in my love life, nor I in his. As for his blind self-centeredness, I figured I could hold my own. I knew I was stubborner than he was, had more staying power. And through our intense letters while he was away, we had become friends; he knew me better, I felt, than anyone except Freddie. Certainly better than LeRoi, who never bothered to inquire at all.

There was also the fact that Peter had money, a private trust of some sort. I wasn't sure how much was involved, but it seemed likely he could take care of me and Jeanne, or at least pay Jeanne's private school bills— he had done that once already. He and his leather luggage, a great number of his magick books from storage and a new stereo, moved into my apartment. We hung the demon *t'hanka* over the bed next to the bone necklace, and proceeded to explore our mutual sexuality.

During this brief, idyllic interval, Michael McClure came through town, and stayed with us on Houston Street for a while.

I had read Michael's *Hymns to St. Geryon,* and loved his work. I loved the movement of energy on those pages, the vast abstract tapestry that he wove above and beyond his meaning. A dance of sound, of verbal energies, syllabic powers, vectors and tensors mingling, cutting each other off and flashing light on the page. And we had been corresponding. But I was only partly prepared for the meeting of minds that occurred between us when we met, the instant recognition.

It was a blast. There had been so many poet visitors (male) who were a drag, who had held forth pompously, or come on to me condescendingly, who had thought they were teachers, or rabbis, or revolutionaries, or god knows what. But here at last was a fellow mage, a kindred spirit I could sit up with all night reading Shelley, who matched my energy as we ran from the house on the corner of Houston and Avenue B down to the East River to see the sun come up.

Michael and Peter and I had an enchanted few days together. Freddie was away again, and I lent Michael his apartment. Roi came over with a "spoon" of cocaine that Peter was buying for our entertainment (in those days you bought cocaine by the teaspoon and it was incredibly pure). The spoon, as I recall, cost fifty dollars, and lasted all of us through the visit and on into the winter. It was packaged in two tiny glassine envelopes, one inside the other, that we promptly hid in a plaster of paris mask that was part of a huge collage Jim Dine had given me.

Roi dropped the coke off, visited for a while, and left. I am not sure what he thought of it all—he knew of course I was engaged to Peter, but when we were together we never talked about that. I didn't see any reason why we should, any more than we should talk about his marriage. Didn't see that it was his business, really. We were pushing the envelope of "cool" a little, I guess.

There was another friend visiting at the same time: a Canadian painter named Elsa, who shared Freddie's apartment with Michael. I remember one particularly exquisite night when Michael, Elsa, Peter, and I snorted some coke and went up to the roof of the building to look at the sky. It was one of those clear fall nights you get in New York when it is still warm— balmy as summer, with a light breeze—and we lay out together on blankets all night long, in each other's arms in various groupings, talking softly, watching the stars move, and admiring the pale blue light like magnesium flame that the cocaine drew around the edges of things. The flatness and brightness of shapes. Flat cool clarity of our minds.

● ● ● ● ●

By the time Michael went home, things had become difficult between me and Peter. Our very brief "engagement" had begun to fray at the edges.

We had an argument, as I recall, about some aspect of Jeanne's upbringing, by my standards not a very serious argument—I was used to wildly disagreeing with folks or they with me and both of us thinking nothing of it, going on about our mutual business of friendship or work without missing a beat. However, I had reckoned without Peter.

We were in bed when we disagreed and his first response was to leap up and run up to the roof of the building in his nightshirt, ostensibly to throw himself off. Instead, what he did was to lie on the roof, looking over the edge and shivering fiercely, till I came up and talked him downstairs again. I was more than mildly annoyed; found this kind of acting out uncool, to say the least.

But then—and I am not at all sure how he made the transition—he added insult to injury by folding himself into a sitting position on the bed, with his back against the wall and his knees tucked under his chin, and proceeded to remain in that position, talking to no one, for several days.

Now, as we had but the one bed, this made sleeping mildly difficult for me, and generally conducting the business of life even more so. The bedroom was, after all, also the living room. It was the room with the drawing table where all business got conducted and all meals eaten. It was the room with the couch. I did have a small study off the kitchen, but between a large IBM typewriter on a typing table, a desk, and several bookcases, there wasn't all that much room for living in it. Much less sleeping. However, I did finally withdraw to the study, as Jeanne withdrew to the nursery, leaving Peter grunting and rigid on the bed in the exact center of the action.

To my knowledge, the only time he moved during those days was when Jeanne (who was then not even four) would bring him something to eat and hold it away so that he had to reach out for it. "Well", she would say, severely, "are you going to take it or not"? Peter would move his arm very slowly, inch by inch, and take the plate, and even sometimes eat a little. I am not sure that during those days I ever saw him go to the bathroom.

Finally he must have gotten bored, because with a series of small gestures, half-sentences and grunts, he got me to call his psychiatrist (up to that point I didn't even know he *had* a psychiatrist). Said shrink asked me to hold the phone to Peter's ear, which I did, while he gave him what-for in no uncertain terms.

It seemed to have worked, because Peter came out of his catatonic freeze and took a cab to go see the guy. He saw him once or twice and then announced that he was leaving for the Virgin Islands.

Nice option, I thought. It was starting to get cold, first hint of the coming winter was coloring the air, and I was more than a little mad, and more than a bit envious. How come it was, as we would have said back then, that Peter could sit like a statue on my bed for days, discombobulating my entire household, disturbing my rest, causing endless people to come by and worry about him, and then arise unscathed, like Venus from the waves, and announce he was off to the Virgin Islands, thank you. Not so much as a word of apology. How come, huh?

Of course our engagement was "off", by mutual consent. I wanted no part of a partner who was going to turn into a cabbage at the slightest provocation; and Peter—I am sure he wanted no mate who would disagree with him. Ever.

(The whole thing had already begun to sour for him, I know, some days before the quarrel, when we were out together at some stuck-up restaurant of his choosing, and I made the mistake of moving my empty plate to one side, to get it out of my way. One *never*, he had told me severely, touches one's own dirty dish. One waits for the waiter to move it. This seemed to me to be potentially inconvenient, depending on the service, but I filed the information away at the time and said nothing about it.)

Anyway at that point the prospect of no longer having a statue in my bed was such a relief, that I affected great support and pleasure at the proposed trip to the Virgin Islands—what a great idea, dear! Just the thing. Etc. But I was seething with what I felt was justifiable rage. One of the unforgivable things, in my code, was to force someone else to take care of you. It just wasn't cool. If you were going to flip out, you did it where you wouldn't "bother" anybody. Not throw your emotions all over somebody else's pad.

So it was none too soon that he went, and none too far, and none too long he stayed away. As far as I was concerned, it should have been years.

As soon as Peter was gone, I proceeded to begin to get rid of the various things of his around my house that in my eyes contributed to his breakdown. Righteous indignation, fortified with greed or necessity—I was as usual broke—led me to decide to sell all his vellum-bound, gold-stamped first editions of Aleister Crowley. Crowley, I decided, was partly responsible for Peter's craziness. I trotted down to Weiser's Bookstore with a large armload of the stuff, and turned it to cash. Don Weiser, to his credit, tried to talk me out of it, pointing out that I might regret it later. I assured him I wouldn't.

Just around this time, Freddie, who was still living upstairs and still my daily confidant, brought home another piece of the karmic puzzle, in the form of a young model/actor named Alan Marlowe, whom he had found at a party at Jean Claude van Itallie's house. Jean Claude, a Village playwright, gave a fair number of parties, and Freddie, a theatre person, tended to go to them. Freddie was also given to sleeping with as many people as he could in those carefree and long-gone days and on this occasion he hooked up with Alan Marlowe.

And so, one morning, trotting upstairs as was my wont for my morning coffee and intimate conversation with Freddie, after getting Jeanne off to the Ecole Française, I found Alan Marlowe ensconced at the kitchen table.

Now, this in itself would have been a warning, if I had needed one. Freddie as a rule managed to get rid of his one-night stands before our coffee time, which was the half-hour before he left for dance class. So to see this blond, rather decadent-looking young man sitting there as though he already owned the house and smiling a "Good Morning" at me was enough to set my teeth on edge.

But there was something else, too: perhaps it was the same kind of feeling Freddie had when he looked out his window and saw me handing a cup of coffee to Roi on our first morning together: a kind of sinking feeling, a kind of finality, as if some piece of the puzzle had just fallen into place, and it was a puzzle that was spelling out our fates. Destinies.

Not a good feeling at all, and from that first moment, I didn't "like" Alan Marlowe. Found myself in an adversarial position to him. Freddie introduced us, and I could swear Alan sneered as he took my hand.

Alan moved in upstairs that very day. Within a few days some leavings of Peter's I still had doubts about—the tree-of-demons *t'hanka*, the bone-and-coral necklace—were in Freddie's pad, decorating the walls. Alan had "borrowed" them for a while. Had taken them over as he had taken over Freddie's house, his life.

It all happened so suddenly there was no period of "transition". There was just the time before Alan, and then the time after. My intimacy with Freddie had to find odd moments when Alan was out seeing his agent or doing a modeling job. There was no point any more to our morning coffees, no room for the camaraderie that Freddie and I had nourished each other with for six or seven years: shared puzzlement over the ups and downs of our lives. Instead, no matter what either of us brought up, Alan would hold forth upon it—"pontificating" as we came to call it—telling us what was what, and what we needed to do to put our lives in order.

I learned to tolerate him, as Freddie and I tolerated any of the weirdnesses of each other's path, but something was amiss and both of us knew it.

And so, when Peter finally returned from the Virgin Islands and came to Houston Street, he found his lifetime love, Freddie, totally engaged with Alan, and me refusing to open the front door to him. I was still angry, and let him know it, through my closed door with its changed locks. At one point, when he asked rather reasonably, if he could pick up his stereo—which I had in the interim decided I definitely needed in the bedroom/ living room—I simply said to him in my coolest tone, "Peter, dear, it's the least you can do" and he went away without it. We weren't easy on each other, any of us.

After that we didn't hear from Peter for a while, and then I heard he had gone to live in Europe.

● ● ● ● ●

With Peter gone, and Michael McClure returned to the West Coast, things settled down into a more dreary and predictable pattern. A kind of Winter-in-New-York pattern.

Freddie and Alan lived upstairs, in a welter of Alan's expensive luggage, and Freddie's dancing rags and "schmattas"; and Jeanne and I lived downstairs, doing whatever it was we did. Freddie and Alan didn't always get along too well (sometimes I thought it was the apartment that was the problem—after all hadn't Pauli almost killed Jo up there by throwing a hatchet at her?). One morning that winter, to Jeanne's astonishment, she looked up to see honey dripping down the steam pipe from Freddie's place to ours, slithering along the pipe. It turned out Alan had thrown a honey jar at Freddie. It was that kind of a year.

Freddie and I found time now and then to commiserate. Embroiled as we both were in unhappy love affairs. Freddie for the first time taking somebody seriously, had fixed on Alan Marlowe—a bad choice, I thought then, little realizing *how* bad it would prove to be in the long run. And I— I had gotten warily back together with Roi. With a sense of inevitability, and a kind of wry, half-bitter passion. Grief still running strong between us. None of the flash and excitement of the first days, but just enough feeling to keep us circling each other. Some blind hope that kept us dancing in the dark.

There was less money without Peter, no fancy dinners out or theatres, and more need to work to pay Jeanne's considerable (by my standards) tuition, as well as the monthly bills. I spent a great deal of time at the Phoenix Bookstore, earning my keep.

Everything there was also up in the air. Nervous energy. Larry Wallrich not sure at all what he wanted to do next. He'd been in the merchant marine before he started the store and was thinking a lot about shipping out again. But things had changed: there was the business, and too he had a wife, a beautiful woman named Ruby: "What if", Larry asked me, "I don't want to come back at all"?

"Best find out now", I suggested, "instead of later".

He hung in, but the store felt like a small ship straining at a rope, feeling the wind, the current, wanting to be off.

The Floating Bear immediately became a focus, set a definite rhythm to our lives. In those early months it "came out" every two weeks, and that entailed a continuous and seemingly endless rhythm of editing, typing, proofing, printing, collating, stapling, labeling, and mailing. Keeping track of returns and address changes. Often the editing of the next issue would overlap the mailing of the last.

Roi and I met often and long, reading, picking, arranging sequences of material. It was an amazing time. All kinds of stuff poured in through the mail: great, historically important poems jostled elbows with the usual dreck, and all of it claimed to be poetry. There was a large area of work we were both interested in—for our different reasons, this included the poetry of Robert Duncan, of John Wieners, of Frank O'Hara. There was a certain amount of work Roi always found more interesting than I did, some of it I called to myself "boy poems", hearing an affected macho in the voice. And there was a whole lot of mystical or magickal work that I favored, that Roi couldn't "see" at all. In the areas where we didn't agree, we tended to cut deals: you can put that in, if I put this in.

We seldom tried to talk each other out of anything (probably knew it was pointless), or talk about our different ways of seeing the poem, what we were looking for. Simply, we each respected the other enough to work with the mix. And it proved to be a good mix, have its own balance.

After the editing was over and done with, the rest of the work was chiefly in my hands. I typed the material onto green plastic Gestetner mimeograph stencils with my ancient, heavy IBM typewriter. The good thing about our "format"—eight-and-a-half-by-eleven-inch mimeograph paper—was that it was the same size and shape as the paper used by our authors, so I was seldom if ever confronted with having to change a line break or a stanza. Thus I had almost no layout decisions to make, though sometimes I would seek out a typewriter with smaller type to fit someone's poem as they had it on the page.

Then came the proofreading, which I did sometimes with Roi, sometimes with Jimmy Waring who was a meticulous speller, and had, in fact, worked as a proofreader for *Newsweek* at one time.

Correcting mimeograph stencils was painful and painstaking. You applied a liquid plastic, also green, which closed over the typing as it dried, making a new plastic "skin". You had to make sure that the schmear of fluid didn't adhere to the stencil's backing sheet, or it would tear off again leaving a big hole in the stencil just when you were ready to print. Then, too, the correction fluid needed to be neither too thin (wouldn't cover the previous typing) or too thick (you wouldn't be able to get the new word to "show through" when you typed in the correction). Painful and nerve-wracking, it was the worst part of the process and makes it clear to me that computers came none too soon.

Sometimes Roi assisted at the actual printing—especially for those first issues which were done in the back of the Phoenix Bookstore. It was a kind of social event, printing the *Bear,* was like that from the very first. Folks dropped in to chat, to help. And the run was quite short at first: 250 copies gave us plenty of extras, as well as 50 that we gave Larry Wallrich in "payment" for using his machine.

Sometimes we also collated there, in the small back room where Trocchi had hidden out. Other times, we took the sheets in boxes over to Houston Street and up the stairs to my apartment to collate. I had the stapler, after all. That large industrial thing I'd bought to put my book together served me for years. *Bears* got one staple each in the upper left-hand corner, and then they got folded in half for the mailing labels.

Freddie had a lot to do with keeping up the mailing list. It started out quite manageable, with only 120 names from Roi's address book and mine, and increased very gradually at first. We kept everybody on an index card in a box, and changed the info when needed, and somebody—maybe Jimmy—sometimes typed up labels with carbon copies. Other times we addressed the early *Bears* by hand.

I am telling all this, because I am thinking about and noticing how, though Roi and I coedited the *Bear,* and often it was he who got the credit for the whole thing, most of the actual physical work devolved upon me and those friends I could dig up to help. Most of the time. I am sure this was also true for Hettie, for the Totem Press books, in fact, before things got too sticky between us, I often helped her and witnessed how it was she who typed the camera copy, proofed (most of the time) and pasted up (always), but it was Roi's press, and in this he was not any different from any other male artist of his day. It was just the natural division of labor / and credit.

The work and the work-rhythm of *The Floating Bear* was completely natural to me. There was something familiar about it, almost as if I had, as I later wrote that I had, been a printer in some other time. As if from the beginning of printing in Europe, I had been there for it, been a part of it, that's how it felt. I didn't even think about it then. Only that it was supremely satisfying to watch something—anything—roll off the machine and know you had made two hundred, two thousand of it. Felt right somehow.

I felt this even more strongly a few years later, when I bought an offset press. But its beginnings were there, with the *Bear.*

(Or, no, it had its beginnings when I had a gelatin pad as a kid, from which you could pull ten copies of something, if you wrote on coated paper with the special colored pencils they provided. I remember putting out a street newsletter, a kind of Journal for the Block, Third Place Rag, with articles by me and my brothers. The pencils red, dark blue, and a kind of green, the "newspaper columns" drawn awkwardly down the page. You had to wait a few days for the image to sink down into the gelatin, before you could use it again, print a second page, or maybe another issue. The articles floated there, one under the other like a magic palimpsest, blurring a little as they disappeared.)

Not only the publishing but the networking too felt familiar. The linking of all of us through the magazine: Olson, Duncan, Dorn, myself, John Wieners. A kind of sixth sense of who was actually speaking to whom in a poem, a review, or article. Where it might be heading.

Years later, Charles Olson told me how important it was to him to know in those early days of the *Bear,* that he could send us a new piece of, say, *The Maximus Poems,* and within two weeks a hundred and fifty artists, many of them his friends, would read it. Would not only read it, but answer in their work—incorporate some innovation of line or syntax, and build on that. Like we were all in one big jam session, blowing. The changes happened that fast.

There was this about the networking: like the editing, like the purpose(s) of the *Bear* itself, it was a completely different process for Roi and me. Roi kept the *Bear* correspondence alive. He wove long, weighty letters around important Literary Questions. They were punctuated and spaced like Pound, or some other literary figure: filled with slashes and speculations. I have used my share of Poundian abbreviations, both in letters and poems, but I could never really rise to the Weighty Issues. I was more likely to write the day-to-day news and let the rest go by.

Again, we invented some kind of working balance. I often went to Frank O'Hara's house, there to ferret out poems for the *Bear* from amidst his clean towels, or from under the pillows of his couch (he wrote all the time, the typewriter on the kitchen table, and the poems landed anywhere). I struck up a close friendship with John Wieners which resulted in our publishing a large stack of his remarkable and fugitive work. Roi on the other hand visited Charles Olson a bunch of years before I did. He took up the political and poetic with Ed Dorn in endless letters without a qualm. Between us we managed to put people in touch with each other, and with the *Bear,* and kept the energy moving. Kept all these writers we cared about involved and informed. As the jam session continued.

● ● ● ● ●

There are certain moments that, in happening, immediately stamp their imprint on the gullible stuff of our brains, whispering "This is important. Remember this".

So it was that on a bright and gusty spring day, I walked with James Waring, John Herbert McDowell, LeRoi Jones, and Alan Marlowe to a notary's office, to complete the first steps in the process of founding the New York Poets Theatre. We were, the five of us, the founding members, and looking back I find it significant that Freddie wasn't there.

Alan had come into Freddie's apartment, Freddie's life, and colonized it: mined it for raw materials which he sought now to export to other countries, other social groups within the stratified and complex New York society. He was even then, at that very moment, colonizing the rest of us, though we didn't know it, or see it that way at the time. Perhaps LeRoi did, but he was used to coping with colonizers of one sort or another, and apparently thought he could make use of this arrangement.

What had happened was that Alan, living with Freddie and observing all of our lives, had realized that he was sitting atop a mother lode of unexploited, mostly untapped creativity (us), and saw how he could cash in on it. To do him justice, I believe he thought we could all cash in on it, at least that was the plan, and to do so, we needed to incorporate as a nonprofit organization.

So there we were, walking down the street in the windy sunshine in our trench coats, an envelope of papers in Alan's hand. There was Jimmy, tall and spectral with his pale face and long pointy nose, in his black raincoat (showers were threatening, though the sky was clear); and John Herbert, perky and determined, with his sandy hair consisting almost entirely of cowlicks and his owlish glasses; there was LeRoi moving softly, almost invisible, joking with John; and Alan very modish, in a well-cut raincoat that shouted "designer". He had put on one of his many suits for the occasion, and was, I am sure, more nervous at finding himself among so many of us than he was at the pending paperwork and government proceedings— which, however mild and non-threatening they might actually be, had made all the rest of us vaguely suspicious and paranoid. Alan had already named himself President of the Corporation-to-Be.

There is that moment in the sun. I was there—and also trench coat attired, it turned out, with my long tousled braid—probably trudging quickly to keep up with long-legged Alan who set the pace, probably a bit annoyed and suspicious, but totally loyal to my friends, loyal to the idea of Art.

Plan was, we were going to make a theatre happen. One in which John's music, Jimmy's choreography and plays, Freddie's dances, my own and LeRoi's plays, all would have a place. A theatre where Alan would direct and manage the fund-raising (he had been a gay hustler in Europe, and demimonde/society personality in New York, and seemed to know some of the ropes).

That moment stands out in its high hopes, many of which came, in fact, to be fulfilled over the next four years. Stands out in its harmony and seeming unity of purpose. Energy of our several visions.

Freddie's not being there, though, was telling.

I think that for Alan, who carried the same blind prejudices as most "straight" men, Freddie, by the mere fact of being his lover, was more or less negligible. And Jimmy and John Herbert still saw Freddie as one of their young students, which in fact he was.

What seemed a slight omission then (Alan had suggested that five board members was good, because it was an uneven number, and wouldn't lead to a "tie" vote) becomes enormous from my present perspective.

Freddie would continue to have no real place inside the Poets Theatre. Though he worked with us continuously till his death in 1964.

chapter FOURTEEN

September 7, 1994
San Francisco, 8:15 A.M.

Greyer than night out there. It's as if San Francisco is grey from all the grief all the unfulfilled dreams we brought here; they have splintered into a fine mist, they hang in the air, turn back the sun even at the height of summer. Now as we fall toward autumn and the sun comes up too late for my liking, these clouds continue to oppress me, to egg me on toward those old dreams when it seemed all important to be in a city where you could stand on a hill and simply wait for a bus, views spilling around you, the pavement dropping precipitous to the Bay and the scudding sailboats and gulls and the improbable orange of the bridge. When the rainbows off the beveled glass on a thousand front doors, the stained glass windows and gardens of paradise in even the ghetto announced we had come home, come home to earth.

I remember the miracle it was/and is—to drive through the miles of Golden Gate Park to the sea! The sea! And the waves crashing, while the seals barked and people watched from walkway and sand and the rides— the rides played their tinny tunes and went round and there was even cotton candy. And the Great Highway in those days thrust improbably through the dunes, a fragile ribbon in an ocean of sand, and when it was open and you drove that unlikely stretch you caught glimpses of wave after wave in the breaks, dips, between untamed sand hills spilling everywhere, and the wind and salt and whiteness of the light made whiter by the bank

of fog waiting out there, bending the light, and the unlikely clumsy peli-
cans going north or south according to the whim of the season—all this
washed across your mind the foreground of your mind till you were
blasted with wind and light and colors of the sea.

Anything seemed possible in San Francisco then, still does sometimes
for a moment NOW but that is rare. Anyplace where anything seems pos-
sible is bound to go, crushed by the borderguards of the permissible. But it
gleamed, by god, the roofs and towers, the painted stoops and hilltop parks
while ancient women and barefoot teenage boys chatted together on the
never-crowded buses, and we scoured the grass for evidence of other
worlds, and a parallel universe rode in every night on the fog.

When I got on a prop plane in August 1961 with an almost-four-year-old
Jeanne, I was doing magick. Was breaking a spell, a magick circle that had
been cast around me when my parents had set the parameters for college
"no more than three hundred miles" from New York. I had left college,
but had never left that circle, that radius. Not really. New England tugged
at the north limit a bit, and Washington with Ezra Pound to the south,
but that was it. I had never even tried three hundred miles west, and
three hundred miles east would have landed me in the ocean. It was unconscious. But as the plane moved slowly west it snapped a cord / tore
through a taboo, a curse I didn't even know I was living under.

I had refused Peter's offer of Africa, refused many a trip to Europe and
always with good reason: I didn't like the guy, whatever guy it was, couldn't
trust the situation. But I see now that underlying all the good reasons, all
the rationales, was this hidden and irrational taboo.

It would be a long time more before I actually crossed the ocean, but
this first journey west finally took me outside the Limit.

● ● ● ● ●

It was about noon and we were coming down over Burbank. I had never
really seen anything like it. The light was odd: a pinkish twilight haze, and
the ancient prop plane was landing in this unlikely place, a place that until
ten minutes ago I never even knew existed. My flight was supposed to
have ended in San Francisco, but—as they told us now while we omi-

nously descended in what was obviously the wrong place—they hadn't had enough San Francisco passengers when they left New York. Plenty of Los Angeles passengers though, and so they were taking us all to Burbank, like it or not. When they said "unscheduled" they kind of pushed the limits of that word.

When the next batch of unsuspecting, shanghaied San Francisco–bound passengers arrived in Burbank on the next "non-sched" flight, they would then put us all, or so they said, on a (smaller) plane to Oakland.

The first thing would be to wake Jeanne. She had traveled well—which meant that she had milked the few perks that existed on this no-perk airline (chocolate milk, a pack of playing cards, some crayons and paper) and then promptly fallen asleep against me with all the aplomb of her almost-four years, whilst I stared night-long at the stars, from the air for the first time and guessed at the ground that was going by under me.

Waking Jeanne meant half-dragging her and the carry-on bags to claim our luggage, which I would have to check again, it turned out, when we finally got on a plane to San Francisco. Then I proceeded to search out someone who worked for this accursed airline (luckily the airport was small) and worm out of them with my most acidic New York tones the probable time of the next flight to San Francisco. Turned out we had at least six hours to kill.

This was definitely *not* part of the plan—I was to have come in to San Francisco without a hitch, with all my cool intact, and wended my way easily to Michael McClure's house—but here I was, in a tiny airport, staring at a white plastic wall and a couple of posters of palm trees.

At last I made out, by perusing various gaudy airport ads, that there was in existence a thing called a "day rate" at the nearby airport hotels; that said day rate purported to be very cheap indeed, and that some kind of vehicle would allegedly come by without charge to convey one to same, and hence to bed, bathroom, and shower. With as much aplomb as I could muster, I picked up a labeled motel phone, reserved a "day rate" room, and went outside as directed to sit and wait for the van.

Outside was a whole other story. As long as I stayed inside the terminal building, I could at least pretend that I knew how to cope. But out here the air was a texture and temperature I had never encountered, the sky no color I had ever seen. Whatever it was, the air the sky—the atmosphere, I guess—it surrounded me, wrapped me round. There was no getting away from it.

The airport buildings were the corpse-white of fake adobe. Ungodly looking palm trees straggled along the roadside, like some kind of hellish caricature of California. I sat down and pulled Jeanne on my lap for protection, and we waited for the van.

A few hours later we found ourselves staring out the window of a bus that was taking us across the Bay Bridge from Oakland to San Francisco. Buildings the color of Mediterranean towns outlined the hills they clung to. A scatter of clouds, the colors of the Bay, and just enough wind to keep everything bright. It shone. This San Francisco, gone by my next visit when skyscrapers had begun to hide the contours of the land—this San Francisco 1961 burned itself on my eyes and on my brain. Became a model of the shining city.

Michael and Joanne McClure's place was a welcoming Victorian flat. We sat together in the dining room and watched the trees out back bend and shiver in a summer storm. Lightning, and brief, pouring rain. I had no idea then just how rare that was in August.

The flat was filled with dark wood floors, dark woodwork, and the light shone off the polished wood. Easier and more spacious than anything I'd known, room opened upon room. Jeanne found Janie McClure, only a year older than herself, and the two of them went off into the timeless and unimaginable games of four-year-olds. And Michael, Joanne, and I sat and talked in the sudden chill and dampness. Fresh ozone smells from the wind coming through the gaps in the window frames.

In the days that followed, people dropped in to meet me. Philip Whalen, large and friendly, just back from Japan, and a little terrifying in his knowledge of flora and fauna (in New York it was all just "a tree" or "a bird"— we never bothered with these occult designations) took me out. In his fierce but disarming way, he marched me through Golden Gate Park and up and down the streets of Japantown, pointing out and naming the natural world for me as we went, a magical incantation that brought out all the special qualities of this land.

In Japantown, we ate great fish-dominated lunches for eighty-five cents each, and then explored a garden shop that could have been a museum, full as it was of ancient imported bonsai. The tiny trees two hundred and more years old stood on polished shelves among stone paths and fountains, grey weathered wooden fences and bamboo. You would never know, I thought, that a city was just outside.

The poet Robert Duncan arrived early one morning in his cape before we had even had breakfast, and ate with us. I am sure that Michael and Joanne had invited him to meet me, but he preserved an air of lofty indifference if not downright boredom all through the meal, which made me feel dull and uninteresting and I fell absolutely silent.

Since nothing was shaking, conversation at an all-time low, and I hadn't had time to finish my basic grooming before his visit, I left the table, wandered over to the bay window, and started brushing my more-than-waist-length hair. Whereupon Robert broke off in the midst of a sentence to Michael, and said all in one breath and almost without inflection: "You-have-the-most-beautiful-hair-I've-ever-seen-will-you-come-to-lunch"?

I accepted, and accepted the premise of the invitation as well: it was what I looked like, with my ass-length red hair let down (like a pre-Raphaelite, I figured), not anything I said or thought, and certainly not what I wrote, nor even *The Floating Bear* where we published him often, that Robert was seeking the acquaintance of. My hair and maybe my Italian nose.

He wanted to show me, it turned out, to Jess, his partner, who was a painter. I had hung out with enough gay men back in New York to get the picture. I wasn't hurt, but I certainly wasn't flattered. I went to lunch with them a few days later.

I'm not sure what I had expected of California, but I took what I found and loved it. San Francisco was the most beautiful town I'd ever seen, certainly more beautiful than anything I could have imagined, and I walked the hills tirelessly, checking out numberless views, eating barbecue on Fillmore Street, finding Chinatown, spending hours in City Lights Bookstore, its small downstairs crammed with tattered literary magazines from everywhere, and in the nearby North Beach coffee shops.

I'm not sure what my longtime mail-and-postcard friends from the West Coast had expected of me either: I think I was a bit sharp for them, a bit too fierce—too quick with the repartee, and not all of it kind. I was fast-moving and "witty" and paranoid, and didn't know an ice plant from a fern. And I was more than a little used to going it alone. It was this, I think, they found weirdest. The women of San Francisco were tough as nails, but they had a deceptive softness—they moved easily, spoke throaty and slow, and usually stayed close to their men. Whereas we were alone, Jeanne and I, and even here in this kinder place I sat with my back against a wall and watched the door.

● ● ● ● ●

I was hardly aware of it, but it was terribly important for me to be so far from New York: from the constant intensities of my life there. I certainly knew that I was enjoying San Francisco: the light, the air, the easy exchange between folks, the beauty and relative quiet of the streets, but I was far from consciously realizing just *how* different it was, just how far I had come in that propeller plane.

I had no clear sense of the pressures of my daily life in New York: the unspoken perfectionism I took for granted—together with all my friends and fellow artists; the unspoken agreement to "produce", the tacit belief we held that our only value was in the Work itself. Whatever that might be for each of us. We lived for that—blindly, I might say now. Driven.

Being in San Francisco demanded a shift in my attention. It required me to learn a different rhythm. Quick, constant, witty repartee did not pass for conversation here, and what *was* conversation had holes in it— long gaps and pauses, where nothing was missing and nothing needed to be said. I noticed, too, that folks here were equally loved for their work, or for their not-working. It was people who were valued, rather than their Works, and they were loved for their quirkiness, flavor, their uniqueness. It was savored.

We loved each other for those things on the East Coast too I suppose, but we would never have let it be known. And we never created or allowed gaps—in our conversations or our lives—to savor such quirkiness where and when it occurred. Jimmy Waring did, a little—more than the rest of us—but then Jimmy, as we often reminded each other when he baffled us—Jimmy was from *Oakland*.

But most particularly, it was being away from *my* life that was important, not just leaving behind the "life of art" that New York was. I had in some way invented a world—there on East Houston Street at the start of the 60s—a way of being, that for all its satisfactions was more demanding than I realized. Or than I could sustain, though I was far from admitting that.

There was the commitment to poetry, the commitment to Jeanne, of course, those two I knew about, but, without really acknowledging them or even knowing how they had come about there were also the commitments to Roi (to be available, to be loving, to be cool, not to get in the way of anything that was going on including of course his other affairs, but nonetheless to be utterly present when he wanted me, to be beautiful, to awaken willingly at any hour for love, for conversation, to do my part on *The Floating Bear,* and on time, too); and the commitments to Freddie and Jimmy and the ensuing collection of good friends and artist buddies (to keep an open house except when I was with Roi, to have food available, and grass and counsel, and warmth and kindness, and a "real" home which was real partly because it included a child, which almost nobody else's did, to be unflappable, to write every day but never when they wanted to visit, or needed something, or when it was time for dance class or rehearsal); and the commitments to the larger New York society of artists of all kinds (to be funny, not to lay trips on anyone, not to be gauche in carrying on my love affair(s), not to force anyone to take sides—in love affairs or art controversies, to look nice at parties, to be sexy but know without being told who was and wasn't gay, to be a staunch revolutionary without getting heavy about it, not to make a fuss if my work got ignored because I was a woman).

This was just part of it. Now, writing these lines on a beautiful Indian summer afternoon in San Francisco, all of these things more than thirty years behind me, I find myself wondering who wrote the contract I am describing, and how and when I had agreed to it. What on God's earth was the offer I couldn't refuse?

So, it was very wonderful to have put more than three thousand miles between my actual embodied self and the mysterious and formidable powerhouse I had somehow agreed to be. To be here in San Francisco and appreciated by folks who for whatever reason didn't seem to expect me to be extraordinarily wise, or cool, or have the keys to abundance; who never even asked what I was writing. "Working on".

Michael and Joanne McClure lived on upper Fillmore Street, at a time when the Fillmore district had not yet been gutted. You could walk a continuous curve from the mansions of Pacific Heights to the soul-food restaurants and thriving shops of lower Fillmore. Their flat was upstairs, and right below them Jay DeFeo, the painter, lived and worked. I remember one night we went to visit her; she was at work—her vast, sculptural rose painting hung on the wall, bulging with the thickness of the paint. I almost couldn't believe what I was seeing. The deep layers of oil paint, three-dimensional, glowed in the dim light. Jay herself, reticent but welcoming. Living in that studio, with that work, she radiated power, and she became for me part of the mythos of this northern coast, its mystery.

One day Kirby Doyle came by, handsome and Irish, to visit the McClures and to meet me and Jeanne. Kirby whose rich, melodic prose was already legendary, had brought his lady with him. No doubt they had been invited by Michael and Joanne, kind guides, who, I am now sure, had plotted carefully to reveal the magic of this place to me, one piece at a time.

Kirby and DeeDee invited me and Jeanne to come out to Marin to stay at their place in Larkspur (wherever that was). I was doubtful: I was, after all, a New Yorker to the bone. For me The City was where it was at, was the place to be, and a week had already passed. I had only one more week before I went back, and I wasn't at all sure about spending even a minute of it in The Country.

But Michael and Joanne, Kirby and DeeDee were adamant: I wouldn't have seen anything if I didn't cross the Bridge. Wouldn't know where I was, where I had been. Kirby and DeeDee said they had some errands in the city, would come back and get us tomorrow.

Tomorrow found us crossing a socked-in Golden Gate Bridge in an ancient, dubious car. Halfway across, the fog stopped dramatically and we suddenly found ourselves in brilliant sunshine. Hills of the headlands brown and shapely rose straight out of a turquoise and steel blue sea. Stark and dramatic. No beaches I could see from the car.

Kirby and DeeDee lived on a narrow road that wound around the larger trees: madrone and eucalyptus. It even split into two one-way lanes for some of the really big ones. Their house of old redwood smelled of damp even in the summer. Beautiful light came through the trees, a light of everything crumbling, light of decay: soft wooden porch, cedar shingles, thick leaves underfoot. Windowsills covered with dusty stones, shells, ancient mushrooms. Glass bottles a century old dug from the earth, sand dollars, pine cones, seaweed. Assembled shapes for the hand and colors for the eye.

DeeDee I loved at once: she had that ineffable West Coast woman's glamour I so admired, but could never figure how to emulate. Slanting green eyes, straight brown hair falling into them. Laid back and laughing, soft and wise.

Later that evening her friend Marilyn Rose came by and we talked through the night, just the three of us women; Kirby had gone to bed. Talked woman-talk all night at the kitchen table: lovers and womb-talk, childbirth (I was the only one who had done that yet) and abortions, sickness and herbs, and travel, magick and drugs. Many years after, Kirby told me that he'd lain awake all that night listening and terrified: literally trembling, wondering who and what we were, really. What scared him the most, he said, was when we laughed, and we laughed a lot that night, the three of us.

It was a process of empowerment I was engaged in, though I didn't know it. Self-empowerment, and change. Unforeseen and potent, other lives beckoned me. Contrasting with the fierce streets of New York I'd navigated. These women were free as I was, didn't dream of marriage, or a dinette set, gave their love where they wished, with no hidden agenda. These folks moved slow, but with purpose, their work glinted with highlights of playfulness, their houses were full of collage and carved scraps, bits of glass in the windows flashed new colors on the walls. It seemed there was room and time enough here.

I cut a swath among them with my New York energy; they let me. I cut a swath, but watched them all the same. To see: how did they do it, this intricate dance. To keep the creative, but without so sharp an edge. It almost seemed dangerous, a risk, but a risk I hungered for.

This north country was its own nation, had its own laws. And colors and shades of green I'd never seen anywhere.

We went next day for a drive, visited the mudflats of Larkspur. Where dilapidated boardwalks wound between ancient tiny cottages. Trolls' houses in a never-never land.

We left the car, and walked the rickety wooden boardwalks to visit various friends of Kirby's. I met the moviemaker Larry Jordan, the gallery owner Billy Jahrmark with his wife Joanie and their first baby Jade. (Billy had started the "Batman Gallery", which in its turn had engendered his nickname "Billy Batman".) Gracious folks came out of their mouldering houses into the Marin sun to greet us: me and Jeanne, Kirby and DeeDee, on some mission of discovery.

We wound our way finally to a more secluded cottage, whose front yard, if you could call it that, was surrounded by indescribable "junk sculptures", "assemblages" the art world called them later. All the glowing objects of the local dump—phosphorescence of decay and change—were brought into relation here so that their magickal essence stood revealed. George Herms lived here with his wife Louise and their child Nalota, who was a bit younger than Jeanne.

Inside the cottage was like the outside, only more so. We sat down on sculptures, balanced our coffee cups on others, while Jeanne and Nalota went about rearranging the art and the kitchen as they thought fit. Or drawing on the walls. It was one of those moments of mutual instant recognition. Jeanne and I left that day with sculptures specially signed for each of us, and with an invitation to a party to be held at the Herms' cottage in a couple of days: a "New Sense" party. George and his works having been officially declared a public nuisance, the family was being evicted, and—in what I later learned was George's typical mode when faced with overwhelming problems—he planned to vastly celebrate the event.

As a good New Yorker and a non-driver, I was plenty used to public transportation, and so it was no trouble for me to swing back and forth over the next few days, from Marin to San Francisco on the bus—an easy run, digging the Bridge, the different worlds I could compass in an hour. Watching the interplay of sun and fog, of land and water in this changing place.

Jeanne would come along and do the coffee shops of North Beach with me like she did the ones in the Village. Or she would stay in the woods with DeeDee and keep house. It was all very easy.

On the day of George Herms' party we drove back to the mudflats with Kirby and DeeDee. Nearly everyone I'd met since I'd gotten to San Francisco, and myriad other folks had gathered at the Herms' house. Good California wine—cheap in those days—flowed freely. The plentiful food had been gathered for free from abandoned orchards just north of San Rafael: figs and plums abounded. There were hundreds of clams from Tomales Bay, and someone had baked bread. There was all kinds of music, and young single moms nursed babies in the sun.

We sat on George's sculptures and told each other poems. Someone shot movie footage. It all seemed simple enough: there was no "survival problem". There was certainly enough for all and to spare, and most of it was just there for the picking. Easy, gentle folk kept an eye on the many children. Good local grass came round, and round again.

That afternoon, for the first time, I knew it was possible to have it all. To have the children I wanted, as and when I wanted, and still write the poems. To live without struggle, or to have a different relationship to struggle. Watching these beautiful women with their babies, eating these figs, sitting among George's powerful work that seemed to grow of itself straight out of the ground, I then and there decided to have LeRoi's baby. To end my grieving at last, erase the abortion of last year, with the child of this. It was clear that it was my right. That I need ask no one's advice or permission, simply follow my Will, wherever it now led me.

This insight was burned in my brain, my heart and gut, by the sun, the music. The overflowing love.

The next day I packed my bags and returned immediately with Jeanne into San Francisco. Based at the McClures', ensconced in the bay window on the phone, I arranged to fly home several days early. I knew without question it was time. An urgency in my gut, no doubt in my mind. I had gotten whatever it was I had come to the West Coast for. And I was ready.

Larry Wallrich wired the extra twenty-five dollars I needed in order to change our travel date. I sat at Vesuvio's in North Beach one last time and talked with poet David Meltzer over Italian coffee. And by the next night we had boarded the plane for New York.

The next night, I had safely returned; Jeanne was tucked in her room, content to be back, asleep amongst her toys.

LeRoi came by to say hi, to welcome me reticently home with that renewed passion that separation sometimes stirs in us humans. We talked quietly together in the dark, in a flat I barely remembered, it seemed so strange after San Francisco spaces. And when we made love, I knew we were making a baby. Not the one I'd lost, but the one I had come back to make. Tuned in to my blood, to the ovum that falls like a star. Tuned in to my stars and hers, the newcomer. Love child. I had flown home, swift and early, to keep an ancient appointment. One writ in the stars. The urgency spilled over, into our passion. This time, I knew, I was asking no one's permission.

● ● ● ● ●

As I recall that autumn in New York, it was nothing but trouble.

I knew pretty right away that I was pregnant, almost always did know right away—either while it was happening, or by the next morning. This time I was very glad, but I could see the storm clouds looming ahead and I kept the news to myself for a while.

When I finally did tell Roi he was really angry, and immediately asked me to get an abortion. I said no. He had to be kidding, I figured—I'd done that once and once was more than enough.

I tried to tell him I *wanted* this baby. It wasn't some off-the-wall chance event. I don't know how much he heard, but we wound up not speaking to each other.

"If you *really* loved me", he'd said, "you'd have an abortion". I thought it was the weirdest thing I'd ever heard.

We were at a standoff, managed to get the *Bear* out, working each of us on our own part of it alone, but that was that.

I remembered now that once after making love Roi had said, half-kidding but half-serious, that he didn't ever want me to have his child, because if I did, then I would leave him for sure. I wondered at the time how he could be so sure. I had thought it was probably true, and wondered if he knew me that well. Now I wondered if that sort of thing was still on his mind. It would have been nice to think so.

Then one day, just a few weeks after my missed period, I started bleeding. Out of the blue. Just spotting at first, but there were these cramps, and the blood was getting heavier, and I was afraid. All of me, body and mind—my attention, my focus, and my Will—came together to hang onto this baby.

I found myself going to Bellevue emergency once again. But this time it was a little better. It was daylight for one thing, not the middle of the night, and I wasn't alone. A friend came with me. And Anna Butula, my next-door Hungarian neighbor, took Jeanne over to play with her girls.

Holding tight internally to my womb and its contents, I negotiated the stairs, the streets, and found a cab. Holding tight through the long wait in the emergency room.

This time, a young doctor, compassionate and kind. "Don't worry", he said. "We're going to save your baby". I felt I was in good hands, I could relax. He gave me a shot of something.

I made it home and went to bed. The cramping stopped. Jeanne slept over at Anna's place with her friends.

A day or two later, I called Larry Wallrich and cut my work hours at the bookstore in half. Taking it easy had become a priority: especially, the doctor had said, for the first three months.

The irony was not lost on me. How I was fighting to save a baby that LeRoi and nearly everyone who knew us wanted gone.

Everyone whom I'd told about it by then basically thought it was uncool and disruptive—rude of me—to have this kid just because I wanted it. I was making overt something that had been secret, had pretended to be secret, or at least denied. Not acknowledged. A love affair they could wink at, pretend not to see—and secretly therefore support—was now being shoved in the faces of "everyone". It was selfish of me, self-centered.

I had turned from the accommodating mistress they could all admire, into the one they met most often in their nightmares. The lover they all dreaded ending up with. Self-willed, following her own path at any cost. What the trip West had shown me I could do. Roi was universally pitied.

I had just gotten used to kicking back a little, reading in bed in the mornings with Jeanne, taking it slower so I could "hang onto my baby", when another disruption burst on us, seemingly from nowhere.

Early in the morning one day in October, there was a loud knock on the door. A series of loud knocks. They didn't sound inviting, and so I did nothing at all, having found over the years that the people who arrive unannounced at your door in the morning in New York are usually up to no good. They are landlords, or bill collectors, or Jehovah's Witnesses, or the FBI. This time, it turned out, they were the FBI.

The knocking continued for a while, and then stopped. Then my phone rang, and it was Hettie Jones, LeRoi's wife, calling to tell me that if anyone came knocking at my door I shouldn't let them in. I assured her I hadn't. She then said she had—it was early, and she was half asleep and had opened the door, to what turned out to be FBI men and postal agents and U.S. marshals, whoever they might be, and they had arrested Roi and the mailing list and most of the manuscripts and papers on his desk, turned the study upside down and terrified their kid.

Hettie gave me the name and phone number of Roi's lawyer, a charming man and fervent communist named Stanley Faulkner. She asked me to get in touch with him and arrange to turn myself in. I said I would think about it.

What I did next, instead, was to phone upstairs to Freddie and Alan's apartment and tell them what was happening. They offered to come right down, and since none of us knew for sure whether any feds were still lurking in the hall, I suggested that they use the fire escape which connected our apartments. They climbed through my study window in no time.

We had a confab over coffee, and agreed that it was probably a good idea for me to call the lawyer. When I did I found out to my disgust that one of the many ways the feds were playing dirty was to refuse to set bail on Roi till they had me. Roi was someplace downtown, sitting in a cell till I showed up, which made it clear that I should show up, and soon. What a drag.

I also found out that what the feds were so excited about was issue number nine of *The Floating Bear* which contained "Roosevelt After Inauguration" by William Burroughs and a short homosexual play by LeRoi. The play was actually a section from Roi's prose book, *The System of Dante's Hell,* that was still in progress.

Of course, the *Bear* was not public, not sold on newsstands or even in bookstores, so it never occurred to us that what was in it was anybody's business. What LeRoi and I had failed to take into account was that at least one of the folks on our mailing list was in prison. Harold Carrington, a Black writer in Rahway, New Jersey, never got his copy of *Floating Bear* #9. Instead, a warden who routinely read all the mail, turned it in to the postal authorities, and here we were.

By this time Freddie was sitting on my bed, explaining to a still-sleepy Jeanne that mommy was going to have to go downtown to explain something she had printed to some very stupid men. Seemed like this was as close to the truth as we could come, in kid language.

And I was getting dressed. I put on stockings, and that same "Chanel" dress that had gotten me through a few other difficult times. I put on make-up, too, this time, and a string of pearls, and my low "heels". Alan went out with me to help me find a cab, and Freddie stayed with Jeanne and fixed her some breakfast.

I had arranged to meet Stanley Faulkner on the courthouse steps. I was indignant and nervous—had no idea what was going to happen—and was scared and upset for Roi, who they'd been holding for several hours by this time.

Stanley did what any good lawyer is supposed to do for his client: set me at ease, and made me feel that the whole situation was workable. He had that combination of urbanity and charm, and fire when it was needed, that many of that older generation of left-wingers were so good at. Dignity and bravado. When he explained that this whole thing might come to trial months from now, I found myself telling him I was pregnant, and with Roi's baby, and that the trial had better not be next May or June.

Stanley played my pregnancy for all it was worth, like a lawyer in a black and white movie. He had court clerks and bailiffs and cops running around to make sure I had a seat at all times, and probably cut hours off our bail hearing by his fierce but courtly announcement that his client was pregnant and needed special treatment. She couldn't stand for very long, for example.

After I had gotten a handle on what to expect at this juncture, thanks to Stanley Faulkner's explanations, and realized that he would be shepherding us through the whole procedure, my indignation overrode my fear. I had lived too long in Brooklyn, and in my parents' house, to take seriously any of the ins and outs of the law. Short of being locked up, which I had determined was not going to happen to me today, there was nothing I was particularly afraid of. I became more and more outraged at the whole business: my perceived loss of constitutional rights. I fairly bristled. To the point where the cop who fingerprinted me, said "Excuse me" as he took hold of each and every finger and rolled it in the ink.

It was amazing and a little silly: I *was* fingerprinted, and they *did* do mug shots, and then they took me and Stanley down to where they had LeRoi.

He was sitting alone in a very small cage; some kind of holding cell, I guess. They had refused to give him paper and pencil, and that had made me feel even fiercer. Roi looked scared and tired, and it gave me pause to think that while I had been growing angrier, energized by my sense of my "rights", and the feeling that a remedy of one sort or another lay close at hand, Roi had become more and more worried and silent. I felt protective towards him; felt we were both protected by my righteous outrage.

The whole thing was over in an hour or two. We were released without bail, and after passing a gamut of flashing cameras and questions from reporters (the first time this had ever happened to me, and I really didn't like it), we each went back to our respective homes. Our lives. Jeanne had passed the day with Freddie and then Anna, giving hardly a thought to the inexplicable deeds of the "stupid men".

An offshoot of all this was that Roi and I were friends again. It's hard to stay silent and aloof from a buddy you've shared a bust with. And especially a bust for a good cause, in what you both conceive to be the line of duty.

Roi still wanted me to get an abortion, but we simply didn't talk about that side of things at all.

• • • • •

There was a time not many years back when my son Rudi turned re-proachfully to me to ask "Why didn't somebody tell me it wasn't always going to be like that? That those times were going to end"?

He was talking about his childhood, the freedom and abundance we had all experienced in the 70s. He said, "That's how the world was when I started. I didn't know—how could I—that it was ever going to be different".

There was something like that going on in the early 60s in Manhattan, and sometimes, now, when I find myself in a dearth of the kinds of friendships I had known and had so taken for granted, a mutuality of art and creation, I feel something like heartbreak, something like *Why didn't somebody tell me it wasn't always going to be like that?*

That there weren't always going to be more great poets, musicians, dancers, painters, at my door, on my couch, than I knew what to do with. There wasn't always going to be time later to go back to the conversation, the unfinished collaboration. More time to sit at a rehearsal or a jam session, and scribble in my notebook.

No matter how hard it got in other ways, how painful, there was always the work and the friends. Over the next five years, I would watch the world slowly deconstruct.

But in those days, there were so many friendships, so rich and complex. Complicated and full of intrigue.

There was John Wieners, for instance, a gem who flickered in and out of our minds. Our hearts. I had first encountered John by encountering his work, in Paperback Traffic on Sixth Avenue. A slim volume, *Hotel Wentley Poems,* sold for one dollar. I stood there spellbound, reading the whole thing, recognizing many of the effects I was also at work on: the street language flowing so smoothly it seemed effortless, the almost-cliché shining and made new. A taut nervy lyricism that fooled you—it looked so easy.

I bought *Hotel Wentley Poems,* and then a day or two later I went back and bought it again for James Waring. I had no words to explain why it was so great, and I am not sure he "got" it the way I did.

John drifted into my world from time to time in the 50s. He hit New York after being released from one of the mental hospitals in Boston. Irving Rosenthal brought him over I recall, and we hit it off. John's story was tragic, but familiar, too. His Boston Catholic family had had him committed for being gay, and using dope, maybe junk, now, all those shock treatments later, he was more than a little crazy. Don't know how he had been before the forty or so shocks, but suspect there would have been a wild, fey quality in him from the get-go.

John was one of my tightest friends for about ten years; he and I went through many incarnations together: there was the John Wieners whose play we did at our first theatre, and the one with the fake leather drapes in the always-darkened speed den around the corner from us (this was a few years later, around 1963). There was the John Wieners who lived with the whole slew of extended family Alan Marlowe and I had collected, at the Hotel Albert in 1967, alternately in love with Alan or with Robert Creeley, trying on my size three mini-dresses, ripping the shoulders and smearing them with make-up.

So many others. He was one of my mirrors, and I loved him. His intensity and beauty and playfulness. And his work, always a surprise, and hard to come by. (He often left it behind him, wherever he'd written it.) We shared many winter afternoons, reading or talking or weeping together in the early New York dark.

There was the whole crowd of Black Mountain people and their friends: Norman Solomon, who lived in a basement apartment and made photographs, millions of them, and kept them in boxes; Ray Johnson, who made collages, all of them the same size, stacked neatly, and one day painted all his collages white, as he had also painted his apartment white: floor, walls, ceiling—even the window panes. There was Nicola Cernovich who did theatre lighting, lit many dance companies and worked in Orientalia Books. I found Nick inscrutable, as I did Norman and Ray: they all had the habit of talking in riddles. It was fun, but sometimes it was exhausting.

When he was at Black Mountain, Nick had hand-printed a poem of Robert Duncan's, "The Song of the Border-Guard". It was a large broadside and I first met him when he came into the Phoenix Bookstore with a handful of them to sell Larry Wallrich. He had made a whole lot of these broadsides, and he told me then that he had bundles and bundles of them at his apartment, all wrapped in brown paper and tied with string, and he was using them for chairs. I was impressed, perhaps because that image prefigured what would happen to my house when I started the Poets Press. I must have subconsciously known that I would be printing one day, and would be swamped with books, and I made a mental note to use them for furniture.

There was Remy Charlip, who was Nick's friend and Jimmy's, and a dancer for Merce Cunningham, and all his friends who danced for Merce, and so the Black Mountain people, and the Merce Cunningham people, and the Jimmy Waring people all converged at various points, though each group was distinct in its flavor.

But there was this distinction: everyone talked in riddles, but the Black Mountain people did so more than the rest of us; and Jimmy's riddles tended to be more Zen; and people like Freddie and me affected a street style and used phrases like "treat him with ignortion", while John Wieners and Herbert Huncke in different ways affected a junk / hustler style which was kind of existential, and Roi mumbled or grunted and said "yeah" or "how you doing"? which was more hip.

All of these things and folks and many others were in and out of my house, my world: we wrote collaborative plays to pass the evenings, or collaged together at Jimmy's house, using the stuff he'd saved up in two large trunks, or we helped out with each other's productions: theatre pieces or publications like the *Bear,* and with the one babe on the scene, shared food, money, books, successes and disappointments, and sometimes lovers. We hung out in painting studios, rehearsal spaces, music rooms, and dug each other's work while we contemplated our own. And nobody told me that it would ever stop.

Meanwhile I was coping with being pregnant, and all the various opinions about it, and all the advice, and all the folks who were mad at me, or who weren't. Many friends and acquaintances thought I should have an abortion and said so, Hettie Jones among them. Of course, each time I refused and sometimes I tried to explain myself, but not often. And Hettie and I just stopped talking to each other around that time.

When I told my mother and father that I was expecting a baby, my dad's first reaction was: Why didn't I just marry LeRoi? After all, he said, you've been together for a couple of years, and you seem very close. I was touched that he would sincerely make such a suggestion, but I knew it would never work out.

I had already been through the "Let's live together / leave New York together / etc." stage with Roi long before, and whatever I might have thought I wanted at first, by now I knew that wasn't what was happening. At this point I would never have considered marriage, having seen too much of Roi-the-married-man being silent and surly in his home life with Hettie, and knowing, or making a good guess how trapped he felt in any domestic scene.

Besides, being pregnant wasn't about me and Roi. It was about me and this new baby and Jeanne. We were the ones who were planning to stick together.

When I explained to my father that we wouldn't be getting married, he fell back on the old abortion solution. This time they sent my youngest brother, Richard, over to my house to talk to me. This was a particularly ugly blow, because Richard and I had managed to stay close through all the brouhaha about Jeanne and about my lifestyle, and I don't think he really wanted me to have an abortion but was just doing what he felt was his duty, representing the family. It really made me really sad, and it hurt my feelings.

But I was too "tough" and too busy to notice how much any of this was getting to me. It has taken all these years, and this writing now, for me to feel how alone I was then, in spite of friends and the vast amount of work.

Even Freddie thought this time I'd gone too far, and an abortion was definitely in order. He was quite vociferous about it. Exasperated.

In fact, my pregnancy had polarized the town, the New York I knew at any rate. Nearly everyone thought I was behaving badly. As if I was doing it on purpose to put them on the spot. Only Frank O'Hara and his friends tended to see all this in a larger or more remote context—as if we were nineteenth-century artists in Paris, or somewhere where these things happened. I could count on their playfulness and kindly wit—a gentle backup at parties and gatherings.

And Peter Hartman too, whose context for me and for the whole drama of the Manhattan art world was even larger than one or two centuries, saw no problem with any of it.

Jeanne was at this time going to the Ecole Française, and it was difficult getting her there. There *was* a school bus, but it didn't go to the Lower East Side (she was the only kid from our neck of the woods, it turned out). Peter at that time had an apartment on Sheridan Square, in a large building complete with doorman, and he arranged that I bring Jeanne there every morning, and leave her with his doorman who would put her on the school bus when it arrived. Meanwhile as soon as we got there, the woman at the building switchboard would call Peter's apartment and he would come down, invariably cheerful, and he and I would stroll through the Village, and have breakfast at The Bagel on West Fourth Street.

(Many years later I learned inadvertently that when Peter moved to Europe he told everyone that he had a child in America. Jeanne became the child he never had, as she was Freddie's, and Jo's, and who knows how many others'.)

● ● ● ● ●

That October, around the same time that LeRoi and I were busted for *The Floating Bear,* Alan Marlowe had located the first home for the New York Poets Theatre. It was a large, dark, back room with a stage and little else, located on East Tenth Street, in what was then becoming the downtown art gallery scene. The place had been dubbed the Off-Bowery Theatre by its optimistic owners, who ran an "avant-garde" gallery in front. The back room had minimal stage lighting and very little heat. It had nothing going for it, in fact, except the location (people were coming to East Tenth Street to go to art shows, and therefore might come to a theatre, we reasoned) and the price—it was *very* cheap.

We rented the space as of the first of October, and Alan, in his typical speedy way, announced that we would open our first show in three weeks.

In fact it did take only a month—the first week was spent just cleaning the place up, and getting it workable. No one had used it in years, and it was filled with all the debris you are likely to find in abandoned theatres. From the beginning our idea had been to do plays by some of the new poets, our friends, and since most of the plays the poets were writing consisted of only one act, the plan was to do several of them on each bill. The first program had been planned and cast before the bust, and as luck would have it, it included the very same play of LeRoi's from *Floating Bear* #9 that we were currently going to court about.

Alan, whether from courage or bravado, didn't miss a step. The bust didn't faze him in the least, in fact, I suspect he thought it would be good for business. We went right ahead with the program as we had planned it: *The Discontent of the Russian Prince,* a play I had written about two years earlier, about getting up in the morning, in which Freddie Herko and I were the sole performers; *The Pillow,* a beautiful early verse play by Michael McClure (another of his plays from this same series, *The Feast,* written in "beast language", was published in *Floating Bear #14,* that same eventful October); and LeRoi's play from *The System of Dante's Hell.*

We—actors and stagehands and all—went ahead with some trepidation, none too sure that we were going to be allowed to open, or get through the run without a bust, but go ahead we did, and that felt good and very brave and encouraging.

What was happening with the *Floating Bear* case at this point, was that at Stanley Faulkner's suggestion we had asked for a grand jury hearing. The hearing was, of course, set for many months later. Since only one of us was going to be allowed to testify, LeRoi volunteered to be the one to do it, and I was happy enough to let him, as I figured I'd be mighty pregnant by then. He and Stanley Faulkner were getting the case together, but the hearing was so far in the future that everything except our paranoia was in limbo.

The Off-Bowery Theatre was dark, and gloomy, and I remember it as dirty, but that might just have been my own prejudice. It seemed like we were there day and night, rehearsing or generally carrying on, hashing stuff out. Everything seemed like a big hassle, and Freddie and Alan fought all the time. At one point Alan threw an armload of costumes and props at Freddie who ducked, and they all hit me, like in a grade C slapstick movie. I quit for the day, vowing I'd never come back, but of course I did.

What I remember most clearly about that time is that LeRoi came to almost every rehearsal of his play. He didn't say anything much to anyone, didn't criticize or make suggestions to the director, or generally carry on as some of our playwrights would do in the future—make themselves general pests—but he just sat there, very still and alert in some empty row like an animal about to pounce. Just sat there and watched, and I had the sense he was noting everything that did and didn't work about his script, about the directing, about the whole production. Watching, and listening. Learning a trade. I could feel him doing it, even as it happened. It was after this initial performance at the Poets Theatre that LeRoi began to write the plays he became so quickly well-known for: *The Dutchman, The Toilet,* and so on.

Aside from that, Freddie and Alan fought painfully; actors and directors and backstage folks became more and more hysterical, as we advanced toward November with no heat at all; there was general pandemonium, vows of vengeance and reprisals, and we opened our first plays on October

29, 1961—the day after Jeanne's fourth birthday. She had a part in that first production: the set for *Discontent* was made up entirely of flats which we had covered with her tempera paintings. She and I had chosen them and glued them down together one panel at a time in our apartment—a work we both took very very seriously. As a set it was charming and funky: just the right background to Freddie and me, and our grumpy performance.

The New York Poets Theatre opened its first program with no tickets, no programs, no flyers. Only a one-inch notice in one newspaper (based on the press release we managed to get out on the mimeograph) and word-of-mouth to the various worlds of our friends. There was a night or two when police did come and stand in the back, but they said nothing and did less. And there was many a night when we tried in our paranoia to guess who might be the plainclothes personnel in the audience, but nothing untoward happened. We ran the show a few weeks to reasonable crowds, and then closed uneventfully and without much fanfare. I have never to this day been able to discover any photos of that first program of ours.

In which I tromped about the stage with tousled hair and in dumpy pajamas, and scolded Freddie, who sadly embraced his image in a mirror. In which I pulled blackened wet sheets off and on a clothesline, and sat on the stage with Freddie while we brushed our teeth together, dipping our brushes in a glass of water which slowly turned green.

I loved doing it.

I loved doing it, but didn't again perform in any of the Poets Theatre productions for many years, though I would come on in an emergency as an understudy. And once I was Emma in my own play *Murder Cake* for two whole weeks. I also stopped being stage manager or assistant director, as I had often been for Jimmy Waring or Nick Cernovich at the Living Theatre, and instead became the mostly invisible all-round person: printing the programs and flyers, writing copy, buying props, raising money, and taking tickets, and occasionally cooking for the crew or watching (in later years) the stage manager's babies.

The end of that year found us immersed in theatre. We did a second set of plays at the Off-Bowery in December: James Waring's *Nights at the Tango Palace;* John Wieners' *Still Life;* and the fourth act of Robert Duncan's full-length work *Faust Foutu.* The audiences were a bit smaller; perhaps the work lacked the variety and flash of the first program. And the theatre was certainly *very* cold.

Alan directed the choral fourth act of the *Faust*. It was all performed at the table with one pool hall lamp for lighting, where the characters sat and spoke or screamed at each other, except for Faust who went wandering through the audience stripped to the waist, laying their reluctant hands on his not-too-exciting body. Jimmy's play about a dance palace derived most of its moments of grace from Freddie Herko playing a mute janitor, who knows but can't tell anything of what's going on—Freddie was always brilliant at this sort of thing, it had great significance for him. John Wieners' work *Still Life* was the most haunting, though I am not quite sure that his amazing words were truly realized. But it had a marvelous set and costumes, and a young, very intense Yvonne Rainer (who was then a dancer for Jimmy Waring—she hadn't gone on to film yet); and a fierce, poignant Ann Holt in a box. Ann was Barney Rosset's mistress, and LeRoi's lover: a beautiful mulatto actress, who might well have felt herself in a box most of the time.

The plays were dark, the way that time of the year is dark, as the sun sinks to its lowest point, and in New York you are boxed in by shadows.

● ● ● ● ●

We had only just begun, and it *felt* like we could go on for a long time. Like everything was in equilibrium. There was me and LeRoi, Alan and Freddie. There was *The Floating Bear* and Totem Press, and the New York Poets Theatre. There was dance companies, and the Judson Theatre, and the first "happenings", and all the new experimental films that were being made.

We hadn't heard then about mathematical chaos and its laws; couldn't see that we were a "damped and driven system", and that as such even when things were at their most stable, they are most likely to go out of whack—though the *I Ching* could certainly have told us. Driven by the vision, the ambition and hope, as well as the ideals we each held in our own way for our various arts; damped by the actual needs of the body for sleep, for air and comfort, as well as by the various compulsions of our psyches. And the never-admitted need for quiet: the countryside, and do-nothing days, and sanity. Damped and driven alternately by the need for the rent: for more money, more space, a change of scene.

Freddie and Alan struggled constantly. It was a fight for control, for power. Alan who had never been the "submissive" one in a relationship (back when gay relationships were as much modeled on straight ones as the dyke-femme pattern was)—Alan, as he admitted to any of us who would listen, found himself longing to be the passive partner with Freddie, and so he fought him tooth and nail. Eventually he "won"—if you can ever win by destroying the Other—but that would take years to play out, and at this time the energy swung from smooth to turbulent almost daily in their apartment, and that found its way into the theatre, into rehearsal and production, and into our world on every level.

Roi and I also had an uneasy truce, which grew wobblier and more reticent as my belly grew larger.

And there were all the concomitant struggles and tugs-of-war that such a large and complex group, with ties to so many other worlds, would naturally engender. Jimmy Waring, and in fact all of us, were working with dancers from Merce's company, and Merce's Foundation for Contemporary Art had just turned down Jimmy's grant application on the ground that his work was not "contemporary". And that caused a schism we hadn't expected.

We didn't consciously realize it, but a whole mix of different aesthetics, different ideas of the intent and meaning of the arts, especially the performance arts, was fighting it out among us. Merce's stark, clean line (he never worked with us directly, but, as I said, his dancers did); Jimmy's baroque Chaplinesque ways, his use of gesture; whatever was changing in me, turning me towards the West Coast, its romanticism and love of clutter, sensory overload; Freddie's groping for the allegory, the ultimate fairy tale that could tell his story, could maybe save him; Alan's sense of the "chic" in art, whatever that might be, enlivened and strengthened by Frank O'Hara's unerring homing instinct. (It was during a performance of *Faust Foutu, Act Four* that winter, that Frank leaned over to me and whispered "Alan Marlowe is a genius, you know". Giving me pause.)

Everything from Burlesque to Bauhaus was playing itself out on our stage, in our company, and the work was richer and more exciting for it; though it was also—it had to be—uneven and infuriating.

Even when a damped and driven system reaches seeming stability, I read just this morning in a book on chaos (and they are just talking there about pendulums—never mind anything really complex, never mind *persons*) even when such a system seems stable, it is never stable, and will suddenly revert to turbulent, unpredictable behaviors.

1962 would be the year of the triumph of chaos.

chapter FIFTEEN

That winter, after the second set of plays at the Off-Bowery, Michael and Joanne McClure came briefly to live in New York. They thought of themselves as moving there, but it turned out to be more like an extended visit.

The McClures made quite a stir when they arrived. We didn't have, locally, anything quite like them. Their beauty and nonchalance. A kind of laid-back *intelligence* that some of the Zen-influenced New Yorkers tried to affect, but could never quite get right.

They quickly found an apartment, a bright, airy flat on East Fourth Street between Avenues A and B. The McClures seemed always to be lucky about living spaces. This one turned out to be rather elegant, long and narrow, and reminiscent of San Francisco, with dark woodwork, large windows and finished floors.

Michael was, I think, eager to join in whatever artistic adventures were going on at the moment. He did everything from walk the night streets with Ray Johnson, looking for billboards to alter with a well-thrown can of paint, to going to cocktail parties at Frank O'Hara's house. Good-looking as he was, and a fine writer to boot, everyone was in love with him. He was lionized everywhere, in that enclosed, secretive way that New Yorkers have when they admire someone. Rumor had it that Frank O'Hara had a crush on him, and that he was being propositioned by folks of both sexes, somewhat to his confusion.

It wasn't quite as simple for Joanne, and this made their whole venture into a kind of uneasy truce.

In the San Francisco art scene there was a well-defined place for women and children, a way of taking the family into account, including them all in the picture of the bohemian life. This didn't exist in New York. I had myself blasted a niche of sorts into the stonewall, big enough to fit myself and Jeanne into the picture, and I knew it could be done, but it was hard. It took a certain stridency, a self-confidence that West Coast women might have felt uncomfortable with, or confused with arrogance.

I tried a bit to pass on some of these tools to Joanne, but it didn't seem to work. I think, in retrospect, that the skills I had were nothing she wanted. Perhaps she saw them as too harsh. Perhaps she was right.

Recently at a concert of a group called Mix which consists of David and Tina Meltzer and Clark Coolidge, Tina told me that one of the main reasons the Meltzers came back from England when they went there to live in the early 70s, was that she "didn't know how to survive there". Here, she said (meaning the Bay area), she knew how to work the thrift stores, the food markets, how to take care of things for herself and her family, but there the ground rules were different, and she didn't want to play.

It gave me pause, caused me to look back for a minute at the ground rules, the ways of survival, in Manhattan, Kerhonkson, Millbrook, San Francisco, Marshall. The places I've lived. I had not been aware enough to know that I was assimilating different patterns, dancing a different dance to feed and clothe and house us in each place.

Kyra McClure, which is what Joanne was calling herself at the time, did what she knew best. She set up a school in a small room in their flat: even found small school desks and chairs in some secondhand store, and began to run classes on a daily basis for Janie McClure and Jeanne. Sometimes Anna Butula's younger girl, Rosemary, would join them. Dolly Butula, was, I think, already in first grade by that time. When I came by to bring or pick up Jeanne from "school", Joanne seemed radiant. Educating little ones was, after all, her chosen lifework.

But she never reached out, into the "adult" community. Lord knows we were all kids in more ways than we knew, but I got the impression that she disapproved of us. Or of the New York lifestyle. Found The City (as we arrogantly called it) too harsh and devoid of nature; it lacked the amenities of "real" (meaning green) parks, places to grow things, access to the ocean.

And, I am sure, she missed her friends: the many kinds of creative women (and men) who used their creativity to further the domestic arts (as well as what we in New York persisted in calling the "fine" arts), and to blur the boundaries between humans and nature, civilized and wild, in the quiet, persistent way that the West Coast was going about doing that.

In short, there was in the West a spare but rich and elegant lifestyle that I had glimpsed, and that we in New York had no substitute for—and Joanne found this a sore lack in East Coast life. She made me feel uneasy about it all: defensive and a tad apologetic.

And she was visibly wilting. After a while "school" began to be cancelled. She took to her bed and stayed there for days, with indefinable malaise, elusive symptoms. And then, finally, she announced that if Michael wanted to stay in New York he could, but *she* was going back to San Francisco by the next full moon and taking Janie with her.

I couldn't see him leaving. I was totally involved in all of it. In the sudden and surprising convergence of the various arts around the Poets Theatre, around The Floating Bear. *Was so amazed at what was starting to happen in and around these streets I had known so well, that it seemed unthinkable to be leaving them. I was certain New York was the center, the hub of the action, and fiercely wanted those I loved—those whose work I loved— to hang in with us, to be a part of it. That included Michael, of course, and by inference his whole family.*

A piece of information I was sorely lacking—and which would have saved me much grief had I known it—was that these energies, these movements are worldwide *when they happen. That New York City was* not *the center, but* one *center. But Manhattan, in its inspired parochialism, conspired to keep such a point of view at bay.*

As it turned out, Michael agreed to go back, with minimal resistance. I am sure there was much he too missed from California life: the proximity of nature and the beaches and wild things, and the perpetual burgeoning plant life, physical freedom. It seemed to take no time at all for them to pack up again and be gone with barely a trace. A breath of something else, some other way of doing it, that had blown through our lives and disappeared again.

It wasn't the only time we blew it on that particular dream, but it was the first time. Dream of what Kirby Doyle would later call "cross-pollination": the blending, the close collaboration of the artist-friends of the two coasts. It was an integration we sensed was crucial, but never quite pulled off. Later it would be the Herms family in Manhattan, or Kirby Doyle's old lady run off with Freddie Herko. Later it would be me, in Topanga

Canyon, with Alan Marlowe and Jeanne. But each time we would come away defeated. It seemed no foreign seedling could take hold. Nothing transplanted from across the Great Divide, from the Other Side, would grow, in either place.

There was so much we sensed was going on: in New York, in California. The burgeoning new work in *either* place had to be seen, heard, assimilated, by the Other Place, so we could all take it from there. Something that the *Bear* was doing for the writing: getting the news out every couple of weeks. But when it came to the logistics of the other arts: transporting bodies, families, whole life systems—vast human terraria in a way—the problems were different. And huge.

Our words in the *Bear* somehow didn't get culture shock when they arrived from Max Finstein to Robert Duncan; from Jan Balas to Denise Levertov. They just flew in in mail sacks, they got there, they sat around, and sometimes they changed things when someone got around to reading them. And every someone could take his/her own time. But Joanne McClure or Louise Herms lost and footloose in Manhattan, or the bump and grind of George Herms' set for Michael McClure's *Blossom* up against Frank O'Hara's aesthetic—none of that waited on our readiness, it came when it came, and none of it was terribly comfortable.

In the end we all went home somewhere, chose sides, and set to work. West Coast and East. And all the various middles. And the "cross-pollination" that we dreamed of, attempted, in 1962 has yet to happen. To come into some fruition.

It was Alan Marlowe who kept insisting that it would be a good idea for me to take the McClures' apartment when they left. His arguments were all about me, all taking my needs into consideration: there would be more space, it was cleaner, a better block. I would need the extra space when I had the new baby.

But actually, Alan being Alan, the real considerations were all about him: he wanted the apartment I was then inhabiting, right downstairs from Freddie's, for his own office; wanted, understandably enough, to be with Freddie and yet be able to get away, and I suspect he wanted me well out of the way. Freddie and I had been friends and allies for too many years, had helped each other see through the machinations of far too many friends and lovers, and a lot of Alan's manipulations of their relationship were far less effective when Freddie could come downstairs to talk with me over a cup of coffee. As Roi's painful behaviors were less prone to hit their mark in my heart after I'd hung with Freddie for a while, and we'd had a good laugh or two over our gullibility and our grief.

I see now that my move to East Fourth Street was the tip of the wedge that Alan was deliberately driving between Freddie and me. We would never again be as close as we had, but I didn't know that then, and certainly couldn't foresee the consequences.

I finally did accede to the move. The McClures' place *was* undeniably bigger and on a slightly safer though less convenient block (farther from stores, buses, and the subway). Then, having agreed, I wanted to move slowly, to take things from Houston to Fourth Street a bit at a time and arrange them—get used to the change. But as soon as the lease was signed Alan put the pressure on to rush me out the door.

I managed to get out with most of my stuff, but left two boxes in the closet of what had been my study. One was full of letters from my friends from the early days of O'Reilley onwards—all the letters I'd wanted to keep—and the other held my journals, starting from when I was fourteen and wrote the "No day without a line" notebooks. I returned to the old place a day or so later to get them, but they weren't there. Alan told me with some satisfaction that he'd thrown them out.

He *said* he thought I didn't want them, but I could see he was lying. Outside I tore through the garbage, tore the street apart looking everywhere, in trash bins and gutters. Looking especially for the journals.

Wasn't it a shame, Alan said, just that morning he'd seen some local teenager sitting on the stoop, reading a volume of the journals. And he said it with something like a sneer.

I couldn't answer him. I didn't know how to be angry without going crazy, wrecking everything in sight. Or bursting into tears, which was even worse. Or both at once. All I knew for sure was I wouldn't (like my mother used to say) "give him the satisfaction" of seeing me cry.

I returned empty-handed to my strange new house. It felt awkward: windy and uncomfortable. And cut off from those I knew best, who knew me best. Cut off from Freddie and from Anna Butula. My extended family, mainstays through the first years of being a mom.

The whole place was like a hallway. No one could live there long. A wind-tunnel, it swept you through, and out. The air, the *chi*, a subtle steady breeze. Like a train station, or an airline terminal. Subway platform.

I sat down carefully on my bed. I put my back up against the wall in the room that was now my bedroom, a room I was supposed to appreciate, it was so big, so bright and airy. I felt myself watching and listening like a cat, and at the same time I tried to process the grief I felt, the rage. Being suddenly here in this desolate, echoing space, and without my journals. The chain of words that had linked me to my past. To my earliest conscious writing. All gone now. I was stripped and alone.

Knowing Alan Marlowe at all was dangerous. It could even be fatal. For the first time I was truly afraid of him. From here on out, I thought, I had better keep my distance.

That night, sometime before dawn, Jeanne climbed out of her bed and into mine. "Not that I'm scared or anything", she said, "but the witches are coming out of the walls".

I knew what she meant.

● ● ● ● ●

Michael McClure had so much to do with the New York Poets Theatre over the years, his work so much a part of what we did, that it's hard to believe he never read his poetry there. But he never did read for us, so the McClures must have been in New York, must have come and gone, between our first two theatres: the Off-Bowery where we did our first two sets of plays in 1961, and the miscellaneous series we did at the Maidman theatre.

It was probably soon after the McClures left New York, that someone offered Alan Marlowe the Maidman Playhouse on 44th Street for a couple of months. Whoever it was, they were offering the space to Alan in order to cut their own losses, having engaged the theatre for a play that didn't run.

Alan rented the place cheaply and produced another two-month season, March to May, 1962. This one was quite different from what we'd been doing at the Off-Bowery. For one thing we didn't do, or try to do, any plays, instead we had various people arrange and be in charge of various kinds of performances: we had music, dance, happenings, and movies, on different week nights. There was even a poetry reading: I still have a series of photographs, all in one long frame, which shows the same set-up: table, chair, and glass of water, with Paul Blackburn, LeRoi Jones, myself, and Frank O'Hara, at the table by turns, and then finally the table and empty chair and the glass of water.

I look very pregnant in the photo, so it was probably April or May when we did that reading. I remember another reading we did about the same time (I wore the same maternity dress). This one was at Rutgers with Roi and Frank and some others. None of us wanted to read last, and so we agreed on the train that at the very end we'd each read a poem aloud simultaneously. It seemed like a very natural solution, immersed as we were in the world of cut-ups and chance composition, but it did make the Rutgers audience rather upset. Folks came storming up afterwards to ask us what we were trying to "prove". It was the only time I have ever read at Rutgers.

As I recall, too, it was a bit awkward and strained, the going there with the guys, and being so large and pregnant, and people alternating between being nice about it and ignoring it, not knowing which was the more polite, and Roi still mad but working perforce with me, because that was how it was—we were both part of this reading.

We did the two-month season at the Maidman and I helped backstage a lot, and got larger and larger in the belly though I still didn't gain any weight, and during that time the Phoenix Bookstore changed hands.

Larry Wallrich had been looking for a way out for some time, and he found it in the form of a man named Robert Wilson. Bob Wilson hailed from Baltimore, and had done various things in New York, including being a ballet dancer, and now he was buying the bookstore. Several of us old-timers felt some skepticism: what did he know about books, after all? And would he keep the store an open house for us writers to meet and hang out? And would he help us out when we needed it, buy first editions, or notebooks, as Larry had?

There were some folks who just never got comfortable with the change, but for most of us, and definitely for me, Bob Wilson was soon a part of the scene, and Bob Wilson and the Phoenix Bookstore became inseparable in my mind. Over the next few years, Bob would become my staunch friend, and adviser, and sometimes banker. My buddy through thick and thin and sometimes a readily accessible source of humor and wisdom when I myself was sorely lacking in both.

One thing that a lot of people found difficult was that Bob was moody:

he lacked Larry's surface equanimity. But, like most moody people, there was this advantage: you knew where he was at, and—if you knew how—he was extraordinarily easy to cheer up. A flower on a grey day, a hug, or a joke made all the difference. Whereas Larry, alas, under his seeming affability kept so much inside. You never knew for sure what was on his mind.

The reason I am taking this time to talk about the Phoenix is that it was, and continued for years to be, one of the centers of our lives: a place to rendezvous, a place for writers to meet, for writers from out of town to drop in and see what was going on on the poetry scene. Even after I moved to the West Coast, an afternoon at the Phoenix, checking out what had been published, hearing the news, and generally catching up, was one thing I always scheduled when I was in New York.

Back then, there were these unexpected and welcome encounters: between writer and writer, writer and collector, and Bob (as Larry had done before him) presided over our meetings, or melted discreetly into the background. As soon as we were long enough out of the nest to be publicly noticed, he handled the sales of our papers: letters and manuscripts, to persons and libraries, thereby keeping food on the tables, the lights and heat turned on. Keeping some of us in dope, and enabling others of us to travel, or buy an abortion.

The Phoenix, in short, was one of the threads of continuity in our lives. And when it passed from Larry to Bob, it continued to be the backdrop, the support we needed.

Meanwhile I was getting close to term, and then a few days over.

I had a doctor for this pregnancy, unlike the first one—a woman obstetrician who followed me for most of the nine months, and had been urging a diet of malted milks and hamburgers on me throughout in order to make me gain some weight. (My notion of delicious food when I was carrying Dominique was cold grapefruits, especially the white part of the rinds, heads of iceberg lettuce eaten whole like apples, and cold tofu.)

Dr. Jane, as I called her, was associated with Manhattan General Hospital on Second Avenue near Fourteenth Street, and it was there that I was to go to have this second child. I had an agreement with her: this time I would for sure be allowed to stay awake to see and feel my baby being born.

Finally my labor pains started one night. The schism with me and Roi had grown bigger in those final weeks, and I called Alan and Freddie's house, as I'd arranged with them, so they could come over and help me. They were both there right away: Freddie was to sleep at the house with Jeanne, so someone she knew well would be there when she woke in the morning, while Alan took me to the hospital in a cab.

After the usual red tape and confusion, I was admitted and settled in. Alan didn't wait around. He went on home and Dr. Jane agreed to call him and Freddie as soon as the baby was born.

It was after midnight by the time I got to the hospital, and Dominique was born at 8:30 the next morning. It was a relatively easy labor, partly because I knew what to expect. In my mind to this day I think of her as being born at dawn, but I guess that is just the way it is with time, how it changes when you are in any altered state of mind. And certainly giving birth puts you in an altered state. One of the best, I would say.

All I remember now is looking out the window at the soft pink of the sunrise streaking the sky, the colors of dawn in a warm late spring morning in New York, and then it suddenly seemed she was crowning. I could see her dark, wet hair plastered against her head, in the mirror Dr. Jane had placed for me. And then I was panting, then pushing, and they were putting her in my arms, and the doctor's voice was saying, "She's perfect, dear". It seemed idyllic after the nightmare of Gouverneur Hospital.

After we both were duly cleaned up, Dr. Jane went off to call Alan and Freddie for me. She kept asking me if there was anyone else she should call. I told her no. "Ask Alan or Freddie to call Roi and let him know", I said finally, when I realized what she was getting at. To which she replied, "Poor Roi". But it didn't compute, not really, not for me. I put him out of my mind and attended to settling peacefully in with my infant.

Roi, I knew, was chagrined at having had "only girls" with Hettie. He had spoken of it, and with my usual hubris I had decided ahead of time that I would be the one to have his boy. I had even picked out the name I wanted: Dominic, after my anarchist grandfather.

Of course when they put this tiny gorgeous creature in my arms I lost all thoughts of wanting anything other than Herself. But I decided to stay with the plan, and call her Dominique, which was, I thought, much nicer than Dominic in any case.

When they brought Dominique to me and I put her to the breast, she didn't suck. Just looked at me with her wide dark eyes—it is a lie that newborn babies can't see—her mouth soft, a little open, incurious. I was bewildered, and a little hurt. One easily feels rejected in those first disorderly hours. A nurse's aide came by finally, and saw my dilemma. She didn't speak English, but motioned me to stroke the baby rapidly under the chin a few times. I did and Dominique began to suck, but after a short time she stopped again. I repeated this maneuver till she caught on.

Manhattan General was a blue-collar sort of place. I was on a ward, a huge room with windows on one side, in which there were eight beds lined up, four against each wall. Eight of us who had given birth in the last couple of days shared the space. The women were for the most part Italian, and they spoke various dialects only some of which I could follow. Some, but not all, of the women also spoke English.

But they all agreed about the important things. They had a definite routine and protocol, definite priorities.

During the day they usually lay around, read magazines and talked, watched television and fed their babies. A few of us were nursing, but it was not the general rule there at all. In fact, I narrowly escaped taking pills to "dry my milk" which were routinely handed out to all of us when we came from the delivery room. Being the paranoid sort, I asked the name and purpose of every single pill I was given, and so I caught the offending medicine and got rid of it with much indignation and noise. I was informed by the nurse in attendance that baby formula was more "scientific" than breast milk, and less bother than nursing, and that furthermore if I persisted in my plan of breast-feeding my baby, I was surely going to—horror of horrors—ruin my figure.

The folks on the ward were definitely among the upwardly mobile lower middle class, and both being scientific and not ruining your figure were very serious considerations. I had seen and heard a lot of this before, of course, amongst my relatives and the family friends in Brooklyn. I decided I would just "treat it with ignortion".

I concentrated instead on trying to sort out the various dialects that were being spoken, but when I tried to speak to anyone in my old-fashioned and broken Italian, learned from an ancient grammar and from opera librettos, almost no one could make sense of what I was saying. The exception being one delicate and good-looking girl from Rome, who actually replied to me, to my surprise and delight, so that we held ungrammatical and stilted conversations. All the others were down on the Roman woman for being, as they thought, a snob, and this judgment was automatically extended to include me, too. It didn't matter much to either of us, since there was no way to communicate with the other women, and nothing much to say in any case.

I did understand enough, though, to be quite thoroughly freaked out once or twice. I remember an afternoon that was almost festive: one of the women was going home that evening, her husband was coming for her and the baby after work. The conversation was disturbing: As soon as you get home, someone said, and everyone agreed, get the baby baptized. Before you take him to the park, or let the relatives see him. If God forbid somebody gives him germs and he dies, or if he gets pneumonia in the park, you don't want him to go to hell.

It was the closest I'd ever been to this blind, fundamentalist Catholicism, and I was totally horrified.

The TV was always on on the ward, but I had learned in Brooklyn how to concentrate through any amount of racket, and so I reverted to reading and scribbling as usual to pass the time. It got turned down, but not off, during evening visiting hours, when all the husbands arrived. The women would begin struggling an hour or two beforehand, putting on make-up, brushing their long, tangled hair, getting out of hospital gowns and into their best nightgowns and robes.

I watched them astonished. They did this every night and every night I was astonished. I just plain couldn't understand it. Why, on God's earth, did they care how they looked to these guys? And within days of the birth of a baby. The last thing on earth I could think of wanting right then was to have some guy find me sexually attractive.

I am sure they, on their parts, thought I was weird. Dominique was an odd color, for one thing. And then, too, there was no one particular man arriving nightly, with a flower, or a confection, and a kiss. Instead Freddie, Alan, sometimes no one at all, and one time Roi, who after a perfunctory peck headed down the hall to peer through the glass at his daughter in the nursery.

Mostly New York left me alone, friends and acquaintances didn't quite know what to make of this event, long expected but nonetheless an unpleasantness on their socio-poetic scene. Only Jimmy Waring came more than once to hang out—a gentle presence; and Frank O'Hara and Edwin Denby arrived together, like knights in armor, defiantly bearing gladioli taller than themselves, and sent the nurses scurrying about looking for a hospital vase that could actually hold such blooms.

I took the flowers home with me when I left; they lasted for almost a month.

● ● ● ● ●

October 21, 1994
Totowa, New Jersey, Holiday Inn near Paterson
The "Unsettling America" Conference

On the road again, and even now, after thirty-two years, nothing seems to get any easier. Not really. Holiday Inn in Totowa, New Jersey, and carless, and rather more than a bit broke, not really sure that I have what it's gonna take to finish the gigs I agreed to do this fall.

My room looks out on a parking lot and people like in the Godfather movies keep coming out of brand new cars; the restaurant so-called has these silent huge color TVs facing in all directions and little lights along the edges of everything and there is nothing to eat there for less than fifteen dollars, and I have fifty dollars with me and need to eat for the next four days. Besides that when I get paid for this gig, I need to get the money off to the Bank of America in a big hurry to cover the rent which is late, and then figure out where to stay in Manhattan while I work there, and how to stay at Frankie's without him noticing I'm out of bread.

Now what I can't figure about all this is how I am highly honored and highly professional and getting rather old too, by god, and still it hasn't happened that I can take care of myself. I feel a bit goofy about it, I must say. And maybe rather ashamed. I had a hundred and twenty dollars in my pocket when I left Boston this morning, and the people of New Jersey have already gotten eighty-five of it.

I got out of Manhattan General Hospital after five or six days, which was the standard stay for childbirth back then, and went back to my new pad on East Fourth Street, but I knew I was in no shape to take care of anything. Much less a house and two kids.

I was tired—it always amazed me how tired I was after giving birth, compared to how lively and full of energy I felt right up to the very moment of labor. Something nobody ever warned us women about. I wondered how much exhaustion had to do with what they liked to call "post-partum psychosis".

Then too there was very little money, and no real way that I could see to get right back to earning much. I had a freelance editing job for Simon & Schuster, something I'd gotten through Bettita Sutherland, a friend who was an editor there, but I had to get it finished, obviously, before I could collect on it.

Jeanne was staying in my parents' summer house at Greenwood Lake, New Jersey, and Emma invited me and the new baby to come out too. I decided to take her up on it. I badly needed to be taken care of for a while, and then too, I felt sure that the sooner my mother got to know the baby the more she would love her, and I really wanted my folks to love Dominique. I knew that their hearts would override any prejudice or hesitancy that their heads had set up about her being partly Black, and me still not being married, and all the rest of it.

When my father drove to the Lake for the weekend with some of my cousins, I got a ride with them.

I always had mixed feelings about the "house on the lake"—in many ways, it was too crowded and chaotic for my taste, it lacked privacy, life there lost some of its middle-class veneer and became more tribal than it was in the city. Then too, it was bought with my college money. But as it turned out there were to be several times in my life when "the house on the lake" functioned as a safe house, a retreat or convalescent home for me and/or my friends.

The first time was when I had gone there after chaos broke loose with me and Roi and Hettie. I had written "What I Ate Where" for *Dinners and Nightmares* there while I waited to find out if in fact I needed an abortion.

This visit with Dominique was only the second time I used the place as a refuge, but there would be occasions in the future when I would go there when the family wasn't around to hang out and write, while John Wieners or Kirby Doyle or some other friend tried to cold-turkey from speed or heroin in the spare bedroom, and I kept a kind of watch and sometimes fed them.

When I got there this time with Mini, as we were already calling her—Freddie's nickname for her, from the middle of Do*mini*que—she was about two weeks old. The house was full, as it often was in the summer, cousins of mine in their teens and early twenties were inhabiting all available nooks and crannies. My mother and her sister Ella were there full-time, and my brothers came and went. My father came for the weekends, and spent the weeks working in New York. Jeanne of course was ensconced as a guest of honor: this had been her home away from home since her very first summer, and she lorded it over the neighborhood toddlers and her various relatives with a natural grace.

I was given a bed in one of the side rooms with my kids alongside, but during the day, since I was actually working—and work was regarded by all as sacrosanct—I had privileged use of the living room with its tables and stereo. I proceeded to set it up as my study, installing my electric typewriter.

Various girl cousins slept in the living room at night, and their habit of course was to sleep late. I was an early riser, as also was Emma, and in order to get my workspace cleared out at what I considered to be a reasonable hour, I would go quietly in amongst my sleeping cousins and put Ornette Coleman's *Free Jazz* or some other advanced and cacophonous album on the stereo. They would then arise, the poor dears, amidst groans and curses, but as Emma was morally in agreement with me for once in our lives, my cousins didn't dare complain about any of it.

We'd all together clear the bedding away, and I would get to work.

Aside from the book I was editing for Bettita (with scissors and rubber cement, as was the wont in those primitive times), I was also doing another project on which I pinned some hopes. Bettita had suggested that I do a book of translations of medieval Latin love poems for Simon & Schuster, and at the same time had proposed it to her bosses. They wanted to see a prospectus with five or six translations, and I was working on those. I'd brought along some Latin texts and dictionaries and a reference grammar, and plugged away for hours every day, often uncovering the hidden sexual meaning of a metaphor, or a place where a stanza or two had likely been cut in copying by a prudish monk.

It was perhaps some of the happiest work I've ever done, certainly the happiest job I'd had to date. I love translating, love the absorption in another time and place and mind. And it was real, legitimate work, proposed by a real publishing house, which certainly helped my status in the eyes of my family. As did the fact that I was translating poems from a distant—and therefore surely respectable—past. There was a certain sense of "be quiet, Diane's working" in the air, which contrasted oddly with the mix of nervousness and contempt with which my folks regarded my own literary productions.

In the end, of course, Simon & Schuster decided not to do my book of medieval Latin love songs, but by then I had finished and polished the handful I had been working on, and when I finally got a press of my own and began to publish books, I put them out in a chapbook called *Seven Love Poems from the Middle Latin.*

In the midst of all this activity, Mini was thriving. I nursed her whenever she wanted, in spite of dire predictions from my mother that I was making her self-willed. She had a habit of eating a little, and then going starry-eyed and dreamy at the breast, and I would put her down and in no time at all she'd want to eat some more. This, I was warned, was *giving her her own way*, but I went on doing it, as I pondered Latin syntax.

And, of course, she had completely won over Emma and all the girl cousins, and elicited the interest of Jeanne. A beautiful and happy baby, she went from one pair of arms to another, surrounded by family and summertime.

●　●　●　●　●

I put in two or three good weeks at Greenwood Lake: everything was taken care of. I didn't have to lift a finger to cook, or take care of Jeanne and Mini. They would appear as if by a miracle, clean, clothed, shod, and fed, and I would hang out with them. Breast-feed Mini.

Wonderful meals, too, appeared miraculously in the hot, noisy kitchen, and wondrous girl-cousins with the intense unconscious beauty of early Italian movies set the table. I could translate medieval Latin to my heart's content, write new poems, play cut-and-paste with the manuscript I was editing, and if I wanted a break, a "fall" into the reality of daily life, I could come out of the living room / study and have coffee with my mother and some of her sisters, and we would talk endlessly, at the kitchen table.

I was intensely grateful, took none of this for granted. Something about the past year—the legal battle over *The Floating Bear,* the social battle: bucking public opinion to have Mini, the many struggles that came into focus around the theatre, I am not sure what it was, exactly—but something about the year just past had made me very conscious of ease, of leisure. There was a feeling of having come in out of the rain for a moment.

Though certainly my ways were enough different from the ways of this household, and in particular from the ways of Emma, that often a weird tension would fill the cottage over seemingly nothing at all.

On one such occasion, when my mother and I were sitting in silence at the kitchen table, four-year-old Jeanne came by with an open umbrella and handed it to me. "Hold this over you, mommy", she advised me solemnly, her eyes very wide, "hold this over you, so *things* don't fall on your head". It made me laugh, but it also made me think.

What I thought was that it was time, it was probably time to go home, to go back to my apartment, and to the city. Back to my own life. And this didn't make me feel very good. In fact, it terrified me, and that was a response to my life—the personal freedom so hard-won—that I had never had before.

The idea of going back to take care of two kids on whatever I could manage to earn, however I earned it, of going back to all that *work,* that wonderful but non-paying work: *Floating Bears,* Poets Theatres, whatever—I could feel how exhausted I was, down to my bones—the notion of going back to all those dear friends and other karmic relationships: whatever Roi might be feeling by now about Mini, however Freddie and Alan's lives were coming apart at the seams, whatever might be bothering Jimmy, etc. etc. All that for the first time looked not enticing, but dangerous. More than I could handle, hence frightening.

I had no idea how to do or say anything about my fear. Had no notion even that there was a kind of sanity in it: the voice of the body, saying "Enough".

I was not trained to think in terms of alternatives, other courses of action that might be possible. I felt, myself, that I had chosen this life, chosen each part of it, each friend, involvement, commitment, bill, low-paying-but-freelance job, and that therefore there was nothing for it but to *go through with it,* somehow. Though I couldn't have really said what I was going through with.

Even as I wasn't taught to think of alternatives, so too, at that point in my life I had no way of talking about these feelings. This terror. This knowing I had "bit off more than I could chew", and that I had no sense how to navigate it.

Perhaps if I had been able to bring myself to talk to Emma, had mentioned even a part of what I was feeling—cold mist in my solar plexus, my belly—she might have come up with something, some way of helping. I am sure at this point she could see the problem, and that she wanted to find some way in. I'm sure she and Dick were as baffled as I was by my life.

Perhaps I thought it would have been admitting defeat. Afraid of the many forms of "I told you so", or the door shut in my face again, as it had been when I wanted to go back to college.

In writing this chapter I have come to wonder for the first time, what would have happened if I had said right then: *I'm scared. I hurt and I'm tired. I need to figure out what to do.* Because I know now, finally—and it took me more than fifty years to find out—that there are always human alternatives, parallel pathways, though some of them require that we rely on others. Ask for help.

I am sure I gave the impression that everything was cool, that I knew exactly what I was doing when I announced that it was time to go back to the city. What internal clock I was using I have no idea, but the tension in the cottage was growing: Emma's ways of being with babies and mine were so different. And I knew that if I stayed away any longer the life I'd set in motion in the city, and which only cohered through my effort, my vision (Will), would have slipped too far out of recognizable shape, and it would take more than I had going to retrieve it.

Emma was sad—she was having a good time with the kids. The cousins too were sad, but mightily relieved as well: they'd be able to sleep in without being roused every morning by the Avant-Garde. Jeanne protested loudly, and Dominique looked curious and tranquil. As she usually did at that point.

I had anyway finished the *Seven Love Poems from the Middle Latin,* and written a prospectus for Simon & Schuster, and was hoping for a contract and advance. I had masterfully finished the freelance editing job, too, and so a check would be wending its way down the pipeline sooner or later to help pay for my household. I had definitely recovered from the birth itself—but the tiredness, the exhaustion I was still feeling, went much deeper than that recent event, and I didn't seem to be recovering just yet.

And so me and the kids and a great number of our possessions: papers and books and toys and diapers and suchlike, were delivered to my door on East Fourth Street one Sunday night, and carried on up the stairs.

It seems inevitable now: within a few days I was sick. I woke light-headed and feverish: and found I had developed a breast infection that required antibiotics and interfered with my breast-feeding Mini, at least on one side. I was disconsolate.

On top of that, I had Freddie sleeping on my couch, he and Alan having finally broken up, and Alan—as was his way—winding up with both of the apartments. Freddie had no place to live. He was a distracting roommate at this point, completely distraught, and given to sobbing loudly at all hours of the night. Waking me, and sometimes one or both of the babies.

LeRoi came to visit us almost daily. He too was going through something, though I didn't know what. He'd just come and sit next to my bed, and hold Dominique in his arms, and not say anything at all. I knew he was hurting, but I was exasperated and didn't try to get him to talk about it. He never elucidated, and didn't offer even the slightest help. Just came and sat there in silence, and looked bewildered.

I felt like I was drowning in it all. There were just too many people hanging on for me to go on swimming. Something like that. But the way it manifested was: I was either angry, or depressed. Mostly the latter, but with a cynical cutting edge. Cruel word, cruel thought for nearly everyone.

One day while I was still sick, a phone call came for Freddie. It was from his shrink, a Jungian woman named Maria Rolling who had been Alan Marlowe's friend and therapist in the past. When I answered she could hear from my voice that things were not okay, and asked me what was the matter.

I burst into tears as I told her: I had a breast infection, and I couldn't nurse my baby the way I should, the way she needed. I truly felt I was a total failure and was letting Mini down horribly, not giving her what a newborn baby had the right to expect. I had been brooding about it, feeling really miserable and guilty.

Mrs. Rolling was very gentle. My dear, she said softly, you are an intellectual woman, you write books. In Europe a woman such as you would probably not even *try* to have children. But you, you have two children and you care for them and write your books. This is very wonderful. It is not such a big thing if you cannot nurse your baby for a while. It is quite amazing that you nurse her at all. That you want to—a woman with all the other calls on your time, all your gifts. It is more than enough that you are with her so much. You should be proud.

I wasn't exactly willing to let all that comfort in, all that praise and admiration, had nowhere to put it, but I could hear her a little. I could hear that I was probably doing just fine, and what with everything else that was going on I didn't need to beat up on myself for being ill. As if sickness was a treachery I'd committed on purpose.

And sometimes, in the future, when things would get to be too much, I would hear Maria Rolling's gentle Russian accent, "My dear, you are an intellectual woman. You write books". Putting things into perspective for a while.

●

The other thing I recall from that conversation was that when I asked, Mrs. Rolling would not and could not give me any assurances that Freddie would be okay. Though in the events that followed, I did not remember her words.

When pressed, she said only that it was serious for him, but she hoped he would find a way. I thought she was maybe making too much of how he was being emotional—"exaggerating" as my parents used to say.

● ● ● ● ●

The summer drew to a close and at some point it stopped being Freddie on my couch, and it was Alan instead. I don't remember where Freddie went next—we would never again be as close, or share a living space as we so often had over the past ten years, but of course I didn't know that then. And I don't think I ever found out how Alan managed to lose or get rid of both of the Houston Street apartments so quickly after Freddie and he split up.

At that time all the ins and outs of other people's lives were beyond me—just beyond my grasp. I had enough to do with the ins and outs of my own life; I felt like I was sleepwalking, or moving through a dream.

Having two kids on my own instead of just one was not, I found, a quantitative change, so much as a qualitative one. When there was just Jeanne, she had been my buddy, my companion—the little sister I had never had. She had gone with me everywhere: eaten dinner backstage, fallen asleep at parties and come home at dawn in a taxi, carried upstairs in my own or someone else's arms.

But two babies brought with them perforce the reality of Baby. They became a ballast, an anchor. Some kind of necessary and opposing weight, and I stopped trying to fly so far so fast. In a sense, it was Jeanne and Mini who anchored me—kept me here on the planet—and I knew it, even then.

I am not at all sure why I let Alan Marlowe stay on my couch. I still didn't like him or trust him, and I blamed him for Freddie's breakdown when they split up. Beyond that I had never forgotten or forgiven him for my lost notebooks—those irreplaceable records of my earliest years as a writer. Maybe in a way I saw it as a challenge: could I stand it to have him in the house, grit my teeth and bear it? Or even, could I handle him? I think maybe I hoped to find some kind of revenge for my lost writings, and—even worse—the disrespect: the casual slighting way he told me he'd thrown them out. Hard to say why I let him in, but there he was.

There he was, and with him his full array of games and hustles. The chess pieces he played, and would play, over and over in his life: cars, clothes, crime, sex, travel, money. A lower astral magick. But I was new to it all then, was still naive.

When he moved in, one of his soap operas was already in full swing, and over the three weeks that we lived together on East Fourth Street, an entire melodrama unfolded before my astonished eyes. Little did I know that it would change the course of my life.

There was at that time a health food restaurant on East Seventh Street, where Yoko Ono used to hang out and where she did some art "happenings", complete with installations of her work. I am not sure what the place was called then, it later became the famous macrobiotic restaurant, The Paradox. I am also not sure whether that was where Alan Marlowe met Yoko, but it was where I knew her from. And Alan and she had indeed met someplace.

At the point where his melodrama intersected my life, Alan had lent (or rented, more likely—he always needed money) his car, to a friend of Yoko's, a man named Tony Cox. Unlike most of us Manhattanites, who couldn't care less how we got from one place to another, what kind of transportation moved us around, Alan was always a fanatic about cars, always needed to have one, even in the most unlikely times and neighborhoods, and he liked them to be flashy. This particular one was a white Ford convertible.

Anyway, the time came and went for Tony Cox to return the car to Alan, and nobody heard from him. Yoko Ono said she didn't know where he was either, and we believed her. The rumor then began circulating that Tony, who allegedly did some drug dealing on the side, had burned some guys (his suppliers) and had consequently taken off "perforce", like they say, for parts unknown. We never did find out if the rumor was true or false. But Alan waited a few more days and then reported the car as stolen.

All this was not so very unusual, not very exciting one way or the other, petty crime was just part of the milieu in New York, then as now. Except that back then the whole thing was more casual, the stakes were generally lower—though in this case they must have seemed high enough to Tony Cox. Rumor had it that the gentlemen he burned were out to kill him and that he had lit out for the West Coast (probably in Alan's car).

The whole thing got weird and interesting when the Los Angeles police called my house and told Alan they had found his car. It was, as far as I know, the only time in history that the police actually found a car stolen in New York City—though my statistics on this point are probably not very accurate.

Perhaps Tony Cox wanted it to be found, and parked next to a police station or something as the next best thing to returning it.

In any case, Alan would have to go out to California to identify his car, claim it, and drive it back. He had a bit of money from some TV commercials he had made (residuals for these brief bits concerning cigarettes or perfume seemed to be always coming to him in the mail). He was, he said, going to fly to Los Angeles, pick up the car, and drive back. He asked me to take the two kids and come along with him.

I said okay.

The plan was: we would stay with Wallace and Shirley Berman, friends I had never met but with whom I had an extensive correspondence. Wallace, an assemblage artist, painter, photographer, and magician, had been doing *Semina* magazine for years. *Semina* was a one-man operation on a handpress; each issue of one or two hundred copies was full of poetry, photos and incredible art. I had been trading *The Floating Bear* for *Semina*, and keeping in touch with Wallace via scribbled letters. Wallace's notes were usually scrawled in pencil, in a large hand, on three-inch squares of faded yellow paper. But sometimes instead he would send a beautiful photomontage postcard.

The Bermans lived in Beverly Glen with their son Tosh, and we worked it out that we would stay there while Alan got through the red tape on the car, and then drive the convertible up the California coast, and back to New York City. It was almost autumn equinox, and we thought we could get back before the weather got bad.

What is the real question in hindsight, is why I said yes at all. What I was thinking about, or feeling, that made the trip so feasible. So welcome.

Perhaps it was the knowing I had deep in me that I couldn't manage what I had taken on. That the apartment, the *Bear*, the theatre, the children, my many demanding friendships, the love affair with LeRoi, were all finally beyond me.

Or it was Roi himself coming day after day and holding Mini with such grief on his face. Such despair. His silence, and the sense I got from him that there was no solution. No way out.

Or it was the impossibility of resurrecting the routine, any part of the routine I had known before Dominique's birth, in a city polarized about my baby and mostly hostile.

Or it was the apartment itself, like a corridor, with its winds blowing me out the door. A vast and open space with nowhere to hunker down. No corners.

I was worn out, and I knew it, and I needed to put some distance between me and my lover, me and my friends. All the worlds we'd made. All the adventures, the wonderful work we'd done. To see what was left, what, indeed, I would return to.

I remembered Larry Wallrich, the year before he sold the Phoenix Bookstore, wanting to ship out again, to go back to sea, but saying he was afraid: suppose it turned out he didn't want to come back at all? To his wife Ruby and the baby. Better find out now, I'd told him, don't let it go further.

And I longed to lay eyes on that West Coast again, that magick land which had so bewitched me only a year before, seduced me into believing I could have it all, could follow my heart's deepest wishes.

I needed to be there to regain my strength. Renew my vision. To soak up that power. Touch the big trees again, drink from the Pacific.

What made it all possible, was that Alan had the money: he'd pay for the whole thing, arrange it, all I had to do was say yes, and we'd be off in a trice. In a few days, at any rate. For once in my life I wouldn't have to be the one who dealt with the logistics: where the money was coming from, how to get to the airport, etc. etc. etc. For once in my life somebody else would take care of things. And, after all, we'd be home in a couple of weeks. So what was the big deal?

The thing is, though, that I knew from the start we wouldn't be back in a couple of weeks. That it wasn't that simple. I knew that maybe I wouldn't be back at all.

LeRoi came by one afternoon just before we left, Jeanne was out with Anna Butula and her girls, Dominique was asleep, and we made love in the golden autumn sunlight, Billie Holiday again on the phonograph, every move like light cutting through light, and I knew it was the last time, and I couldn't or wouldn't tell him. Just held my lips for a long time on the smooth indented place under his collarbone.

chapter SIXTEEN

When we touched down at L.A. Airport on September 25, 1962, Wallace Berman was there to greet us: an apparition like nothing I had ever seen, not even on the mudflats of Larkspur the previous summer. Not very tall, he had long flowing hair, lots of huge, chunky Indian jewelry, and a magician's inscrutable eyes. A vast turquoise set in heavy silver covered his left wrist, another piece the color of the sky clung to his black string tie. There was a softness about him—not a gay quality, just a soft female/maleness I couldn't place. I found it disorienting and attractive all at once.

Alan and Jeanne and I piled into Wallace's nondescript car with our baggage. I was carrying a very small bundle of Mini. She had, blessedly, slept through most of the flight. I was blissfully ignorant of the art of toting disgruntled infants through the air, and didn't realize just how gracious she had been. Wallace was euphoric: the mountains east of Los Angeles could be seen, he pointed them out to us vigorously and triumphantly, and evidently thought them a very good omen. L.A. was an unknown quantity, and I had no way of knowing how much of a miracle it was to be able to see the mountains. But I looked at them since he obviously wanted us to, and I liked them okay. They had a kind of rawness to them I hadn't expected.

We went directly to the Bermans' house in Beverly Glen. It was a small place, perched precariously on a dry hillside, overlooking a winding road in a state of terminal disrepair. There was a small shed beside the house, which listed dramatically to one side, and served as Wallace's studio.

Shirley came out of the house to greet us, looking very much like her photo on the cover of *Semina* magazine. Over the next few days she would awe me with the quality of her presence: she could intensely participate in whatever was going on, and at the same time radiate a kind of powerful passivity and acceptance. Some kind of active serenity. An incisive intelligence wrapped in gentleness.

Their son Tosh, a dark-haired dark-eyed tyke, was just a year or two older than Jeanne. The two of them hit it off at once, and went off to do whatever kids of four and six did in Beverly Glen, with Tosh delightedly acting as mentor and guide.

The Bermans' house was innocent of unnecessary or cumbersome furnishings. We sat on mattresses and cushions on the floor amidst our luggage, and had tea on a rug, while I looked around. The place was beautiful, with that distinctive West Coast style I had become enamored of the summer before: the walls were weathered wood, the windows partly overgrown with plants, inside and out, and covered with a thin film of dust which filtered and warmed the light. The windowsills were covered with stones, shells, bits of glass or metal, and there were pictures everywhere: collages, photos, paintings, leaning against the walls and balanced on ledges and beams. It was like living inside an assemblage, and it totally suited me.

Wallace and Shirley were skillful hosts, and they made plenty of space for folks to be whoever they were. They were open to all the various gifts of the travelers who found their way to their hearth, and grateful for whatever these travelers chose to share. Alan, of course, saw this spaciousness as opportunity and filled it: chattering endlessly about his exploits in New York and Europe, his lost and newly found convertible, and whatever else came into his rambling mind. The kids played; I nursed Mini; we had some lunch.

In the afternoon the Bermans announced that they were going to clean house, and we could help them if we liked. The method they used was somewhat different from any I'd ever encountered in New York. The first thing we did (under Wally's direction) was carry everything outside: mattresses and rugs (almost indistinguishable from throws, or blankets), pillows, all got stacked on some rocks, and pictures and vases, collages and small sculptures were then piled on top of them, until we had created a great mountain of household furnishings on the side of the mountain. Toys and a few baskets and footlockers of clothes followed everything else out the door and formed an outer perimeter, a kind of Stonehenge of domestic possessions around the central stack. We emptied that little house of just about everything except for the dishes and miscellaneous items that sat on the high shelves over the kitchen sink.

While we were accomplishing this, Wallace explained rather proudly that he had drilled a bunch of holes in the wooden floor of his place. All he had to do, once we took the stuff out, was hose the house down. No sweeping, no dusting, no scrubbing. The water just ran out the holes in the floor, he said, and down the hill. He proceeded to demonstrate. The holes were about the size of a quarter, and the only drawback to the arrangement was that it was sometimes necessary to encourage some of the water to leave with the aid of a stiff broom.

Afterward we sat on rocks in the sun, amidst cactus and yucca and overgrown jade trees, our backs to a steep, dusty hill, and continued our conversation while the house dried out.

A few days later, we loaded up Alan's newly recovered convertible with luggage and kids, and prepared for the trip north. Wallace helped Alan pack the car: his soft, practical energy and humor temporarily grounding Alan who was as nervous as a big cat. I was already beginning to get the feeling that traveling with Alan was going to be like traveling with a time bomb.

I think the small, close quarters of the Beverly Glen house were a part of it. While I was feeling cozy, tucked in and secure, Alan told me privately, plaintively, that there was no place for him to *stretch out*. It was, he complained, a hobbit house. Though there was certainly plenty of land around us, if we took the trouble to drive even a short distance, and Alan, once he had gotten his car back, drove all the time. We'd gone to the ocean several times, played on the boardwalk at Santa Monica with the kids, strode up and down the beaches. Or Alan strode up and down while me and the kids and the Bermans sat contentedly together, sifting sand through our fingers, and talking.

It was at the ocean that I met Wallace's good friend, Cameron, a woman painter and magician, who was a formidable presence: her long red hair, intense green eyes, and her way of zeroing in to talk to you in full intensity. A real contrast to Wallace's ambling way of garnering what he chose from a given scene. I loved her immediately, with that unreasoning love and loyalty I am given to sometimes, without rhyme or reason: just—they are who they are, these souls, and my heart is theirs. Charles Olson was another such, and Cecil Taylor.

No way I can explain it, this kind of love is beyond personal, but when, on the drive up the coast, I found I had forgotten my portable altar at the Bermans' (a carved soapstone lingam-and-yoni that Peter Hartman had brought me from India the year before), I called Wallace and asked him to give it to Cameron and tell her to hold onto it for me. "She's going to need it", I heard myself telling him. I knew that she was going on a magickal retreat in the desert, and knew instinctively that that particular retreat was going to be a rough one. That she would need all the help she could get.

Some fifteen years later Cameron told me a bit about that time in the desert, and how, indeed, she had used that sacred carving. She said it had helped her through a difficult time.

But now we have just finished packing the convertible, we are about to pile in and take off, but we stop for a last cup of coffee with our friends. Everyone wants to stop, wants this brief moment together, except Alan who is of course already down the road a piece. In his mind's eye. Or perhaps he is just afraid to say goodbye.

We have decided to take the coast road, drive up Route 1. Wallace and Shirley have highly recommended that journey, and they met with no resistance from Alan and me. I am thoroughly pleased and excited—for me there's no end to the joy of looking at landscape as it goes by.

We finally pile into the big white car. The top is down, of course, and will stay down throughout the journey no matter what the weather. Alan likes it that way, and for now that's just fine: it's hot and sunny, a perfect fall day in southern California. Later, sometimes it's okay, and sometimes not. But I will cross those bridges one by one as they arise.

One big drawback is that because there are two separate seats in the front instead of one big one, Jeanne will have to sit by herself in the back. I don't like this too well: she is little and will be isolated from us and the conversation (the more so because of the noise that comes with having the top down). There will also be the problem sometimes in the days ahead that the back seat is just too windy. Occasionally when Mini is asleep I can put her down on the back seat, where she lies low enough to be out of the wind and take Jeanne on my lap in front, but this continues to be a dilemma, both actual and metaphorical, all the way up the coast.

●

But—it is so beautiful! One spot more gorgeous than the next. Beaches of black sand, coves and the fall of the hills. Jade and agate, tumbled by the sea, strewn along the shore. The ocean lavender, azure, turquoise, green with seaweed. Once we were out on the coast road, Alan for once was not in a hurry; he was as enchanted as I was. "Have an adventure" was the last thing Wallace had said, as he kissed us each goodbye.

• • • • •

When we finally got to San Francisco, we stayed only a night or two, and then pushed on. Alan had become totally enamored of the Pacific coastline on the drive north, and he suggested that we find a place in Marin near the water to rent for a month or two. It sounded real good to me, but highly unlikely. I knew from hearsay that it wasn't all that easy. But we decided anyway to give it a try.

We crossed the Golden Gate Bridge, and stayed with Kirby and DeeDee Doyle in Larkspur for a bit, getting our bearings and a good deal of house-hunting advice: where to look and what to look for. Finally we headed over the Panoramic Highway and down to Stinson Beach to try our luck. It was a glorious autumn day, and we felt euphoric. The drive "over the hill", on the road that connects Mill Valley with the coast, was breathtaking.

We had barely arrived and begun to cruise the town, when we spotted a "For Rent" sign in a front yard, and within an hour had arranged to take a furnished cottage one block from the ocean for seventy-five dollars a month. It was a tiny place, almost a doll house, with dilapidated thrift store furniture. It boasted three microscopic bedrooms, a living room with a fireplace, and a kitchen.

The house we'd rented was the front cottage of two that stood on a corner diagonally across from the town's only store, post office and gas station. Both cottages were owned by an ancient white-haired ex-army man who lived in the back one and worked the garden that surrounded us on three sides. Our landlord was one of that oldtime, honorable breed who didn't nose about in other people's business. Which is to say: as long as we paid the rent on time, and kept out of his way, he'd pretend not to notice if the smell of marijuana should waft from our windows in the evenings.

We settled in delightedly.

The house was furnished with gracious mildewed hand-me-downs: a stained pink sofa adorned the living room, and there was a small table I immediately claimed as my desk and set in the front window, where I could look out at the yard and the street beyond. We made a bed for Dominique out of a large, wonderfully clean packing crate of beautiful white wood, which we'd picked up on the street in San Francisco's Chinatown. We lined it with foam rubber covered with velvet, and set it at the foot of our bed. Jeanne had a tiny room of her own behind our bedroom.

On the surface, everything was idyllic, but like most idyllic situations, it came with its own built-in problem which rapidly turned into a crisis and led to the first of many showdowns between Alan and me.

While we were staying in San Francisco, Dominique, who was just four months old at this point, developed a bad case of diarrhea which wouldn't go away. Alan, who was sure it was nothing, opined that the "changes in the water" we had been drinking as we traveled were responsible for her trouble, and we tried using bottled water, but she got no better. Instead, the diarrhea worsened while we were at Kirby and Dee's, and DeeDee must have been quite worried, because she suggested in her gentle way that we take "the baby" to Marin General Hospital, but Alan wouldn't hear of it, and I decided to wait and see.

But Dominique showed no sign of recovery during those first few days at Stinson Beach, and Alan still wasn't budging, and then one afternoon as I was changing her diaper I saw some blood in her stool.

For the first time since I had left New York, I had to look at some hard facts about my immediate situation. In leaving the East Coast with Alan I had surrendered a great deal of control over my life. I didn't know how to drive for one thing, and had very little money of my own for another. I now found myself and my kids in this beautiful but wild spot, from which there were only two means of egress: the Panoramic Highway, back "over the hill" to Mill Valley, or Route 1, down along the coast to the Golden Gate Bridge and the city. Forget public transportation—perhaps one bus a day came to this place. I was, in fact, stuck here, on this beautiful edge of the world.

Nevertheless at that moment my baby was very sick, and I knew it. I wasn't going to sit there and let things take their course. I couldn't. I had a horrible premonition of what that course might be. How pioneer women lost their babies. I flashed on Mary Shelley in Italy.

I also knew it was pointless to argue with Alan. I would only lose precious time, and he would never admit he might be wrong. Never relinquish any stance that gave him power in our relationship. In any relationship. I knew that much from having watched him with Freddie.

It was drizzling, an early fall rain with some possibility of a real downpour later, but I saw nothing for it but to pick up Mini and hitchhike to Marin General Hospital. I set methodically about getting us ready: warm clothes and a raincoat for me, and as many layers and blankets for her as I could reasonably muster. I also brought along Kirby's phone number, in case I needed to stay somewhere overnight.

When it dawned on Alan that I was totally serious, was about to take this sick baby and stand on the road with my thumb out till I got to some medical help, he was furious. His main thought was that I was doing all this just to show him up, to embarrass him. He went through a lengthy process of explaining that there was nothing to worry about—I was being dramatic (which painfully and grotesquely reminded me of my teen years and made me quietly furious). When he finally saw that his storming about didn't even slow me down, he grudgingly announced that, unnecessary as it was, he would drive us to the hospital, and all four of us piled once again into the car.

At Marin General the doctors in the emergency room were impressed enough with Dominique's plight to admit her immediately. They kept her overnight to treat her for dehydration. The rest of us stayed with the Doyles, and came back the next morning to pick her up as instructed. At that point the pediatrician on duty spent a fair amount of time reading me the book on infant diarrhea, complete with instructions on what to feed her, and what to look for in the way of further symptoms, etc. He was also adamant that I should get back in with her *fast* if there was any recurrence. It was abundantly clear that I had not been "dramatic" or exaggerated the seriousness of the situation. On the contrary, I gathered I had maybe been a bit too laid back.

A storm of emotion went through me but there it was: I knew better than to expect men to be capable, or tuned into what was going on, or to care, really, about anything except whatever it was they wanted. So I felt I had no room to be surprised or angry. I just had to watch out. For myself and my kids. It was, as always, war.

Back home, with the aid of some health food books and the diet recommended by the hospital, I finally got Mini's digestion to settle down. What I have always believed did it, actually, was my addition of brewer's yeast mixed with applesauce or yogurt to her daily eats. I read in Adelle Davis that infant diarrhea was often caused by lack of certain B vitamins that were prevalent in brewer's yeast, and Mini seemed to like the stuff: she gobbled it up without protest. She quickly got strong again, and regained the round baby look she had lost.

But I couldn't forget the showdown between me and Alan, or the hard facts that it had brought home to me. I didn't know how to drive; he had the only car; and most of the money that was coming in was his residuals for TV commercials. It kept me as wary, watchful, as I had ever been in my life. I felt my back to the wall even more than I had back East.

In fact, this was precisely the kind of bind I had done my utmost to avoid all those years living on my own in New York: here I was, living with a slightly crazy man who was calling the shots. Though I certainly didn't see it that clearly then. My pride would never have let me. I told myself I was still in control: tough enough for whatever might transpire. Hadn't I been ready to hitchhike over the hill?

We settled down to what certainly was a rather beautiful life. For a few weeks, Jeanne and Dominique and I had a taste of the idyll that northern California could be.

Alan frequently took off for San Francisco, sometimes for days on end, but we didn't miss him. While he cruised the Embarcadero for foreign sailors, we cruised the beach, barely a block away, for shells and sunsets. The general store was diagonally across the road from us, and we had a charge account there, which Alan paid whenever he got back. Our landlord worked placidly in his garden. The autumn sun kept deepening and turning more golden. I wrote every day at my table in the front window, and burned driftwood in the fireplace at night; the flames were blue with sea salt.

Internally there were a couple of things I was wrestling with at that time, and they kept me plenty busy. Preoccupied.

One was the question of whether I was actually a writer. What that really meant and whether I qualified.

The issue had come up for me in New York City over the past year: a shift had gone on for my contemporaries, but not for me. There was no way I could keep up with it—no way I even wanted to. They (LeRoi and his circle, Joel Oppenheimer and the others) had begun to write articles and criticism: some of it for the new literary magazine, *Kulchur,* that Lita

Hornick, a wealthy art patron, had just founded, and some for other, "slick magazines" as we called them then. (LeRoi had acquired an agent, and she got him these "jobs".)

To do my friends justice, they wanted to bring me along, but I just couldn't go. When, for instance, they asked me to write a "retrospective of Denise Levertov's work" for *Kulchur*, there was no way into it that I could find. It was, after all, only 1962. It felt presumptuous—as if I would be burying the lady.

All this brought up a whole barrage of questions: was I, in fact, a writer at all, if I couldn't write on request. A writer, I reasoned, should be able to write. That was the name of the game, and if I couldn't be "professional" about it, and whip out a piece to order, then maybe I just plain wasn't a writer. It wasn't quite that this inability made me a phony—more like a dilettante, maybe.

When I came West with Alan this question was big in my mind; it loomed at least as large as the second one: how to proceed without LeRoi in my life? And what to do with the fact that I still loved him?

The LeRoi question was more immediately painful, but the question of whether I was a writer ran even deeper—it undercut my foundation. Threatened everything my life had been predicated on for the past fourteen years. And so it was a relief when it quietly resolved itself—"like a snake uncoiling itself" as they say in Buddhism.

I had been working on a play in New York just before I left. *Whale Honey* was to be a full-length theatre piece on the death of Shelley, and it had a cast of just three characters: Mary, Shelley, and Byron. I had gotten to a certain point and was somehow stopped, and so I had brought it with me to work on in California.

What I discovered that autumn at Stinson Beach was that each morning, after the routines of dressing and feeding the kids, and eating breakfast, I would simply and without forethought find myself at the window looking out at that small garden and writing on *Whale Honey*. So that it simplemindedly dawned on me over time that maybe that was all there was to it: maybe, just maybe, *a writer was nothing more than someone who wrote*. Gratuitously, and sometimes aimlessly, sat down and wrote—often without design.

It was simply part of her life.

●　●　●　●　●

I don't remember exactly at what point Alan and I became lovers—things just quietly evolved that way. The occasion was not precipitated by passion, but friendliness and a kind of camaraderie between us.

The feeling I had for Alan at this time was close to compassion: he was handsome enough, in his way, or so everyone told me (he was not my type—any one of my several types—so it was hard for me to see it). But close up, sitting next to him in bed at night for instance, I sensed a kind of jadedness, a lonely fatigue as from an aging prostitute, and it made me want to reach out and comfort him. I felt he was lost and deeply sad.

He would certainly never have tolerated such feelings on my part had he been aware of them. I kept them to myself, and nursed along such kindness as I could muster, as I would a reluctant fire. It helped to temper and soften the coldness and distrust I most often felt for my new companion and housemate—he was, after all, the erstwhile destroyer of notebooks, and the nearly lethal ignorer of infant diseases.

But Alan could be kind enough in his way. Those first weeks at Stinson Beach I was in deep mourning for Roi, for the life we might have had. For the dream, the entire world of art I felt I'd left behind. There was one day when—to my embarrassment and chagrin—I could do nothing but sit on the cottage floor and cry. Alan rose to the occasion. He drove me to Mount Tamalpais and we hiked around the top of the mountain together, leaving the kids to be babysat by two East Coast dykes we'd made friends with, who lived in the motel just down the road from our house.

Though we would have indignantly denied it, we were simply two wounded people mending slowly on the far western shore of the continent, as far away from New York as we could get, and we took care of each other as best we could.

Taking care of Alan was not so easy. He had—by my standards at any rate—very peculiar ideas and tastes.

There was the evening he freaked out at the lentil soup—announcing that what he needed was meat and potatoes and he needed it *every night*. There was his high and mighty estimate of himself: his beauty, his importance, the fascination of his adventures, his "connections" (read lovers), his place, I dare say, in history. And there was also in him a simple, almost peasantlike being, who loved the earth, connected directly with animals and kids and had the big, capable hands of a healer and the sad eyes of an abandoned geisha.

●

Once we had all settled in, he and Jeanne immediately began a struggle for power which they never completely abandoned in Alan's lifetime.

Jeanne, who had turned five at Stinson, was not at all sure that she liked Alan. She was at the height of those witchy psychic powers which some little girls come by naturally if allowed to run free. She also had plenty to be stressed out about: her baby sister had just recently arrived on the scene; then within three months she had been uprooted from home and friends and from the city that she knew; and on top of all that she was now obliged to compete with this large, loud egomaniac for her mother's attention. From her point of view, it was one revolting development after the other. But Jeanne was alert, passionate, and resourceful, and she quickly took matters into her own hands.

"I don't think Alan should go anywhere today", she whispered to me one afternoon as he was getting himself ready to run into the city to cruise, and sure enough when—all spruced up—he went out to start the car, it wouldn't turn over.

Now Alan knew nothing at all about the insides of the cars he loved so well, and he also didn't tolerate frustration, so after gingerly trying the few things he did know (such as jiggling the wires that led to the battery terminals, and turning the ignition on and off a few times with the hood up) he went across the road and got the guy from the garage. The guy obligingly came over, and went through his complete Garage Mechanic Ritual, northern California style, while I watched from the window and pretended to type. Finally, when nothing worked he suggested manfully that he and Alan should push the car over to the garage so he could check it out more thoroughly.

This necessitated Alan's climbing out of his city duds and back into his jeans, which he did with much grumbling and cussing. They recruited me to steer—which I found utterly terrifying, as terrifying as if the damn thing was going a hundred miles an hour. It was the first time I'd ever found myself behind the wheel of a car, and Alan kept yelling incomprehensible instructions at me at the top of his voice. Both Alan and the garage guy strained and grunted as they pushed that beast up the small incline to the garage across the way.

Jeanne stood quietly watching the scene from our small front porch.

It turned out the mechanic and his buddies were baffled: they gathered together for a consult, but nobody had any ideas. Nothing seemed to be wrong. Nevertheless the car just sat there like it had never heard of moving. Alan finally gave up for the day and went for a walk on the beach.

The next morning nothing had changed, and there was talk at the garage of towing the beast over the hill, but in the afternoon, as we headed en masse to the post office next door to the garage, Jeanne pulled me down, and whispered very softly, "I think I'll let Alan go now". And so on the round-trip back to the house I suggested to Alan that maybe, just maybe, he should try starting the damned thing one more time.

He did, and the car started up without so much as a hiccup. Alan went home, dolled himself up once again and drove off, blissfully oblivious to the dangers and excitements—indeed, the mysteries—of his life at home.

Later in the day I questioned Jeanne in private, but all she would say was that she didn't know *how* she made it happen, she "just did it with her mind".

Jeanne was practicing her new-found skills in other arenas. At the post office, for instance, no one liked to see us coming, because while we grown-ups were picking up our mail and buying stamps and maybe chatting for a minute with the clerk, Jeanne would go down a long row of mailboxes with their combination locks and open every one of them. When I asked her how she did *that,* she told me she could "just feel it" in her fingertips. I noticed that she never opened the doors all the way or looked inside the boxes. For her the game was just cracking the combinations.

The postmaster scowled, but Alan beamed at her. He was rather proud of her outlaw abilities, and never for a moment dreamed that they were also being used on him. But I have to admit that I have sometimes wondered where and how else in our lives Jeanne's fierce and powerful child's mind was at work back then, molding our world to her vision.

In spite of all these half-hidden paradoxes—games and tensions—it was a really ecstatic time for me. Ever since my childhood summers at Long Beach, I had been in love with the sea, or rather the seashore—the interface where land and water meet—but I had never dreamed that I could actually *live* there. At Stinson I walked endlessly, exploring that small beach, finding at the south end two standing stone circles and even a huge flat stone aligned with the setting sun. I gathered shells and dried seaweeds and pieces of driftwood for my windowsills, and larger driftwood for the fireplace.

Everything was permeated with salt: my hair, my skin, the sand that always lightly covered our floors, the blue flames of the driftwood we burned. It was good, and clean, and slightly harsh, and it drew poisons out:

regret and nostalgia and lost hopes, till I was more or less present, there, in that place, facing into the wind, facing waves and sky and stars in the lengthening nights, or gazing down from Mount Tamalpais on the city sky-line, Alan, who was prone to vertigo, tall and teetering beside me.

The air smelled of salt, and of all the plants of the north coast: sage-brush, and cedar and eucalyptus, and hundreds of herbs. It was a smell particular to that piece of the world, and it seems to me it has slowly re-ceded from the Marin coast as more and more building has been done, but in those days it seeped into the house; it permeated one's dreams.

In late October the first fierce storm of the season hit. The wind came in steadily for three days and nights, and rain fell like I'd never seen it fall anywhere before. I walked to the beach in the midst of it, and was instantly plastered head to foot with wet sand, which clung to my skin and my clothes and weighed me down. I remember staring through the driving rain at broken pieces of crab claws flung onto the ice plants: the same form, in two kinds of life, two "mediums". The same shapes, in two colors, thrown together on the shore. As the earth and water and wind had be-come one element, "one confused mass", like in Ovid's description of chaos. Some alchemy I'd never experienced before.

I walked back to the house, weighted down with wet sand, carrying a whole piece of the beach on my clothes, my person.

It stormed for three days and nights. Filled with the energy of the ele-ments, the sounds of the wind, the rain, Alan and I made love throughout that time—with pauses to eat, build fires, change the records, take care of the kids. When the storm was finally over, something had changed.

●   ●   ●   ●   ●

I had been with Alan Marlowe at Stinson Beach hardly more than a month when I agreed to marry him.

Like coming with him to the West Coast in September, it was a move that made no outward sense at all. Something deeper and other than logic or common sense was at work. For many years after, when asked by my as-tounded or confused friends *why I had married Alan in the first place,* I would say it was *because I didn't love him,* and let it go at that. There were other reasons, but it took me a long time to discover them.

I think that at the time the whole thing made as little sense to Alan as it did to me. I was from a glaringly dysfunctional world, as was he, but neither of us knew it (hardly anybody did, in those days). Alan's father's world of gangsters and racketeers, and his own mix of gay hustlers and international bankers, we both considered as "normal", as my family's hysteria and tribalism. Or my personal clan of artists, junkies, and street people. It was our broad notion of the "normal" which had made both of us comparatively unflappable, even for New Yorkers, had endowed us with what looked from the outside to be "nerves of steel"—what we still called "cool".

And so it just happened at one point in early November, with the golden part of autumn over and the rains starting to loom, as it became clearer and clearer that neither of us was ready to return to New York or to the life that we had known there, that Alan began persistently and energetically proposing marriage.

At first the notion seemed perfectly ridiculous, and I was quite out front about telling him so, vigorously and forthrightly: I didn't love him, nor, I was sure, did he love me; he was mostly gay; we couldn't be more different in tastes or lifestyles, had very little in common; I wasn't even sure we liked each other. I thought most of the time that he was a snob, and he found me unpleasantly lower-class—a street urchin lacking in charm or manners.

Alan was not put out by my tirades on the subject of our incompatibility and continued to pursue the issue in the most unlikely times and places. Whether he actually had a plan, had figured a way that I could be of use to him in the future, be part of his next hustle, or whether something blinder was pushing him, I can't say. All I know is, he kept saying he wanted a family, I was one of the few women he liked to sleep with, and he wanted to be a father to Jeanne and Dominique.

Over time I came to think that our marriage could be simply a contractual agreement, and as such it didn't seem so bad. Alan had, at that time, a little money coming in regularly from TV commercials he had made in New York (the kind of thing I—being twenty-eight and inexperienced in all things monetary—figured would continue forever). It was obvious he could, at any rate, pay the basic bills, and God knows I was tired of trying. He wanted a wife, and the front that would give him, maybe a kid or two of his own (we didn't know yet that I was already pregnant with our son Alexander).

I wanted to be looked after a bit; it was long overdue. To have somebody else take care of some of the physical details for a change: where we lived, where to put the furniture, what it would look like. I was bone-tired, though I didn't know it, and still hurting from giving up on my affair with

Roi. So it seemed pretty clear right then that the only way for anything to work in the long term was for it to have nothing to do with "love" as such. Let "love" fall where it may, for each of us, I thought (and Alan was more than willing to agree to an "open" marriage), but best of all let it fall *outside* of any permanent arrangement.

If I fell in love again, I figured, the last thing I would want would be to live with the person, male or female. Best live with / be married to / a friend, someone who could comfort you in the vicissitudes of your love affairs, a partner of sorts, undemanding and without judgment.

That was the ideal. And it was from there that we started.

In figuring all this out so carefully, over weeks, I did make one serious error in judgment.

One of my most precious and valued possessions was my independence: my struggle for control over my own life had been an epic one, and because the struggle had been so difficult and—yes—dangerous, and because this control was so precious and so hard-won, I mistakenly considered this independence an *objectively* valuable commodity, something which I could now, in the tight corner in which I found myself, barter for what I needed. I didn't see that it had no intrinsic value for anyone but myself, that it was a coin that was precious only *within* the realm, a currency that could not cross borders. (I suspect that other women besides myself have similarly misreckoned from time to time.)

So, when I gave over the reins to Alan in this curious marriage of convenience, I had no doubt of the value of those reins, and no doubt that he knew that I must needs get equal value in exchange, though we never talked about it. Certainly gratitude was warranted, for starters, and acknowledgment. And of course, I assumed I would be cared for, financially and otherwise, would have no particular responsibility for the sustenance or maintenance of our household.

The truth was, although I was a prime survivor with many special skills honed for my life in New York, I knew next to nothing about money in this West, how it came and went, and in the eight months or so that we lived in California together, I never really bothered to find out.

Even before the ceremony, our marriage was to change my life totally, in no way I could have anticipated.

One of the things that Alan and I were in complete agreement about was that there was to be no ordinary marriage ceremony. That was for sure. Neither he nor I had enough respect for government in any form to think of simply going down to City Hall. (Our anarchism was one of the few things we did have in common, and it was to remain a part of the communication system throughout our marriage.) And neither of us had a religion to turn to: no priest or rabbi would suit our various purposes in the least.

In casting about for a solution to this problem, we turned to one of our few friends in the area. One night we went into the city without the kids to visit Donald Allen, who had moved to San Francisco from New York soon after the *New American Poetry* anthology was published, though he still worked for Grove Press from this far-flung outpost. We told him our plan and put the question to him: did he know anyone out here whom we could ask to marry us? It was the first that Don, or indeed anyone connected to the East Coast literary world, had heard of our proposed connection: to Don, as to everyone else from New York, I was still "Roi's mistress"— though I didn't realize till I went back East to what extent this fantasy held sway in people's minds.

Poor Don! He of course wanted to come off as quite the man of the world, just as we wanted (almost forced) him to be wise and cool for us at that moment. Besides, he was more than a little taken with Alan, and probably wanted to impress him a bit—but he was, first and foremost, LeRoi's friend. How much this friendship counted for was something I just hadn't figured on (though perhaps I should have, since it had kept me out of the *New American Poetry* anthology), nor did I realize that it would weigh on his particular sense of loyalty to help us out.

But Don did come through. After his initial astonishment, he suggested that Shunryu Suzuki Roshi perform the ceremony. Suzuki was a Zen master who had just recently come to San Francisco to be the priest for the Japanese community. He spoke a bit of English, and had already gathered around him a small group of American students. Among these was Richard Baker, a poet from the Midwest, whom I already knew because of correspondence about *The Floating Bear.* Richard was a friend of Don's, and it was through him that Don had met Suzuki Roshi, who had apparently impressed him a great deal. Don told us he'd get in touch with Richard Baker, and try to arrange a meeting for us with the Zen teacher.

We passed a long evening at Don's elegant apartment, talking and drinking wine. Don excused himself a few times to make a call or take care of some other business in his study. At one point I had to use the bathroom, and found myself passing through that same study, and there in the typewriter on Don's desk I saw the beginnings of a letter, which he had been hastily typing even as we sat contentedly by his fire: "Dear Roi", it began, "I don't know how to tell you this . . ."

It gave me pause.

A few days later, Alan and I found ourselves in an old, dark wooden building on Bush Street, face-to-face with a diminutive Japanese Roshi, formidable in his Zen robes. Then I looked into his eyes, and was stopped in my tracks.

Shunryu Suzuki Roshi was the first person I ever met for whom I felt immediate and total trust. It was something which I had never expected to experience. Every sense, every brain cell and nerve fiber in me suddenly woke up. I felt alert, and watchful, and euphoric, all at once.

During the previous year, I had read Heinrich Zimmer's *Philosophies of India* and had given a great deal of thought to the idea of a "teacher" or "guru": wondering what it would be like to have one, but knowing with a kind of resigned cynicism that I never would. Of course not. A teacher, a path, belonged to some long-gone romantic age, to far-away places like India. It had nothing to do with me in New York City 1962. Or so I had felt. Now, in San Francisco, suddenly confronted with the wise, kind face of Shunryu Suzuki, there was no doubt in my mind that I trusted him utterly, and no doubt that this in itself made him my teacher. (This trust was the first thing that he taught me without teaching, and for me it was one of the hardest.)

It was that he was so simply and utterly *there*, standing in that dim room, looking at us. There was a nakedness about it. No cover-up, no attitude at all. His gaze was flat, and extraordinarily deep. I felt he saw into and through me, and in spite of, or perhaps *because* of that seeing, he was totally kind.

I knew then and there, that whatever it was he did, I wanted to do it. So that I could begin to see what he saw. Think like him.

The fact was, I had grown up hard and tough, with my back to the wall, and now, when my toughness had led me into a cul-de-sac, I found myself still standing against the wall, trying to cut a deal. A deal for survival, for myself, my kids. A deal was what this proposed marriage was: it was directed by no inner necessity of love—as far as I knew—but by reason and convenience.

And at this very juncture, when I had lost for the first time my sure sense of path, when I was no longer sure that my passion—for art, for love—could be relied on, when, in fact, I suspected I might at that very moment, be compromising my principles, all I had believed in, "selling out" for some safety, a respite, when for the first time since I vowed to be a poet I was certain of nothing at all—I found myself staring mutely at this man, sensing he had knowledge that could take me further.

As I would later express it to whosoever asked: I knew only that I wanted to do what he did. Whatever that was. "If he had picked apples in Northern California, I would have become an apple-picker". Not simply to be near him, but to be him. To be that mind that he was.

I felt as though my world had split open.

● ● ● ● ●

At that first meeting, Suzuki Roshi gave us to understand that he would certainly consider marrying us, but the whole thing was not as simple as we thought. He carefully explained in his Japanese/English that if he did perform our ceremony he was thereafter responsible for us, for our spiritual well-being. He had therefore to determine first of all if we would be helpful to each other on our separate spiritual paths.

Suzuki Roshi arranged to have a private interview with each of us in a few days' time. We drove in again from Marin, and sat down with him one by one at Sokoji while he questioned us about our lives and our intentions. What he liked to call our "understanding". I was scared, of course, shy and self-conscious. But it must have gone okay, because a day or two later, Suzuki sent word through Richard Baker, who called Donald Allen, who got word to us, that it was all right, he would marry us. It seemed he thought we would be more helpful to each other than not.

Many a time in the six and a half rocky years that I was married to Alan I found myself thinking about Roshi's decision, and wondering in exactly what way we were helping each other *this* time.

The marriage ceremony was performed on November 30, 1962 at Sokoji, the Japanese Buddhist temple on Bush Street where we had first met with Suzuki. A small handful of our West Coast friends attended: Michael and Joanne McClure, Kirby Doyle and DeeDee, the Batman family, Donald Allen, Richard Baker, and a few others. We really didn't know that many people in this new land.

In order to fill the temple, so that the wedding would be auspicious,

Okusan, Suzuki's wife, invited many of her friends from the Japanese community. The place was filled with the soft beautiful sound of women's voices speaking in Japanese.

The ritual was brief. We had rehearsed it once before the guests arrived, and we both found it very beautiful. Suzuki sprinkled us with water from a green branch; we circled the temple in opposite directions with lighted tapers in our hands, then came together, and lit a single candle with both of ours. And of course we exchanged rings.

(We had picked them out at the Cost Plus "antiques" counter the day before: Alan had chosen a Persian carnelian with a few names of Allah carved into it, and I had then settled on a bit of old Russian silver into which was set a glowing ancient pearl.)

Throughout the main part of the ceremony, the only words spoken aloud were the Heart Sutra, chanted over and over in rapid and rhythmical Japanese by Okusan and her friends, and by us and our few American buddies as best we could. (The prayer-cards had the Japanese characters and their phonetic approximation, as well as Suzuki's word-for-word English translation. I found myself glued to the Sutra's simple but overwhelming statements: "Because mind no obstacle, no exist fear".)

When the actual ritual was over, Suzuki Roshi gave us instruction in the form of a quick talk—a kind of generic "marriage sermon", which I have since thought should be spoken at all weddings everywhere.

Today, he said, is very happy occasion. He beamed at us, and then at the assembly at large. He paused and stood totally still in his special brocade robes, holding his staff. In this life, he then continued tranquilly, happiness follows unhappiness. Unhappiness follows happiness. He paused again, and seemed to smile at each of us in turn. Then he added the Zen punch line. *Is all the same thing,* he said. Thank you very much. He bowed. We all bowed back.

We filed out of the shrine room. In the outer room I was surrounded by tiny Japanese women, laughing and giving me flowers and wishing me happiness in two languages.

There was a party at Marilyn Rose's house on Gough Street. (Marilyn was a friend of Kirby and Dee's.) We were to proceed from there down the coast to Los Angeles. It was Alan's plan, he was sure there was work for him there. He was very insistent and I had agreed, though every fiber of my being cried out against going. Before the wedding, we had cleared our belongings out of the beach cottage, and packed them into the Ford. Our Stinson Beach life was already receding into the past.

We sat in the car in the driveway of the Gough Street house before we went in to the reception, and Alan announced out of the blue that he/we had no money at all for our trip down the coast, he having spent the last of his cash on our rings. As if on cue I reached into my bra and pulling out forty dollars I had managed to stash away over the two months at the cottage, I handed it to him without a word.

It was an archetypal moment, the true beginning of our marital relationship, and I wouldn't have been so pleased with myself if I had realized how that one small gesture would increase and multiply over the next few years. How Alan would come to rely on the forty dollars that I must inevitably have in my bra. Or somewhere.

LaMonte Young, avant-garde composer and performer, and his lover, the artist Marion Zazeela, were joining us for the trip to L.A. They had flown out from New York, and stayed with us at Stinson Beach during the last frantic week. They were planning to visit LaMonte's mother in some suburb of Los Angeles before they headed on to Juárez where Marion had arranged to divorce her present husband so she would be free to marry LaMonte.

The morning after the party, we all piled into the Ford somehow: Jeanne in the back with "the LaMontes" as Alan called them, and me riding shotgun with Mini in my lap. I was uncomfortable but it didn't have that much to do with the crowding. It was more the idea of going to Los Angeles at all. I definitely didn't want to live there, but we had talked about it for weeks and there it was. Alan was ambitious; he wanted to be an actor, and had movies on the brain. Myself, I was dubious: I knew how long it took him to learn lines—any lines—and how bad an actor he was. Fine as he was as a director, his acting always seemed a little wooden.

Besides my general skepticism, I had no heart for Los Angeles itself. It wasn't my kind of turf. The rough dry hills were a bit too raw, the town a bit too brash. There was nothing subtle about any of it. I didn't know much about geography and/or climate, but after two months at Stinson Beach I had become quite attached to that northern coast.

Nevertheless we set out, as we would time and again over the next few years at some whim of Alan's. Some new plan. We took the coast route so the LaMontes could see it, and I was glad of that. Route 1 from Monterey to Morro Bay is always a vast joy. Alan and I drove it so many times in the next few years that I can't say for sure if this was the time we stopped off to meet Emil White, a friend of Henry Miller's, and spent the afternoon in his house near Monterey, a house he had built himself. Emil passed the day teaching us: talking recent developments in brick making and European philosophy, feeding us herb tea from his garden and homemade bread from his oven before we set out again, continued on our way toward what I thought of as the Land of Mordor.

We pulled into Los Angeles the next afternoon in a gloomy magenta sunset as the car radio reported a hundred-car pile-up on one of the major freeways. By then I was certain we were driving into hell itself. The San Fernando Valley its gaping maw.

When we finally arrived at LaMonte's mother's house, I sat rigid in the parked car as a thick purple twilight gathered over the insipid town of Glendale. My body had gone stiff with despair. I couldn't move. Couldn't bring myself to get out and meet the mom in the cottage, have coffee, smile.

Instead I held on tight to Mini and cried my eyes out, looking at those lawns bought and rolled out by the square foot like carpet. For the first time I wholeheartedly gave myself over to the fantasy of a coming revolution. Imagined with relish that bland oblivious world razed to the ground, those front lawns pitted and torn by bombs. By grenades. I could almost feel them in my hands.

• • • • •

In less than a week we had found a house in Topanga Canyon, and embarked on the process of buying it.

[Looking back now, I can hardly believe the whirlwind that that December must have been, though I don't remember feeling particularly rushed at the time. But somehow before Christmas Alan and I had: found a house, agreed on a price, gotten some small bank in the Valley to finance it, and arranged with my father to cover the down payment. We had also in that same month driven to New York and back in Alan's by-now famous white Ford; picked up said down payment in person from my family; and packed and moved all our earthly goods, either to the West Coast or (neatly boxed and labeled) to my parents' basement. We had then returned to Los Angeles with a car full of our stuff and stacks of presents for the kids, and pulled into the Herms' driveway in the middle of the night on Christmas Eve—just in time to be there for the Christmas morning scramble.]

But that was later.

Soon after we arrived in Los Angeles with the LaMontes, Alan and Wallace figured out between them that the place we were meant to be was Topanga Canyon. Not too close to L.A., not too far either. Wild, and beautiful, and still cheap. And it was, as they used to say, "above the smog line". We proceeded to look for a house there.

I let the men do the figuring. I was too bewildered to hold to my usually strong and vociferous opinions. I had no idea at all of the lay of the land around Los Angeles, where anything was—ocean, valley, township, or city—much less which of these dry, brown hills with their arrogant unlikely houses perched in the wind was "better" to live on than the others. What the difference was. I just disliked them all.

What I did know was that I would much prefer to live right on the water, thank you (there were still plenty of cheap dilapidated houses for rent along the Pacific Coast Highway), to be able to walk to the store when I wanted (since I didn't drive), and maybe even do a few other things by myself once in a while. But I had already noticed that these archaic preferences of mine were not going to count for too much in the men's serious business of relocating my family as they thought fit, so I held still and waited to see what was coming down.

Someone the Bermans knew—maybe Dean Stockwell—knew a real estate man named Bob DeWitt, who lived in Topanga Canyon and had his office there. Bob was a genuine California eccentric: a barefoot millionaire—his dad before him had owned the land a Lockheed plant was built on. Needless to say, Bob still held that piece of property. He was a communist, a friend of Will Geer and the Seegers; he lived at the east end of the Canyon and made pots, and had five kids and a wife who wove and painted.

Bob DeWitt took us under his wing immediately: he and his wife Doë practically adopted us. He found us a house that we could actually afford—the selling price was just $12,500, and our mortgage payments would be seventy dollars a month. He then cajoled a bank in the Valley where everyone knew him into lending us the money, and my father into agreeing to give us the down payment for a wedding present.

My father Dick trusted Bob DeWitt a whole lot more than he trusted me or Alan, or any of "my crowd": Bob was a businessman after all, something Dick could make sense of. They had several long, confidential, man-to-man phone conversations, arranging things for us like we were babes in the woods.

(At this point while everyone else in New York was mad at me, I had strangely fallen back into favor with my family. A marriage, obviously, was the thing that my parents most desired for me. Evidently it was something they had long since given up on, and now here it was. They were delighted. It's a shame in a way that it never occurred to me, and probably not to Alan either, to invite them out for the wedding.

In fact, in the beginning before they actually got to know him, my husband was much esteemed among all my Italian relatives: they would have given him the store: lock, stock, and barrel.)

There was nothing particularly prepossessing about the Topanga Canyon house, but I figured it would have to do. It was small by my standards, and built into the hillside, so that there was a lower floor, a single room dug into the hill. The whole thing was brown, painted to emulate brown shingle, and wrapped charmingly around a tree which stood smack in the middle of the doorway. The tree turned out that spring to be an acacia, with gorgeous yellow flowers that made me sneeze.

The place was dark and small—or it seemed even smaller and darker than it was, I don't really know, and I've never been back to visit since we left. But Alan and Bob DeWitt were insistent this was the best "deal" we would find. Wallace and Shirley congratulated us effusively, and George and Louise Herms were ecstatic, so I figured I'd get used to it. Somehow.

Alan and I signed some initial papers, left the kids with George and Louise, and hastily hit the road for New York.

It was a given, a never spoken but well-understood fact, that if we were actually going to get this down payment money from my dad, we would have to go back there to pick it up. Both of my parents wanted to formally meet my husband and properly acknowledge my change in marital status. Then too, we needed to close out my Fourth Street apartment, gather Alan's scattered possessions, and tie up a whole bunch of loose ends.

We took the "southern route", as Alan called it, and "The LaMontes" were with us again. Having done whatever had to be done in Glendale, LaMonte Young and Marion Zazeela Schleifer now had to stop in Juárez for a day to pick up Marion's divorce, so that they could get married when they got back to New York. That was okay with me: the LaMontes were good company, and they kept Alan amused. Certainly neither he nor I had any wish to be alone and honeymoony. The one big advantage over our previous trip with them was that this time there would be a bit more room in the car since the kids were staying out west.

The LaMontes amused Alan, but they also drove him nuts. He was all his life a compulsive neatnik, and they—they turned the back of the Ford into something comfy and unfathomable. They snuggled down amongst layer upon layer of Items: blankets, crackers, tchotchkas, postcards, cheese, books, kleenex. Alan, when he was out of earshot, would rant and rave, call them "some kind of small nesting animals".

As for me, since I didn't drive, I was looking forward to more than three thousand miles of landscapes and scribbling. It promised to be a great trip.

Except for a couple of little things. We were barely out of California when to my great surprise it became clear that my "late period" was in fact a pregnancy. I had assumed—as we mostly all did in those backward times—that I couldn't possibly conceive while I was nursing, and had therefore taken no precautions at Stinson Beach. I had obviously assumed wrong. An early stage of morning sickness plagued my journey east, a dull nagging nausea that I ignored as much as I could, while I (mostly silently) adjusted my plans to this new fact.

(Having another kid at this point didn't seem to be a problem—three not so different from two, I figured—but being nauseous and sleepy for over six thousand miles of cross-country travel, and whilst packing my house and dealing with New York—that did seem a bit much. But there it was, we were already headed East—and I was definitely pregnant.)

The other obstacle to our total travel enjoyment was the fact that Alan liked to drive as fast as whatever car he had his paws on would allow. Sometimes I frankly enjoyed it; sometimes it scared the shit out of me, and often it was just a downer: a small cloud over the journey. But all too often over the next few years, it landed us at 3 A.M. in some Justice of the Peace's home in some small town, in some terribly American state—said home inevitably complete with doilies, upright piano, wooden mottoes on the walls, and bric-a-brac. We would wind up doling out some part of our meager supply of cash to line said Justice's pockets (and/or the pockets of the cop who pulled us over in the first place). Alan would then drive on at a careful seventy miles per hour, and I would sleepily watch the speedometer creep upward again as the towns, and wayside bars, and gas stations slipped by like beads on a rosary.

•

On this trip we only got stopped a couple of times for speeding, and aside from these small problems, the journey was uneventful. With the LaMontes in the back seat Alan was on what I later came to realize was his best behavior. We made our way across Arizona and New Mexico; stopped overnight in El Paso so Marion could go to the Mexican court in the morning; spent a few hours at the Old Market in Juárez (it was my first sight of Mexico); and continued on through the fermenting South of the early Freedom Riders. In Mississippi I got my first glimpse of the rapidly obsolescing three-bathroom system of the southern gas stations of that unbelievable period ("Men", "Women", and "Colored") and (with Marion standing staunchly by my side) warily picked up greasy delicious food-to-go at a squalid restaurant with fat white guys at the counter and unfriendly signs on the walls.

When we finally got to the Atlantic Coast somewhere around Georgia, Alan pulled out all stops, and we tore north up the edge of the North American continent in a kind of wild hysteria. The Jersey Turnpike was just a blur of lights we navigated way beyond any speed limits.

We entered the city, like entering another dimension; dropped LaMonte and his lady off at his loft, and then went looking for food, espresso, and conversation. We were in the Village, and it felt like coming home. Alan for some reason was backing the white Ford into traffic at the crazy intersection of Sixth Avenue and Eighth Street, and we were once more stopped by a cop.

"Thou shalt not", intoned the man in blue patiently, "back into intersections. Especially not this intersection. Especially not before midnight". He waved us on our way.

chapter SEVENTEEN

What I *didn't* do in New York was deal with the karma of my recent marriage: talk to my friends and explain what I was doing. Instead I concentrated on tying up physical loose ends, like packing the apartment.

I couldn't have explained much in any case: because I didn't know the real reasons for what I was doing. Don't know some of them to this day. What I did know or feel was, that if I slowed down enough to talk the situation over with, say, Jimmy Waring or Frank O'Hara, I might never go back to that dark little house in Topanga.

Our basic speediness was my protection. We had developed it on the road, tearing across the continent, and continued a breathless mode of existence through our brief days in New York. Years later I learned from Trungpa Rinpoche, another of my teachers, that we use speediness to maintain ego, keep our hard shell intact. That was certainly what I was doing then. I was just plain too *busy* to see anyone, and since everyone in Manhattan used that same excuse, and often, my friends had little to say that could have broken through that bulwark. Even if they had wanted to. I think they were still too bewildered by my about-face—marrying at all, and then, marrying Alan Marlowe of all people—to try very hard.

Roi was the most persistent. Messages that he wanted to talk to me were delivered daily by nearly everyone who came by East Fourth Street to help me pack. My own sense—or the story line I told myself—was that I couldn't see him because if he so much as asked me to leave Alan and stay in Manhattan I would have to do it. Would have had no choice since I loved him but to do what he asked. And some distortion of that same ancient code of love said that if I didn't see him, if he didn't ask me face-to-face, then I could blithely and blindly go ahead with the move I was making.

As it was, things were hard enough: my apartment had been ripped off while I was gone. I had sublet my place to Soren Agenoux, a young man on the edge of Jimmy Waring's scene, a type that was beginning to spring up in larger and larger numbers in our various circles. He was a dilettante hustler who made various kinds of collage and photo art, and wrote a little. Mostly he was into drugs, but then we all were in our own ways, so I had paid no particular attention to that aspect of his life, just seen it as part of the whole picture: gay-artist-hustler-druggie.

When it came down to actually packing the apartment, I found that stuff was missing. I suppose that shouldn't have been a surprise, but it was. The rip-off had been careful—I'd even have to say thoughtful and selective.

In the narrow room which Joanne McClure had used as a classroom for Jeanne and Janie, and which I had turned into the Gestetner room, where we produced *The Floating Bear,* there were bookshelves, floor to ceiling. A large portion of said shelves now gaped emptily at me—every art book I had ever managed to get my hands on had been sold. It didn't seem so bad at the time—I was used to being in New York where painting was to be found everywhere, and books were easily replaceable, but it became much more of a loss in Topanga where there was no art whatsoever except what was being made right then and there by my friends; and still more, when I moved permanently to the West Coast a few years later. European painting is in short supply out here.

At the time I just noted it, and kept on packing. Maybe a bit faster for the fury I felt, the betrayal.

What was harder to accept was the non-presence of my small collection of Egyptian scarabs, some old, some new, some probably fakes, of various sizes, colors, and materials. They had been in a box in the top drawer of my dresser, but I found to my sorrow that they were not going to accompany me out West.

I could understand the art books—they would have brought in immediate money, but the scarabs were probably not worth very much, I had not paid much for most of them, would sometimes just give one to a friend, like giving a piece of my energy. I felt that part of my magick, part of my power, was stolen, and perhaps it had been.

Other batches of stuff were missing: Lalique jewelry, and a few things from India and Tibet that Peter Hartman had given me. Whatever was gone, was gone in its entirety. There was not a single art book left on the shelves, a single scarab in the drawer. It was as if nothing of all this had actually existed.

Besides this, there was the small matter of the *Bear*.

Part of the deal when I sublet my apartment to Soren in September, was that he would take care of getting the next *Floating Bear* out. It was already typed; he was to print it on the Gestetner in the apartment, and get it into the mail: the labels were all ready. Instead he'd printed half the normal run on really cheap, thin paper, and mailed very few of those. Probably used the rest of the money for dope. I didn't ask.

The copies he hadn't mailed, which were most of them, got stored in somebody's closet in Brooklyn, and were subsequently thrown out by somebody's mother. I never got it all straight. To this day, *Floating Bear #24* is an elusive and sought-after item.

I was confronting all this while I crammed everything into boxes with a fierce and wrathful energy. Alan helped me when he wasn't running around, but he seemed to have a million plans, and dozens of places he thought he had to be. I coped by grounding myself in the actual, material work that had to be done: store this, wrap that in newspapers. And let my fury at him, at Soren, at my entire New York community—after all, who were *they* to decide who I should marry? It's not as if any of them had offered to help me in any real way after Mini's birth—let my fury become efficiency and precision, room after room.

Sometimes some friends did come by to help and when they did they had the sense to be cheerful and more or less "cool"—not ask too many questions. We would put music on the stereo and talk as if nothing untoward was going on.

And by night Alan and I would go back to Brooklyn, to my parents' house, and listen to the teary and sentimental effusions of Emma, whose only wish, she said, was that *we* would be as happy as *she* had always been with Dick. A "happy" that, when I witnessed it in my youth, had pushed me out the door and driven all ideas of marital joy from my mind.

I didn't have the heart to disabuse her: tell her my version of what this marriage was about.

I did see a lot of Freddie and what I saw I didn't like very much. There *was* all that tension, unspoken stuff between us, of my having in his eyes "stolen" Alan from him, but there was something else too, and it was definitely something new. After a while he told me that he had upped the ante: he was snorting a lot of speed, and shooting a little.

We had, as I've said, all done plenty of dexedrine, and dexamyl by then, but crystal methedrine was a whole different story. It seemed to "get" you in a way that the pills didn't. You kept increasing the dosage, for one thing. There were a whole lot of stories already out there about what crystal amphetamines did to your liver, your brain—you name it.

And Freddie was really into it. He told me he *needed* speed to push his body so he could dance the way he wanted to. He felt otherwise he didn't have a chance; he had come to dance too late in life to make it work for him.

It did cross my mind that heavier drugs might have been his way of dealing with the loss of Alan. Like an old blues song with the genders reversed: his best friend (me) running off with his lover (Alan). But I didn't know anything about the psychological side of addiction, and I didn't think about all this for too long. It was Freddie's choice. I certainly didn't allow myself to feel responsible. I couldn't afford to.

The last exchange before we set out again for the West was with Jimmy Waring who had come to say goodbye.

We were alone for a minute. I was standing yet again beside that packed white Ford.

"Jimmy", I said, "stop Freddie from using speed".

"No", said Jimmy, and I didn't question him.

I figured he either meant that Freddie had to figure it out for himself, or that Freddie was actually dancing better with the drug, or that no one could stop anyone else, or . . .

I didn't say anything. Instead I just kissed him on the cheek. Then Alan came out of the house, and we got back into that car.

● ● ● ● ●

It is New Years Day 1963 in Topanga Canyon, and we are expecting the Hermses to join us for a celebratory lunch. I have been in the kitchen for a while, preparing the meal. It is at any rate more interesting than trying to unpack the rest of our possessions.

The fact is, we have just barely moved in. We are surrounded by cardboard boxes, cloth bags, and miscellaneous art works looking for a place of their own in this little house. We have no money, and almost no food. The Hermses are apprised of all this, so we will not be disappointing them, or anything like that, but still, it is New Years Day, and I want to make it as festive as possible.

The main thing we seem to have is a whole lot of brown rice, and brown rice is what the dinner will consist of. I have a box of large teabag-like things, filled with dried fish flakes and seaweeds, a kind of Japanese instant soup called *dashi-no-moto*. Our first course, I figure, will be *dashi-no-moto* with rice, with a little seaweed crumbled on top.

The main course takes a bit of ingenuity, but thanks to Altadena Dairy, which delivers now and bills us later, there are milk and eggs, and with a few spices I can make a bunch of yesterday's rice into rice croquettes. Voilà! I'll serve said croquettes with a side of fresh hot brown rice.

I have been working on the dessert since yesterday, and it is the pièce de résistance: rice pudding. I've cooked the rice in apple juice from Altadena, added handfuls of raisins, a bit of tahini and tons of cinnamon. A feast!

It is certainly a far cry from Alan's "I-must-have-meat-and-potatoes-every-day", but it's what there is, and since Alan hasn't brought in any money or food for a while, he has the sense not to complain.

We made a fire in the smoky fireplace, sat on cartons of books in the midst of the living room, and toasted the future with coffee and herb tea.

There were two styles of life in Topanga, two ways of being there. There was the old style: kind of funky California, even more given to front yard assemblage than anything up north because here the rainy season was shorter.

This was the way of life of Wallace and Shirley Berman, George and Louise Herms, Jack and Ruth Hirschman, when we came to know them, and dozens of their friends and neighbors. These folks were hanging out in timeless space, in a generous climate, making what art work they would with no thought for the morrow. They were as selfless a bunch as I have ever encountered: given to appreciating the sky, the ground, each other, with total quiet absorption. They were for me a lesson and a healing, and I absorbed a great deal of unspoken wisdom from them.

Then there was the Southern California of Alan's fantasy, what he came West to be part of. There was a bit of it in Topanga Canyon, but it was mainly south and east of us: a world full of agents, and modeling contracts, and movie auditions. A world of expensive restaurants and dubious health clubs. Beverly Hills and Laurel Canyon. This was not just Alan's fantasy, it was the fantasy of millions. But Alan was willingly seduced by it.

There was always the next audition to go to, the expensive suit to get pressed for the next important opening or party. Alan was always speeding off. And he soon found out that speeding off in his white Ford didn't work as well as he would have liked. He needed something more sporty, something that would cling to the curves of Topanga Canyon Boulevard, add to his flair. He decided to trade the Ford for an old MG.

Over my protests, naturally. The Ford was bad enough when it came to the kids: the top always down, the back seat always windy. But the proposed MG barely had a back seat at all. When we all had to go somewhere, Jeanne and Mini were squeezed onto the back bench.

I guess the operative phrase here is "when *we* had to go somewhere". Now that he had acquired a family, Alan felt more than ever the need to go forth as a single man in search of adventure. Hence he bought himself a one-person car, into which he could invite the occasional passenger, instead of being saddled with "the family" as a matter of course.

Occasionally, when it was more seemly to show up with a mate at one of these fashionable excursions, he would ask me along.

At this point I was beginning to "show", and I had a red and purple maternity dress with full, slashed sleeves, that Marilyn Rose had sent me. I would wear it to openings and such. On the drive home from one event Alan told me proudly that Cecil Beaton had asked him "Who is that beautiful woman, with the red hair, the red eyes, and the red dress?" I wasn't so sure that that was a compliment: my eyes, were they red that night from crying—I cried a lot in Topanga—or from allergies? From smoke?

I settled down to making some kind of relationship with the house. The winter turned out to be foggier and colder than usual, and each morning I woke in our bedroom which was dug into the hill and looked out of its small high window at the branches of a pine tree obscured by layers of mist, and dripping dolorously onto the brown shingles of our roof. It was not my favorite waking, just as going to bed in that room—turning on the light as you walked in and waiting for various beetles and whatever else to scuttle and slither out of sight—was not my favorite going to bed.

It was almost as if we were sleeping outside, and yet the bedroom closet was full of these elegant suits of Alan's all hung in a row: his polished shoes on a rack. I would lie there under our double sleeping bag and watch a spider dangling a few feet above my nose.

Upstairs, the main part of the house was just barely adequate. The kitchen was small, the living room large but usually crowded. The kids' room was off the kitchen.

I had my so-called study next to the living room, but it was not really private and there was no way to make it so. Even with the door shut I could hear everything that was going on in the living room. Every word that was said. I did very little writing in Topanga except for letters.

A lot was constantly going on in the living room. We were not in Topanga for even a month when we started to have visitors—the kind that come and stay. We had acquired some furniture with the house: a sofa long enough to stretch out on, a few wicker chairs, and a low coffee table—all clustered around the grey stone fireplace. When it was not being a dormitory, the living room was the center of the action.

We used the fireplace a lot: the foggy mornings were cold, and the evenings freezing as soon as the sun disappeared behind the hills. We would have used it a lot more, except that it smoked incessantly. The house was permeated with the aroma of woodsmoke, and sometimes an actual cloud of the stuff hung in the air. We tried everything we could think of to no avail: no matter what we did, the damned thing persistently smoked. Dark stains on its stone front when we moved in should have warned us there was something wrong with it.

My guess is the chimney simply wasn't high enough above the surrounding land to catch a cross draft so it would "draw" (the clearing behind the house was level with the roof). In any case, the fireplace smoked for whatever reason, and Alan, who was never as cold as the rest of us, opined that we should refrain from making fires. No one paid him much mind. We sat around that smoky living room, drinking coffee, eating Altadena yogurt, listening to music, with red eyes and streaming noses.

Altadena was a continuous presence in our lives. My mother had evidently decided that she wanted to help us out. What she really wanted to do, like any reasonable woman, was make sure her grandchildren had food. So when I mentioned on the phone that there was this great dairy that delivered all kinds of food to your door three or four times a week, and billed you once a month, she generously offered to cover the bill. When times were tough in Topanga, we lived on yogurt and raw milk cheese and eggs and kefir. That and potatoes and onions. It wasn't half bad.

● ● ● ● ●

There were a whole lot of things I learned in Topanga Canyon, but mainly what I learned was the basic fact of married life: *if he was bigger than you, you couldn't stop him doing it.* For two people who actually agreed about almost nothing, Alan and I managed fairly well: we had some shouting matches, and then learned quickly that a good way to get everything out of our systems was to smash china against the nearest wall. We had an un-limited supply of awkward pottery with thick, heavy bottoms, gifts of the real estate agent Bob DeWitt—created by him at his own kiln—and we made use of these cups and bowls whenever we needed to express our utter frustration with each other and with our situation.

And the situation was indeed frustrating. Soon after we moved to Los Angeles, the flow of residual checks to Alan slowed to a trickle. Moreover, we found ourselves in a place where I, for one, had no idea whatsoever of how to make any money—I didn't even drive—and Alan's only ideas had to do with making it big in the movies, or finding a millionaire lover (some-thing, to hear him tell it, he had been good at in Europe a few years back). But, of course, L.A. was not Europe, nor was Alan at twenty-five the same person that Alan age eighteen had been, and so he muddled along trying his charms on this one and that, making a friend or two in Bel Aire, or at some "good" restaurant or bar, and generally living on hope.

What money did come in, he quickly spent on such amenities as mem-bership in a Beverly Hills gym. Or getting the right haircut, sunglasses, driving gloves.

Then too, my actual, physical situation was even more isolated than at Stinson Beach. Here there was no store within walking distance of the house, and everything domestic had to be done by mutual consent: gro-ceries, laundry, etc. Although Alan was never physically violent as such, it was clear to me from the beginning—he made it clear right after we moved in—that there was no way in hell I could *make* him do anything. He only needed to tower over me and refuse.

I began to look at my situation as endemic: what women were up against, more or less everywhere. I was, I grant, a bit more immobilized than some because I couldn't drive: couldn't just pick up and do what was needed: but it would not have been all that different if I *had* been able to go where I pleased. I would still have had to deal with this larger, more volatile being when I got back with, say, the pampers, when he had been planning to spend the same money on gasoline. Or scotch. And there was only one car.

I knew I was better off than many women because he never physically hurt me. It wasn't violence, but the hidden potential of violence, lurking under the surface of the relationship, that kept me watchful, made me manipulate where before I would simply have asked.

It was really, I figured, only what I had bargained for. A contractual marriage. Only somehow I had figured into that equation some acknowledgment of the freedoms I'd given up. Some respect for the woman/artist I was, and some gratitude for coming to meet this man halfway. None of these things was forthcoming, and I knew better than to feel sorry for myself.

I had hardly been married two months before I knew I had made a mistake—shouldn't have gotten into this at all. Alan was out somewhere partying, hadn't called, of course, to say where or when he'd be back, and I was alone in a dark house in a small clearing, on a dusty and ominous mountain, with no money and almost no food, aware that my mate's benevolent but nutty whims could take us all anytime in any direction.

Part of me wanted to pick up the phone and call my parents. Tell them what was what, ask for their help in getting out of it all. But I was far too proud to let them in on my misgivings, to admit to them, of all people, that I had made a mistake. And a kind of ancient Italian wisdom told me that asking for help might produce many effects, but would not most likely produce the desired one.

They would certainly *not* be sympathetic. Although they were not Catholic, mom and dad definitely believed that marriage was for life. "She made her bed, now let her lie in it" had been a frequently muttered axiom in my childhood home. Besides, Alan was still a hero in their eyes. Had he not married me (read: rescued me from disgrace) even though I had two kids by other men? And one of the kids half Black? Should I be looking a gift horse in the mouth? No, I was in this with no one but myself to rely on. I would have to figure it out.

I remember sitting at the table that night while the kids slept, and staring at the phone in the dimly lit room, and deciding not to use it. Acknowledging that the wall between my parents and me could not be bridged that simply.

Luckily for me, plenty of friends came in and out of the Topanga house. I began to rely on them: for a trip to the beach, the store, for the five dollars necessary for groceries or laundry. For a little extra help with the kids. For keeping Alan cooled out. He was very much a social being, and much more likely to be sane and funny, outgoing and more or less on an even keel when others were present. Throughout our marriage, one of my ploys was to see to it that plenty of others were present.

By mid-February some of the East Coast crowd had begun to find their way up our mountain. I am not really sure to this day whether their pain and shock at my behavior was actually already behind them, or whether it was simply overruled by their curiosity. Their desire to see the West Coast, or get a free vacation in "the country".

Billy Linich arrived the earliest and stayed the longest. He was an old friend: a part of that world of hip casual art and even more casual drug-taking that Andy Warhol had just discovered and was beginning to exploit. Billy (who later became Billy Name in Andy's gang) was at that time doing a bit of everything: writing, collaging, taking odd combinations of drugs, making mots that sounded way hipper than they probably were, and mostly *looking* wise with a little half-smile and crinkly eyes.

When he arrived at our door, though, he just looked ashen and gaunt—no doubt the effect of months of speed—and immediately took up residence on the living room couch.

Alan and I mutually took him on. (For once we agreed on something.) We felt it our mission to bring him back to health. The only question was: how to manage it?

I myself wasn't in the best of shape: perhaps this pregnancy had come too soon after my last one, but I was wracked with "morning" sickness all day long, and so anemic that the doctor we finally went to suggested blood transfusions. I refused of course, but going on what I knew about anemia, I started to eat beef liver for breakfast whenever I could get it. It seemed a perfectly foul idea, but whenever I fried and devoured the stuff first thing in the morning, my nausea vanished like magic, and usually stayed away for the rest of the day.

Now, it was no mean feat keeping me in beef liver, and Dominique in baby food, and all of us eating, especially since the checks had become so scarce. Clearly, an emaciated Billy Linich was one thing too many to think about—but there he was.

We relied on Altadena Dairy to heal Billy. My mother, bless her heart, kept right on paying that one bill no matter how absurdly huge it got. We feared that we would become utterly bovine, but it worked. Color began to come back into Billy's face, and he spent more of his time sitting up on the couch instead of lying down. He began to tell the kids stories, and draw with Jeanne, and build the smoky fire in the evenings. So that when Michael Malcé and Freddie Herko arrived at our door ready for adventure, Billy was ready too.

It was spring by then, and I was hungry for a change of scene. Freddie and Michael had been traveling together in Mexico, having a brief fling, and they stopped on their way up the coast to San Francisco. I'd never seen Freddie so tan and healthy. His muscular leanness somehow more balanced and solid than a dancer's, from all the hiking and trekking about in the out-of-doors.

Perhaps this was for Freddie his moment of triumph: arriving at our house—most especially Alan's house—looking so well and so happy, an international traveler in the midst of a new affair. Give Alan a taste of his own medicine for a change. Perhaps. I didn't think of it then, was only glad to see him, to know that he and I could still be friends.

He and Michael Malcé proposed that we all drive up the coast to San Francisco, but Alan was pursuing something he couldn't leave—a movie role, or a millionaire, or some young trick. Or perhaps all three. So Billy and I and the two kids climbed into Michael and Freddie's rented car and set out, leaving Alan undisguisedly pleased at having the house to himself.

It was spring, the beaches were glorious, we would often stop along the way for no reason but the sheer beauty of the spot, let Jeanne run wild while Freddie played his flute, perched on a rock. It was promise, as of the beginning of the world, I picked up agates and jade in the sand, Freddie swam naked into a sea cave and came back out with his arms full of abalone shells. All along the San Francisco peninsula fruit orchards were in bloom, the air was full of color, and laughter, and perfume.

We arrived in San Francisco in a state of exaltation.

At Marilyn Rose's house where we had arranged to stay—she had fourteen rooms on two floors, on the corner of Post and Laguna—we found Kirby Doyle and the poet Lewis Welch, getting ready for a big poetry reading. The place was buzzing with excitement: Kirby and Lew rehearsing together at the big round kitchen table, Freddie and Michael bringing in huge bags of groceries for all, kids and grownups toddling about in various states of wonderment and undress. Sheerly agog.

Nobody had to tell me this was one of those memorable moments: conjunction of folks and energies to match anything I'd ever found in New York. Marilyn and DeeDee and I took up our conversation where we had left off more than a year ago.

Two nights later I sat with a great crowd of friends in a large-ish hall while Kirby and Lew read wondrous poems, most of them now lost, and Philip Lamantia stood up in the audience during Lew's reading and began to scream and scream and scream, dispassionately and all on one piercing note, till Michael McClure and a few others took him outside to calm him down, and the reading resumed.

●   ●   ●   ●   ●

After the reading, Lew was heading north, back to his cabin on the Salmon River, but Kirby and DeeDee came south to Topanga Canyon with us. I think we drove two cars down, but I don't really remember.

A fairly large tribe of us came together at my house to celebrate Easter. There were George and Louise Herms with Nalota, and me and Alan with Jeanne and Dominique; there was Jack and Ruth Hirschman with their son; and there was the tribe from New York: Freddie, Michael Malcé, Billy Linich, and there was Jim Elliott who took our picture. Jim was a friend of George and Wallace, an art collector who often bought their work when they most needed it bought.

Anyway, that Easter, we all gathered at this huge rock that stood on the side of our driveway, and Jim took photos. Some of us climbed the rock in order to be seen above the others, some of us have babies or squirming kids in our arms, some of us are pregnant, and everyone looks tanned and healthy and very young.

It was at this very party, that very night, that Freddie who was mostly gay fell in love with DeeDee Doyle. As they told it later, they started dancing together and couldn't stop, much to Kirby's chagrin and eventual fury, and a few days later they eloped—hitchhiked back to New York City looking like a hipster version of Bonnie and Clyde.

When Freddie and DeeDee took off without a word of warning, it caused a great deal of consternation and endless conversation. People just didn't behave that precipitously out here, it seemed. Things proceeded for the most part at a more leisurely and considered pace, with a great deal of talking and mutual consideration. Kirby was devastated, of course, but

many of my other new friends were quite put out. They felt us New Yorkers were rude, and they were right.

[A year or so after this torrid and narcissistic romance had blossomed and
played itself out cross-country and then in the amphetamine pads of Manhattan, Kirby himself arrived in New York for a lengthy stay and encountered Freddie soon after his arrival. Freddie was sleeping face down on a
couch in John Daley's apartment in the afternoon sun.

Kirby sat down on the edge of the couch without a word and started
massaging Freddie's shoulders. Freddie woke. He turned and saw with a
shock who was sitting beside him. His surprised, "Hi, Kirby, what are you
doing in New York"? was met with Kirby's half-joking reply: "I've come to
fuck you and kill you".

This exchange became part of the legend.]

*All that was later. Now we are standing in the sun in that dusty driveway,
our backs to a huge rock, smiling and energetic and very young, and
squinting a little against the brightness of the day.*

We made at least one more flying trip up the coast to San Francisco, car-
avaning in different vehicles, with Alan driving his MG this time and
leading the way. The point of this particular trip was to make the final
arrangements with Auerhahn Press for the publication of my new poetry
book, *The New Handbook of Heaven.* It was mostly the poems I'd written
while LeRoi and I were together, and I thought of it as my book of love
poems to him.

I had been in love with Auerhahn Press books since I'd first seen
Michael McClure's *Hymns to St. Geryon,* and had longed to have them do
something of mine. While we were still living in Stinson I'd given Dave
Haselwood this manuscript to read. He and Andrew Hoyem both liked it
and wanted to publish it, but they were seriously broke.

I wrote to Peter Hartman about backing the book for me, and he had
been amenable. He flew out and met me and Alan in San Francisco. We
sat down with the Auerhahn people, and the whole thing was quickly
arranged. A beautiful blue book, and an even more beautiful limited edition with stars on the cover, came out by that fall.

We split up from there. Peter had family to see in Los Angeles, and Alan
and I went back to Topanga Canyon, and once more went through the

motions of playing house: being settled married folk who owned their dwelling place and soberly took care of business.

Another month or so went by. Jeanne was going to the local kindergarten, where she quite upset her teacher by refusing to paint houses or flowers as instructed. "I paint the way *real* artists paint" she informed the bewildered woman, and calmly continued to produce New York style abstract expressionism with her crayons and finger paints and tempera. She also ran wild on the hills in the afternoons. The pale city child was long gone; she looked tanned and healthy. The out-of-doors had done its magic for her.

As for me, I studied this same out-of-doors, these low mountains, large rocks—studied them both straight and stoned, but never quite made them out, came to terms with them. It often seemed to me that at dusk I could see prehistoric beasts walking on their crests, silhouetted against the sky. And there was something odd about the human habitations we had plopped down on these same forbidding hills. The houses were much too bright for the browns and dark greens of the landscape. They stuck out too much from the slope of the hillsides, poked themselves into the wind with a kind of hubris.

I was never sure we humans were meant to be there at all. I had been told by some friend of Wally's that Topanga Canyon had once been an Indian burial ground, no one had lived there, he said, before us whites. It made sense to me.

Meanwhile Alan went his way oblivious, navigating triumphantly through tempests of his own creation, which he stirred up like some emanation of Puck in the swimming pools of Bel Aire, the gardens of Beverly Hills. Once he pulled into our crumbling driveway in a Rolls Royce someone had lent him for a couple of days. He piloted us about in it, using huge amounts of gasoline and making me seasick. We drove Mulholland Drive, looking down at the lights of the city, drove past Houdini's spooky burned-out house in Laurel Canyon, zipped up and down the Pacific Coast Highway, and went back home. It all seemed a bit sad to me, like taking the measure of one's cage.

Some days we would all squeeze into the MG and drive off in the afternoon to visit the Hermses in Encinal Canyon where they lived in a tiny hunting cabin on some remote estate—surrounded by George's huge assemblage pieces at the end of a dirt road.

Or we'd go in the evening to Jack and Ruth Hirschman's beachside cottage in Venice. The Venice Arcade still intact and already mythical. We'd park blocks away from their place and stroll through the warm air, amidst painted plaster faces, arches, gargoyles, blue shops, and multicolored rides; pick our way amongst the new box-shaped buildings going up here and there, and the old charming beach bungalows with flowers on the porches, and kids' swings in the yards, and settle in with Jack and Ruth for an evening of talk and wine, while outside the silhouettes of oil pumps like great strange beasts, swung silently up and down against the backdrop of the sea, and sometimes that special algae would be in that lights the sea and we would walk out on the sand stained black with oil to watch the waves break with phosphorescent fire.

It all came to an end abruptly, and without warning, as our lives—especially the artificially constructed ones—are wont to do.

It was a quiet night in the late spring when we received a surprise visit from Clarisse, Larry Rivers' wife. There had been an opening for Larry that evening in one of the fancy downtown galleries; Alan had gone to it, but I had begged off.

Alan had been back for some time when Clarisse suddenly appeared at our door. (People didn't usually appear at the door in Topanga just like that, without their cars, without even a phone call.) Clarisse was British and her icy calm betokened strong emotion—rage, I suspected. She informed us she had taken a hundred-dollar ride to get to our place from the post-opening party. (She described a sumptuous balcony on some hill or other, as though we would know exactly where she'd been, but it might have been anywhere.) She had left in a huff, called a cab and charged it no doubt to Larry and here she was. She was mad at Larry for flirting, or more than flirting, with some Hollywood dame or dames.

We made her a bed of sorts. I think Billy moved to the floor as he often did and she took the couch. When in the morning Larry himself arrived, looking earnest and a bit hungover and not in the least contrite, no one was surprised, and we all had breakfast together in front of the fire.

Larry took in the scene for a while: the clearing behind the house, the view, the cats, the school bus dropping Jeanne off, the smoking chimney, the dusty driveway, the strange, haunted land. We made small talk as if we were all sitting in his studio, or one of my New York kitchens.

Then out of the blue came his question, incised and jagged as his profile:

"*What*" he asked, "are *you people* doing *here*"?

There was the Poets Theatre behind his question, there was *The Floating
Bear.* There was, I suppose, everything that Larry and others had pro-
jected on us, had seen us, and especially me, as standing for—all we had
made, done, in New York. All in fact that we still saw *ourselves* as standing
for, hadn't managed in the least to leave behind.

"A man is what he *does*", Charles Olson had memorably said, and we
certainly hadn't managed to leave definition behind. Or our hunger for
definition.

Alan and I just looked at each other. We had no answer for Larry, but in
light of his question we could admit to each other that we were both just
killing time.

A few weeks later we were back in New York.

●　●　●　●　●

Now, the Riverses came to visit in early May, and my baby was due in August, and if I had had the sense god gave little green apples, or in fact any
compassion for myself and my own physical needs, I certainly wouldn't
have gone ahead with this notion of moving yet again. I would have dug
my heels in and said, firmly but with, I hope, some humor: "Wait a minute.
Hold on a second here. I've got a house, a school for Jeanne, a whole bunch
of good friends, and there is no reason on earth, with a third child just
around the corner and these last two of them going to be only fourteen
months apart, for me to make even more work for myself by packing and
moving this circus: let alone, moving it back to *New York* of all places,
where surely more theatres and newsletters and god knows what else
awaits me than I can possibly desire or imagine".

But the truth is, I was just as glamorized by Art and Doing as Alan
was at that point, maybe more, and I despised my little smoky house
on its questionable and haunted hill; and Jeanne was fighting with
her kindergarten teachers about hard-core questions of aesthetics; and
a whole family of Seventh-Day Adventists had moved in just across
the road; and almost all my "nearby" friends lived at least seventy miles
away; and my writing room was only a few feet and a thin plywood board

away from all the family noise and all the visitors; and New York sounded good.

What I really needed was to learn to drive and get my own car. Then I could have made myself a life right where I was. Or made one temporarily till the baby came, and grew to toddler age, but simple solutions didn't occur to me then. They rarely do to this day.

I actually tried to learn to drive two or three times that spring, with Alan as my instructor, but his idea of how to train a fearful novice was to share with her what little he had picked up in Europe about driving racing cars. And so, as we careened down the hills of Topanga, with me terrified, going five to ten miles an hour but feeling like it was breakneck speed and I was about to go over a cliff, desperately swerving with huge exaggerated swings in all directions to keep the car on that scary road and avoid hitting trees and houses and other large stationary objects—while all this was going on, Alan, riding shotgun beside me, would be shouting into my ear,

"Hug the center line! Hug the center line"! (there was no line at all on those roads, that I could see) or

"Accelerate! Step on the gas as you go into a curve"! Now this sounded very dangerous, and I was not about to attempt it. Besides, I silently wondered, when am I *not* going into a curve on this hill? Where does one curve end and the next one begin? How would I *know*?

It definitely seemed easier to move East again.

I think, too, that though Alan was not ready to admit it, he was genuinely discouraged with his stab at Hollywood fame and fortune. To do him justice, he'd gone to a fair number of auditions, before many of which I'd held copy while he tried to memorize lines. It was a job I would have found funny if we hadn't been so totally poor. Alan had the mind and imagination of a director: theatre or film, I'm fairly sure he could have done either. He could move people around and arrange space like it was three-dimensional chess, but he had almost no memory at all, and when he opened his mouth to deliver lines his speech was robotic.

He'd also "made the rounds" of innumerable modeling agencies, sometimes armed with a letter of recommendation from some highly placed new-made "friend"—but so far to no avail. We thus were left to the tender mercies of Altadena Dairy, an occasional reluctant residual from an old TV commercial, and an even rarer infinitesmal contribution drifting in from somewhere for *The Floating Bear*. (Thomas Merton sent us stamps once or twice, lifted from the monastery office.) The *Bear* had survived the move West and my marriage and was still going strong: albeit with one editor now instead of two, LeRoi having resigned "for personal reasons" soon after I got settled in Topanga.

So it had to be admitted that on the survival level nothing we tried so far was working: we were clearly without resources, and maybe it was a good idea to go back to Manhattan where both of us knew how to hustle. The land had given us no new vision to put out, no work to set our hands to. And that, as I was to learn over time, was the main thing that this marriage to Alan was about: us working together, making theatres and presses—making situations for various folks to shine in.

Another thing that made moving so easy then was that with the hubris of youth we were certain we weren't actually giving anything up—we could have it all. Obviously, we could come back here anytime: after all, we weren't selling the house. With a seventy-dollar-a-month mortgage, it would have been madness to let it go.

It was clear to us that George and Louise, Wallace and Shirley, and all our other friends would be here, would be just as they were when we left, when and if we chose to return. This world of dry dusty canyons and sports cars and oil pumps on the beach was ours now too. Simply by dint of having lived in it, we claimed it, sure that nothing would ever change.

May 15, 1995

> *I am writing this in a small beach cottage at Carpintería, where I came to read for the Santa Barbara Poetry Festival and stayed to work on this book. As I write about leaving Topanga Canyon in 1963, my own household in San Francisco is under siege: a new owner is trying to evict us and move into my pad. I mentally see my four thousand books in labeled boxes, me trying to manage that, to find what I need when I need it in great catacombs of "storage". My old vinyl records in Alex's garage perhaps, art works by famous people that one can never sell when one really needs to, all wrapped in plastic and stacked in Laura Stortoni's attic.*
>
> *Actually, it is not all that difficult this time. There are at least no kids to move about, no crazy husband. What makes it seem hard is that at my age I have absolutely no sense that I can have it all again. Come back to anything I leave behind. This is a kind*

of un-hubris, perhaps, the opposite of what I felt in Topanga, packing those boxes with Alan for shipping to New York. Back to my long-suffering parents' basement till we found a place. Again. I had two small kids and was very pregnant then, but I felt none of the hesitation I feel now.

Now there is a storm about me, storm of regret, storm of definition and redefinition of lifestyles for myself, for my partner, Sheppard. We stare at each other down long corridors of Art. Or stand silent in rooms whose walls are awash in books. Blinking at dust motes, at shrines cluttered with garnets and multicultural gods, we wonder what we are doing, who is right.

Which way to go. Which life to salvage out of the many that surround us.

• • • • •

In spite of all the years I knew Alan, and all the adventures and amazing lives we shared, in spite of the gargantuan anger and the struggles of mythological proportions between us, when I think of him I inevitably flash first on *possessions I lost* through his agency: things gone but not forgotten, as they say, that Alan in high-handed and unilateral manner, or through the tactic of heavy pressuring, left behind or got me to leave behind on one of our many moves. I am barely willing to admit that I attach such importance to these objects, but—there it is, there they are, gone, and I still at times reach out a hand for them.

We did better than this together, and we did worse, but for me these missing artifacts define our interaction in some way.

• • • • •

Somehow in three weeks we were packed and out of there. After innumerable goodbye lunches, dinners, cups of coffee, drinks along the Pacific Coast Highway. Innumerable vows and promises that we'd be back.

Alan put the kids on a plane with Billy Linich, and my parents met them at what was then Idlewild Airport. Somehow the moving van got up our hill, and the movers loaded on the furniture we were sending by truck. Somehow we found Greyhound Shipping for our clothes and household goods, and then mailed the books fourth class at the post office—boxes and boxes of them—and stood finally together in an almost empty house; stripped back to the dilapidated furnishings: couch, kitchen table, that had been there when we moved in.

As I made the last trips in and out of the house, I saw our cat, slight, black and unmoving, sitting in the clearing behind the house that was level with our roof. With her back to the house and all the activity therein, she was contemplating the brush and the empty hill behind us. Later, when we looked for her, she was gone.

Bob and Doë DeWitt and the Seventh-Day Adventists were the last to come to the house to say goodbye. Then we put our suitcases for the road trip in the tiny back seat and tinier trunk of the MG, and headed down to Santa Monica.

Jim Elliott had an apartment on the pier, right over the carousel, and he'd made up bed space for us on the sofa and the floor. A few more folks dropped by that evening, and conversation went long and low-key into the wee hours.

In the early morning light I walked out to the end of the pier and said goodbye for the time being to the Pacific. Then I climbed into the passenger seat of that white MG, looking more enormous than ever in my red-and-purple maternity dress, my figure, such as it was, made definitely larger by the sporty lowness of the bucket seat which made my stomach stick both *up* and *out*.

Alan put on his coolest sunglasses, the pair that made him think he was a racer, pulled on his driving gloves, gave himself a final check in the rear-view mirror, and gunned the engine in the early quiet.

We took off, and aimed in the direction of New York: mountains and deserts, Mormons and horse thieves and priests, dark nighttime towns and eagles and asphalt and thunderheads, gas stations, cornfields, and jazz clubs in Chicago, all flashing alongside the car like a magic lantern show.

chapter EIGHTEEN

Over the next two years, downtown Manhattan was agog with excitement: plays, dances, films, music of all sorts, abounded: and it was all new. Each art, like poetry when we started the *Bear* just two years earlier, was trying out a new syntax. Oil paint, sound, film, the human body, language—all were being stretched to their limits and beyond, and we were to be part of all that through the Poets Theatre, and soon the Poets Press.

No one was counting, no one was keeping score. Almost nothing of all this activity was recorded or tracked. There was no time for journal writing, and video had yet to become anyone's second nature. Video cameras were huge and unwieldy, and the medium required an inordinate amount of light. Except for the black and white photography, the archival work, that Peter and Barbara Moore did, and the more occasional photographs of Karl Bissinger, Daniel Entin, Peter Hujar, and a few others, there is no visual record of our doings at that time.

There were the flyers, there were announcements and programs. I have a handful and can hardly believe what I read there. How we managed to do all that. But even these are mostly gone—sold through Bob Wilson at the Phoenix Bookstore to some collector, on the occasion of some financial crisis.

Everything we had was grist for the mill. To keep the theatre open, the presses running. To keep the new work flowing, and flowing out, so that it would communicate to those others who really mattered: fellow artists, fellow experimenters and risk-takers. So that they in turn would communicate back to us in the form of more and other work: more scripts, happenings, art shows in dusty spaces.

There would come a time in the next couple of years when I would sell my first editions of *Howl* by Allen Ginsberg and *Gasoline* by Gregory Corso—for thirty-five dollars each—to pay the electric bill at the Poets Theatre, so we could stay open, and the show go on that night. The way I figured it, the work that was done was already done, and if it could help pay for the stuff that was still to happen, so be it. I would have sold the paintings off the walls for the ones yet to be made.

Alan and I were in accord about that one thing. We were both in the service of the going-forwardness of things. Though he was better at no-regrets than I was. I still occasionally turn to what isn't there, remember with some surprise the day I let it go. And the reason why.

We regrouped in Manhattan. Michael Goldberg generously lent us his West Village apartment for a while, and it was there that a few folks gathered one evening to welcome us back. It was a scary and tentative welcome, for them as well as for us. Frank O'Hara came, and Edwin Denby, both of them still backing me unquestioningly in my erratic-nesses (it would take a lot more craziness on Alan's part to finally burn Frank out). Jimmy Waring arrived and, briefly, Freddie. We mixed cocktails at the kitchen counter. Many of the old crowd were significantly absent, though there had been no overt breaks with anyone, in spite of my zigzag course through the manners and morals of that time and place over the past eight months.

We stayed briefly at Mike's while we house-hunted. I was supremely uncomfortable there: it was all so beautiful and well arranged, and I was painfully aware that I had two totally wild and messy kids in tow. I did what I could to keep track of them (make sure they didn't write on the walls or spill stuff on the sofa), and at the same time write, house-hunt, figure out about money, and do what we now call "damage control" with the entire New York arts community.

A prominent poet and translator lived upstairs from Mike Goldberg and heartily disapproved of our being there, though he did borrow one of my electric typewriters (I had two) and kept it till we moved. He came downstairs to get it, as I recall, but he wouldn't come inside. Perhaps he disliked children. Many years later, I was told by a prospective editor at Knopf, who had put together my "Selected Poems" only to have it turned down by the powers-that-be, that this same writer had been vociferously against publishing my work, which—he declared—wasn't poetry at all. I wondered then, as I still do now, if Alan and the kids and I had been too noisy, too arrogant. Too lower class. Or perhaps it was just that pregnant women with long red hair in red and purple dresses or embroidered Jordanian robes just weren't to his taste.

Actually, it may be that I had run into one of my first real encounters with class prejudice in the literary world. This is something that nobody talks about much, but it is very very real. There are to this day accepted and prestigious modes of entry into that world that are based simply on race, gender, class and/or money, and everybody knows about them and nobody acknowledges them.

Take, for example, the simple expedient of going to one of the "right" literary colleges, and while there using family dollars to start a slick but arty literary magazine. Many prestigious writers will happily send you work, if your "product" looks tasteful and expensive. And one name leads to another, of course. Presto, before you know it you are not only an editor and publisher, but a *writer,* for god's sake, a literary personage to be reckoned with (whether you can really write a word or not). You instantaneously wield a certain amount of power, and—unless you do something unspeakably gauche—no one is going to venture a word against you.

And this is only one of the more innocent and harmless methods of becoming part of the literary landscape.

Look at what it takes in the way of financial backup to be available to travel and read your work at the ridiculously low rates they offer at first. How much money you need to show up in the right places at the right times: poetry conferences, arts festivals, or to publish endlessly in nonpaying "little magazines", spend a small fortune on postage, spend the equivalent of a part-time job in work hours on gratuitous (often inane and pompous) literary correspondence, etc. There is simply no way to persist in all these activities, and not only persist but convey a sense of ease and pleasure in them, in the "literary life", per se, no way, I tell you, to have the time, space, and finances to continue these games indefinitely, without some kind of private income. So that you are free to make your decisions not based on what will help you survive for the next month, what will get the rent paid and food on the table, but on what will aid and abet your literary career, keep you visible, by god, put you at the right conference, in the right city, the right anthology or magazine, the right agent's or publisher's office at the right moment.

And all the other denizens of that world, your fellow-literary-playmates-whatever want and need your unspoken assurance that the living is easy, that no unsightly issue such as the bills, or medicine for the kids, or the bouncing check you wrote the airline to get there to do that reading in the first place, is on your mind when you show up to play with them. They crave this assurance of ease.

It is a gentleman's life for sure, and my upstairs neighbor—who had no doubt won his own place in that life with just the right mixture of money and academia, subservience and arrogance—was quite right in sensing that I was an upstart who had no place in it at all.

In years to come I would encounter the same barriers time and again; they would rise up in response to my politics, my mode of dress, my deliberately cultivated Italian/American manner, New York accent, the concerns of the characters in my short stories, the street slang in my poems.

Or I would stand stubbornly in the wings at some powerful and prestigious university, refusing to go on, demanding payment in front for some lecture or reading, while the powers-that-be assured me that the check would arrive in the mail in about two months. It was painfully clear at those moments that I was *not* one of the boys, and it worked against me. It still does, in spite of the alleged gains of the women's movement. In spite of the vague prestige and respect that simply surviving to the frontier of old age brings an artist, and especially a woman artist, in this all-devouring century.

In 1978, Audre Lorde stayed at my house when she was in San Francisco to speak at a women's march and rally. Audre came back to the house that night more than a little bemused and we talked late. Was it possible, she asked me, that she had made a mistake, that perhaps the deepest most underlying rift we were dealing with was class, not sex or race. Class.

"Diane", she said, "I was sitting with two of our friends this afternoon, and a woman got up to speak. She was white and she was obviously poor. She was wearing a cotton housedress, and carried a plastic purse on stage. And she spoke bad English. I noticed that neither of the women I was with could *hear* her at all. It was like she didn't exist. They talked to each other all the while she was speaking.

"Suppose it's *class* that's the biggest blind spot we have. Not race or gender. Is it possible I've made a mistake and the deepest prejudice is *class*"?

I already knew that it was. Had already talked about this with Bobbie Louise Hawkins: how no matter our education, or self-education, if we chose to write the language and speech of the blue-collar family or street folks we had grown up around, we were automatically invisible to a large part of the literary world.

Audre and I never really had a chance to follow up on that conversation. She left a day or two later for New York.

But in 1963, I tiptoed around that elegant West Village apartment, praying the kids wouldn't get jam on the drapes, or play loud enough to disturb my upstairs neighbor, and not knowing exactly why I felt so intimidated.

●　●　●　●　●

We had been back for about two weeks when we found our new place. It was an old, dilapidated house on Cooper Square, which had an empty store on the ground floor, and above it a two-story apartment with rough wide-plank floors and working fireplaces. The rent was forty-seven dollars a month, and you had to take care of your own heat, hot water, and repairs, but it had a rough elegance and enough room for all our needs, real and imaginary.

The current tenants were moving out of town, going to Los Angeles to become important art dealers, and they were asking a thousand dollars "key money", which was quite a bit in those days.

Now, I still owned that huge Jim Dine assemblage that he had made from a double-bed spring. It was the only piece that had survived from his first show at the Reuben Gallery; he had given it to me after the show closed because he knew I dug it, and he had no place to keep any of the work he had made for that occasion. I had dragged that monster assemblage to California and back, just because I loved it. It was my good luck piece, my connection to the artists and writers of New York, and for years on Houston Street we had hidden all our drugs except pot in the nooks and crevices of its cloth-and-plaster masks.

I loved the piece a lot, but we certainly didn't have a thousand dollars, and so I reluctantly offered it to the art dealer couple in lieu of the key money, Jim Dine having become prestigious in the course of the past two or three years.

Once the would-be art dealers saw the piece, they jumped at the offer. It probably made their art reputation when they got to the other coast. And so it came about, that I traded my one and only Jim Dine art work for the last real apartment I would ever have in New York.

.
.

We moved in. Thirty-Five Cooper Square was on a wide and busy thoroughfare which, just a block or two south of the house, became the Bowery. There were shiny brass numbers nailed to the red door, and a black doorknob, and you stepped into a tiny foyer, and found yourself looking dizzily upward at an enormous and crooked flight of stairs. They ran straight up without pause or bend, though there was, I recall, a kind of "landing" area, a large shelf-like space, to the right of the bannister and the stairs halfway up, an area which would later house many works of art—pieces of sets and props from the plays we had done at Poets Theatre piled helter-skelter.

You came out into a kind of hall that led on one side to the kitchen/dining room. The kitchen sported bare wood floors—wide, unfinished grey planks of some soft wood that had warped a great deal—and one of its walls, a large chimney, was stripped down to the brick, the plaster removed by the previous tenants. To look more arty, I suppose. There was a gas heater set against the brick chimney and vented through it, and a row of ancient oak cabinets separated the actual cooking area from this "dining room", where we soon placed a large round table, which, with its leaves, could open out to feed sixteen folks more or less, on important occasions.

There was a door on the far side of the kitchen which opened onto a roof—a baroque fantasy of Roof, of what a roof should be. Huge and dotted by strangely shaped skylights: pyramids and rhomboids, with here and there a panel of glass broken out, it was edged like many New York roofs with a low wall, and crisscrossed with clotheslines. A few random ledges sprouted here and there, with dubious dead plant material in broken ceramic pots. It did not take me long to try my hand at a garden, as others had before me, and with the indomitable optimism of a New Yorker I covered those ledges with potted plants.

The roof itself owed its existence to the fact that the store below us jutted out much farther in the back than our apartment did. Going out on it was a kind of casual way of going outside: one step up from the kitchen, through a street-sized street-style door, and down two or three steps on the other side, onto The Roof. It became an important adjunct to the house.

From the dining area, you went over another step that led nowhere, like some threshold stone at Newgrange, and found yourself in the living room. There, stripped down to the brick, was the one fireplace that *did* work. It was a true hearth, destined to become the center of our home and of most of the activities that would soon be sprouting there. The living room was spacious, with large niches on either side of the fireplace for large easy chairs. This was a *house* and most especially these were rooms (the dining room and living room in particular) built for large and ritual acts, and such did indeed take place there over the next two years.

If you went back out into the hall and then turned to your right you came upon two bedrooms: one, with yet another fireplace (this one not working), we gave to Jeanne, and the other we immediately dubbed "the nursery". It would be the base of operations for Dominique and the baby still on the way.

You could then proceed up rickety, slanting stairs to the upper floor. The stairs made a turn this time. There was a skimpy landing where you could climb out onto a much smaller roof, bare except for a large brick wall to your right. When you made it up to the top floor, you found a large space dominated by its slanting ceilings: eaves. There was a tiny room tucked completely away, a room in which one could only stand up straight in the center where the ceiling rose steeply. We made this our bedroom.

Then there was a huge, L-shaped attic space. We divided it in two with a wall of bookcases. Alan took the larger front half with a view of the street, and the highest parts of the ceiling. He rather liked the plywood backing of the bookshelves and had it stained so that he could contemplate the wood grain when he got high.

(And he did get high there a whole lot in the next few years. A beautiful old samovar tray from Russia, together with antique hashish pipe and accouterments all in sterling silver, became an essential part of this room and its hospitality. At various times Herbert Huncke and/or William Burroughs would come by to shoot smack with him, or several of us would take LSD together—though when we first moved in acid was just a rumor.)

He also had a couch in his study, and would languish on it in various poses and watch TV when the world got to be too much for him. A stereo with enormous speakers found its way to his room, and when the mood took him recorded music would shake the entire house.

I got the smaller space in back. It had a potbellied stove, a long built-in table and low eaves. I immediately dubbed it "The Study" and began to spend most of my time there.

I stuck the Gestetner mimeograph machine on the long table, placed my desk so that I faced a wall of my books, and set to work. I had a bright red IBM typewriter with an extra-long carriage for putting legal-size paper or mimeograph stencils in sideways and "doing layout" for small chapbooks right there in the machine. It was in The Study over the next two years that I would write the remaining sections of *The Calculus of Variations,* and all of *Spring and Autumn Annals.*

This was my refuge. It even had a bed: a fairly large and sturdy "studio couch" with a purple cover, where I would sleep when I was writing intently and wanted to wake up in the midst of the chaos of the work. Or when I wanted to get away from Alan.

It was a kind of precarious perch on the very edge of the space, but The Study served me well over the next two years. Sitting at that desk, staring blindly at those Mermaid editions of Elizabethan playwrights and poets, my only window a small one, set into the long low eaves at my back, I got a lot of writing done, some of it unexpectedly tragic.

From the moment when I first laid eyes on 35 Cooper Square, I knew it was the fulfillment of all those fantasies of art and the artist's life, *la vie de bohème,* harking all the way back to my high school years. Or before.

It was dusty, it listed to one side, the wide board floors would later prove to be rotten here and there, giving way suddenly under high heels, snapping them off and upsetting our would-be theatre patrons, the traffic was a loud, incessant roar under our windows, which I eventually came to think of as the ocean—but it was my dream house. As close as I'd ever come to that early vision. It came complete with garret rooms, roof gardens. It came with potbellied stove and fireplace, and tiny dormer windows, and a ridiculously low rent.

The only other house I'd ever love as much I lived in ten years later on the foggy northern coast of California, suspended over the tides of Tomales Bay. But that is another story.

This *vie de bohème* I was once more so wholeheartedly embracing included two (soon to be three) kids and a mad gay husband. All of which certainly wasn't part of the original script, but I was never one to quibble with destiny.

We were back in town, and with a style (largeness of household, spaciousness of quarters) that was unusual for Manhattan, to say the least. People just plain didn't have kids there, or if they did, it was *one* kid, carefully nurtured like a hothouse plant, not a bunch of them, noisy and scrambling up any way they could. And in the midst of all that "serious" art activity, too.

My friends had spent the three months or so that I lived on East Fourth Street avoiding the issues that Dominique's birth had stirred up by the classic device of not visiting, or not talking about those issues if they did visit. Mostly they never showed up and so from their perspective it must have seemed that I had suddenly gone from being a single mom with one precocious and wise four-year-old, to being the matriarch of a diverse and disreputable brood. Jeanne, taken singly, they could relate to—they *had* related to her, as a fellow artist, confidante, and playmate. But Jeanne plus Mini—and, soon, Alex—were something else. Not to mention that the ménage included Alan.

Also people in New York didn't have fireplaces, roof gardens, duplexes, except nice clean elegant ones they paid a bunch of money for, usually in the West Village or uptown. We, on the other hand, were as poor as church mice, but the spaciousness and location of our house belied all that. It displayed a kind of ramshackle elegance that was to become a trademark of Alan and me as a couple. Of our peculiar marriage. A blending of two wildly disparate fantasies of living in New York.

To add to the complexity, and to the legendary quality of that time and place, just down the street on the same block, at 29 Cooper Square, lived LeRoi and Hettie Jones with *their* two kids. I had known they were there before we first came to look at our place, but given the shortage of reasonable living spaces in Manhattan, I couldn't see that their presence should be a consideration in deciding whether or not to take the house. I figured we could all handle or ignore each other's proximity. The way I saw it, there was no way LeRoi and Hettie should keep me and Alan and the kids from such a perfect pad.

● ● ● ● ●

We dealt more or less summarily with the rest of the house. It was not, compared to our work spaces, all that important.

Oddments of furniture had been left behind by the last tenants, as part of the deal: a "federal" desk, which Alan pronounced elegant and immediately appropriated for his office; a rather uncomfortable but beautiful love seat, stuffed with horsehair and upholstered with worn gold velvet, which found its way to the living room; and a huge round oak table with many leaves, which opened into an oval that would seat sixteen on the Winter Solstices to come.

It all seemed to come together effortlessly. We gathered beds and dressers and kitchen chairs from anywhere. Our "stuff" arrived from the West Coast, and even more came out of my mother's cellar. We quickly threw together something that truly and miraculously felt like home.

The first and most pressing issue of course was to get some money. Alan dutifully made rounds to his agent, dropped in on a few auditions, and schemed a great deal on and off the telephone.

I put out the word, and got a job typing some manuscript or other for someone who lived nearby. Everything escapes me about that particular piece of gainful employment except that I had to do it at my employer's place, whoever he was, and that his place was dark and up a great many stairs. Making it up these stairs—with a kicking eight-month embryo inside me—was not as easy as it once had been. I noted that fact somewhere deep under the conscious surface of my mind, but would never have copped to it. Since pregnancy was a natural state, after all, there was no problem, right? Or if there should happen to be even a tiny problem, given my premise I would be forced to conclude there was something wrong with me. Not with the situation.

We squeaked by on what I made, and a little help from my family. The kids settled into their rooms. Alan somewhere acquired, and proudly presented me with, an ancient washing machine with a hand-cranked wringer on the top. He and I thought it a miracle of technology and proof, should such be needed, of the success of our hunter-gatherer activities. We put it in the kitchen, and a few times a week I happily scrunched the wet clothes through the ancient rollers before hanging them out on the grey and fraying clotheslines that some previous tenant had strung across the roof like a maze.

This roof, with its ledges and jutting skylights, was as close as we came to a garden, an out-of-doors space of our own. From time to time I'd give a whirl to growing basil, or mint, or Italian parsley there, with only medium success. In clement weather, I'd also hang out the clothes. The kids, especially Dominique and Alex, used it as their playground and private park. It had a few disadvantages: There were holes in the dirty, opaque glass of the skylights which jutted up randomly here and there, and on occasion one or another of the kids would thoughtfully drop a single sneaker, the only can-opener in the house, or some other essential object through one of those holes into the back of the empty and inaccessible store below us.

That summer was somewhat hotter than usual, and it was with relief and glee that Alan and I accepted an invitation from our friend Jack Smith, the experimental filmmaker. Jack asked us to go with him and a bunch of his people to Old Lyme, Connecticut, for three days in August, to shoot some scenes for his new movie, *Normal Love*. His previous black and white film, *Flaming Creatures*, had already achieved fame and some notoriety through showings at Jonas Mekas' Cinematheque.

Alan and I liked *Flaming Creatures* very much: its visual richness and complexity, the chaos of contiguous flesh, the jumble of genders and costumes were pretty much in tune with our own aesthetic interests—things we were trying and trying out in the theatre. *Normal Love* promised to go way beyond *Flaming Creatures*: it was in color, for one thing, and from the few stills we'd seen it was obvious that Jack Smith was a master of color in film. And the cast of characters, the splendor of dress and props and setting, the so-called plot—which was constantly shifting and changing— were matters of great excitement amongst those of us who were watching the progress of this flick. It seemed bound to be the movie epic of our time.

Actually, the difference between Flaming Creatures *and* Normal Love *was the difference that was everywhere in the air when we got back to New York.* Flaming Creatures: *black and white, stylized in its baroqueness, was held in check or given structure by the hint of old forms from which it led us. But* Normal Love, *blazing with gorgeous color, left no holds barred. The plot, the scenes, wandered where they would: through Bowery lofts and Connecticut woods. So many sequins, lizards, rhinestones, pythons, so much stained glass, make-up, art, flesh, costume jewelry, papier-mâché, spray paint, had never before seduced the film-goer's eye.*

In retrospect, there was a difficulty that would prove to be telling: Whereas Flaming Creatures *was finished,* Normal Love *never was. By the time Jack Smith was in the editing process, he was bedazzled by speed and the glamour of the footage. It literally cast a spell from which the artist never emerged to shape and name his work. It seems now to be a metaphor for the aesthetic dilemmas that beset those particular years, filled as they were with creative invention, and with amphetamine.*

We were, as the poet Ed Dorn said of another time and place, another people, "Crazy with permission".

Jack had arranged to shoot at Wynn Chamberlain's place in Connecticut. Wynn was one of a new group of figurative painters who were taking their subjects straight out of conventional portrait photography, projecting a photo right on the canvas and tracing it, and then painting the figure in oils. I didn't really like the work, though I was assured it was "good"—but Wynn was a nice enough guy, and very generous with his resources.

Alan and I sent the kids off to my parents' summer cottage at Greenwood Lake, and drove up to Old Lyme. It was a relief to get out of the city: the constant noise of the traffic, and the black, oily soot and dust that came with it, killing my plants and blackening the windows. Nothing to rest my eyes on but brick and dirt-stained stone.

The green was a relief. I had gotten more used to it than I realized in California. But this was better than anything Topanga had to offer: here, in the midst of an idyllic landscape a whole gang of my favorite urban freaks were at work, preparing for a show—for all the world as if they were backstage in a particularly elegant theatre on the Lower East Side. It was beautiful and amazing. A study in contrasts.

Besides the large and elegant house, Wynn's place boasted a three-story barn, and it was in the barn, against the backdrop of rough board walls with the green of the fields showing through gaps in the planks, that the various drag queens, ballet dancers, performance artists, painters, and what-not were hard at work: sewing costumes, hammering at props, painting cloth on the grass out front, their hot pinks and saffrons, whites, chartreuses, and lavenders contrasting with the many greens of late summer in Connecticut. In the mid-August heat they were all in various stages of dress and undress, various stages of make-up and bits of jewelry, and they sat there, utterly unselfconscious, fiercely ascetic, almost austere, in the slanting light that fell through chinks in the barn roof, fell through the trees.

They sat there, mending a tear in an overskirt, stuffing and darning the stiff toes of their ballet shoes, brushing some rouge onto each other's cheekbones, and it was there, for the first time, that I found myself wishing I held a camera in my hands. To shoot what I saw. From that day to this, some of my favorite pictures to shoot or to see are production shots, backstage or in the wings, in the alley behind the stage door or just getting ready for a shoot.

Claes Oldenburg had constructed a huge many-tiered wedding cake for Jack Smith on the edge of the woods, and my part in this particular shoot was to dance vigorously on the lowest tier of said cake, a print skirt tied under my huge belly (the baby was due any day now and my navel had popped out), and tiny pasties on my nipples. I danced, we danced—there were many of us dancing on all levels of this multicolored wedding cake. Andy Warhol was twisting rather tentatively and stiffly behind me, there was some scratchy rhythm and blues on a phonograph egging us on and on—until lo and behold, an *extremely* ugly Green Mummy (sewed into his green gauze outfit, and hence not able to get out of it through all the takes of the day in that August heat)—the Green Mummy, I tell you, came hulking out of the woods and we screamed and fainted, or did something of the sort. We all fell off the cake in any case, feigning various campy approximations of terror.

Now, from the lowest tier where I was dancing, it wasn't a very long way to the grass, and before we started I had figured out a fairly safe and comfortable way to land, but nevertheless, doing that routine over and over till we got it right may have somehow convinced the baby inside of me that my womb was no longer the most convenient and quiet place to hang out.

In any case, Alan and I drove home late that Sunday evening and I woke up at two in the morning with labor pains.

● ● ● ● ●

I woke up suddenly with mild but insistent pain. Urgent. And Alan was nowhere to be found. This was often the case: I was tired at night and crashed early, and he would go out and cruise: roaming the streets of mysterious New Yorks I had long since lost the desire to know anything about.

As I awoke, I remembered him saying he was going dancing with Gerry Malanga. I was annoyed, but not surprised: I'd kind of figured that Alan might not be around the night his kid got born. It was a good chance for me to play macho, tough and superior, and I took it. The kids were still at Greenwood Lake, so all I had to do was get dressed and pack for the hospital. I went about this slowly, with a certain deliberateness. I have to admit I was pretty calm, and felt fairly smug about it.

The labor pains were strong, but they were still about fifteen minutes apart, so it was all workable. I had just finished packing my overnight bag, and was writing a note to Alan before leaving to get a cab, when I heard voices on the lower floor, and Alan showed up with Gerry.

I never did find out whether they were lovers or just good friends in those days, and I didn't care much: Alan and I had already stopped being lovers. As far as I was concerned he could do what he pleased, with whomever he pleased, as long as he didn't do any of it in the house. Those were the carefree, freewheeling days before AIDS, when we prided ourselves on our freedom, but on this particular night I *was* glad to see him. I think I'd had it by then with taking taxis alone to hospitals in the middle of the night.

The plan was that I would have this baby at New York Hospital. Alan had good insurance with one of the acting or modeling unions he belonged to, and so for the first time I'd arranged everything ahead of time: registered with a hospital, and even gone through the red tape that would allow Alan into the delivery room (not so easy in those times).

Alan said a hasty goodbye to Gerry, who was standing in the kitchen not knowing quite what he should be doing. Then Alan got his car from wherever he had parked it and drove me to New York Hospital. But when we got to the buildings: institutional grey stone, and a bit grim-looking, he kind of balked at the idea of actually going in, and suggested that since my pains weren't too bad we might stay outside for a while.

It was getting light by then. We walked a little ways and watched the dawn break over the East River. It sure was pretty, but as we were standing there, me leaning on a railing for support, all of a sudden I felt a rush of warm liquid down my leg, and then the cold of the morning breeze on my wet skirt and legs. My "water had broken" as we used to say, and I watched a stain grow and darken on the cement. I informed Alan it was indeed time for us to go inside.

New York Hospital prided itself on being progressive. It had a program whereby the father could be in the delivery room while his baby was being born, and we had signed up for it. Little did I realize that it would make the whole proceeding even more bureaucratic and confusing, taking my attention from the main project on hand (giving birth to a baby) and putting a great deal of it into alternatively soothing the bureaucracy, and soothing my mate. But that is how it turned out.

First, there was the paperwork. Even though I was already registered, and my obstetrician worked there, the paperwork was endless. It seemed even more complicated and obscene than before my first two deliveries. When I had no money or insurance, the powers-that-be had fewer questions to ask me.

On top of that there were their ridiculous precautions. Once they heard my "water had broken" they insisted on sticking me in a wheelchair. My female macho told me this was clearly unnecessary (childbirth is a natural process, etc., ad infinitum). I protested mildly, but Alan was ready in his nervousness to turn this issue into a cause célèbre. Did I indeed need a wheelchair? Was I being coerced?

I quieted him down, but his fear and hatred of all institutional proceedings then turned toward the papers I was gingerly filling out. Lord knows, I was capable of enough paranoia on my own, without his fanning the flames.

We finally got through all that and I was wheeled up to a labor room where Alan could hang out with me, and where nurses, coming in from time to time to check my dilation, assured me I had "plenty of time" before the birth. I in turn assured them I did not. I could tell from the strength of my contractions. I pointed out that this was not my first labor, that I knew whereof I spoke and they should call my doctor. But they just shook their kindly understanding liberal heads at me, as if I was being unreasonable but they could dig it, and went on their several ways.

Of course I was right, and Alex began to arrive rather quickly, and I was moved to the delivery room long before the doctor arrived, and he was quite chagrined at not having been called sooner, but got there more or less in time anyhow.

Meanwhile, at the door of said delivery room a great ruckus was in progress. Alan was being refused admittance because he had refused to remove his shoes and put some sterile paper thingies on his feet. Nobody had forewarned him about this, and I guess it took him off guard. I heard him shouting in the doorway behind my head, offering to knock the nurse down if she didn't let him in.

They stationed him in the far corner of the room, where he could see everything, but would be nowhere near me or the doctor—whether because of his shoes, or because his hospital etiquette left something to be desired, I am not exactly sure. He, to do him credit, stayed where he was put, and when I called his name during the proceedings, he would answer loud and clear—fiercely even—that he was right there. It was a definite help.

I had told my doctor beforehand that I wanted to be awake throughout the birth. He had agreed, and even suggested that I might want to have a mirror placed so that I could see the baby come out. This was a pretty advanced idea for 1963. I was most grateful for his softness and understanding. This gentleness extended to his approach to birthing. I knew from talking with him that he was completely opposed to the use of forceps. On the delivery table it became more than a theoretical issue.

Alexander it turned out was coming out face up—instead of presenting the back of his head to my cervix, he would be presenting his face, unless he could be turned in the birth canal. This was no easy manipulation, for me or for the doctor, but he did it with no tools but his hands touching the baby. In the process, he had to cut me more than once, so that he could get a hand in high up, and guide the turning of the baby. I was awake for all this, and he told me every step of the way what he was doing. Amazingly, I remember only the usual amount of discomfort: I'd no doubt been given a strong local anesthetic.

What I do remember is the triumph when Alex finally made it into the light of day about 9:30 in the morning—only a few hours after that dawn over the River. I could see him crowning in the mirror, then bursting through. The joy of that. And the subsequent fear when it took a moment for him to breathe or cry (they had to clear a plug of mucus out of his nose and throat).

The "completely natural process" had been a little tricky this time, and I was never so glad to get a baby into my arms.

But it still wasn't over. Alex was okay and the placenta came through, but there was a good deal of stitching up to be done. The doctor suggested that, since I'd seen the birth in the mirror and held my baby, maybe I wouldn't mind if they put me out for the sutures. I said okay and they gave me gas.

The next thing I remember is from very far away being told by a stern voice to "Breathe". I took a deep breath: it felt wonderful, like having a drink of water when you are very very thirsty. But I guess it didn't occur to me to keep going. The voice said "Breathe" again, and I did, with some deep wonder at how amazing breathing was. I don't know how many times this happened. Finally the same voice said clearly, "Breathe and keep breathing". That was a directive I understood and could focus on. Focus my Will on. I paid careful attention. I kept breathing, and after a while I opened my eyes.

They told me later that the anesthesiologist had overdosed me, and for a little while there it had been touch and go.

New York Hospital had "rooming in", which was new, and considered experimental. Your baby in its cradle stayed in the room with you all day, but was taken away at night to assure that you got plenty of sleep. The best of two worlds. In those benevolent times, Alan's medical insurance was willing to pay for me to stay up to ten days in the hospital after a delivery, and the doctor had strongly suggested that I take advantage of this and rest up.

I had had enough experience by then of how bone-tired one is after the baby is born, so I had concurred, albeit a bit guiltily, thinking I should be home, taking care of business. It turned out that I took care of plenty of business from my hospital bed: Alan managed to arrive almost every night with a new crisis for me to solve.

•

It was around midnight on the sixth night after Alexander's birth that I started hemorrhaging. I rang for the nurse and finally got someone who frantically called for the night doctor. The doctor took his time getting there. Meanwhile I was soaking through everything they could slide under me. All it took was moving my legs, even slightly, to precipitate a torrent. I felt like everything inside me was rushing out.

During all this hullabaloo, a nurse's aide appeared out of nowhere. She was a short, thickset woman with a German accent. I had never seen her before. She took one look at my pale face and the red sheets and disappeared, returning in a moment with a large rubber glove which she'd filled with ice. She placed the glove with the palm on my lower stomach over my womb, its icy fingers reaching down toward my cunt, and left it there, and my bleeding slowed to a trickle. I breathed easier, and wondered once again at the innate wisdom of some of the women who work the lowlier positions in these places.

Of course, when the doctor on duty finally arrived the first thing he did was throw away the glove of ice in disgust. I explained to him it was helping and he looked at me like I was mad. Like he was caught in a conspiracy of madwomen. I was starting to bleed more heavily again as, without doing anything whatsoever to improve the situation, he ordered me off to the intensive care unit, so "they" could do a scraping of my womb as soon as the operating room was free.

It was about two and a half days before they got around to the surgery, during which time I was bleeding—though somewhat more slowly—and nursing the baby they brought in to me every four or five hours. I was not to eat anything, they informed me, so I'd be ready whenever there was a break in the action and an operating room freed up. I could sip a little water if I must, but really shouldn't drink anything either.

I proclaimed loudly as I could (I was starting to get weak) that you can't keep on nursing a baby and fasting indefinitely. Especially without fluids. And bleeding, too, by the way. I assured them that my milk, strength, and sanity were all about to give out.

I tried to describe the glove-of-ice device that had slowed down the bleeding. I explained it insistently to anyone who would listen. They all just peered at me as if they thought I was crazy, or some low but vaguely interesting form of life, or they ignored me, as one might a vociferous rat in an expensive experiment.

•

In the midst of all this, they had also neglected to call Alan and let him know where I was, so when he arrived for a visit the next evening, he found my bed empty and promptly decided I was dead, and that he was left with three kids to raise. On his own. By the time someone figured out who he was and showed him where to find me, he was blind with terror and rage.

"I FORBID YOU", he thundered, as though it was in any way up to him, "TO HAVE ANY MORE CHILDREN. It is too risky". (My soft-spoken obstetrician that same afternoon had told me the same thing only more politely. I had decided that he was nuts, and now I decided the same thing once again, this time about Alan. I was silently and smugly pleased that, Alan and the doctor both being men, these decisions did not in any way rest with them.)

I listened while Alan ranted for a while. I was starving, weak, lonely, scared, facing, I figured, imminent death from bureaucracy (since the powers-that-be couldn't manage to clear an operating room for the very short procedure I needed to survive) but I pulled it together long enough to console Alan for getting so scared, as well as for the fact that, having spent all our spare money on his car, he now couldn't figure out how to pay the rent.

I sent him home as soon as I decently could.

● ● ● ● ●

Alan hired someone to help me when I finally got home, a Black woman named Harriet who came in every day to clean and take care of the kids.

She also spent hours holding Mini on her lap, the two of them the picture of contentment, neither saying a word. She also tried to teach me what some of my postpartum rights were, though I'm afraid I made a poor student.

If we were in the South, she told me, after a hard birth like you had, you wouldn't be allowed to touch your foot to the floor for at least three months. At least. She had stories of childbirth amongst her cousins and neighbors to back this up.

It gave me pause. I was exhausted. And being married to Alan had isolated me more thoroughly than I had ever been isolated before: there were no friends dropping by to see if I needed groceries, or to hold the baby. There was nothing informal going on—people didn't just drop in on us—though

I wasn't sure if this was a function of a married state in general, or more particularly because I was married to Alan. Visits happened, when they did happen, more or less as they would in straight middle-class houses. We invited someone or they made arrangements, often a week in advance. But the extended family I was used to—everyone setting their hands to whatever was needed: whether it was licking envelopes, or hanging clothes—that was lacking. I guess it just doesn't come along with marriage. Isn't part of the package. And, too, Alan was a much more formal guy than that.

My job, Harriet insisted, was to stay in bed and heal, and nurse my baby. Many a time I wished it was that simple.

Alan had been shocked and shaken by Alex's birth. He told me often that what he had seen made it impossible for him to sleep with me again. We had actually stopped being lovers sometime before the birth. Our celibate marriage would go on for almost six more years.

This was fine with me. The last thing I needed was to sleep with anybody. It was all I could do to try to regain my strength, to get past needing to sit or lie down most of the time, and get back to work with the vigor and interest I had always had—and had come to rely on.

Alan soon insisted that Alex sleep in the nursery with Mini. Alex was about six weeks old when this came up, was still of course not sleeping through the night, but Alan didn't want him on the upper floor, in or near the bedroom. He said that Alex was keeping him awake, and he probably was, but I had always considered that part of the normal dues of parenthood.

Alex was moved downstairs, I was too weak to argue much, and was powerless in the situation, something I couldn't quite bring myself to admit. I developed the habit of sleeping very lightly, going downstairs in the middle of the night, and sometimes sleeping with Jeanne in her room next to the nursery.

Needless to say, all this was not conducive to my quick recovery, nor to Alexander's sense of the all-rightness of things, though Alan if pressed would have claimed he had made the change for me: so that I could rest and recover more quickly.

Harriet would wax eloquent at times about the beauty and closeness, the strength of the Black culture of the deep South where she had grown up. Once she said, "Oh, honey, I wish you could see it like it was! Folks were just so *kind*"—Then a change came over her where we sat talking;

both face and body changed. She straightened imperceptibly, squared her shoulders. Her voice, her expression became fierce and stern. "But when I was going to have my first baby", she went on, "I crossed that Mason-Dixon Line".

I learned a lot from Harriet that autumn, though it took me quite a while to put it all together. All she was trying to tell me.

chapter NINETEEN

Certain times, certain epochs, live on in the imagination as more than what they "actually" were, and there is always a price to pay for them. They are, if you look close, times when the boundary between myth-ology and everyday life is blurred. The archetypes break out of prison, as it were, and by some collective consent we or many of us, simply choose a myth and live it, heedless of the restrictions of the so-called "real world". Or we are somehow chosen by the myth we were born to live. Sometimes with deadly rapidity.

This meeting of world and myth is where we all thought we were going. Where we thought we wanted to be; it was so beautiful. Vivid, bright, and deadly, like some tropical flowers. Not human. Not cut to our measure.

But we—we couldn't see that. Thought we were gods. . . .

"The 60s" are often referred to as such a time, though what is usually meant by the term is merely "The Summer of Love" and its aftermath: 1967 and 68. Tip of the iceberg, if you ask me.

For me most of the 1960s, and on to about 1976, was a time bathed in the mythic. It was a time when the archetypes stalked the streets of Manhattan, numinous and often deadly. When angels, incubi, and other dreams of what *could be* settled in your hair and refused to be brushed aside. When we saw the creatures that lived in the fog worlds of San Francisco as casually as you see your corner grocer.

·

We had struggled so long and so furiously to find, reach into, the world of our feelings, our secret knowledges, and intuitions, and it was as if Something had caught us up, caught the hand we had slipped through some gap, and that Something was now pulling us in. Pulling us under. For as certainly as we knew that behind the facades our parents had lived there was the world of human feeling, behind that world was yet another that sought to claim us. What I have called the World of Archetypes. Inexorable bundles of soul purpose, often wearing human or humanoid form, sometimes walking among us. Without conscience and without regret. And so beautiful!

As I can tell you now, behind the Archetypes are vast impersonal patterns or textures of energies we might call Orisha. Or Yidam.

And behind that, perhaps the Void dances, not black, cold, or empty as we have believed, but dancing with light, sheet lightnings spread as a series of surfaces over nothing. And moving faster than the eye can register. Even the eye of the mind.

Our downfall was—it was *so beautiful.* For us, who had replaced religion, family, society, ethics with Beauty, who saw ourselves as in the service of Beauty, no warnings were understood, no traps anticipated. To go down, in the service of That—that was the ultimate grace.

But archetypes have their own drama: a vast uncharted cycle of Comedia dell'Arte, which they play out through us, without our informed consent. And with, ultimately, no concern for human purpose.

And it is not without reason that we have been handed by the science of our time the image, the fact or metaphor, of tectonic plates. Earth continents floating on a core of molten magma. As we ourselves float, melting a little, changing shape. Bumping against each other, lifted by, dependent on, in total chemical exchange with, the molten soul stuff I have here called Archetypes. That seeks to break through to the surface wherever the plates are thin.

The plates were very thin in 1964.

It is Winter Solstice 1963, and we are gathered around the kitchen table. Its Round Table quality has been stretched out into an oval by adding the several leaves that came with it—and there are now sixteen people seated at it.

It is the first time I have celebrated Winter Solstice. Nobody did back then, but I—I had long been aware of it as a holy day. Perhaps it was shown to me as such with the flashlight, the orange, my grandfather had used to represent the sun and the earth, respectively, as he demonstrated the tilting of the earth's axis and the resultant lengthening and shortening of the days. Implicit in all this was a sense of the sacred.

Implicit, too, in my mother's solemn annual pronouncement. "This is the longest night of the year". (How she hated winter!) "Tomorrow the days start getting longer".

It seems to me some long-lost but never quite forgotten sun religion, some religion of light from southern Italy that shone even in my family's eyes, spoke in the ritual greetings of the season. In the Brooklyn of my childhood where I had come to know the sacred interplay of dark and light.

Now we have gathered in the house on Cooper Square to celebrate the return of the sun. Freddie is there, and Alan of course. The kids are all abed, though Jeanne did come out of her room to join us for a while. I have invited Merce Cunningham, Jimmy Waring, and John Herbert McDowell. Remy Charlip is there and perhaps Nick Cernovich. I know John Wieners is present: he has come out from his hermitage in John Daley's house around the corner. Cecil Taylor is there, too.

I have made a burgundy beef stew with chestnuts, and there is salad and huge loaves of Italian bread. We drink wine together in the candlelight, talking and laughing, the light from the fireplace in the living room throwing long shadows among us.

I had delved deep into the fourteen volumes of *The Golden Bough*, in preparation. It was a birthday gift I had given myself in 1961, and this is the first time I really got to use it. (The year before, on a hint from John Cage—his "Music of Changes"—I had given myself the two-volume, boxed *I Ching*.) I had been eclectic with *The Golden Bough*, picking and choosing from different times and cultures whatever pleased me, or seemed possible to do in a house in Manhattan, and adding a bit of Pound to the rite for emphasis:

> *As the sun*
> *Makes it new*
> *Day by day*
> *Make it new*
> *Yet again*
> *Make it new.*

A chant we use on the Winter Solstice to this day.

After we ate, we moved close to the fire. I stuck an orange covered with cloves into the flames to represent the dying sun and its rays, and to fill the house with fragrance. I passed out long skinny strips of paper, blank and rolled up, tied with a ribbon, and invited everyone to write the names of their demons, the things they wanted to be rid of in the year to come. What could afford to die with the dying sun.

Everyone wrote but Merce. He handed me back the scroll, still rolled and blank, said he had no demons, and departed shortly thereafter, thanking me politely for dinner.

The rest of us wrote, and some of us read our lists aloud, and then we all rolled our scrolls up again, tied them with the pale blue ribbons, and one by one consigned our demons to the flames.

We sat in that magical living room, with its gold velvet love seat gleaming in the firelight, the huge Christmas tree already set up and thickly decorated, and the bare wood floors partly covered by a black goatskin someone had just given Alan. It was a space made for ritual, for miracles or tripping. A space made for funerals, too, but we didn't know that yet.

We lit candles in the windows to help the sun find its way back; it had to wander so far tonight. We cast an *I Ching* together for the year to come, and duly recorded it in a new red and gold notebook. Then we threw more *Chings* one by one for our separate fates in the year ahead. We sat talking a long while, smoking strong pot from the West Coast, or hashish out of Alan's silver water pipe, and snorting a bit of speed to keep us awake.

At some point, those of us who were left wandered through the kitchen and out onto the roof. To see the stars grow pale, dawn break. The sun had indeed made it back.

• • • • •

New Years Eve, 1963, Cooper Square:

It was as if the sun had risen after a long darkness. Longer than I could imagine—I couldn't even guess how long I'd lived in the dark. I watched the sun peek over some dark hill and then blaze out, watched its white intensity illuminate my interior spaces: body and mind. Illuminate the world.

Just then it was the world I was interested in. I watched each familiar thing in my familiar house retain its shape but change constantly. Flicker through time, as a flame flickers in wind. Holding its shape, the basic shape of the dark it clung to (for fuel), each object in the world flickered into and in the time-wind and disappeared. Like time was a fluid utterly mobile dimension visited upon us, upon the world. Disparate. Each several thing in its own time, arose and went. I thought I could understand now what Dogen Zenji had meant, by what we coarsely translate as "Being-Time".

I had come home to a place in the mind that I had never left. It was familiar as the palm of my hand, but I hadn't even been able to recall it. Hadn't remembered anything about it, or even thought of this place for these many lives. And yet it was instantly, luminously familiar. "Oh, of course"! Nothing to think about here. Nowhere else to go. Only one terrible worry, terribly present:

"I don't want", I said to Jo—Jo was there with me, we were sitting on the stiff golden love seat by the fire; we were sitting alone on a couch in Alan's study. We had moved from spot to spot without doing anything, or that's how it seemed. We moved by thinking the next place around us.

"I don't want", I said to Jo, "to ever come down". And it was then she gave me a great gift, something I carry with me to this day.

"I don't ever want to come down", I said, seeing far below me the world I once thought I lived in.

"You won't", said Jo. As certain as any sibyl.

Like passing an amulet millions of years old into my hands.

I don't want to ever come back down, I said.
You won't, she said.
And somehow I knew she was right. I never would.

She gave me entrée, permission to go on. If none of this was to be taken away from me, ever, ever again, then I didn't have to hang onto it with both hands, try to remember every last detail. It was my kingdom, the kingdom of heaven within, and by all the goddesses and gods, by the Solstice sun I'd greeted just ten days before, I would come back here whenever I liked.

I turned my attention to the trip at hand.

It was ten nights or so after the Solstice party, and I had just taken my first acid. I'd been hearing about acid all year, but tended to discount it. Alan had told me several times about a trip he'd had the previous summer somewhere out in the country when he'd lain all night under the stars watching small candles gutter where he'd placed them in holes in the earth. The melted wax, the blinking lights above/below, ancient cup-holes reflecting the sky, and then the dawn.

Alan tended to exaggerate, and I to be wary, so I had decided to set the whole thing aside, at least for a while.

But this stuff had come so easy: a call from a friend, did we want any sugar cubes for New Years Eve? and Alan said yes, of course, and I ordered four thinking that John McDowell and Jimmy Waring, who were spending New Years Eve with us, would trip too.

Someone came to the house and dropped off four cubes, each wrapped in tin foil. It came with the briefest of instructions: something about not eating for a few hours before you took it. I put the four cubes in the top drawer of my desk until the kids were asleep.

They were asleep, they didn't know from New Years: their holiday was Christmas and we had just played that one to excess. Now it was our turn, the grownups, and I came downstairs with the four cubes in hand, wondering what to do, because now there were five of us: Jo had come over unexpectedly to spend the holiday. It turned out though that neither Jo nor John McDowell nor Jimmy Waring wanted to try this new drug. I coaxed and cajoled, but then I left them talking at my kitchen table and went upstairs to eat a sugar cube in my study.

When I came down they were still talking, but something had changed. The light in the room for one thing: light around, thrown off by, all objects, but more and stronger around living things: plants, people. I tried to describe this and was of course ridiculed, so I did the smart thing and started listening instead to what my guests were saying.

It seemed Jimmy was taking John McDowell to task for his lifestyle, telling him that he, John, would never be a serious composer till he stopped cruising the streets. John, in his turn, was fiercely defending his lifestyle.

As I watched, they became caricatures of themselves: Jimmy's pinched, serious ascetic face became positively medieval, like the idea he was pushing, that one gives up everything for art. John's face went from jovial to dissolute, and yes, maybe a little sly. He looked like a ferret, or a weasel, I thought. And attached as these creatures are to getting his own way. The argument itself seemed eternal and unwinnable. I realized that neither of my friends knew that they were just mouthing ancient philosophies. Meanwhile the acid was coming on clearer and clearer.

I put one hand on either of their shoulders. I stood between them, in the electric stream of their dispute. "Do you know", I asked, "that you guys have been having the same argument for hundreds and hundreds of lives"?

Jimmy made an annoyed sound. I looked at him, and for the first time I think I saw him clearly. I saw him moving down a dead-end street, saw how desperately he needed this acid, or something, anything, to open him to possibility, to the real *force* in things. How he was drying out, cut off from his sources of nurture, relentlessly driving himself: creating and teaching and counseling us all, but with no nutrients coming back in.

I again offered him some acid. Though this was hardly the right moment, I tried to tell him about the flames that all matter was, but that just made him nervous. He put his small hand up against his fine, thin nose, in one of his characteristic gestures that signaled he was at his wit's end. Then I did something which shocked even me, even then: I tried to force a cube between his lips, but he clenched his teeth. I felt that I was trying beyond all reason to save his life, and perhaps it was true.

I gave up after that, amazed that I had actually tried to use force. John McDowell had meanwhile barfed on the kitchen floor, "from the energy", he told me (and possibly too from cheap wine). I made no attempt to clean it up. Wandered back to the living room to pursue my trip.

The house was jeweled, gilded. The bare brick sparkled like gold dust, and the fire (someone, Jo I suppose, had started a fire) threw its magical light over the walls, the furniture, the stairs.

The house had the splendor of a bare and medieval castle: the sudden niches, vaultings and fallings of ceiling, access to the stars from various ramparts (roofs) all marked it so.

The bare wide plank floors with beautifully warped boards were marbled, multicolored, and they disappeared under a most beautiful and medieval fur—black goatskin rug spread out in front of the hearth. I found that my task was to sit, or lie, on that rug. My task was to watch the fire.

I knew without question I had broken through into some world of truth I had always longed for. World of Eternal Verities. Stepped over some invisible threshold, through some insubstantial *tori'i* gate, same landscape on either side. Everything was as it always was, but now I saw it clearly. Saw with "new eyes".

I saw that the world—my house, the streets when I went out (how ancient they were! More ancient and layered than Rome, time moved so fast here)—I saw that the world was indescribably beautiful. That fact, while delightful, was not exactly news. But beyond that I also saw it sacred, and vast—much vaster than I had suspected.

I saw that we were still in the world's First Day, inventing Fire, giving Names to things, saw our tribes, our various myths, what we each held dear, how much of that was ancestors speaking through us. How much was the place where we stood. A wedding of order and chaos. Seamless. So well done we had never even noticed.

Beyond that, so much of what I had ever read or studied of Eastern thought was now suddenly available to my senses. Right here. Palpable. Aura, the living light around things. The emptiness, insubstantialness of being. Everything flickered, quivered and warped around me. I stood in a wind of change, which was wind of time, and I could smell the past in that wind. Could smell the future.

● ● ● ● ●

By mid-February 1964 the New York Poets Theatre was back in action. We had prepared for months: chosen plays, arranged them in programs, and cast them, and Alan had gone into full swing right after New Years, raising money based on our nonprofit status. But it would be a mistake to think that this was business as usual. We had by this time no business as usual, found ourselves making up each day from scratch as it came along. And no two of them were alike.

Now there is excitement in this, but there are also terrible disadvantages. It takes a lot of energy to re-invent the world on a daily basis.

Alan found us a venue, the New Bowery Theatre on St. Marks Place off of Third Avenue, and we rented it for a four-month season, February through May. Unlike the East Tenth Street scene of 1961, this was a real theatre, with a hanging sign, and a stoop, entry and lobby and seats and a proscenium stage.

We started immediately. Our first program (true to our formula of only doing one-act plays by poets) consisted of *Loves Labor, an eclogue* by Frank O'Hara, *Three Travellers Watch a Sunrise* by Wallace Stevens (which nobody bothered to get permission for) and *Murder Cake* by me.

Jimmy Waring had already directed a version of *Murder Cake* at the Judson Poets Theatre while I was in California, and he still had most of this cast, and a pretty good idea of what he wanted to do. (My plays have no plot, or stage directions—they are "word scores" for a director to do with as s/he wills.) It had to be re-blocked, of course, needed a new set, and a new "Dante" character (Alan, who came to unending grief in the part). But that one was easy.

In *Three Travellers Watch a Sunrise* Alan made the mistake of both directing and acting in the same work. The play's simplicity and genius was emphasized by a set by Peter Agostini—an elegant sculpture of a tree with a hanged man in its branches. The sculpture, and the words, carried the piece in spite of forgotten lines and other disasters.

But the pièce de résistance was *Loves Labor* by Frank O'Hara. In contrast to the small cast in my play and in Wallace Stevens', Frank seemed to require a cast of thousands. There was a screaming queen in a tiger skin playing a shepherd, with many dancers for his sheep; Freddie Herko in a black cape was Paris; John Vaccaro, slim and monocled, with a top hat, played Metternich, and no less a personage than the "great" freak show artist and drag queen Frankie Francine portrayed Venus. Alan cast and directed this play, and he did himself proud. There were moments when twenty or more people were cavorting separately on that little stage—a great demonstration of the harmony of chaos. And Frank had given us the entire Decline of the West in less than four typewritten pages of hilarious poetry.

Of course, many folks who had come along with us this far absolutely *hated Loves Labor.* Jimmy Waring was one. I had long, and earnest arguments with Jimmy about the merit of Frankie Francine's performance: Frankie could never remember a line, and whenever he had to speak he'd whip open his fan with a great flourish, his wig and its tiara atremble, peer shortsightedly at the spot where he'd written those particular lines, and read them in a 1930s radio voice, pausing portentously after each line to refind his place.

The audience loved it, but Jimmy thought it was horribly embarrassing and reflected badly on all of us. There was a difference, he said, between *seeming* to be amateurish, and really *being* amateurish. He couldn't stand Larry Ree either, who was the first to come onstage, wrapped in his tiger skin with shepherd's crook in hand, to intone in an indescribable accent "OH FAYMED OF THE ANCIENTS, HOW DAAARE YOU SWEAT IN THE GLAAAMOROUS SUN"? I wonder now whether it all wasn't just a bit too "out" for Jimmy. Not subtle enough. He preferred the light-handed gay references of a Cocteau movie. Or the innuendoes of the great silent comedians.

We did the plays on weekends, mostly Friday and Saturday nights, and turned the week nights over to various other programs. Jonas Mekas' Cinematheque showed short experimental movies on Monday nights; and there was a night for new dance, and a night for new music (mostly taped, played on the new "synthesizers", or composed using random techniques). John McDowell organized these for a while and then for a time LeRoi ran a jazz series. On Sunday afternoons we had poetry readings, often in the midst of the set of one of the plays. If there was a "dark" night we used it to rehearse the plays, as not everyone could come to the afternoon rehearsals that we mainly depended on.

We used the place around the clock, and used every inch of the space. The lobby became a de facto art gallery, and we had a couple of art shows, though we had the problem that our audience, many of whom were on speed, lacked a certain quality of discrimination and a couple of times made off with their favorite collage. There was very little moral sense in at least the fringe of this crowd. Things simply disappeared. We called it "knick-knacking" and mostly laughed it off, though when what was missing was a prop we needed that very night, or a serious painting or photo by a master artist, we took it a bit more seriously.

Somewhere around this time, a friend of Alan's and Freddie's, an Italian gay man named Sergio, died in Rome from an OD or suicide, it was unclear. And Freddie scheduled himself to do a memorial on one of the dance nights. He was going on last, but even so, he was late, and we had an audience waiting in the dark. Goofy as we all were, we were pretty good about theatre protocol: things started more or less on time, and performers showed up when they should. So that night Alan and I stalked the lobby, pretty freaked, or hung out on the stoop, looking for Freddie's cab.

He arrived in black tights and a leotard, with a fierce archaic face mask painted on his face, and whispered to us to kill *all* the lights: house lights, stage lights, everything. I noticed he was in toe shoes. Then I stood silent, in awe of what was about to happen—something sacred and diabolical all at once.

Freddie had an antique wall sconce with a mirror, the kind that used to hold a candle, and he lit the taper he had placed in it. And in that dark and suddenly silent theatre with his back to the audience, he began laboriously and slowly to go down one side aisle of the theatre, across the front below the proscenium, and up the other side. *En pointe.* The only music was the sound of his deliberately exaggerated and labored breathing. And the slow scraping of his toe shoes on the rough floor. The light, the flickering light of the candle reflected his painted face in the mirror in his hand.

He was gone again before any of us could move. No doubt he grabbed another cab and went back to his loft.

It was a birth, or death. It was the bardo none of us had heard of. It was one shaman accompanying another across. It was a rite of mourning.

The thing that rankled in me later was that when Freddie arrived late in the theatre lobby I growled at him about it, and never saw him afterwards to tell him what he had done, how great it was. That in itself should have warned me we were out of whack. We who had once put so much stock in "swinging"—an easy never spoken syncopation, moving apart and to-gether with no mistakes—had lost even the knack of speaking to each other.

● ● ● ● ●

Checking the old flyers and programs, I see that all this happened in a shorter time than I imagined. No more than two months and the New Bowery Theatre was lost to us, a sign on the locked door saying "This Poets' Theater Closed By Order of Police".

How we got there is more complex, but suffice it to say that our land-lady proved to be a nervous type who was steadily and unswervingly sus-picious of the avant-garde. I don't know what Alan told her when we got the lease, but she didn't like the look of our performers, she didn't like the look of our press, and when she got the bright idea that she would come visit our house a couple of blocks from the theatre, she for sure didn't like us.

(She told us in one of her moments of supreme hysteria that she was sure that the stains on her red theatre curtain were caused by the ejacula-tions of the men who sat in the front row when we showed experimental films.)

So it does seem likely that she was the force behind the police showing up at the theatre one Monday night just as Jonas Mekas' crew was setting up. The film that night was to be *Chant d'Amour* by Jean Genet. It was in-tensely erotic: passionate, angry, and political all at once.

I was there taking tickets when the police arrived. I had seen the film before, and had been looking forward to seeing it again, but this turned out to be the wrong night for it. The police were befuddled. They knew they had to take somebody in, but it wasn't quite clear who: I was the only one there who was actually involved with renting the theatre, Jonas had no clear arrangement with us. (He gave us some money on the nights he actually broke even.) However it *was* Cinematheque's program and they owned the film.

It was too good an opportunity to miss, and Jonas and I further confused the police by each insisting that he/she be arrested instead of the other, in a fine contest of Sicilian vs. East-European bravado. They finally decided to *arrest* Jonas and *cite* the Poets Theatre.

The bust gave our landlady just the leverage she needed to close us down, and she did it immediately. When we went to the theatre the next morning, we found a padlock on the door, and painted unprofessionally on the lintel above was a sign: THIS POETS' THEATRE CLOSED BY ORDER OF POLICE.

It didn't take us long to recoup our losses. We were a large and diverse group with many talents. By that night we had people picketing in front of the locked theatre, and others handing out information flyers, and refunding the rare ticket that had been bought in advance. We covered all the weekday performances, and let a lot of people know what was going on.

Others of us, at a much later hour, broke into the place and stole back our sets, costumes, lights, props, scripts. We didn't leave much. We had a borrowed truck waiting and Alan had made an arrangement with Joe Chaikin, who had a loft theatre, the Open Theater, for us to store our stuff there and to finish the run of the three plays there on the weekends (the Open Theater was between productions).

The arrangement didn't last long. Alan didn't get along with Joe, or the members of his company, or much of anyone else for that matter. He had a tendency to ignore everyone and do things his way, even if he was in someone else's space. But we did have the satisfaction of opening in Joe's loft on Friday night in spite of everything.

Johnny Dodd blew the lights trying to set up that night, and no one could find the fuse box: the Open Theater was in a commercial building, and the janitors had gone home for the weekend. We worked in candlelight. Each actor walked on with a candle and placed it where it would serve him or her best during the performance. These and a row of candle "footlights" were all the lighting we had, and it was very moving to see the plays in this way.

Stan Brakhage, the great experimental filmmaker, was in the audience that night. He had come to town with his family, and he and Jane and the kids had gone down to the New Bowery Theatre where the pickets directed them to the Open Theater (we started late so that everyone could make that double journey). It was the first time I'd ever met Stan or Jane. They loved the plays' being done this way, and all four of us struck up a friendship.

We had a wide and varied audience altogether. In fact if our landlady had ever come off her high horse and stopped smelling the theatre curtain, even she might have found some of it impressive. Bankers, Broadway producers, an East European princess, and many patrons of the arts and gallery owners supported us and came to all the plays, as well as famous and not so famous musicians, painters, and writers. A typical evening in the lobby that had been so ungraciously closed to us would have seen Larry Rivers, Morris Golde, Panna Grady, Cecil Taylor, Richard Lippold, Joan Mitchell, any number of dancers, poets, what-have-you hobnobbing and flirting as they waited for the lights to flicker.

The trial was still pending when we set to work to find another venue. We looked at several, but they were very expensive and there was a lot wrong with them, even at first sight. Most of them wouldn't have stood up to the city building inspectors who inevitably came to make trouble wherever something was happening.

That year the city was preparing for its first "New York Is a Summer Festival" publicity campaign, and making more trouble than ever. It was hounding the street people, trying to close down a lot of the small arts places and grungier cafes, and generally making life miserable for all of us. We held a protest march that spring, the Poets Theatre and Peter Schumann's Bread and Puppet Theatre, marching from the Lower East Side to the newly completed Lincoln Center with Peter's huge puppets and dragging a coffin. We called it a "funeral for the arts in Manhattan", and Alan had made a sign that said "New York Is a Summer Police State". We all carried lighted candles, or lit them at the end of the march, and extinguished them in a fountain at Lincoln Center, to point up that state art (Lincoln Center) was putting out the light of the arts in our town.

We had just made arrangements to take a space, were about to sign a lease, and were there cleaning up, when an Inspector appeared as if on cue, and gave us a list of what we would have to do to get permission to open. It was the last straw. Alan decided to try an outflanking maneuver.

There are laws on the books in New York that exist to cover "neighborhood clubs": those usually ethnic, sometimes shady, storefronts with "Sons of Romania" or some such painted on the curtained window. These laws governing private clubs allowed members to hold all kinds of events for themselves and their families, without having to obey the stringent rules governing theatres and other "public" meeting places. The salient points were: (1) that you had to have a book with the members' names in it; (2) that the members be issued some kind of identification; and (3) that they pay dues of some kind. Becoming a member and paying dues could not take place at the club (the space where the events occurred).

We promptly became the American Arts Project. Membership cost a dollar a year, and entitled you to go to all programs free. As a club we couldn't charge members for events, but we could take donations. We printed a couple of thousand little green membership cards, and set out to publicize the AAP and find it a home.

This time our hands weren't tied by the rules and regulations governing theatres, and we quickly rented a loft space in the Village, on Bleecker Street, right over Gerde's Folk City. It was just a big, bare room, which Alan and George Herms (who had joined us) found most exciting. A large number of extra-thick four-by-eight plywood sheets outfitted with pipe fittings on their undersides, and a great number of pipes cut to various lengths and threaded to the fittings gave us a flexible and workable stage. We could put all the plywood together at one height, or raise parts of the "stage" to different heights; have an island of stage in the middle of the audience, stage all around the edges of the room, whatever suited the piece we were doing.

Of necessity the stage lights were on poles, and there were fewer of them than in our "real" theatres, though some dramatic effects could be achieved. Given the vagaries of staging and stage managing, it seemed more sensible with this arrangement to do just one play at a time. We made up for the shortness of the programs, though: the productions were the most elaborate and beautiful we would ever come up with, and we added an "opener" to each show.

American Arts Project went on for two months, and we did one play each month. First was Kenneth Koch's *Guinevere, or the Death of the Kangaroo,* with sets and costumes by Red Grooms. Red outdid himself, creating huge towering gorgeous costumes for kangaroos and rhinoceri and others, and even arranged for Venus (Deborah Lee) to arise from the sea, golden hair and all. The whole thing was visually perfect, and satisfied and delighted everyone, even Kenneth who was an unconscionable fussbudget. For "openers" we used various short movies: George Méliès' *Trip to the Moon* was the most popular.

The next play we did was Michael McClure's *The Blossom, or Billy the Kid*. George Herms designed it, and Alan directed it and played the lead role. We opened those nights with an audiotape: Antonin Artaud doing his radio piece *To Have Done with the Judgement of God,* complete with gongs and blood-curdling screams.

We also managed to continue with a lot of what we had been doing on weekday nights at the New Bowery; though some acts traveled better than others.

It was very interesting to me that American Arts Project, where we never charged for admission if you had your one-dollar-a-year membership card, was the only theatre we ever ran that broke even. In the same way, *The Floating Bear,* which had no subscription rate, and which you couldn't buy anywhere for any amount of money, though you got a free subscription if you asked and we liked you—*The Floating Bear* never lost money, even counting in all the postage it took to mail it. My guess is that there's some magic in truly asking for donations, with truly no strings attached.

● ● ● ● ●

From the time we started reviving New York Poets Theatre, Alan and I had been in agreement about one main point: we needed George Herms in New York with us to make it happen. George and Louise and Alan and I had gotten very close in Topanga; we were used to doing things together, pooling resources, watching each other's babies. And, too, Alan had a genuine quixotic streak when it came to helping those he considered to be great unrecognized artists. Alan thought that if George were in New York he might make the connections he needed so that his work could support his family.

We sent the airline tickets, and the Hermses arrived while the first plays were already in production. We put them up in the living room on mattresses, and pooled all household resources and babysitting. Alan gave George his study for an art studio.

The plan was that George would make the sets for McClure's *The Blossom*. He would also work on wood blocks for a limited edition of a book that he and I were collaborating on. I had written thirty-two haiku—eight for each season—and George was going to carve a woodblock for each haiku. We would print a hundred copies of the book on George's letter-press, and twelve more copies with just the woodblocks, and in these I would write the poems by hand. We figured we could sell them all for an exorbitant sum (something like twenty-five dollars for the regular edition, and fifty for the handwritten one).

There was a special supplier in New England for hardwood blocks—you could get them type-high, if you so specified. George opted for pear wood, or perhaps it was cherry. We were looking at needing thirty-six blocks for starters (there were to be part titles for each season) so Alan and I bought forty to allow for mistakes.

George was in seventh heaven. He loved to work and loved good mate-rials, and we were fortunately able to skim enough off the theatre money to get him what he required. He set up an old easel and did some paint-ing, and worked on the haiku, often all night. For an assemblage artist the streets of New York were a wealth of free materials. His hunter-gatherer instincts kicked in, and he brought home boxes of fur scraps, sheets of old tin, bales of cloth remnants. He also rapidly found that there were plenty of good drugs in town, and got into most of them.

Louise, though, found it difficult to be there. She had never had to raise her babies in an inside where there was no real outside in which to turn them loose, and there are special techniques for that, which I took so for granted I didn't even think to try to communicate them. Just got freaked out when my various possessions were inadvertently cannibalized.

On our part, Alan and I had never taken into account that the cultural dif-ferences between the two coasts would be so telling. Having come back to Manhattan so quickly—in less than a year—we had slipped naturally back into a New York mode of living together and thought nothing of it. But to have the permissive methods of West Coast mothering smear my stairs with noodles and my books with jam, or undo some corner that was carefully arranged with little objets d'art—that was too much. I grumped and clunked about, and made everybody miserable, having never acquired the skills I needed to sit down and talk anything out. We didn't do that in Brooklyn.

Luckily I was grouchy only a small part of the time. I spent most of my waking hours feeling elated. I was a bit in love with George, I think, and he with me, and both of us had the good sense to say and do nothing about it, but often after the theatre was closed for the night and the kids and even the other grownups had gone to sleep, we would both find ourselves working: he in Alan's study, and I across the plywood bookcase in mine, while music and scraps of conversation flew back and forth.

It was good, and it was enough.

I was working at that time on a long prose book, *The Calculus of Variation*, coming to the end of it, and beginning to be aware that it was something extraordinary. It was exhilarating and more than a bit scary, and just the proximity of another artist, a real risk-taker, in the next room, carving a woodblock for my book of haiku, or working on a painting: it was an energy I rode through the last pages, and beyond.

Later, when I sat down to revise and clean up the prose as I had planned, I realized that I wasn't going to do that after all—that the rough edges and awkwardnesses of *The Calculus* were indeed *entrances* into a piece that was otherwise too abstract, and that though I could see exactly how to turn this particular book into a pyrotechnic piece of experimental prose, I just wasn't going to do it. This was important. A turning point in my life as a writer. It made me understand that I was no longer interested in so-called "good writing", but in letting the work lead me where it would.

But that spring we were riding a wave of creative power, me and George, and everyone else who was part of the dance with us at home and in the theatre, and no one warned us that it would ever end, or told us how precious it was.

There has never in my time been anything like those two "theatre seasons" as I think of them. Those four months: February through May 1964. I find I measure all other peak times by them. A kind of secret yardstick nothing comes up to.

It felt like that in early Venice, twelfth-century Provence, at Ficino's school outside of Florence maybe, in some years of Heian Japan. It might have felt something like that in Lascaux.

Closeness vision energy exaltation. Some kind of peak of camaraderie and hope. Some confidence that we understood each other (in all our disparateness) and that we were working in tandem with all of physico/ psycho/history. No kidding. The secret ways of Art would change the world. And there was no need at all for us to agree with each other. There was room and to spare for all our different ways.

Around the beginning of the year I started doing Wednesday night readings at our house on Cooper Square. I began by inviting just a few people, and letting it spread by word of mouth. Often I didn't know most of the people who came, and since we didn't speak I never found out who they were. Once in a while I'll do a poetry reading now, someplace like Tacoma, or Pueblo, and somebody will come up afterwards and tell me s/he had been at my house for one of those Wednesdays.

What would happen was that around a quarter to midnight I'd go downstairs and unlock the front door, and at midnight I'd start reading texts. Anything that interested me, that I was reading or studying. Or old poems that I loved. Sometimes other people would bring things to read. More and more people did, as time went on.

After a while it started to be that we would open the reading by throwing an *I Ching* for the week to come. Sometimes I would throw it, sometimes six of us would each throw a line. And later it began to be that I would follow the *Ching* with reading a story from Milarepa, and these two things became a predictable starting point, but from there it could go anywhere, and did. People would drift in, and sit at the round table, or stand around it, or sometimes we'd make a fire and all sit in the living room, and some people would come in during the reading, and some of them would leave before it was over. No refreshments were served and no one was introduced.

Some people came every week, some I saw once and never saw again. Freddie came every week but he hated Milarepa; he would rail against him while I was reading. He thought Milarepa was a terrible egoist.

But by then Freddie was getting more and more out of control altogether. He was still using speed, and now that Kirby was in town they used it together. It was needles now, not snorting or drinking a little in coffee, and needles scared me, they still do. I wrote him a poem that year that began "Dear Freddie, It's your birthday and you are crazy", and Frank O'Hara was shocked that I read it at a public reading at NYU, but I didn't see that it made any difference since everybody already knew.

But anyway the Wednesday Night Readings, as we called them, kept going right up until the time we lost the Cooper Square house in the fall of 1965. One night just before the end I read all the *Duino Elegies* by the fire, the Stephen Spender translation, while people came and went silently in the rain.

How Milarepa came to be part of the Wednesday Night Readings is another story.

One night that spring I was out in the city, just walking around and alone. I had the night off from the theatre, and with Louise at the house I had a lot more freedom. I didn't have to be around so much for the kids.

Louise didn't like to go anywhere, being afraid of New York, and I took advantage of this and got out whenever I could. Wandering footloose was an essential part of living in the city.

That night I felt called out in some way, and wended my way over to the Village. There was a store there that Alan and I liked to window-shop at, sometimes buying things we couldn't afford: things like ancient Mesopotamian snake bracelets or art nouveau jewelry. It was after ten when I got there, and the store usually closed by seven, but there it was—all lit up, and the door stood open. I walked right in.

I was looking for whatever had pulled me there, so I stirred restlessly about. The woman who owned the place didn't seem at all surprised to see me. There was the usual glass case with its green-bronze crescent moon, its carved semiprecious stones, its occasional ancient iridescent cup or goblet from ancient Rome. Hapsburg pendants. Lalique necklaces. I'd seen most of the stuff before, and no, what was calling wasn't any of this.

Then I noticed a small round table with a glass top, a showcase really, had just been added to the store. I went over and leaned on it, and peered down, and there I saw something very odd, and at the same time very familiar: a kind of thick silver locket, with a window in it through which you could see a tiny carved skull. The eye sockets of the skull were painted red, the carved flame coming out of his head was painted blue. And there was a piece of turquoise set in the top of the locket. "That", I said, and my friend took it out of the case and put it in my hands.

My storekeeper friend told me what she knew. That it was Tibetan, that the rolled up pieces of paper behind the carved bone relic were probably mantras, though they could also be some piece of scripture.

I felt enormous power in the thing, and didn't for an instant doubt that it was what had called me out. Had even seen to it that the store stayed open. But I was also a bit afraid of it too, and so when she said "Thirty-five dollars", I was only too glad to put the locket back in her hands and ask her to hold it for me. I'd pick it up later when I got some money.

But no, she said, I should take it now and pay when I could. She wrapped it in a piece of brown rice paper and put it back in my hands. I got the impression that she, too, was a little afraid of it, and glad to see it leave her shop.

When I got home I went straight to my study, and it was as if the *gau* (that's what they're called, I found out years later) was speaking in my ear. No—more like it was talking from someplace inside my head.

It told me it was hungry, needed some incense. (Grouchy sort, I thought.)

Showed me where in the room to set it (apparently I wasn't to wear it, but keep it as if on a shrine). And when I had it all set up I offered incense, and got told no, this would do for now, but it really wanted to sit on a bit of fur. Yak fur would be best, but failing that, whatever I could find. And no, I wasn't tripping, dear reader, in case you are wondering by now.

I got a piece of black fur from George's collection the next day, and set up my relic, who seemed pleased. I took to referring to it as The-Fingerbone-of-a-Dead-Sage in my mind and sometimes aloud. It brought a kind of order into my chaos. When I got up in the morning, I would quickly go offer it some incense. I mixed my religious metaphors as we were all prone to do in those days, saying my own private mantra "I take my refuge in Shiva and Kali" as I lit the stick. What that meant to me was taking refuge in the still eye of the hurricane, the heart of the dissolution of the world. It was as close as I could come.

And then one day, as I stood in front of this eye-level shrine staring into the carved eye-sockets of the tiny skull, I heard/saw the word MILAREPA in my head. Had no idea what it meant, but noted it down.

It took me a week or two to get around to it, but I went to visit my old friend, the magus of stage lights, Nicola Cernovich, at Orientalia Bookstore where he worked—it was then the only place in town to find out about things Eastern—and asked him, "What's a Milarepa"?

"Oh", he said, delighted, "you must be wanting this". And pulled a beautiful boxed two-volume hardcover set off the shelf and handed it to me. *The Hundred Thousand Songs of Milarepa.* An hour or so later I brought the books home.

Soon after I found I was getting up to burn incense, read Milarepa, and then sit for a half hour or so on my *zafu* from San Francisco Zen Center. It gave my days some kind of shape and they needed it badly.

What with theatre, writing, kids, fund-raising, the *Bear* and all the regular entanglements of life, there was no predictable order to things and it was driving me a little crazy. When I try to describe this time I sometimes feel that I must be making it up. That much couldn't have been going on at once. But that much was.

● ● ● ● ●

George being primarily an assemblage artist and thinking mostly in three dimensions, it was natural for him to sculpt the entire space at American

Arts Project into the set for *The Blossom, or Billy the Kid.* The play took place around, about, and inside of an exotic, brooding, and oddly humorous art piece. George even made six "Theatre Goers": an assortment of assemblages that more or less resembled humans and "sat" in the front row. They were the only audience that never failed us, and it was cozy always having the first row filled before you opened the door.

George made a round oil painting, *The Blossom,* and a huge sculptural flower from some Hawaii of the Titans—it had these thin carbon typewriter ribbons bursting from its center as pistils and stamens, and gigantic petals made of cloth and wire. And he hung paintings all around: flowers bursting out of cunts. Guns bursting out of flowers. To walk into the space was to become part of the piece.

Alan blocked the play so that it happened all around the audience. Toward the end, when Billy the Kid was hunted down and killed, the hunt wove through the entire room. There was a drum crescendo throughout the hunt, which took about twenty minutes. I did the drumming, using what I was given: a partially hollowed-out tree stump and a large stick. John Herbert McDowell told me later that what I did was impossible, that no musician could keep crescendo-ing gradually for twenty minutes like that, but I wasn't thinking of sound, or *listening,* at all. I was doing a dance. First with just the ends of my fingers, then my hands, then my wrists. Slowly my forearms would come into it, then my elbows, and so on. By the time I was making the full-out sound of the tree stump, I was throwing my whole body behind every beat.

The kinds of film that had worked to open for *Guinevere* wouldn't do here at all, so as an opener we ran an audiotape made for radio by Antonin Artaud, called in English *To Have Done with the Judgement of God* on which Artaud imprecates, screams, plays gongs, and rumbles his rrr's quite nicely. Allen Ginsberg had given it to me. A kind of nice touch was that Alan Marlowe brought over the two enormous speakers from his room and set them up in the front windows of the theatre, so that all of Bleecker Street within a couple of blocks of Gerde's Folk City was treated to the howling of Antonin Artaud each night that *The Blossom* was running. It sounded above the traffic, above the rest of the city racket, and in the long dusk Artaud's work, like he always meant it to be, was a magickal act.

Many folks came up to find out what we were up to, and wound up going around the corner to join the "club" at the house of one of our friends.

I've always loved the three early plays Michael McClure calls *The Mammals,* and of the three of them, *The Blossom* is the richest and most complex. In George's set, with Alan's direction, with the hunt in almost total darkness, and with the slow eerie drumming, it was quite an experience. Closer perhaps to ritual than theatre. I felt it go through me and change me every night.

But interestingly, a lot of our New York friends didn't like it at all. They thought it was self-conscious or too "heavy", and they had a thing in New York about not being heavy. Frank O'Hara told me sadly that he thought the play was a big mistake, and the critics seemed to agree. It certainly came from a different *Weltanschauung* than, say, *Guinevere, or the Death of the Kangaroo*. In fact, if you wanted to put two pieces side by side which compared and contrasted where the two coasts were in 1964, you couldn't have chosen better examples.

Guinevere, or the Death of the Kangaroo was witty, urbane, upbeat, silly, irresistibly charming, easy on the eyes. Gorgeous in fact. One came through delighted, with one's sophistication intact. And *The Blossom?* Dark, charged, romantic, existential, awkward, cosmic, grappling with questions to which there are no answers. Alan and I loved both of the plays and I thought both productions were perfect. But if I had had to choose just one perfection—I'd have gone with *The Blossom*.

This split goes deep down, close to the root. Art as magick, or art as entertainment. Not that there *had* to be dichotomy at all, but that there *was*. At least in people's minds. There was no getting around it.

When Freddie danced *For Sergio* at the New Bowery, he made a dance that was also a ritual. That magickally "did" something. Transformed something. It seems so simple now. But at that point many of us were groping our way backward to art as magick.

But all this was too new, we had no clear sense of where we were going, where we were being led. Only that we had to follow. Had chosen to have to follow, even though there were these good ways of making art we already knew and loved that weren't so murky, and that gave us lots of perks. Plenty of room you'd have thought.

After *For Sergio*, Freddie wasn't around all that much. He came by the American Arts Project once or twice during afternoon rehearsals, but he was too jittery from speed and constantly misplacing props and breaking things and I scolded him. We talked about his doing a dance program there, but it never happened.

What he did do was give a dance concert in his loft at 28 Bond Street. He invited a lot of people, the folks who would normally have come to see his work, and when we got there it seemed to be some kind of party. Dips and wine. And Freddie was nowhere in sight.

He had disappeared into his room, from which he eventually emerged in an odd-looking costume, and did a bunch of stuff: some dance, some playing the hostess. He then retreated to his private space, and continued to come out at irregular intervals, each time in a different costume, and performing a handful of anomalous actions. Or dance steps. What looked like "real" choreography sometimes. Many of the costumes were drag, but not all of them, and no one was asked to pay attention to any of it, but it *was* the concert.

This was art or it was not.
It was a lifestyle choice or simply madness.
This was a boundary, but it moved like a snake.
And Peter Hartman, the only one of us who knew anything at all about Western magick had fled to Europe two years back, hearing voices, he said, whenever he lived in the States.

Each of us took what s/he could from the innovations that were breaking in on us, and drew a line at that point. For Jimmy Waring, *Loves Labor* with Frankie Francine was a disaster. Frank O'Hara himself found it delightful, but thought *The Blossom* had strayed too far into schmaltz. Some people liked both plays, but got nothing at all from the concert at Bond Street. Boundary-less.

And there were of course other events that were happening all over town. Political demonstrations that were also theatre pieces. Censorship trials that were in essence happenings. *Normal Love* film sequences shot on a swing in a Bowery loft, the only performance the night of the shoot, the footage itself turned to celluloid dust on a cutting room floor before there were even rushes for the actors.

No one was sure that s/he couldn't or wouldn't manifest soon as Who they knew they really were. Or for that matter, the whole scene: a new society. Numinous. The gods we knew we were, who walked among us.

That's us, baby.

We had no way to talk about any of this. We were at the same time terribly intimate and terribly aloof. We could work shoulder to shoulder for days on end, on what we knew for sure were battle lines; we knew the smell and taste of each other's breath and sweat, but we never stopped, we never paused long enough to look each other in the eye.

And we had no vocabulary for these things. No concepts, really, for what was happening. Another world was breaking through to ours, and we were awash in it. We had in fact invited it and here it was, and mostly we saw it as good. We set blind boundaries, changed them, made impromptu rules, forgot them, quarreled, worked together. While some of us drifted out of reach on hard drugs, or the pure chemistry of denial and need.

But we had no words, not even the thought to look for words to speak what was happening. OR

before we identified the weather pattern, the storm had already broken. You could put it like that.

• • • • •

Freddie made one more dance.

He called it *The Palace of the Dragon Prince* and based it on some Russian fairy tale he'd found somewhere. It was to be huge, an epic, and use most of the dancers he'd worked with over the years, from his own company and from Jimmy's. A full evening, to be performed at the Judson Dance Theatre.

Kirby Doyle agreed to be the Dragon Prince, which meant he sat in a gorgeous costume in a chair that George Herms had sculpted into a throne by jigsawing out of plywood a background of bright flames, which framed and set off Kirby's beautiful head and body.

The piece was long and rich and complex with lots of ensembles and duets and trios, and solos galore. Nowadays we'd call it "a record of the soul's journey", or some such, and take it on its own terms. Whether or not it made any sense to us. Maybe we would ask "Is it dance"? but maybe we wouldn't bother.

But then it was just some place we'd come to, a parting of the ways where we were splitting off from our mentors, interested in something entirely else, but it was all so complicated because some of us were on drugs, and was it just that, and plenty of us were crazy.

There was lots of Romantic music. There were flowing costumes, *shmottas,* what somebody called the "junk store aesthetic". There was a long list of titles made by me at the last minute at Freddie's request after earnestly going over with him how he saw each part of the dance. And then letting the titles arise. I had no idea what they meant, but Freddie seemed to:

Return of the Two Headed Serpent
Rite of the Five Transits
Dawn of Diminishing Winds
Way of Bright Maze:
  Hamadryad's Dance
  Dance of the Five Faces
  Hall of Blue Columns
  Ring of Dark Mist
Oracle for the Brothers
Slope of Fire (Zenith)
   INTERMISSION
Slope of Fire (Nadir)
White Forest Dance
Night Litany:
  Pavanne for the Widows
  Word of the White Cat
  Pause for Jade
  Point of Deepening
Black Wine Uncovered
Five Transits Concluded

There were all sorts of trials and tribulations. At one point the dancers quit en masse. They were *not* on speed, thank you, and couldn't keep up with the hours, the physical demands, etc. It got patched up somehow— John McDowell and Jimmy Waring were the usual patchers but at this point Jimmy wasn't talking to Freddie at all.

I was used to these opening night crises from Alan's way of "working with his actors" as he euphemistically called it, but this was much wilder. I can't remember ever being as nervous on my way to the theatre as I was that night.

Alan and Jeanne and I came in full Renaissance costumes we'd borrowed from somewhere, and Freddie immediately put Jeanne in the piece. He carried her to the front, where she was to sit, on the raised platform that held Kirby's throne. She and Kirby anchored the piece.

Almost everyone we'd worked with in the theatre world was there that night: either dancing or in the audience. The place was full. Then the dance began and I could tell at once that almost nobody was getting it.

A full-out work—I thought it was extraordinary. Oh, I could see as well as anyone the flaws, the places that needed to be cut, the technical mistakes. Or the places where it got corny: too much emotion and you had to say no in self-defense. I could see all this, 'cause these were the kinds of things I'd come to recognize as necessary risks. (Like in my long book *Calculus of Variation,* for instance.) I saw the dance as extraordinarily brave. Mapping internal journeys no one else was looking at.

But the audience didn't know what to make of it.

"I thought it was appalling, just appalling", is what Remy Charlip said the next day when I asked him. I thought then that he was talking aesthetics, but now I do wonder was he perhaps appalled by the drugs? The impending madness? Perhaps he saw something that the rest of us missed.

So Kirby Doyle sat on a throne made by George Herms at the Judson Dance Theatre and was the Dragon King. He had worked with us in the theatre a great deal, performed in *Guinevere,* and had a pad on Ridge Street, south of Houston, in what wasn't SoHo yet. We called his place "The Opulent Tower" and Freddie lived there with him part of the time. That summer they made a second space on the roof, complete with carpets and old sofas, just like we do in California in the summer, only of course in New York it rains in the summer and everything got soggy and mildewed.

Freddie had a crush on some boy, a young actor, and he was planning to take him up to the roof and seduce him on that sofa, all hung with lace, like a high school doo-wop dream from his past or mine, only then it rained and the boy didn't come. George Herms took beautiful shots of Freddie dancing on that roof and I used three later in a a book called *Freddie Poems,* and Jess, the painter, used one of them to make a beautiful oil painting which I just saw again a few months ago at Paula Anglim's gallery. It stopped me in my tracks, it always does.

Freddie was getting pretty far out: wearing his black cape everywhere and black ballet shoes and carrying his flute in a black case. If somebody bugged him he would growl and snarl and raise the flute case as if to strike them, but as far as I know he never hit anybody. He never had to. The Puerto Rican hoods were afraid of him, or fond of him, or both, they called him Zorro, and many a diner on the Lower East Side gave him a free meal whenever he walked in. He had this set of Pan pipes too that someone gave him. I remember him walking down the middle of Third Avenue, playing them while the buses and cars went around him.

• • • • •

That was the summer the Living Theatre left for Europe. They were giving a lot of their stuff away, and had left the apartment door open and had clearly marked which stuff was up for grabs, and what they were taking with them. We went up there on the subway so we couldn't carry a lot. We got a chair for The Opulent Tower and Kirby got a silk tie to tie off with when shooting up. Freddie picked up some velvet and a mirror. There were boxes and boxes of printed lines for fortune cookies written by John Ashbery and Frank O'Hara and other poets for a fancy fund-raiser which had either happened or not, and I stood reading them for quite a while. While we were there I watched a guy I knew go into what was clearly marked as the Becks' private boxes and lift a signed Cocteau print in a frame. Later sold it when he opened a gallery, and it was the foundation of his fortune.

I hung out at The Opulent Tower a lot; it was my refuge from all the busyness and hustle that Alan loved—at one point we had four phones on Cooper Square, one dedicated to outgoing calls only. . . . So I hung, listened, talked, and watched folks come and go and sometimes I snorted a bit of speed or coke, whatever was around. I had tried snorting heroin once and hated it, so I stayed with the uppers and as always stayed away from needles.

Kirby and I had a thing for each other, but it was more or less up to me and I decided against it. I wasn't in love with Alan nor he with me, and we both agreed we could do pretty much what we wanted, as long as it didn't impinge on our lives at home, but I felt like my plate was pretty full, what with the kids, the writing, the theatre, and managing Alan's various insanities. He had a way of making the rent money vanish on a champagne party for opening night, or a new car, or vacation on Fire Island. . . . When I thought it over, I decided I couldn't give a lover the attention he/she deserved, and though this affair would have been fairly simple I thought I'd just try to keep doing the stuff I was already doing. Keep the world from exploding.

It turned out to be a little too late for that.

chapter TWENTY

On October 27, 1964, I was restless, out in the city, walking. I was preoccupied because tomorrow was Jeanne's seventh birthday. Trying to get the pieces of the party together, and thinking about her and me and Freddie the day before. We had met up with Freddie by chance near Cooper Union, where there was a bunch of wood piled up at a construction site. I wanted to take some home for the fireplace, and I got Freddie to help me, though he grumbled a bit and was saying a bunch of strange stuff.

He wasn't living anywhere at the moment, always an unwelcome situation in New York, especially when winter's coming. Kirby Doyle had gone back to the West Coast—following George and his family, who left in the early summer. Freddie had been living with his friend Deborah Lee, a dancer, but that hadn't worked out and just about two weeks ago she had asked him to leave. Now he was sleeping on the street, and using amphetamine and talking strange.

For instance, yesterday he asked me what had happened to the children, and when I wanted to know what he was talking about, he said we had killed all the children in the world.

Anyway we got the wood home, and put it on the roof off the kitchen to be sawed up fireplace-size and then Freddie was off to take dance class and he took Jeanne with him, like he sometimes did. They would take class together; Jeanne seemed to understand him and he took good care of her.

·

Freddie had gotten crazier when he started taking acid. Acid for me had been totally beneficent—even when what I learned was painful, it was always something true, something to work on. But not everyone had the tools to stick with a hard trip and learn from it, instead of just freaking out. And lots of folks were just getting high to have a good time. I don't know why Freddie was tripping, I never tripped with him as it turned out but he talked to me once about a trip he'd had.

He had seen his dancer's body with acid eyes, and seen how he had ravaged it with speed and neglect. Or, as he put it, he had "Destroyed his house". Now at this time neither I nor anybody I was running with knew beans about the body: its amazing regenerative strengths. Later I was to learn about macrobiotics, Bach flower remedies, and homeopathy in a fight to save my own life, but I didn't know any of those things then. So when Freddie said he had destroyed his House, I believed him. All I could do was look him in the eye and share his horror.

My own nature tends to be overly optimistic, and in Freddie's circumstance I'd probably have been looking for what I might do next: what new art I might follow if dance was gone. But for Freddie dance was an absolute. He had turned his back on music when he left Juilliard, and nothing but dance would satisfy him. Nothing but the dance he imagined he would do with time and practice. A kind of hubris we all shared in our different ways.

What Freddie didn't do was give up speed, or stop tripping.

On this occasion, I was walking along, worrying and mulling, when I found myself at Samuel Weiser's big, sprawling bookstore on Broadway, and went in to browse, not sure what I was looking for, or if in fact I was looking for anything. I always entered Weiser's with some trepidation: curious about those worlds of magick and the Far East, but not yet truly at home in them.

At one of the front tables, a book came into my hands, and I spent some time reading around in it. *The Tibetan Book of the Dead*, translated by Evans-Wentz. It looked interesting, but at $3.75 was too expensive, so I put it back and ambled on home through a kind of dull grey twilight.

I was bustling around, getting dinner and taking care of kids, preoccupied with all the usual domestic hassles, feeling put upon and not able to handle one more thing, when the phone rang. Alan was shouting something from the next room, so when I picked up the receiver I was already annoyed. It was Charles Stanley, artist and performer, who worked with us and with Joe Cino at the already famous Cino theatre.

Charles said flatly, but rather slowly and carefully, "Diane? I'm sorry to have to tell you this, but around five o'clock Freddie Herko jumped out of Johnny Dodd's window".

Johnny lived in a sixth-floor walk-up. I felt my irrational annoyance deepen: Oh God, he probably broke something, probably needs to be taken care of. Maybe he's even paralyzed—he'll be in a wheelchair, what a drag! Then I heard the silence around Charles' words.

"Oh Charles!" I said. "Oh Charles, is Freddie dead"?

It was the finality of it I remember. A kind of stuck place—the end of the film cut off and burned so you never see it. Never know what was supposed to happen. All of a sudden it was too late to fix anything. To explain later, to let him in when Alan wasn't home. To let him use the shower. To be his friend.

And no one will ever *see* me like he did. I already knew this. You don't forge links like that after your teens. Your early twenties. Good things happen, but not that intimacy. The jokes. Our private words: "Treat it with ignortion". How tender and scared I was, bringing Jeanne home. Our deepest loves.

How tender and scared we both were, two battered kids trying to make sense of the world, make some beauty in it.

Word spread quickly through the city and people began to gather at our house. Alan, unpredictable and out of control in ordinary times, suddenly became steady as a rock. He made some calls. Made a fire, cleaned up a bit for our guests, put out glasses and cups, put on water for tea. Lit candles.

People came in silence, it was a bit like the Wednesday Night Readings. They sat on the floor, or on pillows or rugs. They watched the fire, they drank tea, brought wine. Very little was said, as the room got slowly full.

I slipped upstairs and called Audre Lorde from Alan's study. Instinctively knowing she would know what this meant for me. More than any of these others who were closer to other Freddies. Freddie the dancer, Freddie the faggot, the junkie. Freddie the great actor, Freddie the wit. Mine felt too tender to share, to talk about in that room.

Audre said she was coming to get me out of the house. I protested, but knew she was right. She lived on the Upper West Side, but in what seemed a few minutes her big brown car was at the front door, and I went out with her into the city night. Passing on the way beautiful firelit faces, honed to new pain: Ondine, Johnny Dodd, Jimmy Waring, Deborah Lee, Michael Smith.

Audre drove me to Central Park, into a leafy, uninhabited space of trees and silence, and then she opened the car windows to let in the sharp smell of fallen leaves, and took me in her arms. A line from *The Blossom* by Michael McClure kept repeating in my head, OH, YOU ARE DEAD, it said. Oh you are dead, I said in my mind to Freddie. To all of us. Then nestled against her, smelling the good smells of her body, I let myself cry like a child.

When I got back to Cooper Square, an all-night vigil was in progress. I sat with everyone for a while by the fire and then I went upstairs to Alan's study and hung out in the darkness. Just in time to catch a phone call: it was Peter Hartman calling from Rome. Peter had never called us before but there he was, he had suddenly felt he had to call.

"What's happening"? he asked, and I told him.

Freddie's body was in the morgue that night, and was later turned over to his family for the funeral. They lived in Ossining, and we were a carless crew for the most part, but almost everyone made it up to the wake, or the funeral service, or both. The undertaker had had quite a job on his hands. The family wanted an open coffin, and in the fall Freddie had symmetrically broken both ankles, hips, both sides of his pelvis, both wrists. I had the image of him holding his ballet pose till he hit the ground. The family had very much wanted to be able to show his hands; they were still fixated on Freddie the concert pianist, never having acknowledged Freddie the dancer, and they had placed a huge display of roses in the form of a grand piano right up against the coffin.

Going to the funeral was good in that it lifted us out of context, out of that city. It was autumn for real in Westchester: pale blue skies and trees already almost bare. My friend Anna Butula drove me one of the times I went, and after viewing the body we went outside and stood looking down at the river that ran between steep banks behind the funeral home. Anna didn't say anything for a long time, just looked at the water, and then, in her fierce Hungarian peasant way spat out "And the scum of the earth still lives".

● ● ● ● ●

Johnny Dodd told us that Freddie had called, and come up to his house to take a shower. After, he turned on the stereo, put on Mozart's *Great Mass in C,* and danced naked to it, while Johnny sat hunched on the couch

watching him, knowing that something was going to happen, but not knowing what, or what he should do about it.

*That was the feeling we all had had for weeks, I think, but being for the
most part only fragments of our battered children selves, that feeling just
paralyzed us, as it had always done when we were little. As it must have
paralyzed Johnny on the couch.*

The bottom half of the front window was open, and Freddie just leaped
out not hitting the frame, jumped out and went straight UP before he
came down. Johnny said it was an impossible move, there was no way it
could have happened, but it did. Even as he watched.

Of course, it took Johnny a while to say all that. Years in fact. All we
knew at the time of the funeral was that Freddie had gone to Johnny's,
showered, danced naked, and then jumped.

● ● ● ● ●

The week before he died, Freddie had called for a big party to be held on
the roof of Kirby's old Ridge Street house, The Opulent Tower. Kirby was
gone, but the people who lived there now would let us use the roof, he
said. He was going to dance a new dance for us, a "flying dance" he called
it, and he wanted me to bring my recently finished manuscript of *The Calculus of Variation* along, so I could read some "flying poetry" while he
danced. I stayed away that night, as did almost everyone. Two or three
people came, but there was no party: Freddie had gone on from Ridge
Street to other adventures. Not sleeping, apparently, from that night until
his death.

On the day of the burial, I stayed alone with Freddie for a minute, just before they closed the coffin. I put a ring and a lock of my hair in his hands.
His flesh had gone by then from quiescent to cold and waxen, so I figured
his spirit was no longer there, but I whispered, "Don't be afraid, Freddie".
It was the only for-sure death instructions that I knew.

I had dressed for the occasion, thinking How would Freddie like me to
look? I had put on a long robe, and my full-length black velvet cape, and I
had taken my hair down for him. It was long enough for me to sit on.

Freddie's magickal consort Ariane was there, with her black hair and
black eyes. She was a sacred prostitute, streetwalker and speed-sister of
Freddie's and she came all in white and put a rose in my hands.

Alan Marlowe was one of the pallbearers, as was Bret Rohmer. And several young male dancers, dressed in suits, with red haunted eyes.

It was neither the beginning nor the end of anything, but it was a hinge. A turning point for many of us. People, I think, came to realize they would die, and they began to take steps, to move toward the work they most wanted to do.

It had a ripple effect. For the next couple of years friends kept leaving for foreign lands, or quitting their jobs to become full-time actors, or painters. Whatever. Deciding to lay what they had on the line and take their chances.

● ● ● ● ●

The morning after Freddie's suicide I went back to Weiser's as soon as it opened. I bought that copy of *The Tibetan Book of the Dead*.

Over the next two days, while serving as information headquarters, ride arranger, counselor, and whatever else was needed, I tried to make heads or tails of this great religious classic. I skipped around in it, read it through, pondered, read Jung's introduction, pondered some more. Neither the book itself nor the commentaries said anything specific about suicide or violent death. I had the feeling there was special stuff I should know, but I'd have to do without it.

I finally did figure a few things out: (1) that no one ever knows for certain exactly when to start this ritual (unless they are enlightened, and can "see" what's going on), but one usually began somewhere around three days after the death; and (2) one would never know for sure (unless one was a great lama) whether the person who died had gotten off the Bardo Train, as it were, by some fortuitous realization, and hence, when one might stop the daily prayers. I figured that in this case I'd better play it safe. I'd start three days after Freddie's death and go the whole forty-nine-day course. I had even figured out which prayers got repeated each day and which constantly changed: no mean feat, as Evans-Wentz and Carl Jung threw little or no light on actual procedure. I decided to read the prayers for forty-nine days.

A surprising number of people joined me. We were a singularly unreligious bunch, and I had expected ridicule or silence when I mentioned the book, but instead I got a handful of earnest New Yorkers, buying their own copies, or reading over my shoulder, struggling with Tibetan names and alien concepts, and melting away again into the autumn dusk.

We would do the prayers in the kitchen in the evening. I would unlock the front door and people would just come in. Johnny Dodd and Michael Smith came every night. Others, like Frank O'Hara, came once in a while. Some people arrived straight from work in suits and ties. I had to cut through my own tendency to apologize for the material—it was so intense. My need to make sure it was okay with everyone.

It was okay. It would be dark when we started, between seven and eight. I'd light a candle on the kitchen table. We would begin to read:

Ye Compassionate Ones, Fred Herko is passing from this world to the world beyond. He is leaving this world. He is taking a great leap. No friends hath he. Misery is great. He is without defenders, without protectors, without forces and kinsmen. The light of this world hath set. He goeth to another place. He entereth thick darkness. He falleth down a steep precipice. He entereth into a jungle solitude. He is pursued by karmic forces. He goeth into the Vast Silence. He is borne away by the Great Ocean. He is wafted on the Wind of Karma. He goeth in the direction where stability existeth not. He is caught by the Great Conflict. He is obsessed by the Great Afflicting Spirit. He is awed and terrified by the Messengers of the Lord of Death. Existing Karma putteth him into repeated existence. No strength hath he. He hath come upon a time when he hath to go alone.

At the very first prayer, each time, I knew we were doing the right thing, saying the right words. Freddie *was* taking a great leap. The winds of karma *did* blow him from place to place. He had indeed come upon a time where he had to go alone. Oh, Freddie, I thought, can you hear us? Don't be afraid. I concentrated on keeping my voice strong.

We got Jeanne's birthday party in there somehow, but Jeanne was neither fooled nor placated. She thought it a lousy thing for Freddie to do the night before her birthday, and she said so, loud and often. Freddie was her best friend, she had been his confidante and playmate. And she couldn't understand how he could do that to her.

For weeks she would only go to sleep if she was completely surrounded by lighted candles. She would lie on her back with her hands on her stomach or chest, like she was herself some kind of sarcophagus. All she would say about it was that it was "like Egypt". It was disturbing, but we didn't try to dissuade her. Had no idea what to say.

●

●

After the funeral I went to Deborah Lee's apartment. Freddie's stuff was still stored there from when he had lived with her, and she and I went through it together.

Black velvet everywhere. Many shards of mirrors. Magick wands made out of old bedposts. Feathers. Lace. Broken statuary. Scraps of fabric, or carpet. Everything thick with some dark energy. There was one whole attaché case of male pornography carefully cut out of magazines, as if for use in collage.

On the floor in his room there was a book by Mary Renault open at the page where the king leaps into the sea. Where the ritual to renew the world is described. It was the closest we found to a suicide note.

We each took a few things for ourselves. I took a pencil holder made of a frozen-orange-juice can dipped in marbleized oil paint. I still have it, have just moved it to my new house filled with old ballpoint pens for making lists.

Mostly I took old clothes, tattered tee shirts, things I remembered him in. It would be like wearing his skin, the skin of the victim. Was it the priestess who kills who does that in *The Golden Bough*? I took a few things for Alan and Jeanne, too, and later someone brought me a box of stuff people thought I should have. Rhinestones and tarot cards. For years I carried that box everywhere with me. Unwilling to disperse it, undo that final ideogram, unravel that persona, turn it to mist. Then, one day I just did.

Debbie planned to open the house the next day so all Freddie's friends—anyone who wanted something of his—could take what they would. We used to do that whenever somebody moved away and left stuff behind. Or if they went to jail. If they had no special person, or after their special person had taken what s/he wanted, everyone came and helped themselves. We called it Scavenging, and it helped keep our households going.

I got home from Deborah's that day to find LeRoi at my house. Over the past year we had only spoken a few times, but Roi had known and loved Freddie. He hadn't come to the wake or the funeral, but he wanted to hear what had happened. I told him best as I could, and then told him a great deal more. Now that it was really too late for us, I finally told him why I had married Alan, how we were living a contractual marriage. How the reason I hadn't met with Roi when he asked to see me back in '62, when Alan and I were here to pack, was because I was afraid if I saw him I might not leave New York. Not leave him. There was no point to any of this now except the telling, and in the pain of the moment any telling was a relief. I don't know how much of what I said he actually heard and how much he shut out. It didn't seem to matter.

I saw I was hurting him by saying all this, but I had begun to feel that silence and coolness was costing us our lives. Had cost Freddie his.

There were these dreams. They would change a little, but were substantially like this: I am standing on a pier somewhere with Freddie, who is about to leave on a boat and asks me to go with him. I tell him I can't leave just yet, I have the kids, have my work, etc., and he asks, tauntingly: "WHERE'S YOUR SENSE OF ADVENTURE, DI PRIMA"?

Or I am standing on a wharf with Freddie who intends to leave on a boat that is moored there. He is going somewhere far from here. We have been talking and are hugging goodbye, and I think if I can just hug him long enough, hang on till the "moment for death" passes, then we'll be safe. We'll be past that particular juncture of fate/stars/karma/ whatever, past some gap he means to use to slip through, and he'll still be alive. I hold onto him desperately, hoping he won't notice the passing time.

I found I had to look to my own salvation. That I woke in a kind of despair, blackness, that didn't lighten. I was often lost somewhere in my mind, far from the task at hand. Of course I knew nothing of the process of grieving, none of us would have even thought of grieving as a process, but I knew something was going on, something that I'd better make room for. So as to avoid going completely crazy.

Early in November, just a week after Freddie died I began writing a book to him in the form of a long letter/journal. It was the one thing I could think of doing. Most of the time the pain was too much to hold still for, and I went around in a haze from one thing to another. But I knew from doing Zen meditation: *one can hold still, hold the mind still, if it is a task. Even better if it is a finite task, has a foreseeable end.* So when the loss got to be too much, I would go into my study, light a stick of incense and tell myself I'd type (write) till it had burned away. That particular incense took about forty minutes, and that seemed a possible time span, though not easy. I could always look up and see how much incense was left. It made more sense than a clock.

I wrote the book for a year, though not every day, and ended on the anniversary of his death.

.

.

.

Nothing was well with us. At Cooper Square we did another Solstice, used white birch logs for the fire this time, but only a few friends came to dine with us. They went home early, though Alan and I did stay up and see the sun come back. Mostly each of us kept to ourselves. Unsure how to act, we chose isolation.

We did a Christmas for the kids of course. The tree touched the ceiling as always, and the grownups came for my special eggnog, so thick you had to eat it with a spoon, and they stayed to decorate the tree. At one point out of the blue, I found myself crying in Joel Oppenheimer's arms. I was crying for the Christmas before, he had been here then, and he was here now, and it reminded me how it would never be like that again.

I'd been keeping a tight hold for more than a year, moving from task to task with no particular expectation beyond getting it done. No clear satisfaction or pleasure was built in: stuff was there to do and I did it—theatre, kids, press. But there *had* been some few friends with whom I shared a mind-set: silly, inventive. Maybe a little Dada. Of them, George Herms and Kirby Doyle had gone back to the West Coast. Jimmy Waring and his friends had become more and more remote. The writers I knew were turning pompous or domesticated. And now my oldest friend, my playmate and brother, had split for good, leaving me in an utterly boring universe full of fund-raising and household chores, art patrons and cocktail parties. I wasn't sure what to do with any of it.

● ● ● ● ●

As time passed, I found that the world we had made by working together was an entity unto itself, with its own rules and demands, and its own *intention to continue,* and we naturally continued to feed it. Nothing came to a halt except momentarily, but there was a twist, a torque to the action—for a long time afterward everything happened at an odd angle. Or that's what it felt like.

In the early winter there was a memorial service for Freddie at the Judson Church. John Herbert McDowell wrote a short choral piece called "God Has Gone Up with a Shout", and LeRoi and Frank O'Hara and I read poems. Deborah Lee danced her solo from *The Palace of the Dragon Prince,* and there were dances by Jimmy Waring and others. It felt odd, as these memorial things always did. For me, anyway, there needed to be more ritual—a fire maybe, big smells, the burning of things, or a speaking into space or to the ocean. Even the dead person's corpse would have been a help, and barring that, his or her likeness: a statue or photo. Keening would have helped.

Later Jimmy Waring made a long dance for Freddie. Very beautiful and restrained, with veiled women dancing as if between worlds, and all to the music of Mahler. It was performed the following summer in the Berkshires.

For the most part we all went on with what we were already doing—only, the tone had changed. We were more conscious that we were engaged in a life-and-death business.

For some that meant the scope of their work expanded. For others, it meant focusing down closely into what most mattered. But mostly we just kept going. So that I wasn't all that surprised when in January, three months after Freddie's death, Alan told me he'd found another theatre.

Not surprised, but not eager. I was deep into the letter-book to Freddie, which had taken an interesting shape. Years before Donald Allen had suggested I do a book that used the seasons for its structure, because they seemed to define so much for me, and now I found myself writing this book to Freddie talking to him about all the autumns we'd spent together, then all the winters. I planned to write for a year, and I had already titled it *Spring and Autumn Annals*, after the ancient Chinese court genealogies.

I was also typing a clean copy of *The Calculus of Variation*, and what with writing poems, and taking care of kids, and doing the Wednesday nights and the *Bear*, and writing stuff for Jimmy Waring and John Herbert McDowell to perform, I was busy enough. But I joined in with Alan on the theatre once it got started: I don't even remember feeling any real hesitation.

What Alan had rented this time was a Ukrainian dance hall on East Fourth Street. "The Ukrainians" owned the building, and they had a dance hall on the first floor, and a bar and club room upstairs, but everybody in the neighborhood referred to the entire building as the Ukrainian Dance Hall. Alan persuaded the owners to rent us the dance hall for a theatre. They readily agreed. Besides the rent, it meant extra business for their bar upstairs. They opened the bar during play intermissions, and before and after the Sunday poetry readings.

The place had a small lobby (not big enough for an art gallery), and a large empty space with a stage at the far end. Folding chairs came with it.

But Alan was obsessed with the plant itself—as he had never been with any of our other spaces. He raised and spent a great deal of money: buying used theatre seats, "real" red velvet theatre curtains, redesigning the stage, and covering the stage floor with hardwood ("for the dancers" he said). He even laid cork under the hardwood so that the floor would have more "spring". And he built the rectangular stage into a "U" so that the two sides extended into the audience. He then further strained our budget by buying handblown Steuben lampshades (secondhand) for the theatre walls.

When he was done, the place looked extraordinary. "A jewelbox of a theatre", Frank O'Hara told me, "like the best of the art theatres of Europe".

Not having been to Europe I didn't really have too good an idea of what Frank was talking about, but it gave me a way to explain the place to myself.

I thought I knew what Alan was up to, even if he didn't. The stage floor gave him away. Now that Freddie was dead, he was making a theatre for him, the kind of place Freddie had always wanted. Freddie, who had constantly complained about the dance floors he performed on—what they did to his arches, his knees—and who loved smooth hardwood floors laid over cork.

It stood to reason that George Herms would come out from California again. He came alone this time, and it was a shorter stay. There was no play for him to design, but Alan arranged for him to have a one-man show ("Spring Visions" he called it) at one of the East Tenth Street galleries, and I read from *The Calculus of Variation* at the opening.

I didn't have the heart to talk much, even to George. I felt deeply and unreasonably that if only we'd fully realized and manifested the power of that previous spring and summer, Freddie might not have died. Nothing less than a full renaissance and revolution is what I had had in mind—and I had felt defeated when George and then Kirby had gone back to the West Coast. I had sensed we were passing up one of those rare perfect conjunctions of time, space, and people. Chance of a lifetime.

Back then, I hadn't had a goodbye present for George, and had instead written him a poem:

> *I'd give you my works*
> *if I had them*
> *I don't got works*

Now it was too late for any of that. I loved George but could barely communicate. I wrote my book to Freddie in my study while George finished the last of the woodblocks for the *Haiku* book on the other side of the wall. One of the woodblocks was of Freddie leaping with the city for background. It had something of the quality of the Fool card about it.

> *stage set for deathscene*
> *hero's voice offstage:*
> *November grey this city*

This theatre season was not nearly as exciting as the earlier ones. It was very East Coast, for one thing. We did all New York writers, and the plays were smooth and witty but with not much bite to them. We did a take-off on murder mysteries by Barbara Guest called *Port* and a play by James Schuyler called *Shopping and Waiting* that had a set by Alex Katz, and a play by Kenward Elmslie and James Schuyler called *Unpacking the Black Trunk*. The poet Helen Adam was in New York that spring and she and I performed *Unpacking* together. There was no action—all we did was unpack a trunk and talk. Helen and I performed in front of the curtain on the right; the left half of the stage had a movie screen on which we showed a silent black and white film of the two of us doing the same play. Of course the timing and action between the two was always a little different, and that was part of what made it interesting.

Alan directed *Port* which had a lot of people in it, and it started out okay, except for some complicated problems with the lighting, but once it opened Alan refused to rehearse anymore, and the damned thing definitely needed a lot of rehearsal so it started to fall apart. The performances got worse and worse and so did Alan. He lay on the couch in his study with an ill-defined malady, with swollen glands and melancholia, and slept. He also continued to spend a great deal more money than we had, and more and more frequently it was I who signed the bad checks on our joint theatre account—much against my will.

Finally I figured if Alan wouldn't rehearse *Port* maybe I'd better, and the play got better for a while after that. More and more that season I found myself directing, or standing in at the last minute for an actor who didn't show up, stage-managing and then going on in a part I had just memorized that day. Or figuring out in the morning how to cover the checks I'd written the night before.

Something was broke and we couldn't fix it. Alan slapped Jimmy Waring in the theatre lobby one day for some trivial or nonexistent reason, and after that Jimmy was no longer a part of the New York Poets Theatre. A bunch of his people—dancers, designers, and just plain friends—left with him.

Around this time Alan bought two huge Great Dane puppies, and a whole lot of Hungarian Empire jewelry from the woman who had sold me my Tibetan *gau*. He would go about in a camel-hair coat, or one of his capes, wearing all this jewelry and leading these Great Danes, who were a pain in the butt because they were not toilet trained, and also because they had a habit of sitting down on top of the kids. Not Jeanne, who was a little too tall for them to land on, but Mini and Alex they sat down on a lot.

Obviously our household was getting out of hand, in size and content. As some of our old theatre friends went away for good, they were replaced with whomever Alan could find. We had a stage manager from "Arista", one of the first spiritual communes to spring up in New York. She was a young single mom and in lieu of salary, which we certainly couldn't pay, she and her baby moved in with us.

Next, we acquired two guys, friends of an Englishman who ran an antique shop in our neighborhood. They moved in and became the handymen for both household and theatre. Ed was a very large blond man, a "dropout" from Canada, where he had been an industrial engineer. Zen was a very small, quiet man with reddish hair, who had just finished a stint in the marines. It was there that he got his nickname because when he was in boot camp he was reading a book with the word "Zen" in the title, and because he didn't say much. Zen was from Louisiana, very soft-spoken and precise.

Ed and Zen met at our house and became good friends. We thought of the two of them as a kind of "Mutt and Jeff".

● ● ● ● ●

Sometime in February or March, a maroon and white brochure came across my desk, from the Castalia Foundation in Millbrook, New York. Castalia was Timothy Leary's latest venture. A few of his students from Harvard had bought a large empty estate in upstate New York and turned it over to him for his ongoing explorations. Acid was still legal, and the Castalia Foundation ran workshops on tripping for various professionals who wanted to know more about it. Many a minister, doctor, writer, psychiatrist, and professor crossed Millbrook's threshold in those early days, took LSD under the kindly auspices of Timothy and his folks, and re-emerged two or three days later, utterly changed.

I had heard a bit about the workshops. When they arrived, everyone traded their clothes for similar but not identical blue and white cotton kimonos and paper slippers. They were then requested not to speak at all for the first evening. Stripped of the marks of rank and the insignia of their various trades, people gathered in the kitchen to prepare supper together. Then in the course of the weekend they tripped together, in the particular ritual mode that Timothy had developed.

I wasn't a part of the target audience for whom the brochure was written, but I felt that our meeting was long overdue. So I sat down at my big red typewriter and wrote a letter containing the kind of information that was requested in the brochure: Who I was, what I had done (writing, publishing, etc.) and whether I had ever tripped. I mirrored the straight, academic style, partly to point up that the brochure was a bit stiff and forbidding. In less than a week, I got a handwritten note from Timothy. It said,

"Come on, Diane! Take another dose of LSD and reread your letter. And then—come on, Diane"!

A few weeks later, Alan and I took the train to Poughkeepsie and were met by two gorgeous and friendly women who drove us to the Millbrook estate. They pointed out the beginnings of the domain as we drove along an old stone wall. Then we stopped at a gatehouse, and our driver checked in before traveling the half mile of "driveway" to the main house—all sixty-four rooms of it.

There were towers and lawns, and a spacious, welcoming front porch. There were gilded mirrors and a huge bell in the entry hall. There were magic carpets and crystals, tapestries and flowers, and excellent wine and foods. Odd buildings had been dropped here and there in the landscape—ten square miles of woods and lawns and water. We drove around, walked, explored, feasted with everyone, spent the night.

It was a world made for Freddie, where all his capes and feathers and flutes would fit right in. It made me sad that such a world should have manifested so soon after he died. It seemed if he only waited a little, he could have been, and had, whatever he wanted. Or maybe his death was part of what was ushering in the changes.

I was too cool to ask about acid, and Alan was too. Several visits later the folks who lived there told us that we had confused Timothy and everyone else. Usually visitors asked for drugs straight off.

I guess the people there were so used to tripping that they seemed pretty normal to us. At least, as normal as most of the folks we knew. We had a wonderful two days, and returned a couple of times after that. It became a new refuge for us, a home out of town.

We had begun to think, and to live, beyond the limits of the city.

chapter TWENTY-ONE

As for me, I had begun to turn my attention away from the theatre, and back toward the world of books. The anarchist dream of being a printer had long been with me, and that spring I found and bought a press.

Owning a press and printing books seemed a natural next step after mimeographing *The Floating Bear* for so many years, and most recently turning out programs and flyers for the theatre on the Gestetner. It became a kind of obsession. I began to read the ads in the newspapers, and after a while I found myself going out and looking at actual presses.

Bret Rohmer was back in town and he helped me. He had learned to print in the army and he knew a fair bit about methods and machines. He himself had become interested in doing fine printing, and was in the market for a Vandercook proof press.

I just wanted an offset press—not too big, the next step up from the Gestetner mimeograph really, but something solid. I had done some printing at Columbia Electronics Labs, and I knew for certain that I did *not* want a Multilith. They were tinny, and the whole unit was sealed so that you couldn't get inside them to adjust or fix anything yourself. To my mind they weren't "real" presses. As luck would have it there were tons of used Multis for sale, and quite a few very big four-color offset presses, but a small-to-medium-size used offset press was hard to come by.

One finally did show up, a Fairchild-Davidson, and I went to see it. The guys who were selling ran a secondhand press business out of a loft. There was some kind of warranty that came with this machine, and best of all there was a week's free training with purchase. The press of my dreams stood there, only a foot or two taller than I was, and gleamed blackly at me. Good, solid metal, really heavy, not rickety at all. It cost twelve hundred dollars.

That was a lot of money in those days, but I got on the phone and started fund-raising. It felt good. This was the first time I'd raised money for something *I* actually wanted, and perhaps for this reason I was very successful. I called people I knew well, mostly well-known painters and sculptors, and I told them that I'd found the press of my dreams. Told them what kind of books I wanted to print, and how I would get trained for free for a week. They mostly got pretty excited about it themselves. I had only made six or seven calls when I had the whole twelve hundred dollars, plus sales tax and moving costs, in my hands.

I paid cash, and rented a storefront on East Fourth Street, across the street from our new theatre. The store was a few steps below street level and a bit musty, but I painted it bright yellow, and arranged for the press to be moved in as soon I finished the class.

It was an evening class, four hours a night, in the sellers' business loft with lots of machinery all around. I learned on my own press—the one I had just bought. I was the only girl in that class; all the others were big machinist-type guys, very blue-collar and gruff, and not too articulate. They acted a little funny at first about me being there, but then they got used to me.

The only thing that was a little embarrassing was that I was so short I had to stand on a stool to adjust the drum pressure. There might have been a few other things that I would probably be too weak to do, but I bought a service contract with the press, and figured not to worry about any of that for the time being.

The first thing I printed was an announcement for the theatre. It had a drawing on one side, and I remember the feeling of power as I watched two thousand of those drawings come into the world. This was a tool I could really relate to.

I called myself Poets Press, and did the first book of poetry. It was by A.B. Spellman, the friend who had almost edited *The Horse at the Window* with me, and then resigned, which had led to LeRoi and me editing *The Floating Bear.* He called his book *The Beautiful Days.*

We had no drawing table as yet, no straightedges or T-squares in the house. Zen sat at the round kitchen table doing the paste-up with nothing to guide him but two index cards with little marks on them. The margins looked straight enough—Zen was meticulous. In a remnant shop I found a nice ivory paper for forty dollars that would give us a run of 750 copies for *The Beautiful Days.* New York in those days was full of stores that sold broken cartons and odd lots of paper.

For me, one of the interesting things about making that book was that the first place we sent our camera-copy to, to have aluminum plates made, refused to do the job. The guy had apparently skimmed through the poems and decided that we were publishing pornography. He had detected the word "dick" in a poem, and explained angrily and at great length that he had churches for customers and wanted nothing to do with us.

We found another place easily enough, but it made me think a lot about getting more control by buying more equipment. Buying a copy camera and plate-maker seemed to be important. I was hooked.

Over that year a bunch of saddle-stitched poetry books came out of the yellow store. I still had the ancient stapler I had used on *This Kind of Bird Flies Backward,* and I put it back to work.

We did a small run of Jean Genet's *Le Condamné à Mort,* put into English by me and Alan, and Bret and Harriet Rohmer. Alan's method of translating Genet was to pick up French gay hustlers on 42nd Street and bring them back to Cooper Square to help with the slang. (A great pick-up line, no? "Come home with me, baby, and help me translate Genet".) We did a bilingual edition, and had to pirate the French, as Gallimard owned the rights. They sent us an acid letter at some later point. I am not sure who got the letter, as we purposely left publisher and place off the title page, just put the alchemical logo of Poets Press: a dragon eating its tail, flanked by the sun and the moon.

I also published the *Seven Love Poems from the Middle Latin* that I had translated in Greenwood Lake after Dominique was born, and that Simon & Schuster had long since rejected. It was a bilingual book, with one of Bret's unicorns on the cover. And I did *Huncke's Journal,* a first book of short stories by Herbert Huncke, who was Allen Ginsberg's mentor and friend. Huncke's book was a technical tour-de-force for Poets Press, and took a long time. Since it was prose, I wanted it to look like prose, with a justified right-hand margin. The way to do that with an "executive" typewriter was to count the hairline spaces that were needed to even out the margin of a particular line. You then pieced out said hairline spaces among the word breaks of the line, writing the numbers onto your typewritten copy. Then you retyped the whole page, adding the tiny spaces with the space bar as you went along. Each line was different, of course—it was a nerve-wracking process.

That was the first batch. I went on from there to do Clive Matson's first poem book, *Mainline to the Heart,* with a John Wieners introduction; and David Henderson's *Felix of the Silent Forest.* Later there was *Sappho-bones* by Kirby Doyle, Audre Lorde's first book, *The First Cities,* and many others. But most of those happened after we left the city.

The shop with the press became a refuge for me. A center that held steady for a while even, in the fall, when we lost the Cooper Square house and had to move on.

There was a huge flood in the city that August: a water main burst at the intersection of Third Avenue and Fourth Street, leaving an apartment-sized hole in the middle of the street. Our shop was just downhill from the break, and below street level, and it was flooded and muddy. I remember going there that night. The scene was unearthly: in the summer heat, and under a huge saffron-colored moon, a torrent was running down Fourth Street toward the East River so fast it was carrying bricks and stones on the surface of the water. It did feel apocalyptic.

Luckily most of the books and paper in the shop were up on tables or shelves, so nothing much got hurt, but over the next few days, in the last heat wave of that summer, the stench of the mud and the size of the bugs who moved in from the sewers were both beyond my powers of belief. But I stuck with it, and with the help of Ed and Zen, we dug out, cleaned up, and got the press running again.

Some of the blank paper we had bought was ruined from the dampness in the shop, and had to be discarded.

● ● ● ● ●

That spring during our theatre season we were pretty broke, so I put my new printing skills on the job market. A man named Zeb Delaire ran a small "cold type house" in the West Twenties. He liked to keep his place humming twenty-four hours a day, to get maximum profit from his many (rented) IBM executive typewriters. I came on part-time as part of the midnight crew. I usually did a four-hour stint and quit at four in the morning, but if there was a rush job and the theatre could do without me I'd come in at 8 P.M. and stay till dawn. I rather liked being there.

For one thing, I was learning a lot, getting quite good with light box and straightedge razor, "stripping in" corrections. (We also stripped in italics or any other typefaces, because they each had to be typed on a different typewriter.)

The radio was on all night, and the music varied according to who got to pick the station. If Zeb was working it was country/western stuff, but usually there was just a jazz crowd in the place after 1 A.M., and we had a ball. People who took jobs typesetting on Ninth Avenue in the wee small hours tended to be a bit unusual, and I found plenty of odd and off-the-wall conversation as well as good music amongst my fellow workers.

The only problem with the job was going home by myself at four in the morning. I usually took the Ninth Avenue bus to Fourteenth Street, and the Fourteenth Street crosstown to Third Avenue, but that left me walking about eight blocks down Third Avenue to the Bowery—through some heavy dealing and pimping turf before I got to the house. I learned a new level of centering for this walk, a kind of self-contained but kindly feeling: that these folks were after all okay, they were going about their business, and besides, I was looking inward right now, thank you; I was completely self-absorbed and wanted and needed nothing from anyone. Nobody ever bothered me.

After a while Zen got a job at Zeb's. He couldn't type worth a damn, but was really great doing the tiny stuff, like stripping in six-point numbers on math and physics texts, and his dry quiet humor was appreciated by everyone. When he worked, Zen and I would leave together, so I had somebody to walk back to the house with.

The money I made at Zeb's took care of our basic bills, but the theatre was definitely going under. The plays were pretty good, the other weeknight programs had as much pizzazz as ever, but people weren't coming out. They just weren't. Some nights there were just three people in the audience. We of course came up with all sorts of reasons: there had been riots over the summer and people were staying closer to home; there was less money around; there was more television, etc. But what I think now is that there was a backlash from Freddie's death. I think that we, the people closest to him, might have been seen as jinxed in some way. Or taboo. It was anyway too soon to get close to any of us again.

Alan tried to fix it by throwing money at it—money that we didn't have. We could both sign checks on the theatre account, but more and more of the time he was asking me to sign them, and more and more of the time I was doing it against my will. I knew he figured *someone* was going to get in trouble eventually, and he much preferred it to be me. When confronted he even said it would be easier to get *me* out of a jam than him, because of my reputation as a writer. These machinations took any last sense of trust or camaraderie out of our strange marriage.

I signed the checks because I knew he could make me sign them, and I wanted to avoid a showdown. It had never come down to brute force between us, but that possibility was always there, subtly or not so subtly. At this point we were totally at war.

At the theatre we kept changing the programs, partly to see what—if anything—would draw, and partly because whole bunches of actors and technicians took their stuff and left. Abandoned ship. I wound up performing a couple of staged readings that had been hastily patched together in lieu of whatever else had been announced.

While all this was going on, we got the news that our house had been put up for sale. At first I thought this would be no problem at all—we could simply buy the place.

When—at his insistence—we had signed the papers that permitted him to sell our house in Topanga Canyon, my father had promised that the down payment for another house would be ours whenever we needed it. It had, after all, been our wedding present. But now it became clear that that wasn't going to happen. Relations between my dad and Alan had gone from bad to worse, and I don't think Dick would have given us money no matter what place we found. For starters, he claimed that the Cooper Square house was not a good deal at the $35,000 asking price, and refused to help us buy it.

I never got clear on exactly what created the bitter feud between Alan and Dick. It all began with Alan yelling at Dick one time in front of my mother and others in the family. Dick never forgot or forgave him for that, and things just continued to escalate between them. At times it felt like they were fighting over *me*—each of them claimed the other was treating me badly, and they were both right.

As for me, I felt a kind of quiet contempt. I didn't really *like* either of them very much. As far as I was concerned they were both mean, stingy, spoiled, self-centered guys who deserved each other. But in the process, me and the kids got done out of what should have been ours.

In the midst of all this confusion and hidden grief over Freddie, a stranger showed up, sent by Jonas Mekas, who wanted nothing to do with him, but sent him along to us—knowing as he did that the theatre was broke. The stranger offered us money for some mysterious project, and Alan flew off to Berkeley to recruit people for an only partly explained scam of some sort. No real money materialized, though for a time Alan was sure there would be a lot—enough to rescue the Poets Theatre and buy our house.

There was some reality gap here. I would stand in my study, trying to reason with Alan over the phone, while he talked about sending a limousine for Philip Whalen, the most unpretentious of men, to offer him a lifetime contract for his poetry. Meanwhile, downstairs at Cooper Square, Bertha, a young woman from Millbrook who was staying with us, would be cooking a mess of collard greens and pork to feed the ten or fifteen theatre people who were living on nothing and sleeping on the floor of a house from which we were all about to be evicted. Said theatre commune (that's what it had become) would then go open a theatre one more time to do a play to which almost nobody came. Nothing made sense.

Finally Jonas Mekas unilaterally decided that he and I needed to go to California to rescue Alan. Jonas, I think, felt responsible for the whole situation.

The stranger, it turned out, was simply crazy, but it took three days and the combined powers of Jonas and myself to pry Alan loose and fly back to our crumbling East Coast theatre, our disappearing home, and our publishing projects.

● ● ● ● ●

Alan had a "breakdown" when we got back—or at least he announced it was a breakdown—and he decided to leave the city and go recover on his father's farm in Pennsylvania. (His dad, an ex-gangster from the Bronx, who had made his money in "construction" during World War II, was now raising veal calves in the mountains of Western Pennsylvania.)

I was left with the failing theatre, the press, the kids, and all the various theatre workers and other dependents who were living at the house, or at the storefront with the press. (Albert Fine, an erstwhile pianist and composer who'd recently gotten out of the madhouse, spent one night at the press and managed to gather the metal dial on the wall telephone into a kind of crumpled flower, and *braid* the metal arms of the chandelier.) Basically, though, I was in better shape without Alan than with him: my work crew had Ed and Zen at its core: they could, between them, fix almost anything, and we weren't impeded by Alan's mercurial, ever-changing vision.

●

It was clear the Poets Theatre couldn't keep going and, left to my own devices, I decided to close it with a flair. We announced the last nights of the plays, and then spent the Easter weekend deconstructing the place and giving it all away. First we gave the lights and the curtains to various small theatres, and then the fun began. We did a marathon round-the-clock reading from noon on Good Friday to dawn on Easter Sunday: people were invited to read their favorite works in their entirety, everyone was welcome to drop in and listen and carry away whatever they could use. Every prop, every can of paint and gallon of glue, every staple gun, made its way out the door, while various folks regaled us with the classics.

I was served with a warrant for bad checks on Holy Saturday while reading "Prometheus Unbound" from beginning to end, not breaking Shelley's rhythm as I took the papers with one hand. *Winnie the Pooh, Journey to the East, Catcher in the Rye*—we read day and night, under work lights on a stage that grew barer and barer, whilst folks put quarters and nickels in a leaded crystal dish labeled "Donations". At sunrise on Easter we locked up the place for good, took the donations money we had gathered, and went to Ratner's for breakfast.

It took a while after that to get the creditors off our backs, to persuade Alan (when he got back) to return his unpaid-for Great Dane puppies and all his Hungarian Empire jewelry, but eventually we were more or less in the clear, and looking at what to do next.

It is interesting to me now that at that time we never for a minute thought of all this insanity and confusion as being in any way related to Freddie's death. For instance, I never really thought about the escalation of Alan's nuttiness in that light. Generally in those days we tended to live in an acausal world, in which discrete events happened out of the blue— perhaps a leftover from the existentialism of the 1950s—but it *is* amazing now to think we were that blind.

I naturally turned to what I had left to work with: The Poets Press.

The interesting thing about it was that the books were selling. I had begun to build up a list of libraries and bookstores which had standing orders for everything I printed. In a very short time I was mailing out literally hundreds of books as soon as they came back from being trimmed at the bindery. (We hand-collated and stapled them at the shop.) At the height of the Press, a year or so later, I was mailing out six hundred copies as soon as a book was ready, and I had to up the first printing of each book from one to two thousand copies, to have enough for the stores.

The Press was a wonderful cottage industry. Ed and Zen worked at proofreading and sometimes did the printing, we all did the collating, stapling, and mailing, and nearly everyone helped with errands. Eventually we acquired a secondhand plate-maker, and then we bought a copy-camera from a guy who was going out of business. Alan loved the copy-camera, and he became the photo person and plate maker. Meanwhile, eviction was looming.

We looked at houses in Brooklyn, where they were less expensive, to see if we could find anything that would fit us and our press, and placate my dad. We found some beautiful places in Bedford-Stuyvesant which he refused to help us with because the neighborhood was "dangerous" (read "Black").

We toyed with migrating to Canada, and even made inquiries. Our plan was to move to the coast of Nova Scotia, and there set up our print shop. Print birth announcements and wedding invitations for the locals, and keep doing Poets Press books. It made sense to us at the time.

However we soon found that much as the Canadian government would like to have us, they wanted us sans shop, so they could employ us in some large printing outfit of their choosing. They kept suggesting we move to Saint John. Meanwhile the customs fees they proposed to levy on our modest equipment came to much more than the machinery was worth, and when we looked into it we found out that we couldn't pay over time, or even get a loan on the machines from a Canadian bank in order to square our account with customs. We struggled with that bureaucracy for a while and then gave up.

Then I got sick: something was really wrong with my stomach. Probably it was rebelling against all the amphetamine I'd dropped into cups of coffee and drunk down with sweet pastry for breakfast over the past couple of years. I couldn't eat anything without pain, and often diarrhea. Doctors muttered about ulcers, and wanted to do expensive tests, and our health insurance was by now gone with everything else, Alan not having kept up his union dues.

Then my good friend Billy Linich, who had lived with us in Topanga, showed up out of the blue. He was mostly a Warhol recluse by this time, but he came over and took care of me, cooking strange concoctions I could actually digest. On questioning him, I discovered they were macrobiotic. It turned out to be the only food that didn't hurt to eat, and I learned how to cook it. I got some books, and connected with the really outré macrobiotic community in New York. At that time "the diet" was suspect, and the stores that sold the products (whole grains, seaweeds, salt plums, ginseng tea, etc.) were operating under a constant threat of invasion: in the months before I left New York there were police raids and wholesale rampages where FDA agents tore open bags of organic grain, poured them on the floor, and then sprayed them with pesticide. If a store contained both books about the foods (what they could heal) and the foods themselves— that was definitely considered illegal. The owner was threatened with arrest for "practicing medicine without a license".

But I was learning how to take care of myself, and Billy and the macro community were helping me do it. I was opting against x rays and barium enemas, and choosing a first glimmer of sanity in my life. The food felt good inside of me; I could digest it. I knew that much.

I decided it was time to give up speed in all its forms, and quit it cold, while doing a week-long brown rice fast. It wasn't hard—all my life I've had this piece of luck, that when I want to stop something—some drug or even coffee—I just do it, and nothing in me cries out for more.

Meanwhile, of course, everything else kept keeping on. Tides of folks flowed in and out of the house. The theatre people gradually left: the stage-manager and her baby were among the first to go. Then Bertha found out she was pregnant and went to stay with her relatives in the South. LeRoi, who had moved to Harlem and started the Black Arts Movement, arrived one day with a battalion of young men to print his newsletter *In-Formation* on the old Gestetner. And I kept on writing *Spring and Autumn Annals,* my year-long letter to Freddie.

By August it was clear we were going to have to move.

Now it is August, 1995, and we are moving again. I am sorting out things for the bookstores, things for storage. Things for the Poetry Archive, maybe, at SF State. Things for the free box, for the Mother Teresa nuns. For the Community Thrift shop, the Friends of the Library. The Street. My friend Laura's attic. Butterfield's auction block.

In those days, perhaps we had fewer choices. Or perhaps we were just a bit clearer about leaving it all for the wind.

It has never but once been hard for me to leave a place. Perhaps it's my nature, or having Sagittarius rising, but I am always more curious about what's to come than sad about losing what I've had. What I know has already slipped through my fingers.

•

At Cooper Square I was living in a museum: a gilded palace filled with theatre sets. Huge painting by Alex Katz on the living room wall. Backdrops
and ten-foot-tall puppets by Red Grooms. George Herms' sculptures
overhanging the stairs and the hall. Peter Agostini's *Hanged Man* swinging
in Alan's study. Boxes of drawings, of sketches, many of them never used
in any production. Costume drawings by Larry Rivers; odds and ends by
Michael Goldberg and Alfred Leslie.

When it became clear we were leaving I called the Whitney Museum,
and offered to give them the stuff. The guy on the phone was quite snotty
and wouldn't even come downtown to take a look. We wound up putting
boxes of the smaller pieces out on the street, knowing at least the speed
freaks would get them. Would decorate their pads. Some of the big stuff
the artists themselves took home. If they had the space. George Herms'
set for *The Blossom* was scattered everywhere.

What was most painful was walking by the house one day after we had
moved, and seeing my old upright piano, smashed, on the sidewalk, and
draped over it the broken plaster torso of the *Hanged Man* sculpture.
White trails of plaster dust in the cement.

*So there was some way it happened, some way it all came together and
came apart in those two years in that luminous and ancient house: press,
theatre, revolution. Prose and poetry. LSD and speed.*

●　●　●　●　●

The tempo picked up, and before we knew it everything was stored once
again in my parents' cellar, and we went with a few boxes to the Broadway
Central Hotel. A "housekeeping unit": one large room and a kitchen. Me
and Alan and the three kids lived there about two months.

We were there on the first anniversary of Freddie's death. On that day
I finished *Spring and Autumn Annals,* while the three kids played around
me in the same room, in the October sunlight.

Alan had a hard time at the Broadway Central. By that time he too was on
the macrobiotic diet, partly by choice, and partly because it was all I was
cooking, and he'd have had to work hard to avoid it. "The diet" wasn't easy
on him: he had lots of aches and pains, mostly in his kidneys, that he was
sure were brought on by the change in food, and there were days when he
was certain that me and my macrobiotic friends were conspiring to kill

him. The macrobiotic community was very tight-knit, partly because of the legal troubles, and partly because they were all such mavericks, and kindly patient souls clothed in eccentric garb and odd demeanor would come to the hotel to put hot ginger compresses on Alan's kidneys and speak soothingly to him, sometimes to his utter consternation.

He recovered after a while, though, and seemed to be much healthier for the process.

As for me, over time the "diet" did restore me to health, but for me the most important part of macrobiotics was the idea of a "unifying principle" or worldview (for macros it was, of course, yin/yang polarity). The notion that a unifying principle in culture, art, history, was not only possible but *necessary,* deepened and changed the nature of my journey. How I looked at my work, my life. How I saw the world. I began to look for the structure(s) on which I could hang my own experience, my knowledge. The principle(s) that could shape and inform my Will.

We went up to Millbrook again, and this time Timothy took us aside and gave us some brown bread soaked in acid, instructing us on how much of the bread to take for one trip. We thanked him, and took the carefully wrapped bread back to the city, where we proceeded to forget about it till Thanksgiving morning.

Peter Hartman was back in town for a few days, and we were getting ready to go with him and the kids and a few other friends to Brooklyn, to have Thanksgiving dinner with my family, when we decided the thing to do was eat the bread from Timothy before we set out ("before it got moldy" was my thought, but I didn't want to turn everybody off). We portioned it out, each of us taking about a quarter of the amount that Timothy had recommended, and certain that we would, at the most, get a slight buzz, we set out for the family table.

Everything was going as well as could be expected: there was only the usual amount of strain, and the usual ominous gaps in the family conversation, until I decided to fill one of said gaps with a profound and (I thought) extremely interesting observation. "Have you noticed", I inquired, "how the shrimp are exactly the same color as the gladiolas"? "Yes", one of my friends brightly responded, "and almost exactly the same curled shape". We all stared mutely back and forth from our plates to the centerpiece.

My folks were nonplussed, but managed to take this and other disjointed and meaningful remarks in stride. I'm not sure to this day if they noticed when Peter excused himself and retired to my parents' bedrooom to have a baby, which he proceeded to push into the world with great groans and thumps, while Deborah Lee acted as his midwife. The new mother and child, and the midwife, were all so taken aback by this turn of events that they decided not to wait for dessert, but to take the subway immediately back to Manhattan, much to everyone's relief.

Shortly after our Thanksgiving adventure, Alan decided to do the *sesshin* (long Zen meditation retreat) that the First Zen Institute held every year during the first eight days of December to celebrate Buddha's enlightenment. Alan was very attracted to the First Zen Institute, partly because it had a mostly upper-class clientele, and the first time we went there Antony Tudor was one of the practitioners. Alan had been sitting there from time to time since the theatre closed.

This would be the first time either of us had done a *sesshin*. It sounded strenuous, but I thought it was a great idea, and encouraged him mightily. He went, and to his credit got through the whole thing.

I wasn't really aware of it then, but as so often happens, new threads were coming into our hands as the old ones slipped away.

● ● ● ● ●

It was at this point that Felix Morrow contacted me, and asked me to do some work for him.

Felix was an older guy, who owned University Books out on Long Island. I knew about University Books because they had published the Milarepa I still studied. And now, Felix wanted to print two volumes of Paracelsus that A. E. Waite had translated in the nineteenth century. He wanted a new introduction for this edition and asked me to write it. He offered the princely sum of two hundred dollars, and of course I said yes.

We signed a contract, and Felix came to the hotel carrying two gorgeous, huge volumes bound in red and stamped with gold, which he loaned me. They were a first edition, his personal copy from which he was going to offset the new printing. I had heard vaguely of Paracelsus, the fifteenth-century alchemist, but now, given the assignment and having the books in hand, I read the two volumes straight through.

I didn't guess that Paracelsus would change forever my way of seeing the world. When I actually began to read him, there was that part of me that recognized even what was most obscure in those pages as inevitable and *true*. It was the same organ of recognition that is at work when one's whole being says "yes" to a painting, a piece of music, even though it is like nothing we've known before, even though it takes an incredible stretch to stay with it, to actually *hear* it, or see it. There is some infallible mechanism in us, something like a dowsing rod of the heart, and it moves in us sometimes—moves seldom, but with total authority.

I wasn't at all sure then what alchemy "meant"—if indeed it meant anything that I could ever express—but I *recognized* it, and I knew from then on it would be a part of my life.

● ● ● ● ●

In early November, we had first made our way up to Rammurti Mishra's Ananda Ashram in Monroe, New York, for a weekend of talks and meditation. We visited a few more times and made friends with some of the regular students. After Alan came back from the *sesshin,* we met privately with Dr. Mishra. We asked for and got permission to live at the Ashram with the kids, while we looked for a new home somewhere in upstate New York. (It was at Ananda Ashram that I wrote the introduction to Paracelsus for Felix.)

We had come to the conclusion by then, and probably correctly, that we would never be able to afford the space we needed—for kids, Poets Press, meditation—and with a study for each of us besides—in New York City, and that we would have to go farther afield. We left the Broadway Central quite easily, almost lightheartedly, not realizing in some sense we were leaving Manhattan for good, not looking back, but eager for the new.

We went on. Thrived in upstate New York; lived at Millbrook with Timothy Leary; moved West (twice); in between tried hotel life (where I had a baby comfortably, at home in bed).

We moved West. Worked with the Diggers and studied with Shunryu Suzuki. I shed Alan. Hid people out and ran them across borders. Left town. Wrote lots of revolutionary poems. Tried commune living. Had my fifth baby.

Hung with the guys who made Sunshine acid; hid them out; left town. (Again). Wrote *Loba* on Tomales Bay and lived on fish. Taught at the opening of Naropa Institute.

Came "home" to San Francisco. Found my lifelong mate (art and dharma brother). Did psychic work; healing work; taught Poetics; got to hang a bunch with Robert Duncan. Founded a Magick school with friends; studied with Chögyam Trungpa and Lama Tharchin. Began to paint watercolors.

Now I mostly meditate and paint and write. Teach a bit. Try to keep up with correspondence and type up poems. Have lunch with Michael McClure and Philip Whalen.

Life in the West has been very good to me. Maybe I'll write about some of it sometime.